I0008329

Golang Pro Whisperer: Code Smarter, Build Faster

By Mike Zephalon

Golang Pro Whisperer: Code Smarter, Build Faster

Copyright © 2024 Mike Zephalon

All rights reserved.

No part of this book may be reproduced, distributed, or transmitted in any form or by any means, including photocopying, recording, or other electronic or mechanical methods, without the prior written permission of the publisher, except in the case of brief quotations embodied in critical reviews and certain other non-commercial uses permitted by copyright law. For permission requests, write to the publisher, addressed "Attention: Permissions Coordinator," at the address below.

For permissions or inquiries, please contact: **mikezephalon@gmail.com.**
Published by **Mike Zephalon**

This book is a work of non-fiction. While the author has made every effort to ensure the accuracy and completeness of the information contained within, the author assumes no responsibility for errors, omissions, or damages resulting from the use of the information. The views expressed in this book are those of the author and do not necessarily reflect the official policy or position of any affiliated entity.

ABOUT AUTHOR

Mike Zephalon was born in Toronto, Canada, and developed a passion for technology and programming at an early age. His journey into the world of coding began when he was just a teenager, experimenting with simple scripts and exploring the vast possibilities of web development. Mike pursued his studies at the University of Toronto, where he majored in Computer Science. During his time at university, he became deeply interested in JavaScript, captivated by its versatility and power in building dynamic, interactive web applications.

Over the years, Mike has worked with several tech startups and companies, where he honed his skills as a front-end developer. His dedication to mastering JavaScript and its frameworks has made him a respected voice in the developer community. Through his books and tutorials, Mike aims to empower new and experienced developers alike, helping them unlock the full potential of JavaScript in their projects.

Table of Contents

1. Getting Started with Go
2. Go: The Basic Types, Values, Pointers, Operations and Conversions
3. Go: Operations and Conversions
4. Go: Function and Control flows
5. Go: Data Structures
6. Go: Concurrency
7. Go: Error Handling and Reflection
8. Go: Structs and Interfaces
9. Go: Packages and Core Packages
10. Go: Harness Time, Manage Data, and Handle Input
11. Go: Reflection, Mutex and Channels
12. Go: Testing and Tooling
13. Go: The Art of Testing Technical Requirements
14. Go: File Handling and Data Processing
15. Go: Building REST APIs
16. Go: Mutex and Channels
17. Go: Strengthening Database Interactions

1. Getting Started with Go

Introduction to Go and Golang Tools

Go, also known as Golang, is a statically typed, compiled programming language designed by Google. It was created by Robert Griesemer, Rob Pike, and Ken Thompson and first released in 2009. Go was designed with simplicity, efficiency, and ease of use in mind, and it has gained popularity for being an excellent choice for developing scalable and high-performance software. The language combines the simplicity of Python with the efficiency of C, making it particularly useful for system-level programming and server-side applications.

Go has a robust standard library, excellent concurrency support, and efficient garbage collection. Its main aim is to simplify software development, allowing developers to write clear and efficient code quickly. Go is particularly well-suited for developing web servers, cloud services, microservices, and distributed systems. The language also encourages the use of best practices, including clean code, simplicity, and effective error handling.

History and Evolution of Go

Go was developed in response to the growing complexity of software systems and the need for a language that could simplify software development without sacrificing performance. The creators wanted a language that could offer:

- **Efficiency:** Comparable to languages like C/C++.
- **Simplicity:** Easy to learn and write, similar to Python or JavaScript.
- **Concurrency:** Built-in support for modern, multicore processors.
- **Safety:** Elimination of common programming errors such as null pointer dereferencing.

Since its inception, Go has evolved to include several powerful features, such as improved package management, enhanced performance, and refined language constructs. The language has seen widespread adoption by companies like Google, Uber, Dropbox, and Netflix for building reliable, scalable software.

Core Features of Go

1. **Simple Syntax**: Go has a clean and readable syntax that emphasizes clarity. This makes it easier to write and maintain code.
2. **Concurrency Support**: Go provides native support for concurrent programming with goroutines, which allow functions to run concurrently. Channels facilitate safe communication between goroutines, making concurrency easier to manage.
3. **Garbage Collection**: Go includes automatic memory management, which helps to manage resources efficiently without burdening developers with manual memory allocation and deallocation.
4. **Compiled Language**: Being a compiled language, Go turns code into machine language, making programs faster to run compared to interpreted languages.

5. **Cross-Platform**: Go programs can be compiled to run on different platforms, making it easy to develop cross-platform applications.
6. **Robust Standard Library**: Go's standard library is extensive and covers areas such as networking, web servers, I/O, text processing, and more. It allows developers to build powerful applications without needing third-party packages.

Why Use Go in 2024?

The modern software landscape has changed dramatically since Go's introduction, with increased demand for scalable, cloud-native applications. Go remains highly relevant in 2024 due to several key advantages:

- **Efficiency and Speed**: Go's compiled nature allows developers to build fast, efficient applications that can handle significant workloads.
- **Microservices-Friendly**: Go is ideal for building microservices due to its simplicity, fast start-up time, and small memory footprint.
- **Cloud-Native Development**: Go is commonly used to build cloud-based services, containers, and serverless applications. It's the language behind Docker and Kubernetes, two of the most critical tools in cloud computing.
- **Growing Ecosystem**: Go has a growing ecosystem of libraries, tools, and frameworks, making it easier to build a wide range of applications.
- **Easy to Learn**: Go's simplicity makes it accessible for beginners, and experienced developers can quickly adapt and become productive.

Golang Tools Introduction

To get the most out of Go, developers rely on various tools that streamline the development process, improve productivity, and ensure code quality. Here are some of the essential tools and technologies in the Go ecosystem as of 2024:

1. Go Modules

Introduced in Go 1.11, **Go Modules** is the standard package management system. It manages dependencies by defining module requirements and versions in a go.mod file. Go Modules support versioning, ensuring that applications use the right versions of dependencies, and facilitate building reproducible builds. In 2024, Go Modules remain the de facto standard for dependency management, replacing older methods like GOPATH.

Key Features:
- **Versioning**: Specify versions of dependencies.
- **Reproducibility**: Ensure builds are consistent across environments.
- **Compatibility**: Works well with existing GOPATH-based projects.

2. GoLand and Visual Studio Code (VS Code)

GoLand (by JetBrains) and **Visual Studio Code** are two popular IDEs for Go development. GoLand offers a range of features, including smart code completion, code navigation, refactoring tools, and robust debugging capabilities. VS Code, on the other hand, is an open-source editor that supports Go through plugins like gopls (Go Language Server), which offers similar features to GoLand. Both IDEs ensure smooth development, debugging, and code management.

Key Features:

- **Code Completion**: Smart suggestions to speed up development.
- **Integrated Debugging**: Identify and fix issues easily.
- **Code Navigation**: Quickly jump between functions, classes, and files.

3. Docker and Kubernetes

Since Go is the language behind Docker and Kubernetes, it's essential for developers working in cloud environments. **Docker** is a tool that allows developers to package applications and their dependencies into containers. **Kubernetes** is a container orchestration platform that automates deploying, scaling, and managing containerized applications.

Go developers often use Docker to build and deploy Go applications, and Kubernetes to manage them at scale. In 2024, the integration between Go, Docker, and Kubernetes has become even more seamless, making Go the preferred language for containerized applications.

4. Go Linters (GolangCI-Lint)
Linters are tools that analyze code to identify potential issues, style violations, or bugs. **GolangCI-Lint** is one of the most popular linters for Go and includes multiple linters in one package. It can identify issues such as dead code, unused variables, and code that doesn't conform to best practices. Running linting tools ensures that code adheres to high standards, reducing bugs and improving maintainability.

Key Features:

- **Static Analysis**: Identify issues without running the code.
- **Customizable**: Enable or disable specific linters.
- **Integration**: Works well with CI/CD pipelines.

5. GoDoc and Go Generate

GoDoc is a tool that extracts and generates documentation from Go source code. It encourages developers to write clear and concise code comments, which can be turned into detailed documentation. In 2024, documentation remains a critical aspect of software development, and GoDoc ensures that code is easily understandable by others.
Go Generate is a command that runs code generation tools. Developers use it to create boilerplate code, manage repetitive tasks, and reduce manual errors. It is particularly useful when working with APIs, protocol buffers, or database models.

Key Features:

- **Documentation**: Auto-generate clean, readable documentation.
- **Code Generation**: Automate repetitive coding tasks.

6. Delve (Go Debugger)

Delve is a powerful debugger designed for Go. It helps developers debug their programs by allowing them to inspect variables, set breakpoints, and step through code. Debugging is an essential part of software development, and Delve integrates seamlessly with major IDEs to provide a smooth debugging experience.

Key Features:

- **Breakpoint Management**: Pause execution at specific points.
- **Variable Inspection**: View variable values at runtime.
- **Step Execution**: Execute code line by line to trace errors.

7. CI/CD Tools: GitHub Actions, Jenkins, CircleCI

Continuous Integration/Continuous Deployment (CI/CD) is a practice that allows developers to automatically build, test, and deploy code changes. Tools like **GitHub Actions**, **Jenkins**, and **CircleCI** are commonly used with Go projects to automate these processes. By integrating these tools, developers can streamline their workflow, reduce errors, and ensure that code is always in a deployable state.

Key Features:

- **Automated Builds**: Compile and test code automatically.
- **Testing Integration**: Run unit tests to ensure code quality.
- **Deployment Pipelines**: Seamlessly deploy applications to production.

8. Go Testing and Benchmarking

Go has built-in support for testing with the testing package. Developers can write unit tests, integration tests, and benchmarks directly in Go. Go encourages a **test-driven development** (TDD) approach, where tests are written alongside the code. In 2024, tools like go test, go bench, and third-party libraries like **Testify** are commonly used for testing and asserting Go code.

Key Features:

- **Unit Testing**: Write tests for individual functions.
- **Benchmarking**: Measure code performance.
- **Test Suites**: Organize and run comprehensive test suites.

9. Go Server Frameworks: Gin, Echo, Fiber

Several frameworks have emerged to simplify web server development in Go. **Gin**, **Echo**, and **Fiber** are three popular frameworks that make building REST APIs and web services easier. Each offers unique features, such as middleware support, routing, and templating, allowing developers to choose the one that best fits their needs.

Key Features:

- **Routing**: Define URL endpoints and route requests.
- **Middleware Support**: Easily add logging, authentication, and other middleware.
- **Performance**: Lightweight and fast frameworks.

Go is a general-purpose programming language created with systems programming in mind. It was invented in 2007 by Google's Robert Griesemer, Rob Pike, and Ken Thompson. It is strongly and statically typed, has built-in garbage collection support, and supports concurrent programming.

Packages are used to construct programs to manage dependencies efficiently. Go programming implementations employ a traditional compile and link model to generate executable binaries. The Go programming language was introduced in November 2009 and is currently used in some of Google's production systems.

GO PROGRAMMING FEATURES

- **Language Design:** The language's designers made a conscious decision to keep the language simple and easy to understand. The entire detailing is contained within a few pages, and some interesting design decisions were made using the language's Object-Oriented support. The language is opinionated, recommending a conversational method of accomplishing things. Composition is preferred over Inheritance. The mantra in Go Language is "Do More with Less."

- **Package Management:** Go incorporates modern developer workflows for working with Open Source projects into managing external packages. Support for getting external packages and publishing our packages is provided directly in the tooling via a set of simple commands.

- **Powerful Standard Library:** Go has a robust standard library, distributed in the form of packages.

- **Static Typing:** Go is a language that is static typed. As a result, not only does this compiler work on successfully compiling code, but it also ensures type conversions and compatibility. Go avoids all of the issues we see in dynamically typed languages because of this feature.

- **Testing Support:** Go includes unit testing features by default, such as a simple mechanism for writing unit tests in parallel with our code, allowing us to understand code coverage through our tests. As an example, we can easily use this to generate code documentation.

- **Platform Independence:** Like the Java language, the Go Language supports platform independence. Because of its modular design and modularity, the code is compiled and converted into a binary form that is as small as possible, requiring no dependency. Its code can compile in any platform, server, or application on which we work.

WHY IS GoLang BETTER THAN THE OTHER PROGRAMMING LANGUAGES?

There is no respite for innovations and breakthroughs in the world of programming languages. Developers are constantly looking for a more straightforward, sophisticated, and project-friendly language. GoLang emerged as an amazing new programming language with a plethora of solutions. GoLang has taken the programming world by surprise since its introduction.

Many of the surprises that distinguish this language from others will be revealed here. Let's begin with an overview of the core capability in brief.

GoLang's Core Capability

Google developers reportedly conceived the GoLang while waiting for a code compilation project. This is why GoLang is the only language that combines all three desired features, namely ease of coding, efficient code compilation, and efficient execution. The fact that one can set all these capabilities together in a single language distinguishes GoLang from other programming languages.

Go, also known as GoLang, is a robust system-level language used for programming across large-scale network servers and large distributed systems. In simple words, through the context of what Google required for its network servers and distributed systems, GoLang emerged as an alternative to C++ and Java for app developers. The language was designed to eliminate the slowness and difficulties associated with programming for large and scalable servers and software systems. To be more specific, Go arrived at Google to provide the following solutions:

- Compilation and execution in a blink.
- Eliminating the need to work with different subsets of languages for a single project.
- Improved code readability and documentation.
- Providing an utterly consistent language.
- Allowing for simple program versioning.
- The ability to develop in multiple languages.
- Facilitating dependency management.

Multithreading and Concurrency

As hardware becomes more sophisticated over time, manufacturers add cores to the system to improve performance. When you come across with huge number of cores, the system must maintain database connections via microservices, manage queues, and maintain caches. This is why today's hardware requires a programming language that can better support concurrency and scale-up performance as the number of cores increases over time.

When working with multiple threads, most programming languages lack concurrent execution, which often slows down the pace of programming, compiling, and execution. This is where Go emerges as the most viable option for supporting both multithreading and concurrency.

When multi-core processors were widely available on sophisticated hardware, Go as a programming language came into existence. Naturally, the creators of Go placed a premium on concurrency. Go uses goroutines rather than threads, allowing it to handle many tasks simultaneously.

Go Empowers Hardware from Within

Because hardware processors only understand binaries, any application written in Java or JVM is interpreted into binaries. This interpretation at the hardware level increases the execution time. This is why compiled languages such as C/C++, which eliminate the step of understanding, can improve performance and speed of execution.

However, extracting and allocating variables in C/C++ involve a significant amount of complication and time. This is where Go shines as the ideal solution, combining the best of both worlds. Go, like C/C++, is a compiled language, which makes it as fast as they are. On the other hand, it uses garbage collection and object removal, just like Java, for variable allocation. As a result, Go is an ideal language for working within any hardware system.

The Unmatched Simplicity of Go

One of the primary benefits of adopting Go is its simplicity. Despite being a highly sophisticated language with a rich feature set, Go stands out from the group due to its simplicity and straightforward approach.

- **No Generics:** Generics or templates, which have long been a staple of various programming languages, often add to the obscurity and difficulty of understanding. By deciding to forego it, designers simplified things.

- **Single Executable:** GoLang does not include a runtime library. It can generate a single executable file that can be deployed simply by copying. This alleviates any concerns about making mistakes due to dependencies or version mismatches.

- **No Dynamic Libraries:** Go decided to forego any dynamic libraries to keep the language simple. However, in the latest Go 1.10 version, developers can upload dynamic libraries via plug-in packages. This has only been included as an added feature.

Inbuilt Testing and Profiling Framework

When developing a JavaScript application, many of us have encountered the complexities of selecting a testing framework through a series of analyses. The fact that we do not use more than 20% of the chosen framework most of the time is true. The same issue arises when good profiling is required for evaluation.

Go includes an inbuilt testing and profiling tool to help us test the application quickly and easily. Apart from providing ready-to-execute code examples, the tool can use for all types of testing and profiling needs.

Easy Learning Curve

One of the important advantages of Go is its low learning curve. We shouldn't be surprised if we say that all of GoLang's features can learn in just a few hours. Once we've mastered these fundamentals, we'll need to understand the best programming practices for specific needs as well as the standard library. However, a two- to three-hour session is sufficient to learn the language.

BEGINNING WITH Go

Several online IDEs, such as The Go Playground, repl.it, and others, can run Go programs without installing anything.
To install Go on our PCs or laptops, we will need the following two pieces of software: Text editor and Compiler.

Text Editor

A text editor provides a platform for us to write our source code. The following is a list of text editors:

- Windows notepad
- Brief
- OS Edit command
- Epsilon
- VS Code
- vm or vi
- Emacs

Finding a Go Compiler

The Go distribution is available as a binary installable for FreeBSD, Mac OS X, Linux, and Windows operating systems with 32-bit (386) and 64-bit (amd64) x86 processor architectures.

INSTALL Go ON WINDOWS

Before we begin, we must first install GoLang on our system. We need firsthand knowledge of what the Go Language is and what it does. Go is an open-source, statically typed programming language created in 2007 by Google's Robert Griesemer, Rob Pike, and Ken Thompson, but released in 2009. It also goes by the name GoLang and supports the procedural programming language. It was initially designed to boost programming productivity on large codebases, multi-core, and networked machines.

GoLang programs are easy to write. They can be written in any plain text editor such as notepad, notepad++, or something similar. One can also use an online IDE to write GoLang code or install one on their system to do writing and working on these codes easier. The best thing is that the IDE makes it easier to write the GoLang code because IDEs include many features such as an intuitive code editor, debugger, compiler, etc.

First, one must have the Go Language installed on their system to write GoLang Codes and perform various intriguing and valuable operations.

How Do We Determine the Go Language Version That Is Preinstalled?
Before we begin installing Go, it is good to check if it is already installed on our system. To see if our device has GoLang preinstalled, go to the command line (for Windows), search for cmd in the Run dialogue (+ R).

Execute following command: go version

If GoLang is already installed on your PC, it will generate a message containing all of the GoLang version's details; otherwise, if GoLang is not installed on your PC, an error stating "Bad command or file name" will appear.

Downloading and Installing Go

Before we begin the installation procedure, we must first download it.
Download GoLang for our system architecture and then follow the installation instructions for GoLang.

- **Step 1:** Unzip the downloaded archive file after it has been downloaded. After unzipping, we'll find a go folder in our current directory.

- **Step 2:** Copy and paste the extracted folder wherever we put it. In this case, we're installing it on the C drive.

- **Step 3:** Now, configure the environment variables. Right-click My PC and choose Properties. Select the Advanced System Settings from left menu and then Environment Variables.

- **Step 4:** From the system variables, select Path and then Edit. Then select New and enter the Path with bin directory where we pasted the Go folder. Here, we're going to change the path and click OK.

- **Step 5:** Create a new user variable that tells the Go command where the GoLang libraries are located. To do so, go to User Variables and select New.

Now enter GOROOT as the Variable name and the path to our GoLang folder as the Variable value. So, in this case, the Variable Value is C:\go\. After we've finished filling out the form, click OK.
Then, on Environment Variables, click OK, and our setup is complete. Now, check the GoLang version by typing go version into the command prompt.

After completing the installation process, any text editor or IDE can use to write GoLang Codes, which can then run on the IDE or the Command prompt using the command: **go run filename.go**

WRITING THE FIRST Go PROGRAM

package main import "fmt" func main() {   // print

fmt.Println("Hello, everyone") }

Explanation of Go program syntax:

Line 1: contains the program's main package, including its overall content. It is the starting point for the program, so it must be written.

- **Line 2:** contains import "fmt," a preprocessor command that instructs the compiler to include the files in the package.

- **Line 3:** main function; this is the start of the program's execution.

- **Line 4:** fmt.

- **Println():** is a standard library function for printing something to the screen.

- **The fmt package:** has transmitted the Println method, which displays the output in this case.

- **Comments:** are used to explain code in the same way that they are in Java, C, or C++. Comment entries are ignored by compilers and are not executed. Comments can be single or multiple lines long.

Single-Line Comment **Syntax:**
  // single-line-comment

Multiline Comment **Syntax:**
  /* multiline-comment */

  Example:
  package main import "fmt" func main() {
    fmt.Println("2 + 2 =", 2 + 2) }

Explanation of the Preceding Program

The preceding program uses the same package line, import line, function declaration, and Println function as the first Go program. Instead of printing the string "Hello, everyone," we print 2 + 2 = followed by the result of the expression 2 + 2. This expression comprises three parts: the int numeric literal 2, the + operator (which represents addition), and another int numeric literal 2.

Why Is There a "Go Language"?

Go is an attempt to combine the programming ease of an interpreted language and the safety of a statically typed, dynamically typed language with the efficiency of a compiled language. It also aspires to be cutting-edge, with networked and multi-core computing support.

What Is Absent in Go That Is Present in Other Languages?

- Go makes an effort to reduce typing in both senses of the word. Developers worked hard to keep clutter and complexity to a minimum throughout the design process.

- There are no forward declarations or header files; everything is only declared once.

- Simple type derivation using the: = declare-and-initialize construct reduces stuttering.

- There is no type hierarchy: types simply exist; they are not required to announce their relationships.

Hardware Restrictions

We have observed that hardware and processing configuration change at a prolonged rate over a decade. In 2004, the P4 had a clock speed of 3.0 GHz. In 2018, the Macbook Pro has a clock speed of approximately (2.3 GHz vs. 2.66 GHz). We use more processors to speed up functionality, but the cost of using more processors also rises. As a result, we use limited processors, and with few processors, we have a heavy programming language whose threading consumes more memory and slows down our system's performance.

To address this issue, GoLang was designed so that instead of threading, it uses goroutine, which is similar to threading but consumes much less memory. Because threading consumes 1 MB of memory and goroutines 2 KB, it is easy to trigger millions of goroutines simultaneously. As a result of the points above, GoLang is a powerful language that handles concurrency in the same way that C++ and Java do.

Benefits and Drawbacks of the Go Language Benefits:

- **Flexible:** It is adaptable because concise, straightforward, and simple to read.

- **Concurrency:** It allows multiple processes to run concurrently and effectively.

- **Quick Compilation:** Its compilation time is very short.

- **Library:** It includes an extensive standard library.

- Garbage collection is an essential feature of go. Go excels at providing a high level of control over memory allocation, and the garbage collector's latency has been dramatically reduced in recent versions.

- It checks for interface and type embedding.

Drawbacks:

- Even though many discussions about it, it does not support generics.

- Although the packages included with this programming language are pretty helpful, Go is not an object-oriented programming language in the traditional sense.

- Some libraries, particularly a UI toolkit, are missing.

Some popular Go Language applications include:

- **Docker:** It is a set of tools for managing and deploying Linux containers.
- **Red Hat:** It is Openshift and is a cloud computing platform as a service.
- **Kubernetes:** The Future of Seamlessly Automated Deployment.
- **Dropbox:** It shifted some of its critical components from Python to Go.
- **Netflix:** For two different aspects of their server architecture.
- **InfluxDB:** It is a time-series database that is open source and developed by InfluxData.
- **GoLang:** The language was created in Go.

TERMINAL

GoLand features an integrated terminal emulator that allows us to interact with our command-line shell from within the IDE. It may run Git commands, modify file permissions, and conduct other command-line functions without switching to a specialized terminal program.

The terminal emulator starts with our normal system shell, but it supports a variety of alternative shells, including Windows PowerShell, Command Prompt cmd.exe, sh, bash, zsh, csh, and others. See Configure the terminal emulator for further information on changing the shell.

The Open Terminal Tool Window

Select View | Tool Windows | Terminal from the main menu, or press Alt+F12.
By default, the terminal emulator runs with the current directory set to the current project's root directory.
Alternatively, we may right-click any file (for example, in the Project tool window or any open tab) and choose Open in Terminal from the context menu to launch the Terminal tool window with a new session in the file's directory.

Start New Session

Click Add button to create a new session in a new tab on the toolbar.
   To run several sessions within a tab, right-click it and choose Split Right or Split Down from the context menu.
   When we close the project or GoLand, the Terminal remembers tabs and sessions. Tab names, shell history, and the current working directory, are all saved.
   Use the Terminal toolbar's Close button or right-click the tab and pick Close Tab from the context menu to close a tab.
   To move between active tabs, press Alt+Right and Alt+Left. We may also press Alt+Down to get a list of all terminal tabs.
   Right-click a tab and pick Rename Session from the context menu to rename it.

Ctrl+F will search for a specific string in a Terminal session. This searches the entire session's text, including the prompt, commands, and output.

Configure the terminal emulator as follows:

To open the IDE settings, press Ctrl+Alt+S and then select Tools | Terminal.

INSTALL Go ON MAC

Before we begin, we must first install GoLang on our system. We need firsthand knowledge of what the Go Language is and what it does. Go is an open-source, statically typed programming language created in 2007 by Google's Robert Griesemer, Rob Pike, and Ken Thompson but released in 2009. It also goes by the name GoLang and supports the procedural programming language. It was originally designed to boost programming productivity on large codebases, multi-core, and networked machines.

GoLang programs can be created in any plain text editor such as TextEdit, Sublime Text, or something similar. One can also use an online IDE to write GoLang code or install one on their system to make writing and working on these codes easier. For convenience, using an IDE makes it easier to write the GoLang code because IDEs include many features such as an intuitive code editor, debugger, compiler, etc.

The following are the steps for installing GoLang on MacOS:

- **Step 1:** Determine whether Go is installed or not. Before we begin installing Go, it is good to check to see if it is already installed on our system. To see if our device is preinstalled with GoLang, open the Terminal and type the following command: **go version**

  If GoLang is already installed on your PC, it will generate a message with all of the GoLang version details available; otherwise, it will show an error.

- **Step 2:** Before we begin the installation process, we must first download it.
  Download GoLang based on our system architecture. For the system, we have downloaded go1.13.1drawin-amd64.pkg.

- **Step 3:** Once the package has been downloaded, install it on our system.

- **Step 4:** Following the completion of the installation processes. Open Terminal (a command-line interface for MacOS) and use the GoLang version command to see if Go is installed correctly. It displays the GoLang version information, indicating that Go is successfully installed on our system.

After successfully installing Go on our system, we will now configure the Go workspace. A Go workspace is a folder on our computer that will house all of our Go code.

- **Step 1:** Make a folder called Go in our documents (or wherever we want in our system).

- **Step 2:** Tell the Go tools where to look for this folder. To begin, use the following command to navigate to our home directory:

cd ~

After that, use the following command to set the folder's path:

echo "export GOPATH=/Users/anki/Documents/go" >> .bash_profile

In this case, we add export OPATH=/Users/anki/Documents/go to .bash_profile. The .bash profile file is automatically loaded when we log into our Mac account and contains all of our command-line interface startup configurations and preferences (CLI).

- **Step 3:** Run the following command to ensure that our .bash_profile contains the following path:

  cat. bash_profile

- **Step 4:** Now, we'll use the following command to verify our go path. We can also skip this step if we prefer.

  echo $GOPATH

Making Our First Program

- **Step 1:** Download and then install a text editor of your choice. Create a folder in Documents called Go (or whatever name we want) after installation (or wherever we want in our system). Create another folder called source in this folder and another folder called welcome in this source folder. All of our Go programs will save in this folder.

- **Step 2:** Let us write our first Go program. Open a text editor and type the Go program.

- **Step 3:** After creating the Go program, save it with the extension. go.

- **Step 4:** Launch the terminal to execute your first Go program.

- **Step 5:** Change the location of our program's files.

- **Step 6:** After changing directories, use the following command to run the Go program:

  go run name_of_the_program.go

Execute a Go Program

Let's go over how to save the source code in a file, compile it, and then run the program. Please follow the instructions below:

- Open a text editor and paste the above code into it.

- Save the file with the name helloo.go

- Open the command prompt.

- Navigate to the location of saved file.

- Enter go run helloo.

- To run our code, go ahead and press enter.

- If your code is error-free, we will see "Hello Everyone" printed on the screen.

$ go run helloo.go

Hello, everyone

Ascertain that the Go compiler is in our path and that it is running in the directory containing the source file helloo.go.

Do Programs in Go Link with the C/C++ Programming Language?

It is indeed possible to use C and Go in the same address space, but it is not a natural fit and may necessitate the use of special interface software. In addition, linking C code with Go code sacrifices Go's memory safety and stack management properties. Sometimes using C libraries to solve a problem is necessary, but doing so always introduces an element of risk that is not present in pure Go code, so proceed with caution.

If we must use C with Go, how you proceed is determined by the Go compiler implementation. The Go team provides support for three Go compiler implementations.

The default compiler is GC, followed by gccgo, which uses the GCC back end, and a slightly less mature gollvm, which uses the LLVM infra structure.

Because gc has a different calling convention and linker than C, it cannot be called directly from C programs and vice versa. The cgo program implements a "foreign function interface" that allows Go code to call C libraries safely. This capability is extended to C++ libraries by SWIG.

Gccgo and gollvm can also be used with cgo and SWIG. Because they use a traditional API, it is possible to link code from these compilers directly with GCC/LLVM-compiled C or C++ programs with caution. However, doing so safely necessitates familiarity with all languages' calling conventions and consideration for stack limits when calling C or C++ from Go.

IN GoLang, HOW DO WE CREATE AN EMPTY FILE?

Go Language, like other computer languages, allows us to construct files. It offers the Create () function for creating a file, which is used to create or truncate the given named file.
If the specified file already exists, then this method will truncate it.
If a specified file does not exist, this method will create one with mode 0666.
This procedure will return a *PathError exception if the specified path is incorrect.
This function returns a file descriptor that may be read and written.
Because it is specified in the os package, we must import the os package in our program to use the Create () method.

Syntax: func Create (file-name string) (*File, error)

First example:
package main import ("log"

```go
    "os"
)
func main() {
    // empty file Creation
    // Create() function Using     myfile, es := os.Create("helloo.txt")
    if es != nil {        log.Fatal(es)
    }
    log.Println(myfile)     myfile.Close() }
```

Second example:

```go
package main import (    "log"
    "os"
)
func main() {
    // empty file Creation
    // Create() function Using
    myfile, es := os.Create("/Users/anki/
Documents/new_folder/helloo.txt")
    if es != nil {        log.Fatal(es)
    }
    log.Println(myfile)     myfile.Close() }
```

In GoLang, We May Check Whether a Given File Exists or Not

The IsNotExist() function in the Go programming language allows us to determine if a given file exists or not. If the above-mentioned function returns true, then the error is known to report that the specified file or directory does not already exist, and if it returns false, it means that the supplied file or directory does exist. ErrNotExist and several syscall errors also satisfy this procedure. Because it is specified in the os package, we must import the os package in our program to use the IsNotExist() method.

Syntax: func IsNotExist(es error) bool

First example:

```go
package main  import (    "log"    "os"
) var (
    myfile *os.FileInfo    es  error
)
func main() {
    // Stat() function returns the file info and
    //if there is no file, then it will return
error
    myfile, es := os.Stat("helloo.txt")
    if es != nil {
    // Checking if given file exists or not
```

```go
    // Using the IsNotExist() function      if os.IsNotExist(es) {          log.Fatal("File
not Found")
    }
  }
  log.Println("File Exist")    log.Println("File Detail is:")    log.Println("Name is: ",
myfile.Name())    log.Println("Size is: ", myfile.Size())    }
```

Second example:

```go
package main
 import (    "log"
  "os"
) var (
   myfile *os.FileInfo    es  error
)
func main() {
   // Stat() function returns the file info and
   // if there is no file, then it will return error
   myfile, es := os.Stat("/Users/anki/Documents/
new_folder/myfolder/helloo.txt")
   if es != nil {
     // Checking if given file exists or not
       // Using IsNotExist() function        if os.IsNotExist(es) {
   log.Fatal("File not Found")
       }
     }
   log.Println("File Exist")    log.Println("File Detail is:")    log.Println("Name is: ",
myfile.Name())    log.Println("Size is: ", myfile.Size()) }
```

CREATE A DIRECTORY IN Go

In Go, use the os.Mkdir() method to create a single directory. Use os.MkdirAll() to establish a folder hierarchy (nested directories). Both methods need a path and the folder's permission bits as parameters.

Make a Single Directory **package main import (**
"log"
  "os"
) func main() {
```go
   if er := os.Mkdir("a", os.ModePerm); er != nil {
     log.Fatal(er)
   }}
```

Make a Directory Hierarchy (Nested Directories)
package main import ("log"

```
    "os"
) func main() {
    if er := os.MkdirAll("a/b/c/d", os.ModePerm); er
!= nil {
        log.Fatal(er)
    } }
```

The os.Mkdir() function generates a new directory with the specified name but does not allow for the creation of subdirectories.

In this chapter, we covered the introduction of Go with its features, advantages, and disadvantages. We also covered Go installation in Windows and Mac. Moreover, we covered Files and Folders, The Terminal, and Text Editors.

GoLang Tools

HOW TO READ AND WRITE PROGRAMS IN Go

GoLang includes an extensive built-in library that may use to conduct file read and write operations. The io/ioutil module is all about reading from files on the local system. Onc can use the io/ioutil module to save data to a file.

The fmt module supports formatted I/O by providing methods for reading input from stdin and printing output to stdout. The log module is a basic logging package that is implemented.
It introduces a Logger type with methods for formatting output. The os module allows us to use native operating-system functions. Buffered I/O is implemented by the bufio module, which helps to enhance CPU speed.

- **os.Create():** This function creates a file with the specified name. If another file with the same name already exists, the create method truncates it.

- **ioutil.ReadFile():** The only parameter to the ioutil.ReadFile() function is the path to the file to be read. This procedure either returns the file's contents or an error.

- **ioutil.WriteFile():** It returns the ioutil. WriteFile() is a function used to save data to a file. The WriteFile() function accepts three parameters: the location of the file to which we want to write, the data object, and the FileMode, which contains the file's mode and permission bits.log.

- **Fatalf:** Fatalf will terminate the application after printing the log message. It is similar to doing Printf() followed by os.Exit (1).

- **log.Panicf:** Panic is similar to an exception that may occur during runtime. Panicln is the same as Println() followed by a panic() call. The parameter supplied to panic () is displayed when the program exits.

- **bufio.NewReader(os.Stdin):** This function returns a new Reader with the default buffer size (4096 bytes).

- **inputReader.ReadString('n'):** This method reads user input from stdin until the first occurrence of a delimiter in the input and returns a string containing the data up to and including the delimiter. An error before locating a delimiter provides the data read before the fault and the error itself.

First example: For best results, use the offline compiler. Save the file as a. go file. To run the program, follow-up the below given command.

go run file-name.go

```
// program to read and write files
package main
// importing packages
import (    "fmt"
   "io/ioutil"
   "log"
   "os"
)
func CreateFile() {
   // fmt package implements formatted I/O, it
has functions like Printf and Scanf    fmt.Printf("Writing file in Go lang\n")
   // in case error is thrown it is received by
err variable and Fatalf method of
   // log prints error message and stops program
execution
   file, er := os.Create("test1.txt")
   if er != nil {
      log.Fatalf("failed creating file: %s", er)
   }
   // Defer is used for the purposes of cleanup like closing a running file after the file has
// been written and the main function has
completed execution    defer file.Close()    // len variable captures the length of string
written to the file.    len, er := file.WriteString("Welcome
Everyone"+
        " Program demonstrates reading and
writing"+
                 " operations to a file in
the Go lang.")    if er != nil {
      log.Fatalf("failed writing to file: %s", er)
   }
   // Name() method returns name of the file as presented to Create() method.
   fmt.Printf("\nFile Name: %s", file.Name())    fmt.Printf("\nLength: %d bytes", len)
}
func ReadFile() {
   fmt.Printf("\n\nReading a file in the Go
lang\n")
```

```go
    fileName := "test1.txt"
    // The ioutil package contains inbuilt
    // methods like ReadFile that reads
    // filename and returns contents.
    data, er := ioutil.ReadFile("test.txt")
    if er != nil {        log.Panicf("failed reading data from file:
%s", er)
    }
    fmt.Printf("\nFile Name is: %s", fileName)     fmt.Printf("\nSize is: %d bytes", len(data))
    fmt.Printf("\nData is: %s", data)
}
// main function func main() {
    CreateFile()
    ReadFile()
}
```

Second example: GoLang program code reads and writes files based on user input.

```go
// Program to read and write files
package main
// importing requires packages
import (
    "bufio"     "fmt"
    "io/ioutil"
    "log"
    "os"
)
func CreateFile(filename, text string)
{
    // fmt package implements formatted I/O
    // and contains the inbuilt methods like the
Printf and Scanf
    fmt.Printf("Writing to a file in the Go
lang\n")

    // Creating file using Create() method with
user inputted filename and err
    // variable catches any error thrown     file, er := os.Create(filename)
        if er != nil {
        log.Fatalf("failed creating file: %s", er)
    }
    // closing running file after the main method
has completed execution and
    // writing to the file is complete
    defer file.Close()
```

```go
    // writing data to file using     // WriteString() method and
    // length of the string is stored in the len
variable
    len, er := file.WriteString(text)
    if er != nil {
        log.Fatalf("failed writing to file: %s",
er)    }
    fmt.Printf("\nFile Name is: %s", file.Name())     fmt.Printf("\nLength is: %d bytes", len)
}
func ReadFile(filename string) {     fmt.Printf("\n\nReading a file in the Go
lang\n")
    // file is read using ReadFile() method of the
ioutil package
    data, err := ioutil.ReadFile(filename)
    // in case of an error
    // the error statement is printed, program is
stopped     if er != nil {         log.Panicf("failed reading data from file:
%s", er)
    }
    fmt.Printf("\nFile Name is: %s", filename)     fmt.Printf("\nSize is: %d bytes", len(data))
    fmt.Printf("\nData is: %s", data)
}
// main function func main() {
    // user input for the filename     fmt.Println("Enter-filename: ")
    var filename string     fmt.Scanln(&filename)
    // user input for the file content     fmt.Println("Enter-text: ")    inputReader :=
bufio.NewReader(os.Stdin)     input, _ := inputReader.ReadString('\n')
    // file is created then read
    CreateFile(filename, input)
    ReadFile(filename)
}
```

IN GoLang, HOW TO RENAME AND MOVE A FILE

The Rename () function in the Go programming language allows us to rename and transfer an existing file to a new directory. This procedure is used to rename and transfer a file from one path to another.

   If the specified new path already exists and is not in a directory, this procedure will overwrite it. However, OS-specific limitations may apply if the specified old and new paths are in separate directories.

   If the specified path is wrong, type *LinkError will throw an error.

   Because it is specified in the os package, we must import the os package in our program to use the Remove () method.

Syntax: func Rename (old-path, new-path string) error

First example:

```go
// Program to illustrate how to rename, // move a file in the default directory
package main    import (    "log"
    "os"
)  func main() {
    // Rename and Remove a file    // Using Rename() function
    OriginalPath := "helloo.txt"
    NewPath := "abc.txt"
    es := os.Rename(Original_Path, New_Path)
    if es != nil {        log.Fatal(es)
    }
      }
```

Second example:

```go
// Program to illustrate how to rename,
//remove a file in new directory
package main
import (    "log"
    "os"
)
func main() {
    // Rename and Remove file
    // Using Rename() function
    OriginalPath := "/Users/anki/Documents/new_
folder/helloo.txt"
    NewPath := "/Users/anki/Documents/new_folder/
myfolder/abc.txt"
    es := os.Rename(OriginalPath, NewPath)
    if es != nil {        log.Fatal(es)
    } }
```

HOW TO READ FILES LINE BY LINE TO STRING

The bufio package Scanner is used to read a file line by line. Let the text file be called sample1.txt, and the content inside the file is as follows.

The Go programming language is an open-source, statically compiled programming language. Rob Pike, Ken Thompson, and Robert Grieserner created it at Google. It is sometimes referred to as GoLang. The Go programming language is a general-purpose programming language designed to develop large-scale, complicated software.

```go
package main import (
    "bufio"    "fmt"
    "log"
    "os"
```

```go
) func main() {
    // os.Open() opens specific file in the     // read-only mode,
    // this return pointer of type os.     file, er := os.Open("sample1.txt")

    if er != nil {
        log.Fatalf("failed to open")
    }
    // bufio.NewScanner() function is called in which     // object os.File passed as its parameter
    // this returns object bufio.Scanner which is used
on the
    // bufio.Scanner.Split() method     scanner := bufio.NewScanner(file)     //
The bufio.ScanLines is used as
    // input to method bufio.Scanner.Split()     // and then scanning forwards to each
    // new line using bufio.Scanner.Scan() method.     scanner.Split(bufio.ScanLines)
    var text []string     for scanner.Scan() {
        text = append(text, scanner.Text())
    }
    // The method os.File.Close() is called
    // on the os.File object to close file
    file.Close()     // and then a loop iterates through,
    // prints each of the slice values.
    for _, each_ln := range text {     fmt.Println(each_ln)
    } }
```

Conclusion

Go, or Golang, has solidified its position as one of the leading programming languages for developing efficient, scalable, and robust software solutions. Since its inception, it has garnered widespread adoption and support from developers and organizations, making it a language of choice for many modern software applications, especially those centered around cloud computing, web development, microservices, and system-level programming. In 2024, the strengths of Go have only become more pronounced as the language continues to evolve alongside the rapidly growing demands of technology.

Why Go Remains Relevant in 2024

The success and enduring relevance of Go can be attributed to a few key characteristics that make it stand out from other programming languages:

1. **Simplicity and Readability**: One of the main reasons behind Go's success is its clean and simple syntax. Go was designed to be easy to learn and write, making it accessible for both beginners and seasoned developers. This simplicity promotes better readability, which leads to maintainable code. Go eliminates unnecessary language features, focusing on essential constructs that simplify the development process. This approach ensures that code written in Go remains clear and concise, reducing the chances of introducing bugs.

2. **Performance**: Being a statically typed, compiled language, Go produces efficient machine code that runs faster than interpreted languages like Python or JavaScript. This makes Go an excellent choice for applications that require high performance, such as network servers, real-time systems, and large-scale distributed applications. The compiler optimizes the code for speed, which is critical in a world where performance directly impacts user experience and infrastructure costs.

3. **Concurrency Model**: Go's native support for concurrent programming is one of its most distinctive features. The language introduced goroutines, lightweight threads that allow functions to run concurrently. Goroutines are significantly more memory-efficient than traditional threads, enabling developers to write programs that can handle thousands of concurrent tasks without consuming excessive resources. The channel-based communication model simplifies synchronization and data exchange between goroutines, making concurrent programming in Go much safer and more manageable than in other languages. In a world where applications need to handle concurrent requests efficiently, Go's concurrency model remains a crucial advantage.

4. **Cross-Platform Compilation**: Go offers seamless cross-compilation, which allows developers to compile code for different operating systems and architectures from a single codebase. This feature is particularly valuable in the era of diverse computing environments, where applications need to run across various platforms, including cloud servers, desktop computers, and IoT devices. Developers can compile their Go programs for Windows, macOS, Linux, and other operating systems, ensuring wide accessibility without additional overhead.

5. **Rich Standard Library**: Go's standard library is extensive and well-designed, covering a broad range of functionalities from networking, file I/O, and text processing to web servers, cryptography, and concurrency. Developers can build powerful applications without relying heavily on third-party packages, which reduces dependency management issues and enhances code stability. The consistency and reliability of Go's standard library encourage developers to build secure, performant, and scalable applications quickly.

6. **Scalability and Microservices**: Go is an excellent choice for building microservices, which have become a popular architectural pattern for developing scalable, cloud-native applications. Microservices break down complex systems into smaller, independently deployable services that can be developed, tested, and scaled independently. Go's small binary sizes, fast start-up time, and efficient memory usage make it a natural fit for microservices, where resource efficiency is critical. Many companies, including Google, Uber, Netflix, and Dropbox, have used Go to build scalable microservices-based architectures that can handle millions of users.

7. **Cloud-Native Development**: Go's relevance to cloud-native development has grown significantly, given that many of the core tools used for managing cloud infrastructure, such as Docker and Kubernetes, are written in Go. This makes Go a natural choice for developers working on cloud-based solutions. In 2024, as more companies shift to cloud-native approaches, Go continues to provide the performance, scalability, and ease of deployment required for cloud services. Its compatibility with containerization tools like Docker and orchestration platforms like Kubernetes makes it easier for developers to deploy and manage scalable applications in the cloud.

8. **Ease of Learning**: Go's simple syntax and minimalistic design make it easy for new developers to pick up. Unlike languages that require an in-depth understanding of complex programming concepts, Go provides a straightforward learning curve. This ease of learning translates into faster development times and a broader developer base, as teams can quickly onboard new developers to work on Go projects. The language's simplicity does not sacrifice performance, which means developers get the best of both worlds—ease of development and high efficiency.

9. **Ecosystem and Community**: Over the years, Go has built a robust ecosystem of tools, libraries, and frameworks that enhance the development process. From web frameworks like Gin and Echo to testing tools like Golang CI-Lint and Delve, the ecosystem provides everything developers need to build, test, and deploy Go applications efficiently. Moreover, the Go community is active, supportive, and continuously contributing to the improvement of the language and its ecosystem. Regular updates and new releases ensure that Go stays relevant and addresses the needs of modern software development. The strong community presence also provides extensive resources, tutorials, and open-source projects that help developers solve common problems and adopt best practices.

10. **Emphasis on Best Practices**: Go promotes best practices such as clean code, simplicity, and effective error handling. The language discourages complex designs and over-engineering, which aligns with its philosophy of keeping things simple and efficient. Go's unique error-handling approach encourages developers to handle errors explicitly, which reduces the likelihood of unnoticed bugs and unexpected crashes. By enforcing simplicity and promoting robust code practices, Go ensures that projects remain maintainable, scalable, and reliable over time.

Future of Go in the Software Development Industry
The future of Go looks bright as the language continues to adapt and grow with the needs of the software development industry. Several trends and developments indicate that Go will remain a crucial language for developers:

- **Growth of Cloud-Native Technologies**: As cloud computing becomes more pervasive, the need for cloud-native applications that are fast, scalable, and efficient will continue to grow. Go's strengths align perfectly with the requirements of cloud-native applications, making it a go-to language for building cloud-based services, serverless applications, and microservices.

- **Increased Adoption in DevOps**: Go is not just a language for application developers; it has also become a favourite among DevOps engineers. Tools like Docker, Kubernetes, and Prometheus—essential components of the DevOps ecosystem—are built in Go. This has led to an increased adoption of Go within the DevOps community, as developers can contribute to these projects or build their own infrastructure tools with Go's efficiency and simplicity.

- **Continued Improvement and Support**: The Go team at Google, along with the active community, continues to work on improving the language. Regular updates, feature additions, and performance enhancements ensure that Go remains competitive with other languages. Future versions of Go may include improvements to error handling, generics, and performance, making it even more powerful and versatile.

- **Emergence of AI and Data Science**: Although traditionally not associated with data science, there is a growing interest in using Go for machine learning and AI applications due to its performance advantages. Go's simplicity and speed can make it an attractive option for developing machine learning models, especially in production environments where performance is a critical factor. Libraries like Gorgonia are making it easier to implement machine learning algorithms in Go, opening up new possibilities for the language.

- **Adoption in Enterprise Software**: Go is increasingly being used in enterprise environments due to its scalability, performance, and maintainability. Enterprises require robust, scalable solutions that can handle high traffic, and Go's ability to deliver efficient, concurrent software solutions makes it a preferred choice. As businesses continue to adopt microservices architectures, Go's popularity in enterprise software development is expected to rise.

Conclusion: The Language of Simplicity and Efficiency

Go's philosophy of simplicity and efficiency has been the cornerstone of its success. In a world where software development is becoming increasingly complex, Go's straightforward approach allows developers to write code that is clean, maintainable, and scalable. This balance of simplicity and performance has helped Go carve out a niche for itself, particularly in building cloud-native applications, microservices, and distributed systems.

As we move forward in 2024 and beyond, the need for scalable, efficient, and easy-to-deploy software solutions will continue to grow. Go is well-positioned to meet these needs, thanks to its strong concurrency model, performance, cross-platform support, and thriving ecosystem. Whether you are a seasoned developer or just starting, learning Go will open up opportunities in various fields, from web development to cloud computing and infrastructure engineering.

The continuous support and improvement from its development community ensure that Go will remain relevant, adaptable, and capable of handling the challenges of modern software development. With its emphasis on clarity, performance, and concurrency, Go is not just a language but a set of best practices that encourage developers to write efficient, reliable, and scalable software. The future looks promising for Go, and it is poised to remain a critical tool for developers looking to build the next generation of software solutions.

2. Go: The Basic Types, Values, Pointers, Operations and Conversions

Introduction

The Go programming language, commonly known as Golang, is known for its simplicity, performance, and ease of use. One of the core features of Go is its straightforward handling of types, values, and pointers, which forms the foundation for writing efficient and reliable code. This introduction provides an in-depth look at these basic constructs, explaining how they work and why they are essential for Go programming.

1. Understanding Basic Types in Go

Basic types are the building blocks of any Go program. They define how data is stored, processed, and manipulated. Go offers a range of built-in types, including:

- **Numeric Types**:
    - **Integers**: int, int8, int16, int32, int64, uint, uint8 (byte), uint16, uint32, uint64, uintptr
    - **Floating-point numbers**: float32, float64
    - **Complex numbers**: complex64, complex128
- **Boolean Type**: bool
- **String Type**: string
- **Rune Type**: rune, an alias for int32 representing a Unicode character

1.1 Numeric Types

Numeric types in Go are straightforward and cater to various use cases. Unlike some other programming languages, Go emphasizes strict type usage. For instance, int32 and int64 are not interchangeable, even though both are integers. This strict typing helps prevent errors and ensures data is handled appropriately.

Example:
```
var x int = 10
var y float64 = 25.5
```

1.2 Boolean Type

The bool type is used to represent logical values: true and false. It plays a crucial role in control structures like if statements and loops.

Example:
```
var isActive bool = true
```

1.3 String Type

Strings in Go are sequences of bytes that are immutable. They can be used to store text, and Go provides several built-in functions for working with strings, such as concatenation, slicing, and formatting.

Example:
var name string = "Go Programming"

1.4 Rune Type
The rune type is used to represent Unicode code points. It allows Go to handle international characters effectively.

Example:
var letter rune = 'G'

2. Values and Variables

In Go, a variable is a storage location for a value. Understanding how to declare, assign, and manipulate variables is fundamental for any Go programmer.

2.1 Variable Declaration

Variables can be declared using the var keyword, with or without an explicit type.

Example:
var age int = 30
name := "Alice" // Type inferred as string
The short declaration (:=) allows for quick assignment and type inference, simplifying code readability and reducing boilerplate.

2.2 Zero Values

In Go, uninitialized variables have a default "zero value." Understanding these zero values is crucial, as it helps in avoiding errors when variables are not explicitly assigned.

Type	Zero Value
int	0
float64	0.0
bool	false
string	"" (empty string)

3. Pointers in Go

Pointers are a way to reference memory addresses, allowing for more efficient data manipulation, especially with larger data structures. Unlike some languages where pointers are complicated, Go simplifies their usage while retaining the benefits.

3.1 What is a Pointer?

A pointer is a variable that holds the memory address of another variable. By using pointers, you can directly access and modify the value stored at that address.

Example:
```
var x int = 42
var p *int = &x  // p is a pointer to the memory address of x
```

3.2 Dereferencing Pointers

Dereferencing a pointer means accessing the value stored at the memory address to which the pointer points. This is done using the * operator.

Example:
```
fmt.Println(*p)  // Output: 42
```

3.3 Why Use Pointers?

Pointers can be used to:
- Modify variables outside the function scope
- Pass large data structures efficiently
- Avoid copying data unnecessarily

3.4 Nil Pointers

A pointer that has not been initialized or does not point to a valid address is known as a nil pointer. Attempting to dereference a nil pointer will cause a runtime error.

Example:
```
var p *int
if p != nil {
   fmt.Println(*p)
} else {
   fmt.Println("Pointer is nil")
}
```

4. Practical Use Cases
4.1 Using Pointers to Modify Variables

When you pass a variable to a function, Go passes a copy of that variable. However, if you pass a pointer, the function can modify the original variable directly.

Example:
```
func updateValue(num *int) {
    *num = 100
}

func main() {
    value := 50
    updateValue(&value)
    fmt.Println(value)  // Output: 100
}
```

4.2 Pointers and Structs

Pointers are especially useful when working with complex data structures like structs. They allow you to pass and modify large objects without copying them, making the code more efficient.

Example:
```
type User struct {
    name string
    age  int
}

func updateName(user *User, newName string) {
    user.name = newName
}
```

In this chapter, I begin to describe the Go language, focusing on the basic data types before moving on to how they are used to create constants and variables. I also introduce the Go support for pointers. Pointers can be a source of confusion, especially if you are coming to Go from languages such as Java or C#, and I describe how Go pointers work, demonstrate why they can be useful, and explain why they are not to be feared.

The features provided by any programming language are intended to be used together, which makes it difficult to introduce them progressively. Some of the examples in this part of the book rely on features that are described subsequently. These examples contain enough detail to provide context and include references to the part of the book where additional details can be found.

To prepare for this chapter, open a new command prompt, navigate to a convenient location, and create a directory named basic Features. Run the command shown to create a go.mod file for the project.

Creating the Example Project

go mod in it basic features

Add a file named main.go to the basicFeatures folder.

The Contents of the main.go File in the basicFeatures Folder package main
```
import (    "fmt"
    "math/rand"
)
func main() {
    fmt.Println(rand.Int()) }
```

Use the command prompt to run the command shown in the basicFeatures folder.
Running the Example Project go run.

The code in the main.go file will be compiled and executed, producing the following output:

5577006791947779410

The output from the code will always be the same value, even though it is produced by the random number package.

Using the Go Standard Library

Go provides a wide set of useful features through its standard library, which is the term used to describe the built-in API.

I describe the way Go packages are created, but some of the examples rely on the packages in the standard library, and it is important to understand how they are used.

Each package in the standard library groups together a set of related features. The code uses two packages: the fmt package provides features for formatting and writing strings, and the math/rand package deals with random numbers.

The first step in using a package is to define an import statement. Figure illustrates the import statement used.

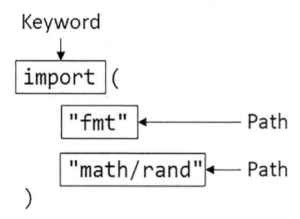

Figure Importing a package

There are two parts to an import statement: the import keyword and the package paths. The paths are grouped with parentheses if more than one package is imported.

The import statement creates a package reference, through which the features provided by the package can be accessed. The name of the package reference is the last segment in the package path. The path for the fmt package has only one segment, so the package reference will be fmt. There are two segments in the math/rand path—math and rand—and so the package reference will be rand.

The fmt package defines a Println function that writes a value to the standard output, and the math/ rand package defines an Int function that generates a random integer. To access these functions, I use their package reference, followed by a period and then the function name, as shown in Figure.

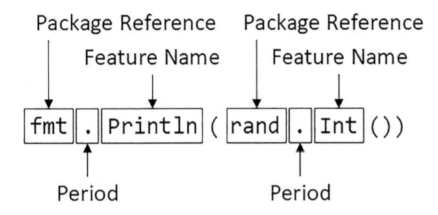

Figure Using a package reference

A related feature provided by the fmt package is the ability to compose strings by combining static content with data values, as shown.

Composing a String in the main.go File in the basicFeatures Folder package main

```
import (    "fmt"
   "math/rand"
)

func main() {    fmt.Println("Value:",
rand.Int()) }
```

The series of comma-separated values passed to the Println function are combined into a single string, which is then written to the standard output. To compile and execute the code, use the command prompt to run the command shown in the basicFeatures folder.

Running the Example Project

go run.

The code in the main.go file will be compiled and executed, producing the following output:

Value: 5577006791947779410

There are more useful ways to compose strings—which I describe in Part 2 —but this is simple and a useful way for me to provide output in the examples.

Understanding the Basic Data Types

Go provides a set of basic data types, which are described. In the sections that follow, I describe these types and explain how they are used. These types are the foundation of Go development, and many of the characteristics of these types will be familiar from other languages.

Table The Go Basic Data Types

Name	Description
int	This type represents a whole number, which can be positive or negative. The int type size is platform-dependent and will be either 32 or 64 bits. There are also integer types that have a specific size, such as int8, int16, int32, and int64, but the int type should be used unless you need a specific size.
uint	This type represents a positive whole number. The uint type size is platformdependent and will be either 32 or 64 bits. There are also unsigned integer types that have a specific size, such as uint8, uint16, uint32, and uint64, but the uint type should be used unless you need a specific size.
byte	This type is an alias for uint8 and is typically used to represent a byte of data.
float32, float64	These types represent numbers with a fraction. These types allocate 32 or 64 bits to store the value.
complex64, complex128	These types represent numbers that have real and imaginary components. These types allocate 64 or 128 bits to store the value.
bool	This type represents a Boolean truth with the values true and false.
string	This type represents a sequence of characters.
rune	This type represents a single Unicode code point. Unicode is complicated, but—loosely—this is the representation of a single character. The rune type is an alias for int32.

Understanding Literal Values

Go values can be expressed literally, where the value is defined directly in the source code file. Common uses for literal values include operands in expressions and arguments to functions, as shown.

Using Literal Values in the main.go File in the basicFeatures Folder package main

```
import (    "fmt"
//"math/rand"
)

func main() {
    fmt.Println("Hello, Go")
fmt.Println(20 + 20)    fmt.Println(20
+ 30) }
```

The first statement in the main function uses a string literal, which is denoted by double quotes, as an argument to the fmt.Println function. The other statements use literal int values in expressions whose results are used as the argument to the fmt.Println function. Compile and execute the code, and you will see the following output:

```
Hello, Go
40
50
```

You don't have to specify a type when using a literal value because the compiler will infer the type based on the way the value is expressed. For quick reference, Table gives examples of literal values for   the   basic   types.

Table Literal Value Examples

Type	Examples
int	20, -20. Values can also be expressed in hex (0x14), octal (0o24), and binary notation (0b0010100).
unit	There are no uint literals. All literal whole numbers are treated as int values.
byte	There are no byte literals. Bytes are typically expressed as integer literals (such as 101) or run literals ('e') since the byte type is an alias for the uint8 type.
float64	20.2, -20.2, 1.2e10, 1.2e-10. Values can also be expressed in hex notation (0x2p10), although the exponent is expressed in decimal digits.
bool	true, false.
string	"Hello". Character sequences escaped with a backslash are interpreted if the value is enclosed in double quotes ("Hello\n"). Escape sequences are not interpreted if the value is enclosed in backquotes (`Hello\n`).
rune	'A', '\n', '\u00A5', '¥'. Characters, glyphs, and escape sequences are enclosed in single quotes (the ' character).

Using Constants

Constants are names for specific values, which allows them to be used repeatedly and consistently. There are two ways to define constants in Go: typed constants and untyped constants. Listing shows the use of typed constants.

Defining Typed Constants in the main.go File in the basicFeatures Folder package main

```
import (    "fmt"
    //"math/rand"
)

func main() {
    const price float32 = 275.00    const tax
float32 = 27.50    fmt.Println(price + tax) }
```

Typed constants are defined using the const keyword, followed by a name, a type, and a value assignment, as illustrated by Figure.

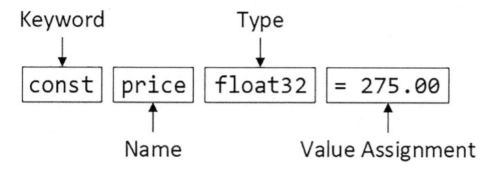

Figure Defining a typed constant

This statement creates a float32 constant named price whose value is 275.00. The code in Listing creates two constants and uses them in an expression that is passed to the fmt.Println function. Compile and run the code, and you will receive the following output:

302.5

Understanding Untyped Constants

Go has strict rules about its data types and doesn't perform automatic type conversions, which can complicate common programming tasks, as Listing demonstrates.

Mixing Data Types in the main.go File in the basicFeatures Folder package main

```
import (    "fmt"
    //"math/rand"
)

func main() {
    const price float32 = 275.00    const tax
float32 = 27.50    const quantity int = 2
    fmt.Println("Total:", quantity * (price + tax)) }
```

The new constant's type is int, which is an appropriate choice for a quantity that can represent only a whole number of products, for example. The constant is used in the expression passed to the fmt.Println function to calculate a total price. But the compiler reports the following error when the code is compiled:

.\main.go:12:26: invalid operation: quantity * (price + tax) (mismatched types int and float32)

Most programming languages would have automatically converted the types to allow the expression to be evaluated, but Go's stricter approach means that int and float32 types cannot be mixed. The untyped constant feature makes constants easier to work with because the Go compiler will perform limited automatic conversion, as shown.

Using an Untyped Constant in the main.go File in the basicFeatures Folder package main

```
import (    "fmt"
    //"math/rand"
)

func main() {
    const price float32 = 275.00    const tax float32 = 27.50
    const quantity = 2    fmt.Println("Total:", quantity * (price +
    tax)) }
```

An untyped constant is defined without a data type, as illustrated in Figure.

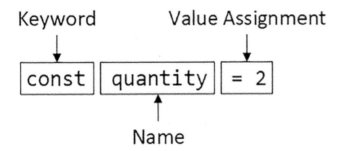

Figure Defining an untyped constant

Omitting the type when defining the quantity constant tells the Go compiler that it should be more flexible about the constant's type. When the expression passed to the fmt.Println function is evaluated, the Go compiler will convert the quantity value to a float32. Compile and execute the code, and you will receive the following output:

Total: 605

Untyped constants will be converted only if the value can be represented in the target type. In practice, this means you can mix untyped integer and floating-point numeric values, but conversions between other data types must be done explicitly.

Understanding Iota

The iota keyword can be used to create a series of successive untyped integer constants without needing to assign individual values to them. here is an iota example:

```
...
const (
    Watersports = iota
    Soccer
    Chess
)
```
... this pattern creates a series of constants, each of which is assigned an integer value, starting at zero. You can see examples of iota in part 3.

Defining Multiple Constants with a Single Statement

A single statement can be used to define several constants, as shown in Listing.

Defining Multiple Constants in the main.go File in the basicFeatures Folder package main

```
import (    "fmt"
    //"math/rand"
)

func main() {
    const price, tax float32 = 275, 27.50    const
quantity, inStock = 2, true
    fmt.Println("Total:", quantity * (price + tax))
fmt.Println("In stock: ", inStock) }
```

The const keyword is followed by a comma-separated list of names, an equal sign, and a comma separated list of values, as illustrated by Figure. If a type is specified, all the constants will be created with this type. If the type is omitted, then untyped constants are created, and each constant's type will be inferred from its value.

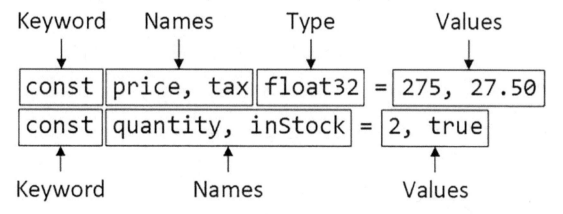

Figure Defining multiple constants

Compiling and executing the code in Listing produces the following output:

Total: 605
In stock: true

Revisiting Literal Values

Untyped constants may seem like an odd feature, but they make working with Go a lot easier, and you will find yourself relying on this feature, often without realizing, because literal values are untyped constants, which means that you can use literal values in expressions and rely on the compiler to deal with mismatched types, as shown.

Using a Literal Value in the main.go File in the basicFeatures Folder package main

```
import (    "fmt"
   //"math/rand"
)

func main() {
   const price, tax float32 = 275, 27.50     const quantity,
inStock = 2, true
   fmt.Println("Total:", 2 * quantity * (price + tax))
   fmt.Println("In stock: ", inStock)
}
```

The highlighted expression uses the literal value 2, which is an int value as described, along with two float32 values. Since the int value can be represented as a float32, the value will be converted automatically. When compiled and executed, this code produces the following output:
Total: 1210
In stock: true

Using Variables

Variables are defined using the var keyword, and, unlike constants, the value assigned to a variable can be changed, as shown.

Using Constants in the main.go File in the basicFeatures Folder package main

```
import "fmt"
func main() {
   var price float32 = 275.00     var tax
float32 = 27.50     fmt.Println(price + tax)
   price = 300     fmt.Println(price +
tax) }
```

Variables are declared using the var keyword, a name, a type, and a value assignment, as illustrated in Figure.

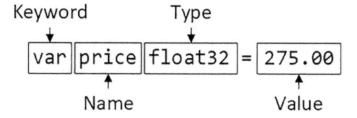

Figure Defining a Variable

Listing defines price and tax variables, both of which are assigned float32 values. A new value is assigned to the price variable using the equal sign, which is the Go assignment operator, as illustrated in Figure. (Notice that I can assign the value 300 to a floating-point variable. This is because the literal value
300 is an untyped constant that can be represented as a float32 value.)

```
Name    Value
  ↓       ↓
price = 300
```

Figure Assigning a new value to a variable

The code writes two strings to the standard out using the fmt.Println function, producing the following output when the code is compiled and executed:

302.5
327.5

Omitting the Variable's Data Type

The Go compiler can infer the type of variables based on the initial value, which allows the type to be omitted, as shown.

Omitting a Variable's Type in the main.go File in the basicFeatures Folder package
main import "fmt"
func main() {   **var price = 275.00**
var price2 = price
fmt.Println(price)
fmt.Println(price2) }

The variable is defined using the var keyword, a name, and a value assignment, but the type is omitted, as illustrated by Figure. The value of the variable can be set using a literal value or the name of a constant or another variable. In the listing, the value of the price variable is set using a literal value, and the value of price2 is set to the current value of price.

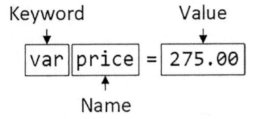

Figure Defining a variable without specifying a type

The compiler will infer the type from the value assigned to the variable. The compiler will inspect the literal value assigned to price and infer its type as float64, as described. The type of price2 will also be inferred as float64 because its value is set using the price value. The code produces the following output when compiled and executed:

```
275
275
```

Omitting a type doesn't have the same effect for variables as it does for constants, and the Go compiler will not allow different types to be mixed, as shows.

Mixing Data Types in the main.go File in the basicFeatures Folder package
main import "fmt"
func main() {   var price = 275.00
var tax float32 = 27.50
fmt.Println(price + tax) }

The compiler will always infer the type of literal floating-point values as float64, which doesn't match the float32 type of the tax variable. Go's strict type enforcement means that the compiler produces the following error when the code is compiled:

.\main.go:10:23: invalid operation: price + tax (mismatched types float64 and float32)

To use the price and tax variables in the same expression, they must have the same type or be convertible to the same type.

Omitting the Variable's Value Assignment

Variables can be defined without an initial value, as shown.
Defining a Variable Without an Initial Value in the main.go File in the basicFeatures Folder package
main import "fmt"

func main() {   **var price float32   fmt.Println(price)   price = 275.00   fmt.Println(price)**
}

Variables are defined using the var keyword followed by a name and a type, as illustrated by Figure. The type cannot be omitted when there is no initial value.

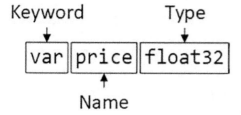

Keyword | Type
var | price | float32
Name

Figure Defining a variable without an initial value

Variables defined this way are assigned the zero value for the specified type, as described.

Table The Zero Values for the Basic
Data Types

Type	Zero Value
int	0
unit	0
byte	0
float64	0
bool	false
string	" " (the empty string)
rune	0

The zero value for numeric types is zero, which you can see by compiling and executing the code. The first value displayed in the output is the zero value, followed by the value assigned explicitly in a subsequent   statement:
0
275

Defining Multiple Variables with a Single Statement

A single statement can be used to define several variables, as shown.

Defining Variables in the main.go File in the basicFeatures Folder package main
import "fmt"
func main() {
   var price, tax = 275.00, 27.50
fmt.Println(price + tax) }

This is the same approach used to define constants, and the initial value assigned to each variable is used to infer its type. A type must be specified if no initial values are assigned, as shown, and all variables will be created using the specified type and assigned their zero value.

Defining Variables Without Initial Values in the main.go File in the basicFeatures Folder package main import "fmt"

```
func main() {    var price, tax float64
price = 275.00    tax = 27.50
fmt.Println(price + tax) }
```

Both produce the same output when compiled and executed:
302.5

Using the Short Variable Declaration Syntax

The short variable declaration provides a shorthand for declaring variables, as shown.

Using the Short Variable Declaration Syntax in the main.go File in the basicFeatures Folder package
main import "fmt"
```
func main() {    price := 275.00
fmt.Println(price)
}
```
　　The shorthand syntax specifies a name for the variable, a colon, an equal sign, and the initial value, as illustrated by Figure. The var keyword is not used, and a data type cannot be specified.

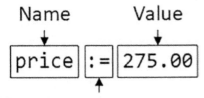

Shorthand Assignment

Figure The short variable declaration syntax

The code produces the following output when the code is compiled and executed:
275

Multiple variables can be defined with a single statement by creating comma-separated lists of names and values, as shown.

Defining Multiple Variables in the main.go File in the basicFeatures Folder package
main import "fmt"
```
func main() {
   price, tax, inStock := 275.00, 27.50, true
fmt.Println("Total:", price + tax)    fmt.Println("In
stock:", inStock) }
```

　　No types are specified in the shorthand syntax, which means that variables of different types can be created, relying on the compiler to infer types from the values assigned to each variable. The code produces the following output when compiled and executed:

Total: 302.5

In stock: true

The short variable declaration syntax can be used only within functions, such as the main.

Using the Short Variable Syntax to Redefine Variables

Go doesn't usually allow variables to be redefined but makes a limited exception when the short syntax is used. To demonstrate the default behavior, Uses the var keyword to define a variable that has the same name as one that already exists within the same function.

Redefining a Variable in the main.go File in the basicFeatures Folder package main import "fmt"

func main() {

   price, tax, inStock := 275.00, 27.50, true   fmt.Println("Total:", price + tax)   fmt.Println("In stock:", inStock)

   var price2, tax = 200.00, 25.00   fmt.Println("Total 2:", price2 + tax) }

The first new statement uses the var keyword to define variables named price2 and tax. There is already a variable named tax in the main function, which causes the following error when the code is compiled:

.\main.go:10:17: tax redeclared in this block

However, redefining a variable is allowed if the short syntax is used, as shown, as long as at least one of the other variables being defined doesn't already exist and the type of the variable doesn't change.

Using the Short Syntax in the main.go File in the basicFeatures Folder package main
import "fmt"
func main() {
   price, tax, inStock := 275.00, 27.50, true
fmt.Println("Total:", price + tax)   fmt.Println("In stock:", inStock)

   price2, tax := 200.00, 25.00   fmt.Println("Total 2:", price2 + tax) }

Compile and execute the project, and you will see the following output:
Total: 302.5
In stock: true
Total 2: 225

Using the Blank Identifier

It is illegal in Go to define a variable and not use it, as shown.

Defining Unused Variables in the main.go File in the basicFeatures Folder package

```
main import "fmt"
func main() {
    price, tax, inStock, discount := 275.00, 27.50, true, true     var
salesPerson = "Alice"     fmt.Println("Total:", price + tax)
fmt.Println("In stock:", inStock) }
```

The listing defines variables named discount and salesperson, neither of which is used in the rest of the code. When the code is compiled, the following error is reported:

```
.\main.go:6:26: discount declared but not used
.\main.go:7:9: salesPerson declared but not used
```

One way to resolve this problem is to remove the unused variables, but this isn't always possible. For these situations, Go provides the blank identifier, which is used to denote a value that won't be used, as shown.

Using the Blank Identifier in the main.go File in the basicFeatures Folder package

```
main import "fmt"
func main() {
    price, tax, inStock, _ := 275.00, 27.50, true, true     var _ =
"Alice"
    fmt.Println("Total:", price + tax)
fmt.Println("In stock:", inStock) }
```

The blank identifier is the underscore (the _ character), and it can be used wherever using a name would create a variable that would not subsequently be used. The code produces the following output when compiled and executed:

```
Total: 302.5
In stock: true
```

This is another feature that appears unusual, but it is important when using functions in Go. Go functions can return multiple results, and the blank identifier is useful when you need some of those result values but not others.

Understanding Pointers

Pointers are often misunderstood, especially if you have come to Go from a language such as Java or C#, where pointers are used behind the scenes but carefully hidden from the developer. To understand how pointers work, the best place to start is understanding what Go does when pointers are not used, as shown.

Defining Variables in the main.go File in the basicFeatures Folder package

```
main import "fmt" func main() {
    first := 100
    second := first
```

```
    first++

    fmt.Println("First:", first)
fmt.Println("Second:", second) }
```

The code produces the following output when compiled and executed:
First: 101
Second: 100

The code creates two variables. The value of the variable named first is set using a string literal. The value of the variable named second is set using the first value, like this:

...
first := 100

second := first ...

Go copies the current value of first when creating second, after which these variables are independent of one another. Each variable is a reference to a separate memory location where its value is   stored,   as   shown   in   Figure.

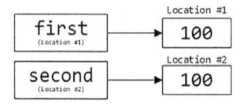

Figure Independent values

When I use the ++ operator to increment the first variable, Go reads the value at the memory location associated with the variable, increments the value, and stores it at the same memory location. The value assigned to the second variable remains the same because the change affects only the value stored by the first variable, as shown in Figure.

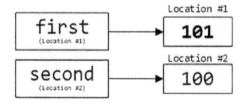

Figure Modifying a value

Understanding Pointer

Arithmetic pointers have a bad reputation because of pointer arithmetic. pointers store memory locations as numeric values, which means they can be manipulated using arithmetic operators, providing access to other memory locations. You can start with a location that points to an int value, for example; increment the value by the number of bits used to store an int; and read the adjacent value. this can be useful but can cause unexpected results, such as trying to access the wrong location or a location outside of the memory allocated to the program.

Go doesn't support pointer arithmetic, which means that a pointer to one location cannot be used to obtain other locations. the compiler will report an error if you try to perform arithmetic using a pointer.

Defining a Pointer

A pointer is a variable whose value is a memory address.

Defining a Pointer in the main.go File in the basicFeatures Folder package main
import "fmt" func main() {

    first := 100   **var second *int = &first**

    first++

    fmt.Println("First:", first)
fmt.Println("Second:", second) }

Pointers are defined using an ampersand (the & character), known as the address operator, followed by the name of a variable, as illustrated by Figure.

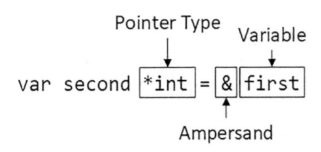

Figure Defining a pointer

Pointers are just like other variables in Go. They have a type and a value. The value of the second variable will be the memory address used by Go to store the value for the first variable. Compile and execute the code, and you will see output like this:

First: 101
Second: 0xc000010088

You will see different output based on where Go has chosen to store the value for the first variable. The specific memory location isn't important, and it is the relationship between the variables that is of interest, illustrated by Figure.

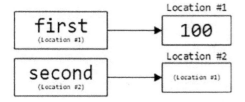

Figure A pointer and its memory location

The type of a pointer is based on the type of the variable from which it is created, prefixed with an asterisk (the * character). The type of variable named second is *int, because it was created by applying the address operator to the first variable, whose value is int. When you see the type *int, you know it is a variable whose value is a memory address that stores an int variable.
A pointer's type is fixed, because all Go types are fixed, which means that when you create a pointer to an int, for example, you change the value that it points to, but you can't use it to point to the memory address used to store a different type, such as a float64. This restriction is important—in Go, pointers are not just memory addresses but, rather, memory addresses that may store a specific type of value.

Following a Pointer

The phrase following a pointer means reading the value at the memory address that the pointer refers to, and it is done using an asterisk (the * character), as shown. I have also used the short variable declaration syntax for the pointer in this example. Go will infer the pointer type just like it does with other types.

Following a Pointer in the main.go File in the basicFeatures Folder package
main import "fmt" func main() {
    first := 100   second := &first
first++

    fmt.Println("First:", first)
fmt.Println("Second:", *second) }

The asterisk tells Go to follow the pointer and get the value at the memory location, as illustrated by Figure. This is known as dereferencing the pointer.

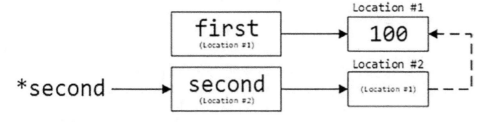

Figure Following a pointer

The code produces the following output when compiled and executed:
First: 101
Second: 101

A common misconception is that the first and second variables have the same value, but that's not what is happening. There are two values. There is an int value that can be accessed using the variable named first. There is also an *int value that stores the memory location of the first value. The *int value can be followed, which will access the stored int value. But, because the *int value is, well, a value, it can be used in its own right, which means that it can be assigned to other variables, used as an argument to invoke a function, and so on.

Demonstrates the first use of the pointer. The pointer is followed, and the value at the memory location is incremented.

Following a Pointer and Changing the Value in the main.go File in the basicFeatures Folder
package main import "fmt" func main() {
   first := 100   second := &first

   first++   ***second++**

   fmt.Println("First:", first)
fmt.Println("Second:", *second) }

This code produces the following output when compiled and executed:
First: 102
Second: 102

This demonstrates the second use of a pointer, which is to use
it as a value in its own right and assign it to another variable.

Assigning a Pointer Value to Another Variable in the main.go File in the basicFeatures Folder package
main import "fmt" func main() {
   first := 100   second := &first

   first++   *second++

   var myNewPointer *int
myNewPointer = second
*myNewPointer++

   fmt.Println("First:", first)
fmt.Println("Second:", *second) }

The first new statement defines a new variable, which I have done with the var keyword to emphasize that the variable type is *int, meaning a pointer to an int value. The next statement assigns the value of the second variable to the new variable, meaning that the values of both second and myNewPointer are the memory location of the first value. Following either pointer accesses the same memory location, which means incrementing myNewPointer affects the value obtained by following the second pointer. Compile and execute the code, and you will see the following output:

First: 103
Second: 103

Understanding Pointer Zero Values

Pointers that are defined but not assigned a value have the zero-value nil, as demonstrated.

Defining an Uninitialized Pointer in the main.go File in the basicFeatures Folder package main import "fmt" func main() {
    first := 100   var second *int

    **fmt.Println(second)   second =
&first   fmt.Println(second)**
}

    The pointer second is defined but not initialized with a value and is written out using the fmt.Println function. The address operator is used to create a pointer to the first variable, and the value of second is written out again. The code produces the following output when compiled and executed (ignore the < and > in the result, which is just to denote nil by the Println function):

<nil>
0xc000010088

A runtime error will occur if you follow a pointer that has not been assigned a value, as shown.

Following an Uninitialized Pointer in the main.go File in the basicFeatures Folder package main import "fmt" func main() {
    first := 100   var second *int

    **fmt.Println(*second)   second =
&first**
    fmt.Println(second == nil) }

This code compiles but produces the following error when executed:

panic: runtime error: invalid memory address or nil pointer dereference [signal 0xc0000005 code=0x0 addr=0x0 pc=0xec798a] goroutine 1 [running]: main.main()
    C:/basicFeatures/main.go:10 +0x2a exit status 2

Pointing at Pointers

Given that pointers store memory locations, it is possible to create a pointer whose value is the memory address of another pointer, as shown.
Creating a Pointer to a Pointer in the main.go File in the basicFeatures Folder package main import "fmt" func main() {
    first := 100   second := &first
third := &second

```
    fmt.Println(first)
fmt.Println(*second)
```
fmt.Println(**third) }

The syntax for following chains of pointers can be awkward. In this case, two asterisks are required. The first asterisk follows the pointer to the memory location to get the value stored by the variable named second, which is an *int value. The second asterisk follows the pointer named second, which gives access to the memory location of the value stored by the first variable. This isn't something you will need to do in most projects, but it does provide a nice confirmation of how pointers work and how you can follow the chain to get to the data value. The code produces the following output when compiled and executed:

```
100
100
100
```

Understanding Why Pointers Are Useful

It is easy to get lost in the detail of how pointers work and lose sight of why they can be a programmer's friend. Pointers are useful because they allow the programmer to choose between passing a value and passing a reference. There are lots of examples that use pointers in later chapters, but to finish this chapter, a quick demonstration is useful. That said, the listings in this section rely on features that are explained in later chapters, so you may want to return to these examples later. It provides an example of when working with values is useful.

Working with Values in the main.go File in the basicFeatures Folder package main

```
import (    "fmt"
    "sort"
)
func main() {    names := [3]string {"Alice", "Charlie",
"Bob"}    secondName := names[1]
fmt.Println(secondName)    sort.Strings(names[:])
    fmt.Println(secondName) }
```

The syntax may be unusual, but this example is simple. An array of three string values is created, and the value in position 1 is assigned to a variable called secondName. The value of the secondName variable is written to the console, the array is sorted, and the value of the secondName variable is written to the console again. This code produces the following output when compiled and executed:

```
Charlie
Charlie
```

When the secondName variable is created, the value of the string in position 1 of the array is copied to a new memory location, which is why the value isn't affected by the sorting operation. Because the value has been copied, it is now entirely unrelated to the array, and sorting the array does not affect the value of the secondName variable.

This introduces a pointer variable to the example.

Using a Pointer in the main.go File in the basicFeatures Folder package main

```
import (    "fmt"
   "sort"
) func main() {    names := [3]string {"Alice", "Charlie",
"Bob"}    secondPosition := &names[1]
fmt.Println(*secondPosition)    sort.Strings(names[:])
   fmt.Println(*secondPosition)
}
```

When the secondPosition variable is created, its value is the memory address used to store the string value in position 1 of the array. When the array is sorted, the order of the items in the array changes, but the pointer still refers to the memory location for position 1, which means that following the pointer returns the sorted value, producing the following output when the code is compiled and executed:

```
Charlie
Bob
```

A pointer means I can keep a reference to location 1 in a way that provides access to the current value, reflecting any changes that are made to the contents of the array. This is a simple example, but it shows how pointers provide the developer with a choice between copying values and using references.

If you are still unsure about pointers, then consider how the value versus reference issue is handled by other languages with which you are familiar. C#, for example, which I use a lot, supports both structs, which are passed by value, and classes, instances of which are passed as references. Go and C# both let me choose whether I want to use a copy or a reference. The difference is that C# makes me choose once when I create a data type, but Go lets me choose each time I use a value. The Go approach is more flexible but requires more consideration from the programmer.

Conclusion: Mastering Basic Types, Values, and Pointers in Go

The journey through the basic types, values, and pointers in Go has been a deep dive into the core components that make the language both powerful and efficient. Go's simplicity lies in its well-defined structure, strict type safety, and intuitive approach to memory management. These features not only make Go easy to learn but also ensure that developers can write clear, readable, and maintainable code.

Understanding these basic concepts is essential for building a solid foundation in Go programming, whether you are developing simple scripts or complex, large-scale systems. Let's revisit the essential components and understand why they play such a critical role in the Go ecosystem.

1. The Importance of Basic Types

Go's basic types are the backbone of data handling within the language. They define how data is stored, manipulated, and passed around in a program. Each of these types serves a distinct purpose, allowing developers to choose the most appropriate representation for their data. Here's a recap of the types we covered:

Numeric Types: Go provides several numeric types, including integers (int, uint), floating-point numbers (float32, float64), and complex numbers (complex64, complex128). Each of these serves different purposes. For example, integer types are ideal for counting or indexing, while floating-point types handle decimal values for precise calculations, and complex types enable scientific computations. The strict separation between these types helps prevent type-related bugs and ensures that mathematical operations behave predictably.

Boolean Type (bool): The boolean type is simple yet fundamental. It is crucial for implementing logical expressions, conditional statements, and loops. By using boolean values (true and false), you can control the flow of your programs effectively, making decisions based on conditions.

String Type (string): Strings are vital for storing and processing text. In Go, strings are sequences of bytes that are immutable, which means once a string is created, it cannot be changed. This immutability makes strings safe and efficient, especially when passing them across different parts of a program. Go also provides several utility functions for string manipulation, allowing developers to work with text easily.

Rune Type (rune): A rune is an alias for int32, and it is used to represent Unicode code points. This enables Go to handle multilingual text effortlessly. Whether you are developing a global application or working with special characters, understanding runes helps you write software that can communicate across language barriers.

By mastering these basic types, you are well-equipped to handle most data-related tasks in Go. You can efficiently manage numbers, control logic, process text, and work with diverse characters, all using simple and consistent syntax.

2. Values and Variables: Building Blocks of Go Programs

Values and variables in Go are straightforward, yet they form the core of every program. A value is any piece of data, while a variable is a named storage location for that value. Go's approach to variable declaration ensures clarity and minimizes errors. With Go's strict type system, the language forces developers to think carefully about how they declare and use variables, which reduces the risk of common bugs.

Zero Values: A Unique Feature of Go

One of the unique aspects of Go is its concept of zero values. When you declare a variable without initializing it, Go automatically assigns it a default zero value based on its type. For example:

int types get 0

float types get 0.0

bool types get false

string types get "" (an empty string)

This feature prevents the usage of uninitialized variables, which is a common source of errors in many programming languages. Zero values make Go programs safer by ensuring that variables always have a predictable state, even if the developer forgets to assign them explicitly.

Variable Declaration: Explicit vs. Implicit

Go allows for both explicit and implicit (type-inferred) variable declarations:

Explicit Declaration: var count int = 10

Implicit Declaration: count: = 10

The ability to infer types can lead to cleaner and shorter code, especially for simple applications. However, it is still essential to be mindful of what types are being inferred to avoid unexpected behavior.

3. Pointers: A Gateway to Efficient Memory Management

Pointers are one of the more advanced features in Go, but they are crucial for writing efficient programs. Unlike basic types, which hold actual values, pointers store the memory address of a value. This allows you to manipulate data more directly and efficiently.

Why Pointers Matter

Efficient Memory Usage: Pointers allow you to avoid copying large data structures. Instead of passing an entire object to a function, you can pass a pointer, which is much smaller and faster to pass around. This can lead to significant performance improvements, especially when dealing with large collections of data.

Direct Data Manipulation: By using pointers, you can directly modify the original data rather than working on a copy. This is particularly useful when you need to make changes to a variable from within a function.

Example:

```
func updateValue(num *int) {

    *num = 100

}
```

In this example, passing a pointer to num allows the function to update the original value, demonstrating how pointers can be used for efficient data manipulation.

Understanding nil Pointers

A pointer that does not point to any valid memory address is known as a nil pointer. Handling nil pointers correctly is essential, as attempting to dereference a nil pointer can lead to runtime errors. Always check if a pointer is nil before using it to avoid crashes and unexpected behavior.

4. The Synergy Between Types, Values, and Pointers

Together, types, values, and pointers create a robust framework for building Go applications. Each of these elements has its role:

Types define the form of data, ensuring that operations are performed correctly.

Values represent actual data and are used in computations, decisions, and actions.

Pointers allow you to handle data more flexibly and efficiently, especially when dealing with complex structures.

By understanding how these elements interact, you can write programs that are not only correct but also perform well. Go's simplicity in managing these concepts means that you can focus more on solving problems rather than worrying about the intricacies of memory management and data handling.

5. Real-World Applications and Benefits

Understanding these concepts is not just about learning syntax; it's about mastering how to build efficient, maintainable, and scalable software. Here's how basic types, values, and pointers translate into real-world programming:

1. Building High-Performance Web Servers

Web servers need to handle thousands of requests per second, and efficient data handling is critical. By understanding how to use basic types and pointers, you can optimize your server to manage large volumes of data without unnecessary overhead. Go's garbage collector and strict type system ensure that your applications are not only fast but also safe and reliable.

2. Developing Microservices

Microservices rely on passing data between different components. Understanding how to use pointers can help you design systems that communicate efficiently. Instead of sending copies of data, you can send pointers, reducing the amount of data being transferred and processed. This leads to faster response times and more efficient resource utilization.

3. Writing High-Concurrency Programs

Go is known for its concurrency features. When writing concurrent programs, you need to be careful about how data is shared between goroutines. Pointers allow you to pass data between goroutines without unnecessary copying, while Go's strict type system ensures that you do not run into common concurrency issues, such as race conditions.

6. Final Thoughts: The Path to Go Mastery

Mastering basic types, values, and pointers is the first step toward becoming proficient in Go. These fundamental concepts form the basis for more advanced features like structs, slices, interfaces, and channels, which you will encounter as you continue your journey into the Go language.

Every programming language has its strengths, and Go's lies in its simplicity, performance, and reliability. Understanding how Go handles basic data will give you the confidence to tackle more complex projects, whether you are building web applications, developing network services, or designing microservices architectures.

As you practice and experiment with these core concepts, you will find that Go's approach to data handling is intuitive yet powerful. The language's philosophy of keeping things simple yet effective will shine through in every piece of code you write. And this is why learning Go is not just about coding; it's about adopting a mindset that emphasizes clarity, precision, and efficiency.

3. Go: Operations and Conversions

Introduction

Begin by introducing the concepts of operations and conversions in Go. Explain why understanding these is fundamental to effective programming in Go, particularly for data manipulation, arithmetic, and type safety. Highlight that Go provides a range of operators and type conversion mechanisms that make it versatile and powerful.

1. Operations in Go

- ### 1.1. Arithmetic Operations
  - Explain the basic arithmetic operators: +, -, *, /, and %.
  - Discuss integer and floating-point arithmetic.
  - Example:

```
a := 10

b := 3

sum := a + b     // Addition

diff := a - b    // Subtraction

prod := a * b    // Multiplication

div := a / b     // Division (integer result)

rem := a % b     // Modulo
```

  - Explain division behavior with integers and floats. Include examples of handling decimal results with float64.

- ### 1.2. Relational Operations
  - Cover relational operators: ==, !=, <, >, <=, >=.
  - Examples and usage scenarios:

```
x, y := 5, 10

fmt.Println(x == y) // false

fmt.Println(x != y) // true

fmt.Println(x < y)  // true
```

- o Explain how these operators return Boolean results, useful in conditional statements and loops.

- **1.3. Logical Operations**

  - o Discuss logical operators: &&, ||, !.

  - o Example of using these operators in conditions:

a, b := true, false

fmt.Println(a && b) // false

fmt.Println(a || b) // true

fmt.Println(!a)   // false

  - o Illustrate real-world scenarios like checking multiple conditions before executing a code block.

- **1.4. Bitwise Operations**

  - o Cover bitwise operators: &, |, ^, &^, <<, >>.

  - o Explain how these operators work on the binary representation of integers.

  - o Example:

a := 12 // 1100 in binary

b := 10 // 1010 in binary

fmt.Println(a & b) // 8 -> 1000 (bitwise AND)

fmt.Println(a | b) // 14 -> 1110 (bitwise OR)

fmt.Println(a ^ b) // 6 -> 0110 (bitwise XOR)

  - o Discuss practical uses like setting, toggling, and clearing bits, and optimizing performance.

- **1.5. Assignment Operations**

  - o Explain assignment operators: =, +=, -=, *=, /=, %= and others.

  - o Example:

x := 5

x += 3 // x = x + 3, result is 8

Highlight that these operators simplify code and make it more readable.

2. Type Conversions in Go

- **2.1. Overview of Type Conversions**
  - Explain Go's strict type system and why explicit type conversions are necessary.
  - Introduce basic syntax for type conversion:

```
var i int = 42
var f float64 = float64(i)
var u uint = uint(f)
```

  - Emphasize that implicit type conversion (automatic casting) does not happen in Go, ensuring clarity and safety.

- **2.2. Numeric Conversions**
  - Discuss converting between integers, floating-point numbers, and unsigned types.
  - Include examples of converting between different sizes of numeric types (e.g., int8, int32, float64).
  - Explain possible issues such as overflow, truncation, and precision loss, with examples.

```
var a int = 300
var b uint8 = uint8(a) // This will cause overflow as uint8 max is 255
fmt.Println(b) // Output will be 44 (300 % 256)
```

- **2.3. String Conversions**
  - Explain how to convert integers and floats to strings using the strconv package.
  - Examples:

```
str := strconv.Itoa(123) // Convert int to string
f, _ := strconv.ParseFloat("123.45", 64) // Convert string to float
```

  - Cover converting runes (Unicode code points) to and from strings.

- **2.4. Boolean Conversions**
  - Mention that direct conversion between numeric types and booleans is not allowed.
  - Explain indirect ways to perform this conversion (e.g., using conditionals).

- **2.5. Type Assertions and Type Switches**

o Introduce the concept of type assertions for interface types.

o Example:

```
var i interface{} = "hello"

s := i.(string)

fmt.Println(s) // "hello"
```

o Discuss ok idiom to safely perform type assertions.

o Explain switch type for handling multiple type possibilities.

```
switch v := i.(type) {

case int:

   fmt.Println("Integer:", v)

case string:

   fmt.Println("String:", v)

default:

   fmt.Println("Unknown type")

}
```

3. Practical Examples and Applications

- **3.1. Mathematical Computations**

  o Illustrate how arithmetic, relational, and bitwise operations can be used in mathematical computations.

  o Example: Building a simple calculator application.

- **3.2. Working with Files and I/O**

  o Show how to convert data types while reading from or writing to files.

  o Example: Reading numeric data from a file and performing arithmetic on it after type conversion.

- **3.3. Encoding and Decoding Data**

  o Discuss encoding data as different types (e.g., converting int to string and vice versa) during serialization and deserialization.

Example: Working with JSON in Go, converting struct fields to strings.

4. Common Mistakes and Best Practices

- ## 4.1. Arithmetic Pitfalls

  - Discuss common issues like integer division, overflow, and underflow.

  - How to handle these issues using Go's built-in constants from math package.

- ## 4.2. Type Conversion Pitfalls

  - Explain common mistakes, such as losing precision when converting from float64 to int.

  - How to use math functions to round or floor values appropriately.

- ## 4.3. Idiomatic Go Practices

  - Encourage using explicit type conversions for clarity.

  - Discuss how to avoid unnecessary conversions to improve performance.

In this chapter, I describe the Go operators, which are used to perform arithmetic, compare values, and create logical expressions that produce true/false results. I also explain the process of converting a value from one type to another, which can be done using a combination of built-in language features and facilities provided by the Go standard library.

Initializing the Project

go mod in it operations
Add a file named main.go to the operations folder, with the contents shown.

The Contents of the main.go File in the operations Folder package main
import "fmt" func main() {
   fmt.Println("Hello, Operations") }

Use the command prompt to run the command shown in the operations folder.

Running the Example Project

go run.
The code in the main.go file will be compiled and executed, producing the following output:

Hello, Operations

Understanding the Go Operators

Go provides a standard set of operators, and Table describes those that you will encounter most often, especially when working with the data types described.

Table The Basic Go Operators

Operator	Description
+, -, *, /, %	These operators are used to perform arithmetic using numeric values, as described in the "Understanding the Arithmetic Operators" section. The + operator can also be used for string concatenation, as described in the "Concatenating Strings" section.
==, !=, <, <=, >, >=	These operators compare two values, as described in the "Understanding the Comparison Operators" section.
||, &&, !	These are the logical operators, which are applied to bool values and return a bool value, as described in the "Understanding the Logical Operators" section.
=, :=	These are the assignment operators. The standard assignment operator (=) is used to set the initial value when a constant or variable is defined, or to change the value assigned to a previously defined variable. The shorthand operator (:=) is used to define a variable and assign a value, as described.
-=, +=, ++, --	These operators increment and decrement numeric values, as described in the "Using the Increment and Decrement Operators" section.
&, |, ^, &^, <<, >>	These are the bitwise operators, which can be applied to integer values. These operators are not often required in mainstream development, but you can see an example, where the | operator is used to configure the Go logging features.

Understanding the Arithmetic Operators

The arithmetic operators can be applied to the numeric data types. The exception is the remainder operator (%), which can be used only on integers. This describes the arithmetic operators.

Table The Arithmetic Operators

Operator	Description
+	This operator returns the sum of two operands.
-	This operator returns the difference between two operands.
*	This operator returns the product of two operands.
/	This product returns the quotient of two operators.
%	This product returns the remainder, which is similar to the modulo operator provided by other programming languages but can return

negative values, as described in the "Using the Remainder Operator" section.

The values used with the arithmetic operators must be of the same type (all int values, for example) or be representable in the same type, such as untyped numeric constants. Shows the use of the arithmetic operators.

Using the Arithmetic Operators in the main.go File in the operations Folder package main import "fmt"

```go
func main() {
  price, tax := 275.00, 27.40

  sum := price + tax    difference := price - tax    product := price * tax    quotient := price / tax

  fmt.Println(sum)
fmt.Println(difference)
fmt.Println(product)
fmt.Println(quotient) }
```

The code produces the following output when compiled and executed:

```
302.4
247.6
7535
10.036496350364963
```

Understanding Arithmetic Overflow

Go allows integer values to overflow by wrapping around, rather than reporting an error. Floating-point values overflow to positive or negative infinity. This shows overflows for both data types. Overflowing Numeric Values in the main.go File in the operations Folder package main

```go
import (    "fmt"
  "math"
) func main() {
  var intVal = math.MaxInt64    var floatVal = math.MaxFloat64

  fmt.Println(intVal * 2)    fmt.Println(floatVal * 2)
fmt.Println(math.IsInf((floatVal * 2), 0)) }
```

Deliberately causing an overflow is most easily achieved using the math package, which is part of the Go standard library. I describe this package in more detail, but for this chapter, I am interested in the constants provided for the smallest and largest values each data type can represent, as well as the IsInf function, which can be used to determine whether a floating-point value has overflowed to infinity. In the listing, I use the MaxInt64 and MaxFloat64 constants to set the value of two variables, which I then overflow in expressions passed to the fmt.Println function. The listing produces the following output when it is compiled and executed:

```
-2
+Inf true
```

The integer value wraps around to produce a value of -2, and the floating-point value overflows to +Inf, which denotes positive infinity. The math.IsInf function is used to detect infinity.

Using the Remainder Operator

Go provides the % operator, which returns the remainder when one integer value is divided by another. This is often mistaken for the modulo operator provided by other programming languages, such as Python, but, unlike those operators, the Go remainder operator can return negative values, as shown.

Using the Remainder Operator in the main.go File in the operations Folder package main

```go
import (    "fmt" "math"

)

func main() {    posResult := 3 % 2    negResult := -3 % 2    absResult :=
math.Abs(float64(negResult))

    fmt.Println(posResult)    fmt.Println(negResult)    fmt.Println(absResult) }
```

The remainder operator is used in two expressions to demonstrate that positive and negative results can be produced. The math package provides the Abs function, which will return an absolute value of a float64, although the result is also a float64. The code produces the following output when it is compiled and executed:

```
1
-1
1
```

Using the Increment and Decrement Operators

Go provides a set of operators for incrementing and decrementing numeric values, as shown. These operators can be applied to integer and floating-point numbers.

Using the Increment and Decrement Operators in the main.go File in the operations Folder package main

```go
import (    "fmt"
//    "math"
```

```
)
func main() {    value := 10.2
value++    fmt.Println(value)
value += 2    fmt.Println(value)
value -= 2    fmt.Println(value)
   value-   fmt.Println(value) }
```

The ++ and -- operators increment or decrement a value by one. The += and -= increment or decrement a value by a specified amount. These operations are subject to the overflow behavior described earlier but are otherwise consistent with comparable operators in other languages, other than the ++ and -- operators, which can be only postfix, meaning there is no support for an expression such as --value. The code produces the following output when it is compiled and executed:

```
11.2 13.2 11.2
10.2
```

Concatenating Strings

The + operator can be used to concatenate strings to produce longer strings, as shown.

Concatenating Strings in the main.go File in the operations Folder package main

```
import (    "fmt"
//   "math"
)

func main() {    greeting := "Hello"    language := "Go"
combinedString := greeting + ", " + language

   fmt.Println(combinedString) }
```

The result of the + operator is a new string, and the code produces the following output when compiled and executed:
Hello, Go
Go won't concatenate strings with other data types, but the standard library does include functions that compose strings from values of different types, as described.

Understanding the Comparison Operators

The comparison operators compare two values, returning the bool value true if they are the same and false otherwise. This describes the comparison performed by each operator.

Table The Comparison Operators

Operator	Description
==	This operator returns true if the operands are equal.

!=	This operator returns true if the operands are not equal.
<	This operator returns true if the first operand is less than the second operand.
>	This operator returns true if the first operand is greater than the second operand.
<=	This operator returns true if the first operand is less than or equal to the second operand.
>=	This operator returns true if the first operand is greater than or equal to the second operand.

The values used with the comparison operators must all be of the same type, or they must be untyped constants that can be represented as the target type, as shown.

Using an Untyped Constant in the main.go File in the operations Folder package main

```
import (    "fmt"
//   "math"
) func main() {
    first := 100    const second =
200.00

    equal := first == second    notEqual := first !=
second    lessThan := first < second
lessThanOrEqual := first <= second    greaterThan :=
first > second    greaterThanOrEqual := first >=
second

    fmt.Println(equal)    fmt.Println(notEqual)
fmt.Println(lessThan)
fmt.Println(lessThanOrEqual)
fmt.Println(greaterThan)
fmt.Println(greaterThanOrEqual) }
```

The untyped constant is a floating-point value but can be represented as an integer value because its fractional digits are zeros. This allows the variable first and the constant second to be used together in comparisons. This would not be possible for a constant value of 200.01, for example, because the floating point value cannot be represented as an integer without discarding the fractional digits and creating a different value. For this, an explicit conversion is required, as described later in this chapter. The code produces the following output when compiled and executed:

false true true true false
false

PERFORMING TERNARY COMPARISONS

Go doesn't provide a ternary operator, which means that expressions like this cannot be used:

max := first > second ? first : second ... instead, one of the comparison operators described in table 5-5 is used with an if statement, like this:

```
...
var max int if (first > second) {    max
= first
} else {    max = second }
...
```

this syntax is less concise, but, like many Go features, you will quickly become used to working without ternary expressions.

Comparing Pointers

Pointers can be compared to see if they point at the same memory location, as shown.

Comparing Pointers in the main.go File in the operations Folder package main

```
import (    "fmt"
//    "math"
) func main() {    first := 100

    second := &first    third :=
&first

    alpha := 100    beta :=
&alpha

    fmt.Println(second == third)
fmt.Println(second == beta) }
```

The Go equality operator (==) is used to compare the memory locations. In this pointer named second and third both point to the same location and are equal. The pointer named beta points to a different memory location. The code produces the following output when compiled and executed:

true false

It is important to understand that it is the memory locations that are being compared and not the values they store. If you want to compare values, then you should follow the pointers, as shown.

Following Pointers in a Comparison in the main.go File in the operations Folder package main

```
import (    "fmt"
//    "math"
) func main() {    first := 100
    second := &first    third := &first

    alpha := 100    beta := &alpha

    fmt.Println(*second == *third)
fmt.Println(*second == *beta) }
```

These comparisons follow the pointers to compare the values stored at the referenced memory locations, producing the following output when the code is compiled and executed:

true true

Understanding the Logical Operators

The logical operators compare bool values, as described. The results produced by these operators can be assigned to variables or used as part of a flow control expression.

The Logical Operators **Operator Description**

	This operator returns true if either operand is true. If the first operand is true, then the second operand will not be evaluated.
&&	This operator returns true if both operands are true. If the first operand is false, then the second operand will not be evaluated.
!	This operator is used with a single operand. It returns true if the operand is false and false if the operand is true.

This shows the logical operators being used to produce values that are assigned to variables.

Using the Logical Operators in the main.go File in the operations Folder package main

```
import (    "fmt"
//    "math"
) func main() {
    maxMph := 50    passengerCapacity := 4
airbags := true

    familyCar := passengerCapacity > 2 && airbags    sportsCar :=
maxMph > 100 || passengerCapacity == 2    canCategorize :=
!familyCar && !sportsCar

    fmt.Println(familyCar)
fmt.Println(sportsCar)
fmt.Println(canCategorize) }
```

Only bool values can be used with the logical operators, and Go will not attempt to convert a value to get a true or false value. If the operand for a logical operator is an expression, then it is evaluated to produce the bool result that is used in the comparison. The code produces the following output when it is compiled and executed:

true false false

Go short-circuits the evaluation process when the logical operators are used, meaning that the smallest number of values is assessed to produce a result. In the case of the && operator, evaluation stops when a false value is encountered. In the case of the || operator, evaluation stops when a true value is encountered. In both cases, no subsequent value can change the outcome of the operation, so additional evaluations are not required.

Converting, Parsing, and Formatting Values

Go doesn't allow types to be mixed in operations and will not automatically convert types, except in the case of untyped constants. To show how the compiler responds to mixed data types, contains a statement that applies the addition operator to values of different types. (You may find your code editor automatically corrects the code, and you may have to undo the correction so the code in the editor matches the listing to see the compiler error.)

Mixing Types in an Operation in the main.go File in the operations Folder package main

```
import (    "fmt"
//    "math"
) func main() {
    kayak := 275    soccerBall := 19.50    total := kayak + soccerBall
    fmt.Println(total) }
```

The literal values used to define the kayak and soccerBall variables result in an int value and a float64 value, which are then used in the addition operation to set the value of the total variable. When the code is compiled, the following error will be reported:

.\main.go:13:20: invalid operation: kayak + soccerBall (mismatched types int and float64)

For such a simple example, I could simply change the literal value used to initialize the kayak variable to 275.00, which would produce a float64 variable. But types are rarely as easy to change in real projects, which is why Go provides the features described in the sections that follow.

Performing Explicit Type Conversions

An explicit conversion transforms a value to change its type, as shown.

Using an Explicit Conversion in the main.go File in the operations Folder package main

```
import (    "fmt"
//    "math"
) func main() {
    kayak := 275    soccerBall := 19.50    total :=
float64(kayak) + soccerBall

    fmt.Println(total) }
```

The syntax for explicit conversions is T(x), where T is the target type and x is the value or expression to convert. I used an explicit conversion to produce a float64 value from the kayak variable,

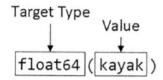

Figure Explicit conversion of a type

The conversion to a float64 value means that the types in the addition operation are consistent. The code produces the following output when compiled and executed:

294.5

Understanding the Limitations of Explicit Conversions

Explicit conversions can be used only when the value can be represented in the target type. This means you can convert between numeric types and between strings and runes, but other combinations, such as converting int values to bool values, are not supported.

Care must be taken when choosing the values to convert because explicit conversions can cause a loss of precision in numeric values or cause overflows, as shown.

Converting Numeric Types in the main.go File in the operations Folder package main

```
import (    "fmt"
//   "math"
) func main() {     kayak :=
275     soccerBall := 19.50
total := kayak +
int(soccerBall)

    fmt.Println(total)
fmt.Println(int8(total)) }
```

This listing converts the float64 value to an int for the addition operation and, separately, converts the int into an int8. The code produces the following output when it is compiled and executed:
294
38

When converting from a floating-point to an integer, the fractional part of the value is discarded so that the floating-point 19.50 becomes the int value 19. The discarded fraction is the reason why the value of the total variable is 294 instead of the 294.5 produced in the previous section.

The int8 used in the second explicit conversion is too small to represent the int value 294 and so the variable overflows, as described in the earlier "Understanding Arithmetic Overflow" section.

Converting Floating-Point Values to Integers

As the previous example demonstrated, explicit conversions can produce unexpected results, especially when converting floating-point values to integers. The safest approach is to convert in the other direction, representing integers and floating-point values, but if that isn't possible, then the math package provides a set of useful functions that can be used to perform conversions in a controlled way, as described in Table.

Table Functions in the math Package for Converting Numeric Types

Function	Description
Ceil(value)	This function returns the smallest integer that is greater than the specified floatingpoint value. The smallest integer that is greater than 27.1, for example, is 28.
Floor(value)	This function returns the largest integer that is less than the specified floating-point value. The largest integer that is less than 27.1, for example, is 28.
Round(value)	This function rounds the specified floating-point value to the nearest integer.
RoundToEven(value)	This function rounds the specified floating-point value to the nearest even integer.

The functions described in the table return float64 values, which can then be explicitly converted to the int type, as shown.

Rounding a Value in the main.go File in the operations Folder package main

```
import (    "fmt"
"math"
) func main() {
   kayak := 275    soccerBall := 19.50    total := kayak +
int(math.Round(soccerBall))

   fmt.Println(total) }
```

The math.Round function will round the soccerBall value from 19.5 to 20, which is then explicitly converted to an int and used in the addition operation. The code produces the following output when compiled and executed:
295

Parsing from Strings

The Go standard library includes the strconv package, which provides functions for converting string values to the other basic data types. Table describes the functions that parse strings into other data types.

Table Functions for Parsing Strings into Other Data Types

Function	Description

ParseBool(str)	This function parses a string into a bool value. Recognized string values are "true", "false", "TRUE", "FALSE", "True", "False", "T", "F", "0", and "1".
ParseFloat(str, size)	This function parses a string into a floating-point value with the specified size, as described in the "Parsing Floating-Point Numbers" section.
ParseInt(str, base, size)	This function parses a string into an int64 with the specified base and size. Acceptable base values are 2 for binary, 8 for octal, 16 for hex, and 10, as described in the "Parsing Integers" section.
ParseUint(str, base, size)	This function parses a string into an unsigned integer value with the specified base and size.
Atoi(str)	This function parses a string into a base 10 int and is equivalent to calling ParseInt(str, 10, 0), as described in the "Using the Integer Convenience Function" section.

This shows the use of the ParseBool function to parse strings into bool values.

Parsing Strings in the main.go File in the operations Folder package main

```
import (
    "fmt"    "strconv"
) func main() {
    val1 := "true"    val2 :=
"false"    val3 := "not true"

    bool1, b1err := strconv.ParseBool(val1)    bool2, b2err
:= strconv.ParseBool(val2)    bool3, b3err :=
strconv.ParseBool(val3)

    fmt.Println("Bool 1", bool1, b1err)
fmt.Println("Bool 2", bool2, b2err)
fmt.Println("Bool 3", bool3, b3err) }
```

As I explain, Go functions can produce multiple result values. The functions described in Table return two result values: the parsed result and an error, as illustrated by Figure.

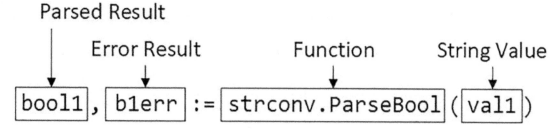

Figure Parsing a string

You may be used to languages that report problems by throwing an exception, which can be caught and processed using a dedicated keyword, such as catch. Go works by assigning an error to the second result produced by the functions. If the error result is nil, then the string has been successfully parsed. If the error result is not nil, then parsing has failed. You can see examples of successful and unsuccessful parsing by compiling and executing the code, which produces the following output:

Bool 1 true <nil>
Bool 2 false <nil>
Bool 3 false strconv.ParseBool: parsing "not true": invalid syntax

The first two strings are parsed into the values true and false, and the error result for both function calls is nil. The third string is not on the list of recognized values described and cannot be parsed. For this operation, the error result provides details of the problem.

Care must be taken to inspect the error result because the other result will default to the zero value when the string cannot be parsed. If you don't check the error result, you will not be able to differentiate between a false value that has been correctly parsed from a string and the zero value that has been used because parsing failed. The check for an error is typically done using the if/else keywords, as shown I describe the if keyword and related features.

Checking for an Error in the main.go File in the operations Folder package main
```go
import (    "fmt"
   "strconv"
) func main() {    val1 := "0"    bool1, b1err :=
strconv.ParseBool(val1)
   if b1err == nil {
      fmt.Println("Parsed value:", bool1)
   } else {
      fmt.Println("Cannot parse", val1)
   }
}
```

The if/else block allows the zero value to be differentiated from a successful processing of a string that parses to the false value. As I explain, Go if statements can define an initialization statement, and this allows a conversion function to be called and its results to be inspected in a single statement, as shown.

Checking an Error in a Single Statement in the main.go File in the operations Folder package main
```go
import (    "fmt"
   "strconv"
) func main() {    val1 := "0"
   if bool1, b1err := strconv.ParseBool(val1); b1err == nil {
      fmt.Println("Parsed value:", bool1)
   } else {
      fmt.Println("Cannot parse", val1)
   }
}
```

Both produce the following output when the project is compiled and executed:
Parsed value: false

Parsing Integers

The ParseInt and ParseUint functions require the base of the number represented by the string and the size of the data type that will be used to represent the parsed value, as shown.

Parsing an Integer in the main.go File in the operations Folder package main

```
import (    "fmt"
    "strconv"
) func main() {    val1 := "100"    int1, int1err :=
strconv.ParseInt(val1, 0, 8)
    if int1err == nil {
        fmt.Println("Parsed value:", int1)
    } else {
        fmt.Println("Cannot parse", val1)
    }
}
```

The first argument to the ParseInt function is the string to parse. The second argument is the base for the number, or zero to let the function detect the base from the string's prefix. The final argument is the size of the data type to which the parsed value will be allocated. In this example, I have left the function to detect the base and specified 8 as the size.

Compile and execute the code, and you will receive the following output, showing the parsed integer value:
Parsed value: 100

You might expect that specifying the size will change the type used for the result, but that's not the case, and the function always returns an int64. The size only specifies the data size that the parsed value must be able to fit into. If the string value contains a number value that cannot be represented within the specified size, then the value won't be parsed. I have changed the string value to contain a larger value.

Increasing the Value in the main.go File in the operations Folder package main

```
import (    "fmt"
    "strconv"
) func main() {    val1 :=
"500"    int1, int1err :=
strconv.ParseInt(val1, 0,
8)
    if int1err == nil {
        fmt.Println("Parsed value:", int1)
    } else {        fmt.Println("Cannot parse", val1, int1err)
    }
```

}

The string "500" can be parsed into an integer, but it is too large to represent as an 8-bit value, which is the size specified by the ParseInt argument. When the code is compiled and executed, the output shows the error returned by the function:

Cannot parse 500 strconv.ParseInt: parsing "500": value out of range

This may seem an indirect approach, but it allows Go to maintain its type rules while ensuring that you can safely perform an explicit conversion on a result if it is successfully parsed, as shown.

Explicitly Converting a Result in the main.go File in the operations Folder package main

```
import (    "fmt"
    "strconv"
) func main() {    val1 := "100"    int1, int1err :=
strconv.ParseInt(val1, 0, 8)
    if int1err == nil {        smallInt :=
int8(int1)
        fmt.Println("Parsed value:", smallInt)
    } else {
        fmt.Println("Cannot parse", val1, int1err)
    }
}
```

Specifying a size of 8 when calling the ParseInt function allows me to perform an explicit conversion to the int8 type without the possibility of overflow. The code produces the following output when compiled and executed:

Parsed value: 100

Parsing Binary, Octal, and Hexadecimal Integers

The base argument received by the Parse<Type> functions allow non decimal number strings to be parsed, as shown.

Parsing a Binary Value in the main.go File in the operations Folder package main

```
import (    "fmt"
    "strconv"
) func main() {    val1 := "100"    int1, int1err :=
strconv.ParseInt(val1, 2, 8)
    if int1err == nil {        smallInt :=
int8(int1)
        fmt.Println("Parsed value:", smallInt)
    } else {
        fmt.Println("Cannot parse", val1, int1err)
    }
```

}

The string value "100" can be parsed into the decimal value 100, but it could also represent the binary value 4. Using the second argument to the ParseInt function, I can specify a base of 2, which means the string will be interpreted as a binary value. Compile and execute the code, and you will see a decimal representation of the number parsed from the binary string:

Parsed value: 4

You can leave the Parse<Type> functions to detect the base for a value using a prefix, as shown.

Using a Prefix in the main.go File in the operations Folder package main

```
import (    "fmt"
    "strconv"
) func main() {    val1 := "0b1100100"    int1, int1err :=
strconv.ParseInt(val1, 0, 8)    if int1err == nil {
smallInt := int8(int1)
    fmt.Println("Parsed value:", smallInt)
  } else {
    fmt.Println("Cannot parse", val1, int1err)
  }
}
```

The functions described in Table can determine the base of the value they are parsing based on its prefix.
Table describes the set of supported prefixes.

Table The Base Prefixes for Numeric Strings

Prefix	Description
0b	This prefix denotes a binary value, such as 0b1100100.
0o	This prefix denotes an octal value, such as 0o144.
0x	This prefix denotes a hex value, such as 0x64.

The string has a 0b prefix, which denotes a binary value. When the code is compiled and executed, the following output is produced:

Parsed value: 100

Using the Integer Convenience Function

For many projects, the most common parsing task is to create int values from strings that contain decimal numbers, as shown.

Performing a Common Parsing Task in the main.go File in the operations Folder package main

```
import (    "fmt"
    "strconv"
) func main() {    val1 := "100"    int1, int1err :=
strconv.ParseInt(val1, 10, 0)    if int1err == nil {
    var intResult int = int(int1)        fmt.Println("Parsed
value:", intResult)
    } else {
        fmt.Println("Cannot parse", val1, int1err)
    }
}
```

This is such a common task that the strconv package provides the Atoi function, which handles the parsing and explicit conversion in a single step, as shown.

Using the Convenience Function in the main.go File in the operations Folder package main

```
import (    "fmt"
    "strconv"
) func main() {    val1 := "100"    int1, int1err :=
strconv.Atoi(val1)
    if int1err == nil {        var intResult int = int1
fmt.Println("Parsed value:", intResult)
    } else {
        fmt.Println("Cannot parse", val1, int1err)
    }
}
```

The Atoi function accepts only the value to be parsed and doesn't support parsing non decimal values. The type of the result is int, instead of the int64 produced by the ParseInt function. The code produces the following output when compiled and executed:

Parsed value: 100

Parsing Floating-Point Numbers

The ParseFloat function is used to parse strings containing floating-point numbers, as shown.

Parsing Floating-Point Values in the main.go File in the operations Folder package
main import (
    "fmt"
    "strconv"

```
) func main() {    val1 := "48.95"    float1, float1err :=
strconv.ParseFloat(val1, 64)
    if float1err == nil {
        fmt.Println("Parsed value:", float1)
    } else {
```

```
        fmt.Println("Cannot parse", val1, float1err)
    }
}
```

The first argument to the ParseFloat function is the value to parse. The second argument specifies the size of the result. The result from the ParseFloat function is a float64 value, but if 32 is specified, then the result can be explicitly converted to a float32 value.

The ParseFloat function can parse values expressed with an exponent, as shown.

Parsing a Value with an Exponent in the main.go File in the operations Folder package main

```
import (    "fmt"
    "strconv"
) func main() {    val1 := "4.895e+01"    float1, float1err :=
strconv.ParseFloat(val1, 64)
    if float1err == nil {
        fmt.Println("Parsed value:", float1)
    } else {
        fmt.Println("Cannot parse", val1, float1err)
    }
}
```

Both produce the same output when compiled and executed:
Parsed value: 48.95

Formatting Values as Strings

The Go standard library also provides functionality for converting basic data values into strings, which can be used directly or composed with other strings. The strconv package provides the functions described in Table.

Table The strconv Functions for Converting Values into Strings

Function	Description
FormatBool(val)	This function returns the string true or false based on the value of the specified bool.
FormatInt(val, base)	This function returns a string representation of the specified int64 value, expressed in the specified base.
FormatUint(val, base)	This function returns a string representation of the specified uint64 value, expressed in the specified base.
FormatFloat(val, format, precision, size)	This function returns a string representation of the specified float64 value, expressed using the specified format, precision, and size.
Itoa(val)	This function returns a string representation of the specified int value, expressed using base 10.

Formatting Boolean Values

The FormatBool function accepts a bool value and returns a string representation, as shown. This is the simplest of the functions described in Table, because it returns only true and false strings.

Formatting a Bool Value in the main.go File in the operations Folder package main

```
import (    "fmt"
    "strconv"
) func main() {
    val1 := true    val2 := false

    str1 := strconv.FormatBool(val1)    str2 := strconv.FormatBool(val2)

    fmt.Println("Formatted value 1: " + str1)
    fmt.Println("Formatted value 2: " + str2)
}
```

Notice that I can use the + operator to concatenate the result from the FormatBool function with a literal string so that only a single argument is passed to the fmt.Println function. The code produces the following output when compiled and executed:

```
Formatted value 1: true
Formatted value 2: false
```

Formatting Integer Values

The FormatInt and FormatUint functions format integer values as strings, as demonstrated.

Formatting an Integer in the main.go File in the operations Folder package main

```
import (    "fmt"
    "strconv"
) func main() {    val := 275
    base10String := strconv.FormatInt(int64(val), 10)
    base2String := strconv.FormatInt(int64(val), 2)

    fmt.Println("Base 10: " + base10String)
    fmt.Println("Base 2: " + base2String) }
```

The FormatInt function accepts only int64 values, so I perform an explicit conversion and specify strings that express the value in base 10 (decimal) and base 2 (binary). The code produces the following output when compiled and executed:

```
Base 10: 275
Base 2: 100010011
```

Using the Integer Convenience Function

Integer values are most commonly represented using the int type and are converted to strings using base 10. The strconv package provides the Itoa function, which is a more convenient way to perform this specific conversion, as shown.

Using the Convenience Function in the main.go File in the operations Folder package main

```
import (    "fmt"
    "strconv"
) func main() {    val := 275
    base10String := strconv.Itoa(val)
    base2String := strconv.FormatInt(int64(val), 2)

    fmt.Println("Base 10: " + base10String)
fmt.Println("Base 2: " + base2String) }
```

The Itoa function accepts an int value, which is explicitly converted to an int64 and passed to the ParseInt function. The code produces the following output:

Base 10: 275
Base 2: 100010011

Formatting Floating-Point Values

Expressing floating-point values as strings requires additional configuration options because different formats are available. This shows a basic formatting operation using the FormatFloat function.

Converting a Floating-Point Number in the main.go File in the operations Folder package main

```
import (    "fmt"
    "strconv"
) func main() {    val := 49.95
    Fstring := strconv.FormatFloat(val, 'f', 2, 64)
    Estring := strconv.FormatFloat(val, 'e', -1, 64)

    fmt.Println("Format F: " + Fstring)
fmt.Println("Format E: " + Estring) }
```

The first argument to the FormatFloat function is the value to process. The second argument is a byte value, which specifies the format of the string. The byte is usually expressed as a rune literal value, and Table describes the most commonly used format runes.

Table Commonly Used Format Options for Floating-Point String Formatting

Function	Description

F as	The floating-point value will be expressed in the form ±ddd.ddd without an exponent, such as 49.95.
e, E	The floating-point value will be expressed in the form ±ddd.ddde±dd, such as 4.995e+01 or 4.995E+01. The case of the letter denoting the exponent is determined by the case of the rune used as the formatting argument.
g, G	The floating-point value will be expressed using format e/E for large exponents or format f for smaller values.

The third argument to the FormatFloat function specifies the number of digits that will follow the decimal point. The special value -1 can be used to select the smallest number of digits that will create a string that can be parsed back into the same floating-point value without a loss of precision. The final argument determines whether the floating-point value is rounded so that it can be expressed as a float32 or a float64 value, using the value 32 or 64.

These arguments mean that this statement formats the value assigned to the variable named val, using the format option f, with two decimal places, and rounded so that the value can be represented using the float64 type:

```
...
Fstring: = strconv.FormatFloat(val, 'f', 2, 64) ...
```

The effect is to format the value into a string that can be used to represent a currency amount. The code produces the following output when compiled and executed:

```
Format F: 49.95
Format E: 4.995e+01
```

Conclusion

In this comprehensive exploration of operations and conversions in Go, we've delved into some of the essential concepts that every Go programmer must master. Understanding these core elements is crucial for anyone aiming to develop efficient, reliable, and maintainable code. Go's simplicity and strict type system ensure that developers write clear, concise, and bug-free programs, and a proper grasp of operations and conversions can further enhance these benefits. Let's revisit the key aspects discussed, highlighting the significance of each topic.

Reiterating the Importance of Operations

Operations form the backbone of any programming language. They enable developers to perform a wide range of tasks, from simple arithmetic to complex logical computations. In Go, operations are designed to be straightforward yet powerful, allowing for precise data manipulation.

1. **Arithmetic Operations**: Arithmetic is fundamental to numerous tasks, from basic calculations to complex data processing. Understanding how Go handles arithmetic operations can help developers write efficient algorithms. For instance, the clarity of integer

division and the implications of using different numeric types (integers vs. floating-point) are crucial for applications requiring accurate calculations, like financial software.

2. **Relational Operations**: Relational operators are essential in controlling the flow of a program. They are the backbone of conditions and loops, which allow developers to implement logic based on comparisons. Go's straightforward approach ensures that comparisons are always explicit, making code easier to read and debug. For example, comparing values in a loop or condition might seem trivial, but understanding the intricacies of Go's type system can prevent unexpected behavior.

3. **Logical Operations**: Logical operators (&&, ||, !) help in creating complex conditional statements. Effective use of these operators can simplify code, making it more readable and maintainable. They play a critical role in scenarios where multiple conditions need to be evaluated simultaneously. For example, when processing user inputs or managing program states, logical operations can determine which part of the code should execute.

4. **Bitwise Operations**: Bitwise operations, while not as commonly used as arithmetic or logical operators, are vital for low-level data manipulation. These operations allow developers to work directly with bits, making them ideal for tasks such as data encoding, compression, and encryption. Understanding how bitwise operators function can unlock new levels of performance optimization, particularly when dealing with hardware interfaces or custom protocols.

5. **Assignment Operations**: Go's assignment operations provide a concise way to update variables. They reduce verbosity and help keep code clean. For example, using += or -= can make arithmetic operations more readable and reduce the risk of mistakes. These operators can also enhance code performance by reducing the number of operations required.

Significance of Type Conversions

Go's strict type system is both a blessing and a challenge. While it ensures that type-related bugs are minimized, it also means that developers need to explicitly convert between types where necessary. This explicitness is an essential aspect of Go's philosophy, emphasizing clarity and simplicity.

1. **The Necessity of Explicit Conversions**: Unlike some languages that perform implicit conversions, Go requires explicit type conversions. This design choice prevents subtle bugs that arise from unexpected type changes. By making type conversions explicit, Go ensures that developers are always aware of the data types they are working with, leading to safer and more predictable code.

2. **Numeric Conversions**: Go provides a range of numeric types, each suited for specific scenarios. Converting between these types allows developers to optimize for precision, range, or memory usage. However, it is essential to understand the implications of each conversion. For instance, converting a float64 to an int can lead to a loss of precision, which could be critical in applications like scientific computing or financial modeling.

3. **String Conversions**: Converting between strings and other data types is a common task in many programs, especially when dealing with user input or file I/O. Go's strconv package provides robust tools for these conversions. Understanding how to convert integers, floats, and Booleans to and from strings enables developers to handle data more flexibly and

efficiently. For instance, converting user input from strings to numeric types can allow for easy validation and processing.

4. **Boolean Conversions**: While Go does not allow direct conversions between numeric types and Booleans, developers can achieve this through logical checks. This approach prevents ambiguities and ensures that conditions are explicitly defined, making the code easier to read and debug.

5. **Type Assertions and Type Switches**: When dealing with interface types, Go's type assertion mechanism allows developers to extract the underlying type. This feature is particularly useful in scenarios where functions return interface types, and the programmer needs to operate on specific types. Type switches extend this functionality, allowing for multiple type checks within a single construct, which can simplify code that handles various types.

Real-World Applications of Operations and Conversions

The concepts of operations and conversions are not limited to theoretical examples. They are used in countless real-world applications across various industries:

1. **Mathematical and Statistical Computations**: Arithmetic and logical operations are essential in developing applications for scientific computing, data analysis, and machine learning. Efficiently implementing these operations can significantly impact the performance of data-heavy applications, such as processing large datasets or running complex simulations.

2. **Data Encoding, Compression, and Cryptography**: Bitwise operations are critical for tasks that require direct manipulation of binary data. Developers can use bitwise shifts and masks to implement efficient data encoding, compression algorithms, and encryption techniques. Understanding how to manipulate bits can lead to performance improvements and unlock advanced capabilities like error detection and correction.

3. **File I/O and Data Processing**: In applications that read from or write to files, it is common to encounter different data formats that need conversion. For example, when reading a CSV file, all data is read as strings, but developers may need to convert these values into integers, floats, or booleans to process them effectively. Understanding Go's conversion mechanisms allows for seamless handling of data across different formats.

4. **User Input Handling**: Programs often need to convert user input, which is typically received as a string, into other types for further processing. For example, a calculator program would need to convert user-provided values into numbers to perform arithmetic. Handling such conversions accurately is crucial to ensure the program behaves as expected.

Best Practices for Effective Use of Operations and Conversions

1. **Write Clear and Readable Code**: Always strive to write code that is easy to understand. Use explicit conversions to make your intentions clear. Avoid relying on implicit behaviors that might be misinterpreted by others who read your code. This clarity is one of Go's core philosophies.

2. **Be Mindful of Overflow and Underflow**: When working with numeric types, especially integers, always be aware of the potential for overflow and underflow. Go does not automatically handle these issues, so it is up to the developer to ensure that calculations are

within safe bounds. This is particularly important when dealing with user inputs or processing large datasets.

3. **Optimize for Performance Where Necessary**: Sometimes, using bitwise operations can offer performance benefits, especially when dealing with low-level data. However, such optimizations should be used judiciously. Always profile your code to identify bottlenecks and ensure that any optimizations you implement provide a measurable improvement.

4. **Handle Type Assertions Safely**: When working with interfaces, always use the ok idiom to safely handle type assertions. This approach prevents runtime panics that can occur if a type assertion fails. Type switches can be a cleaner alternative when multiple type checks are needed.

5. **Test Your Conversions Thoroughly**: Converting between types can lead to unexpected results, especially when working with external data sources. Always test your conversion code with a variety of inputs to ensure that it handles all edge cases correctly. This approach is essential for robust and reliable software.

Final Thoughts

Mastering operations and conversions in Go is more than just understanding how to write correct syntax; it is about grasping how to utilize these tools effectively to solve real-world problems. From simple arithmetic to complex data manipulation, these concepts enable developers to write code that is not only functional but also efficient and maintainable.

By enforcing explicit type conversions and providing a rich set of operations, Go empowers developers to write clear and predictable code. This predictability reduces the likelihood of bugs and makes the development process smoother. While Go's simplicity might make it seem less powerful than other languages, this simplicity is precisely what makes it robust, reliable, and performant.

In conclusion, operations and conversions are foundational skills for any Go programmer. Whether you are building simple scripts, developing web applications, or creating complex systems software, a solid understanding of these concepts will serve as a critical asset. Continue to practice, explore more advanced topics, and refine your skills, and you will find that Go's straightforward yet powerful approach can handle even the most demanding programming tasks.

4. Go: Function and Control flows

Introduction

In the world of programming, understanding how to control the flow of a program and effectively utilize functions is crucial. These two concepts form the backbone of building efficient, maintainable, and scalable software. Go, a statically typed, compiled language developed by Google, emphasizes simplicity, speed, and efficiency. This introduction will explore how functions and control flows are structured in Go, providing insight into why Go's design is ideal for modern programming needs.

What Are Functions?

Functions are fundamental building blocks in programming that allow you to encapsulate reusable code blocks. They enable developers to write modular and organized code, avoid repetition, and promote reusability. In Go, functions are first-class citizens, meaning they can be passed as arguments to other functions, returned from other functions, and assigned to variables.

A typical function in Go consists of:

Function Name: Identifies the function.

Parameters: The inputs passed to the function.

Return Values: The output that the function produces.

Function Body: The block of code executed when the function is called.

Here's a basic example of a function in Go:

```
package main

import "fmt"// Simple function that adds two integers

func add(a int, b int) int {
    return a + b
}

func main() {
    sum := add(3, 5)
    fmt.Println("Sum:", sum)
}
```

In this example, the add function accepts two integer arguments and returns their sum. It is then called in the main function to compute and print the result.

Key Features of Functions in Go

Multiple Return Values: Go allows functions to return multiple values, which is particularly useful for error handling.

Named Return Values: Function results can be named, allowing for more readable code and easier handling of return values.

Variadic Functions: Go supports variadic functions, enabling a function to accept a variable number of arguments. This is often used for functions like fmt.Printf, which can handle multiple arguments seamlessly.

Anonymous Functions and Closures: Go supports anonymous functions (functions without names) and closures (functions that can capture variables from their surrounding scope).

Control Flow in Go

Control flow refers to the order in which individual statements, instructions, or function calls are executed or evaluated in a program. Go's control flow mechanisms provide various constructs to direct the execution of code, such as conditional statements, loops, and branching.

Conditional Statements

Conditional statements are used to execute specific blocks of code based on certain conditions. In Go, the if statement is the most common conditional statement. It works similarly to other programming languages, but Go's syntax promotes clarity and readability.

Example of an if Statement:

```
func main() {
    x := 10
    if x > 5 {
        fmt.Println("x is greater than 5")
    } else {
        fmt.Println("x is 5 or less")
    }
}
```

Key Features of Conditional Statements in Go:

No parentheses required: Unlike many other languages, there's no need to enclose the condition in parentheses.

Support for initialization statements: You can include an initialization statement before the condition, which can help simplify code.

Example:

```go
if x := 10; x > 5 {
    fmt.Println("x is greater than 5")
}
```

In this example, x is declared and initialized within the if statement. Its scope is limited to the if and else blocks, making it easier to manage variables.

switch Statements

Switch statements are another way to handle conditional execution. They are often more concise and readable than multiple if-else statements when dealing with multiple conditions.

Example of a switch Statement:

```go
func main() {
    day := "Monday"
    switch day {
    case "Monday":
        fmt.Println("Start of the work week")
    case "Friday":
        fmt.Println("End of the work week")
    default:
        fmt.Println("Middle of the work week")
    }
}
```

Key Features of switch Statements in Go:

No break needed: Unlike other languages like C or Java, Go's switch statements do not require explicit break statements; they automatically terminate after a case is matched.

Multiple expressions per case: You can group multiple expressions in a single case.

Type switch: A special type of switch that can be used to discover the type of an interface value.

Loops

Loops are essential for executing a block of code multiple times. In Go, the for loop is the only loop construct available, and it can be used in various ways to achieve common looping tasks.

Basic for Loop Example:

```go
func main() {
```

```go
    for i := 0; i < 5; i++ {

        fmt.Println(i)

    }

}
```

In this example, the for loop initializes i to 0, checks if i is less than 5, and increments i after each iteration.

Infinite Loop:

```go
for {

    fmt.Println("This will run forever")

}
```

Looping Through Collections:

Go's for loop can also be used to iterate over collections like arrays, slices, maps, and strings.

```go
arr := []string{"apple", "banana", "cherry"}

for index, value := range arr {

    fmt.Printf("Index: %d, Value: %s\n", index, value)

}
```

In this example, the range keyword allows the loop to iterate over each element of the slice, providing both the index and the value.

Defer, Panic, and Recover

Go provides unique control flow features like defer, panic, and recover that are particularly useful for managing resource cleanup and error handling.

defer: Executes a function after the surrounding function returns, which is useful for resource cleanup.

```go
func main() {

    defer fmt.Println("This will be printed last")

    fmt.Println("This will be printed first")

}
```

panic: Causes the program to crash, typically used when encountering a severe error.

```go
func main() {

    panic("Something went wrong!")

}
```

recover: Allows the program to handle a panic and continue execution.

```go
func main() {
    defer func() {
        if r := recover(); r != nil {
            fmt.Println("Recovered from panic:", r)
        }
    }()
    panic("Unexpected error!")
}
```

A function is an independent section of code that maps input parameters to output parameters. It is a collection of statements that are used to perform a specific task and return the result to the caller.

Functions are the building blocks of a Go program. They have inputs, outputs, and a series of steps called statements that are executed in order.

Function declarations

A function declaration consists of the keyword func, the name of the function, a parameter list (empty for main), a result list (also empty here), and the body of the function—the statements that define what it does—enclosed in braces.
Function declaration has a name, a list of parameters, an optional list of results, and a body as shown below:

```go
func name (parameter-list)(result-list){ //body of the function
}
```

Parameters and returns

The function definition in Go programming language is as follows: func function_name([parameter_list]) [return_types] {

```go
    //Body of function
}
```

Parameters

When a function is invoked, you pass a value to the parameter. A parameter is like a placeholder. This value is referred to as an actual parameter or argument. The parameter list refers to the type, order, and the number of the parameters of a function. Parameters are optional in functions. Hence, a function may contain no parameters.

Returns

A function may return a list of values. The return_types is the list of data types of the values that the function returns. Some functions perform the desired operations without returning a value. In this case, the return_type is not required.

Here is a sample Go program to explain parameters and returns:

Program

```
// Go program to explain parameters and returns package main import "fmt"

func main() {

/* declare local variables*/ var x int = 50 var y int = 40 var sum_value int

/* calling a function to get sum of values */ sum_value = sum(x, y)

fmt.Printf("Sum value is: %d\n", sum_value) }

/* function returns the sum of two numbers */ func sum(num1, num2 int) int {

/* declare local variables */ var result int result = num1 + num2 return result

}
```

The following will be the output for the above program:
Sum value is: 90

While creating a Go function, you define the task that the function will perform. To use a function, you will have to call that function to perform the predefined task.

When a program calls a function, the program control is transferred to the called function. A called function performs a defined task, and when its return statement is executed or when its function-ending closing brace is reached, it returns the program control to the main program.

To call a function, you simply need to pass the required parameters along with its function name. If the function returns a value, then you can store the returned value.

Multiple returns and named return

Golang allows giving names to the return or result parameters of the functions in the function definition. Also, Go has built-in support for multiple return values. This feature is used to return both result and error values from a function.

Multiple returns

In Go, a function can return multiple values using the return statement. The type of return values depends on the type of the parameters defined in the parameter list as shown below:

Program

```go
// Go program to explain multiple returns
package main import "fmt"
// testfunc return 2 values of int type func
testfunc(x, y int) (int, int) {
   return x + y, x - y
}

func main() {
   // Return values are assigned into different variables var
   testvar1, testvar2 = testfunc(10, 20)

   fmt.Printf("addition result: %d", testvar1)
   fmt.Printf("\nsubtraction result: %d", testvar2)
}
```

The following will be the output for the above program:

addition result: 30 subtraction result: -10

Named returns

Golang allows giving names to the return parameters of the functions in the function definition, i.e., explicit naming of return variables in the function definition. It eliminates the need to mention the variable's name with the return statement.

This concept is generally used when a function needs to return multiple values. Golang provides this facility for the user's comfort and to enhance the code readability.

Syntax for named returns:

```go
func func_name(Par-list)(result_par1 data_type, result_par2 data_type, ....){
   // function body

   return
}
```

Let's see an example:

Program

```go
// Golang program to show the use of named return arguments
package main import "fmt"
// Main Method func
main() {

   // calling the function which returns one values x :=
   sum(10, 20)

   fmt.Println("10 + 20 =", x)
}
```

```
// function with named arguments func
sum(a, b int) (add int) { add = a + b

   // return keyword without any resultant parameters return
}
```

The following will be the output for the above program:

10 + 20 = 30

Call by value

Golang supports call by value to pass arguments to the function. Go does not have a call by reference since it doesn't have reference variables. However, we can pass the address of the variable as a value. Golang uses, by default, the call by value way to pass the arguments to the function.

Call by value

The call by value method of passing arguments to a function copies the actual value of an argument into the formal parameter of the function. The values of the actual parameters are copied to the function's formal parameters, and the two types of parameters are stored in different memory locations. The changes made to the parameter inside the function do not affect the argument, i.e., the changes made inside the functions are not reflected in the actual parameters of the caller:

Program

```
// Go program to explain call by value
package main import "fmt"

// function to change the value of given variable func
replace (x int) {
   x = 20
}

// main function func
main() {

   var x int = 10
   fmt.Printf("value of x before function call = %d", x)

   // call by value replace(x)
   fmt.Printf("\nvalue of x after function call = %d", x)
}
```

The following will be the output for the above program:

value of x before function call = 10

value of x after function call = 10

As discussed earlier, Go does not have a call by reference since it doesn't have reference variables. However, we can pass the address of the variable as a value. Here, we will use the concept of pointers and dereference operators. The address operator, & is used to get the address of a variable of any data type and the dereference operator, * is used to access the value at an address.

Since the actual and formal parameters refer to the same locations, any changes made inside the function are reflected in the actual parameters of the caller. This is shown below:

Program

```
// Go program to explain call by passing the address of the variable package
main
import "fmt"

// function to change the value of given variable
func replace(x *int) { *x = 20
}

// main function func
main() {

    var x int = 10
    fmt.Printf("value of x before function call = %d", x)

    // call by reference replace(&x)
    fmt.Printf("\nvalue of x after function call = %d", x)
}
```

The following will be the output for the above program:

value of x before function call = 10
value of x after function call = 20

Variadic functions

Functions, in general, accept only a fixed number of arguments but the variadic function can accept a variable number of arguments.

Only the last parameter of a function can be variadic. If the last parameter of a function definition is prefixed by an ellipsis (…), then the function can accept any number of arguments for that parameter. This is shown as follows:

```
func variadic_function(a int, b …int) { //
    Body of variadic function
}
```

In the above function, the parameter b is variadic since it's prefixed by an ellipsis, and it can accept any number of arguments.

Let's make the first parameter of the variadic_function variadic. The syntax will look like this:

```
func variadic_function(a …int, b int) { //
    Body of variadic function
```

```
}
```

The above variadic_function will fail to compile with an error syntax
error: **cannot use ... with non-final parameter a**

In the above function, it is not possible to pass arguments to the parameter b because whatever argument we pass will be assigned to the first parameter a since it is variadic. Hence, variadic parameters can only be present in last in the function definition. The way variadic functions work is by converting the variable number of arguments to a slice of the type of the variadic parameter.

Program

```
// Go program to explain the variadic function package
main
import (
  "fmt"
  "strings"
)

// Variadic function to join strings func
join(element ...string) string { return
strings.Join(element, "_")
}
func main() {

  // multiple arguments
  fmt.Println(join("GO", "language", "book"))
}
```

The following will be the output for the above program:

GO_language_book

The variadic function increases the readability of your program. It can be used in scenarios such as when the number of parameters is not known.

Let's look at the following program:

Program

```
// Go program to explain the variadic function package
main
import (
  "fmt"
  "strings"
)

// Variadic function to join strings func
join(element ...string) string { return
strings.Join(element, "_")
} func main() {
```

```
   // pass a slice in variadic function element :=
   []string{"GO", "language", "book"}
   fmt.Println(join(element...))
}
```

The following will be the output for the above program:

GO_language_book

Let's look at another program:

Program

```
//Select single argument from all arguments of variadic function
package main import "fmt"
func main() {
   variadicExample("IT", "Finance", "HR", "Recruitement", "Payroll")
}

func variadicExample(x ...string) {
   fmt.Println(x[1]) fmt.Println(x[4])
}
```

The following will be the output for the above program:

Finance
Payroll

Defer

Go has mechanisms for control flow: if, for, switch, goto, etc, but some of the less commonly used ones are deferred, panic, and recover.

A defer statement postpones the execution of a function and pushes a function call onto a list until the surrounding function returns, either normally or through a panic. Defer is commonly used to simplify functions that perform various clean-up actions as shown below:

Program

```
//Program to explain defer
package main import "fmt"
func main() {
   defer fmt.Println("GO") fmt.Println("Book")
}
```

The following will be the output for the above program:

Book

GO

Control flows

In Go, the control flow statements are used to break the flow of execution and enable programs to execute code based on certain conditions. This chapter will cover the concept of control flows in Go. It will cover decision making in Golang using if, if...else, if...else if...else, switch...case and fall through statements. It will also cover the concept of loops - for loops, nested for loops, loop control statements – break, go to, continue, etc.

Decision-making

Golang uses control statements to control the execution flow of the program based on certain conditions. These are used to ensure a logical flow during program execution based on changes to the state of a program.

If statement

A statement executes a piece of code if one condition is found true. If the statement looks as it does in C or Java, there is just one difference which is that we need to use {} instead of (). The variables declared by the statement are only in scope until the end of the if.

Syntax:

```
If condition {
    // piece of code to be executed when the condition is true
}
```

For example, the program given below will print if the variable a is true.

Program

```
// Go program to explain if statement package
main
import (
"fmt" )

func main() { var x =
  "Cricket" a := true
  if a {
    fmt.Println(x)
  }
}
```

The following will be the output for the above program:

Cricket

if...else statement

If the statement executes a block of statements when the condition is true, and if the condition is false, it will move to the else block and execute it.

Syntax:

```
If condition {
   // piece of code to be executed if condition is true
} else {
   // piece of code to be executed if condition is false
}
```

The following example will show the output Capital of India if the x is New Delhi:

Program

```
// Go program to explain if …else statement package
main
import (
"fmt" )

func main() {
   x := "New Delhi"

   if x == "New Delhi" {
      fmt.Println("Capital of India")
   } else { fmt.Println("City is not the capital of
   India") }
}
```

The following will be the output for the above program:

Capital of India

if…else if…else statement

The if…else if…else statement allows for combining multiple if…else statements.

Syntax:

```
if condition-1 {
   // piece of code to be executed if condition-1 is true } else
if condition-2 {
   // piece of code to be executed if condition-2 is true
} else {
   // piece code to be executed if both condition1 and condition2 are false
}
```

The example given below will show the following output:

"Capital of Maharashtra" if x is "Mumbai"
"City of Maharashtra" if x is "Pune" and
"Neither Pune nor Mumbai" if x is other than "Pune" or "Mumbai"

Let's look at the following example:

Program

```
// Go program to explain if …else if..else statement package
main
import (
"fmt" )

func main() {
  x := "Mumbai"

  if x == "Mumbai" {
    fmt.Println("Capital of Maharashtra")
  } else if x == "Pune" { fmt.Println("City of
    Maharshtra")
  } else { fmt.Println("Neither Pune nor
  Mumbai") }
}
```

The above program will show the following output:

Capital of Maharashtra

switch…case

A switch statement is a multiway branch statement. It provides an efficient way of transfering the execution to different parts of a code based on the value of the expression. Switch statements express conditionals across many branches. The cases are evaluated from top to bottom, stopping when a case succeeds. If no case matches and there is a default case, its statements are executed.

The example given below will display the day of the week based on the value of a switch variable:

Program

```
// Go program to explain switch…case statement
package main import "fmt"
func main() { switch day :=
  7; day {
    case 1: fmt.Println("Monday")
    case 2: fmt.Println("Tuesday")
    case 3: fmt.Println("Wednesday")
    case 4: fmt.Println("Thursday")
    case 5: fmt.Println("Friday")
    case 6: fmt.Println("Saturday")
    case 7: fmt.Println("Sunday")
    default:
      fmt.Println("Invalid")
  }
}
```

The above program will show below output:

Sunday

Loops

A loop statement is used to execute a block of code repeatedly. For is the only loop available in Go. Go doesn't have while or do…while loops that are present in other languages like C.

For loops

The for loop is a repetition control structure. It allows you to write a loop that needs to be executed a specific number of times.

Syntax:

for [Initial Statement] ; [Condition] ; [Post Statement] { [Action]
}

The example given below will display the sum of the numbers from 1 to 10 using for loop:

Program

```
// Go program to explain for loops
package main import "fmt"
func main() {
   sum := 0
   for i := 0; i <= 10; i++ {
      sum += i }
   fmt.Println("Sum of numbers from 1 to 10:", sum)
}
```

The above program will show the following output:

Sum of numbers from 1 to 10: 55

Nested for loops

Loops can be nested in Go as they can with other programming languages. A nested loop is a loop that occurs within another loop. These can be useful when you want a looped action performed on every element of a data set.

```
for {
   [Action to be performed] for {
      [Action to be performed]
   }
}
```

The example given below will display the prime number from 1 to 20 using nested for loop:

Program

```
// Go program to explain nested for loops
package main import "fmt"
func main() {
  /* local variable declaration */ var i, j
  int
  for i = 2; i < 20; i++ {
    for j = 2; j <= (i / j); j++ {
      if i%j == 0 {
        break
      }
    }
    if j > (i / j) {
      fmt.Printf("Prime number between 1 to 20: %d\n", i) }
  }
}
```

The above program will show the following output:

Prime number between 1 to 20: 2
Prime number between 1 to 20: 3
Prime number between 1 to 20: 5
Prime number between 1 to 20: 7
Prime number between 1 to 20: 11
Prime number between 1 to 20: 13
Prime number between 1 to 20: 17
Prime number between 1 to 20: 19

Loop control statements

Loop control statements are used to change the execution of the program. When the execution of the given loop leaves its scope, the objects that are created within the scope are also destroyed.

Go language supports 3 types of loop control statements: break, goto, and continue.

Break statements

A break statement is used to terminate the loop or statement in which it presents. The break statement is used to terminate the execution of the current loop.

The example given below gives the output numbers starting from 1 and at x=4, break is encountered and it goes out of the loop:

Program

```
// Go program to explain break statements
package main import "fmt"
```

```
// Main function func
main() {
  for x := 1; x <= 5; x++ { fmt.Println("Number:",
    x)
    // For loop breaks when the value of x = 4 if x
    == 4 {
      break
    }
  }
}
```

The above program will show the following output:

Number: 1
Number: 2
Number: 3
Number: 4

Goto statements

The Goto statement is used to transfer control to the labelled statement in the program. The label is a valid identifier and placed just before the statement from where the control is transferred.

The example given below shows output numbers starting from 1 and at a=3, goto is encountered and without printing 3, control moves to Lable1.

Program

```
// Go program to explain Goto statement
package main import "fmt"
func main() { var a
  int = 1

Lable1:
  for a <= 5 { if a
    == 3 { a = a +
    1
      goto Lable1
    }
    fmt.Printf("Number is: %d\n", a) a++
  }
}
```

The above program will show the following output:
Number is: 1
Number is: 2
Number is: 4
Number is: 5

Continue statements

The continue statement is used to skip over the execution part of the loop on a certain condition. After that, it transfers the control to the beginning of the loop.

The continue statement is used when you want to skip the remaining portion of the loop and return to the top of the loop and continue a new iteration. The example given below shows output numbers starting from 1 and at a=7, the continue statement is encountered and without printing the number 7, the control moves to the top of the loop for the next iteration.

Program

```
// Go program to explain Continue statement
package main import "fmt"
func main() { var a
   int = 1

   for a <= 10 {
     if a == 7 {
       // skip one iteration a++
     continue }
     fmt.Printf("Number is: %d\n", a) a++
   }
}
```

The above program will show the following output:

Number is: 1
Number is: 2
Number is: 3
Number is: 4
Number is: 5
Number is: 6
Number is: 8
Number is: 9
Number is: 10

Infinite loop

In Go, a for loop can work as an infinite loop if you omit the loop condition or use a true boolean. The example given below keeps on printing the Infinite Loop forever:

Program

```
// Go program to explain Infinite loop package
main
import ( "fmt"
   "time" )
```

```
func main() {
  for true {
    fmt.Println("Infinite Loop") time.Sleep(time.Second)
  }
}
```

The above program will show the following output:

Infinite Loop
Infinite Loop
Infinite Loop
Infinite Loop
Infinite Loop

Fallthrough

In Go, the program control comes out of the switch statement just after a case is executed. But by using the Fallthrough statement, control can be transferred to the first statement of the next case clause in an expression "switch" statement.

Program
```
// Go program to explain fallthrough package
main
import (
"fmt" )

func main() { switch
  number := 200; { case
  number < 300:
    fmt.Printf("%d is less than 300\n", number) fallthrough
  case number > 100:
    fmt.Printf("%d is greater than 100", number) }
}
```
The above program will show the following output:

200 is less than 300
200 is greater than 100

Fallthrough cannot be used in the last case of a switch since there are no more cases present. If Fallthrough is used in the last case, it will give the following compilation error:

cannot fallthrough final case in switch

Program
```
// Go program using fallthrough in last case package
main
import (
"fmt" )

func number() int {
```

```
    sum := 10 + 20 return
    sum
} func main() {
    switch sum := number(); { case sum < 40:
    fmt.Printf("%d is lesser than 40\n", sum)
    fallthrough
    case sum > 20: fmt.Printf("%d is greater than
      20", sum) fallthrough
    }
}
```

The above program will show the following output:

cannot fallthrough final case in switch

Conclusion: Mastering Functions and Control Flows in Go

Understanding how to effectively use functions and control flows is crucial for writing efficient and maintainable programs. In Go, the design of these components reflects the language's core philosophy: simplicity, clarity, and efficiency. This conclusion aims to recap and expand on the essential aspects of functions and control flows in Go, providing further insight into why mastering these elements is vital for Go developers.

Recap of Functions in Go

Functions are the fundamental building blocks in Go that allow for code modularity, reusability, and simplicity. Go emphasizes clear and concise syntax, which enables developers to quickly write and understand function definitions. Some of the key features that make Go's functions versatile include:

1. **Multiple Return Values**: One of the unique aspects of Go functions is their ability to return multiple values. This feature is especially useful for error handling, as it allows a function to return both the desired result and an error indicator. It reduces the need for cumbersome error-checking mechanisms and promotes cleaner code.

```
func divide(a, b float64) (float64, error) {

    if b == 0 {

        return 0, fmt.Errorf("cannot divide by zero")

    }

    return a / b, nil

}
```

2. **Named Return Values**: Go supports named return values, which can make function signatures more informative and code more readable. By explicitly naming the return values, the function itself serves as documentation, explaining what each return value represents.

```
func rectangleProperties(length, width float64) (area, perimeter float64) {

    area = length * width
```

```
  perimeter = 2 * (length + width)

  return

}
```

3. **Variadic Functions**: Variadic functions enable developers to pass a variable number of arguments to a function. This flexibility is beneficial in scenarios where the exact number of inputs may not be known in advance, such as when creating utility functions like fmt.Printf.

```
func sum(values ...int) int {

  total := 0

  for _, v := range values {

    total += v

  }

  return total

}
```

4. **Anonymous Functions and Closures**: The ability to define functions without names (anonymous functions) and capture variables from the surrounding scope (closures) adds flexibility and allows for functional programming techniques. Anonymous functions are often used in event handlers, short-lived operations, and as arguments to higher-order functions.

```
func main() {

  adder := func(x, y int) int {

    return x + y

  }

  fmt.Println(adder(3, 4))

}
```

Effective Use of Control Flows in Go

Control flow structures are essential in directing how a program executes and makes decisions. Go provides several mechanisms, including conditional statements, loops, and specialized control flow constructs like defer, panic, and recover.

1. **Conditional Statements**: The if statement in Go allows developers to control which blocks of code are executed based on conditions. Its clean syntax, which does not require parentheses, and support for initialization statements before the condition, simplifies code readability and logic flow.

The switch statement offers a more concise way of handling multiple conditions, often replacing cumbersome if-else chains. It also supports type switches, enabling type-based logic, which is helpful when working with interfaces.

```
switch val := interface{}(someVariable).(type) {

case int:

    fmt.Println("Variable is an integer")

case string:

    fmt.Println("Variable is a string")

default:

    fmt.Println("Unknown type")

}
```

2. **Looping Constructs**: Go's for loop is versatile and can handle many different types of loops, including traditional counter loops, infinite loops, and loops over collections (arrays, slices, maps). By consolidating all loop constructs into a single, flexible for statement, Go reduces the cognitive load on developers, making it easier to understand and manage loops.

The ability to use range for iterating over collections further simplifies code. Combined with Go's support for multi-value returns, iterating over a map or slice is straightforward and intuitive.

```
fruits := []string{"apple", "banana", "cherry"}

for index, fruit := range fruits {

    fmt.Printf("Index: %d, Fruit: %s\n", index, fruit)

}
```

3. **Defer, Panic, and Recover**: These constructs add a layer of control flow that manages resource cleanup, error handling, and program recovery.

   o **defer** is primarily used for tasks that need to be completed before a function exits, such as closing a file or releasing a lock. This makes resource management much more predictable and ensures that necessary cleanup tasks are not missed.

```
func readFile(filename string) {

    file, err := os.Open(filename)

    if err != nil {

        panic(err)

    }

    defer file.Close()

    // Process the file
```

}

- o **panic** forces the program to stop execution and can be used for situations where an error is so severe that the program cannot continue. However, it should be used sparingly, as it disrupts normal program flow.

- o **recover** can be used in deferred functions to catch a panic and handle it gracefully, allowing the program to regain control and continue execution. This is especially useful for building robust systems that can recover from critical errors without crashing completely.

Why Mastering These Concepts is Crucial for Go Developers

1. **Simplicity and Readability**: Go's emphasis on simplicity is reflected in how it handles functions and control flow. The language encourages developers to write clear, concise, and readable code, which makes understanding and maintaining Go programs easier. By mastering functions and control flows, developers can write code that follows Go's idiomatic patterns, leading to more consistent and reliable software.

2. **Efficiency and Performance**: Go is designed to be a fast, efficient language, and its approach to functions and control flows supports that goal. Functions in Go are lightweight, and the language's control flow constructs, such as switch and for, are designed to minimize unnecessary overhead. This allows developers to write high-performance code without needing to resort to complex optimizations.

3. **Scalability and Concurrency**: While not directly related to control flows and functions, Go's concurrency model (goroutines and channels) relies heavily on these constructs. Understanding how to structure functions effectively and manage control flow is essential for writing concurrent code. Functions can be used as goroutines, and clean control flow ensures that concurrent operations do not interfere with each other, making programs more scalable and easier to debug.

4. **Error Handling**: Go's approach to error handling is different from many other languages. Rather than relying on exceptions, Go encourages developers to return errors as values. This design choice makes error handling explicit and helps to prevent errors from being ignored. Functions are a central part of this error-handling mechanism, and knowing how to structure functions to return multiple values or handle errors gracefully with control flow tools is essential for writing robust Go applications.

Conclusion

Mastering functions and control flows in Go is a foundational skill for any developer looking to harness the full power of the language. Go's design encourages simple, clear, and efficient code, and its approach to these concepts embodies that philosophy. Functions in Go are versatile, supporting everything from basic operations to complex logic, thanks to features like multiple return values, closures, and variadic parameters. Similarly, Go's control flow constructs are designed to handle everything from straightforward conditional checks to complex error handling and resource management tasks.

By gaining a deep understanding of these aspects, developers will be well-equipped to write clean, maintainable, and scalable code. Whether you are building a simple script or a large-scale distributed system, the ability to effectively manage functions and control flows will make your Go programs more efficient and easier to manage, leading to a smoother development experience and more robust applications.

5. Go: Data Structures

Introduction

Data structures are fundamental components in software development, allowing developers to organize, manage, and store data effectively. Go, also known as Golang, is a statically typed, compiled programming language designed by Google, which emphasizes simplicity, efficiency, and reliability. Data structures in Go help developers write robust, high-performance programs by providing efficient ways to handle various data types and operations. This introduction will explore common data structures in Go, their applications, and how they can be implemented and used effectively.

1. Understanding Data Structures in Go

Data structures are collections of data organized in a way that enables efficient access, modification, and management. They are crucial for solving problems related to data processing, and their efficiency can significantly affect the overall performance of software applications. In Go, data structures arc built to be straightforward, focusing on simplicity and readability while maintaining high performance.

Go's standard library offers a variety of data structures, such as arrays, slices, maps, and structs. However, Go also allows the creation of custom data structures using structs, which can be tailored to specific use cases.

2. Arrays in Go

Arrays are one of the simplest data structures available in Go. An array is a collection of elements of the same type, arranged in contiguous memory locations. Each element in an array can be accessed via an index, starting from 0.

Example:

var numbers [5]int // array of 5 integers

numbers[0] = 10

numbers[1] = 20

fmt.Println(numbers)

Key Features of Arrays:

- Fixed size: The size of an array is determined at the time of declaration and cannot be changed.

- Homogeneous elements: All elements in an array must be of the same type.

- Efficient access: Elements can be accessed in constant time, $O(1)$.

Applications:

- Arrays are used when the number of elements is known beforehand.
- Suitable for tasks where direct access to elements is required.

3. Slices: Dynamic Arrays in Go

Slices are an abstraction over arrays that provide a dynamic and flexible way to work with sequences of elements. Unlike arrays, slices can grow and shrink in size, making them more versatile. Slices are often used over arrays due to their flexibility.

Example:

numbers := []int{1, 2, 3, 4, 5} // creating a slice

numbers = append(numbers, 6)   // adding an element to the slice

fmt.Println(numbers)

Key Features of Slices:

- Variable size: Slices can dynamically grow and shrink.
- Easy to use: Slices are more user-friendly than arrays, with built-in functions like append, copy, and len.
- Backed by arrays: Under the hood, slices are backed by arrays, and they reference a segment of an array.

Applications:

- Slices are widely used for scenarios where the number of elements can change dynamically.
- Useful for handling collections of data that require modification.

4. Maps: Key-Value Pairs

Maps in Go are collections that store data in key-value pairs. They are similar to dictionaries or hash tables in other programming languages. Maps provide an efficient way to retrieve, update, and delete data based on unique keys.

Example:

personAge := map[string]int{

   "Alice": 30,

   "Bob": 25,

}

personAge["Charlie"] = 35 // adding a new key-value pair

fmt.Println(personAge)

Key Features of Maps:

- Efficient lookup: Maps provide average constant time complexity, $O(1)$, for lookup, insert, and delete operations.

- Keys must be unique: Each key in a map must be unique, but values can be duplicated.

- Flexible types: Both keys and values can be of different types, but keys must be comparable (e.g., integers, strings).

Applications:

- Maps are useful for scenarios where data needs to be accessed or updated based on a unique key, such as databases, caches, and associative arrays.

5. Structs: Custom Data Structures

Structs are custom data structures in Go that allow developers to group related data of different types. They are similar to classes in object-oriented languages but do not support inheritance.

Example:

type Person struct {

   Name string

   Age int

}

person := Person{Name: "Alice", Age: 30}

fmt.Println(person)

Key Features of Structs:

- Composite data types: Structs can contain fields of different types.

- User-defined: Developers can define structs to suit specific requirements.

- Flexibility: Structs can be nested, allowing the creation of complex data structures.

Applications:

- Structs are ideal for representing complex data models, such as records in a database, or objects with various attributes.

6. Linked Lists

Linked lists are data structures consisting of nodes, where each node contains data and a reference (pointer) to the next node in the sequence. Unlike arrays, linked lists are not stored in contiguous memory locations, which allows dynamic memory allocation.

Types of Linked Lists:

- **Singly Linked List:** Each node points to the next node.

- **Doubly Linked List:** Each node points to both the next and the previous nodes.

- **Circular Linked List:** The last node points back to the first node, forming a loop.

Example of a Singly Linked List Implementation:

```
type Node struct {
    data int
    next *Node
}
type LinkedList struct {
    head *Node
}
```

Applications:

- Linked lists are useful when the size of the data set is unpredictable and requires dynamic memory allocation.
- Efficient insertion and deletion, especially when working with large data sets.

7. Stacks: LIFO Data Structures

Stacks are Last In, First Out (LIFO) data structures where the last element added is the first one to be removed. Operations on stacks are limited to the top of the stack, making them suitable for scenarios where the last item needs to be accessed first.

Key Operations:

- **Push:** Add an element to the top of the stack.
- **Pop:** Remove an element from the top of the stack.
- **Peek:** Retrieve the top element without removing it.

Example:

```
stack := []int{}
stack = append(stack, 10) // Push
top := stack[len(stack)-1] // Peek
stack = stack[:len(stack)-1] // Pop
```

Applications:

- Used in recursive algorithms, undo operations, and expression evaluation (e.g., parsing mathematical expressions).

8. Queues: FIFO Data Structures

Queues are First In, First Out (FIFO) data structures where the first element added is the first one to be removed. Queues are similar to lines or waiting lists, where the order of processing is determined by arrival.

Key Operations:

- **Enqueue:** Add an element to the back of the queue.

- **Dequeue:** Remove an element from the front of the queue.

- **Peek:** Retrieve the front element without removing it.

Example:

queue := []int{}

queue = append(queue, 10) // Enqueue

front := queue[0]   // Peek

queue = queue[1:]   // Dequeue

Applications:

- Suitable for task scheduling, buffering, and implementing breadth-first search algorithms.

9. Trees: Hierarchical Data Structures

Trees are hierarchical data structures where each node has a value and references to child nodes. The most common type of tree is a binary tree, where each node has at most two children.

Types of Trees:

- **Binary Search Tree (BST):** Maintains a sorted order, where the left child is less than the parent, and the right child is greater.

- **Balanced Trees (AVL, Red-Black Trees):** Ensure that the tree remains balanced, leading to more efficient operations.

- **Trie:** Specialized tree used for searching words, especially in dictionaries.

Example of a Basic Binary Tree Node:

```
type TreeNode struct {
    value int
    left  *TreeNode
    right *TreeNode
}
```

Applications:

- Trees are used for implementing databases, file systems, and search engines.
- Useful for hierarchical data processing and efficient searching.

10. Graphs: Networked Data Structures

Graphs consist of nodes (vertices) and edges (connections between nodes). They are versatile data structures that can represent a wide range of real-world scenarios, such as social networks, computer networks, and road maps.

Types of Graphs:

- **Directed vs. Undirected Graphs:** In directed graphs, edges have directions; in undirected graphs, edges do not.

- **Weighted vs. Unweighted Graphs:** Weighted graphs have values assigned to edges, representing costs or distances.

Applications:

- Graphs are essential for network routing, pathfinding algorithms, and modeling relationships in social networks.

In the last few chapters, we have seen some of the primitive data types. We also introduced few other advanced data types without going to the details. In this chapter, we are going to look into more data structures.

4.1 Primitive Data Types

Advanced data structures are built on top of primitive data types. This section is going to cover the primitive data types in Go.

Zero Value

In the Quick Start chapter, you have learned various ways to declare a variable. When you declare a variable using the **var** statement without assigning a value, a default Zero value will be assigned for certain types. The Zero value is 0 for integers and floats, empty string for strings, and false for Boolean.

```
import "fmt"

func main() {

var name string

var age int

var tall bool

var weight float64

fmt.Printf("%#v, %#v, %#v, %#v\n", name, age, tall, weight)

}
```

This is the output:

"", 0, false, 0

Variable

In the quick start chapter, we have discussed about variables and its usage. The variable declared outside the function (package level) can access anywhere within the same package.

Here is an example:

Listing: Package level variable

```
package main
import (
"fmt" 5 )
var name string
var country string = "India"
func main() {
name = "Jack"
fmt.Println("Name:", name)
fmt.Println("Country:", country)
}
```

In the above example, the **name** and **country** are two package level variables. As we have seen above the **name** gets zero value, whereas value for **country** variable is explicitly initialized.

If the variable has been defined using the: = syntax, and the user wants to change the value of that variable, they need to use = instead of: = syntax.

If you run the below program, it's going to throw an error:

Listing: Changing value with wrong syntax

```
package main
import (
"fmt" 5 )
func main() {
age := 25
age := 35
fmt.Println(age)
}
```

```
$ go run update.go
# command-line-arguments
./update.go:9:6: no new variables on left side of :=
```

The above can be fixed like this:

Listing: Changing value with wrong syntax

```
1 package main
import (
"fmt" 5 )
func main() {
age := 25
age = 35
fmt.Println(age)
}
```

Now you should see the output:

```
$ go run update.go 35
```

Using the reflect package, you can identify the type of a variable:

Listing: Identifying type of a variable

```
package main
import (
"fmt"
"reflect" 6 )
func main() {
var pi = 3.41
fmt.Println("type:", reflect.TypeOf(pi))
}
```

Using one or two letter variable names inside a function is common practice. If the variable name is multi-word, use lower camelCase (initial letter lower and subsequent words capitalized) for unexported variables. If the variable is an exported one, use upper CamelCase (all the words capitalized). If the variable name contains any abbreviations like ID, use capital letters. Here are few examples: pi, w, r, ErrorCode, nodeToDaemonPods, DB, InstanceID.

Unused variables and imports

If you declare a variable inside a function, use that variable somewhere in the same function where it is declared. Otherwise, you are going to get a compile error. Whereas a global variable declared but unused is not going to throw compile time error.

Any package that is getting imported should find a place to use. Unused import also throws compile time error.

Boolean Type

A boolean type represents a pair of truth values. The truth values are denoted by the constants true and false. These are the three logical operators that can be used with boolean values:

&& – Logical AND

|| – Logical OR

! – Logical NOT

Here is an example:

Listing: Logical operators

```
1 package main

3 import "fmt"

func main() {

yes := true

no := false

fmt.Println(yes && no)

fmt.Println(yes || no)

fmt.Println(!yes)

fmt.Println(!no)

}
```

The output of the above logical operators is like this:

$ go run logical.go

false true false true

Numeric Types

The numeric type includes both integer types and floating-point types. The allowed values of numeric types are same across all the CPU architectures.

These are the unsigned integers:

uint8 – the set of all unsigned 8-bit integers (0 to 255)

uint16 – the set of all unsigned 16-bit integers (0 to 65535)

uint32 – the set of all unsigned 32-bit integers (0 to 4294967295)

uint64 – the set of all unsigned 64-bit integers (0 to 18446744073709551615)

These are the signed integers:

int8 – the set of all signed 8-bit integers (-128 to 127)

int16 – the set of all signed 16-bit integers (-32768 to 32767)

int32 – the set of all signed 32-bit integers (-2147483648 to 2147483647)

int64 – the set of all signed 64-bit integers (-9223372036854775808 to 9223372036854775807)

These are the two floating-point numbers:

float32 – the set of all IEEE-754 32-bit floating-point numbers

4.2. Constants

float64 – the set of all IEEE-754 64-bit floating-point numbers These are the two complex numbers:

complex64 – the set of all complex numbers with float32 real and imaginary parts

complex128 – the set of all complex numbers with float64 real and imaginary parts

These are the two commonly used used aliases:

byte – alias for uint8

rune – alias for int32

String Type

A string type is another most import primitive data type. String type represents string values.

A constant is an unchanging value. Constants are declared like variables, but with the const keyword. Constants can be character, string, boolean, or numeric values. Constants cannot be declared using the: = syntax.

In Go, const is a keyword introducing a name for a scalar value such as 2 or 3.14159 or" scrumptious". Such values, named or otherwise, are called constants in Go. Constants can also be created by expressions built from constants, such as 2+3 or 2+3i or math.Pi/2 or ("go"+"pher"). Constants can be declared are at package level or function level. This is how to declare constants:

package main

```go
import (
"fmt"
)
const Freezing = true const Pi = 3.14
const Name = "Tom"
func main() { fmt.Println(Pi, Freezing, Name)
}
```

You can also use the factored style declaration:

```go
package main
import (
"fmt"
)
const (
Freezing = true
Pi = 3.14
Name = "Tom"
)
func main() { fmt.Println(Pi, Freezing, Name)
}
const (
Freezing = true
Pi = 3.14
Name = "Tom"
)
```

Compiler throws an error if the constant is tried to assign a new value:

```go
package main
import (
"fmt"
)
func main() { const Pi = 3.14 Pi = 6.86
```

```
fmt.Println(Pi)
}
```

The above program throws an error like this:

$ go run constants.go constants:9:5: cannot assign to Pi

iota

The iota keyword is used to define constants of incrementing numbers. This simplify defining many constants. The values of iota is reset to 0 whenever the reserved word const appears. The value increments by one after each line.

Consider this example:

```
// Token represents a lexical token. type Token int
const (
// Illegal represents an illegal/invalid character
Illegal Token = iota
// Whitespace represents a white space
// (" ", \t, \r, \n) character
Whitespace
// EOF represents end of file
EOF
// MarkerID represents '\id' or '\id1' marker MarkerID
// MarkerIde represents '\ide' marker
MarkerIde
)
```

In the above example, the **Token** is custom type defined using the primitive int type. The constants are defined using the factored syntax (many constants within parenthesis). There are comments for each constant values. Each constant value is be incremented starting from **0**. In the above example, **Illegal** is **0**, Whitespace is **1**, **EOF** is **2** and so on.

The **iota** can be used with expressions. The expression will be repeated. Here is a good example taken from Effective Go (**https: //go.dev/doc/effective_go#constants**):

```
type ByteSize float64
const (
// ignore first value (0) by assigning to blank identifier
```

```
_           = iota
KB ByteSize = 1 << (10 * iota)
MB
GB
TB
PB
EB
ZB
YB
)
```

Using _ (blank identifier) you can ignore a value, but iota increments the value. This can be used to skip certain values. As you can see in the above example, you can use an expression with iota.

Iota is reset to **0** whenever the const keyword appears in the source code. This means that if you have multiple const declarations in a single file, iota will start at **0** for each declaration. Iota can only be used in const declarations. It cannot be used in other types of declarations, such as var declarations. The value of iota is only available within the const declaration in which it is used. It cannot be used outside of that declaration.

Blank Identifier

Sometimes you may need to ignore the value returned by a function. Go provides a special identifier called blank identifier to ignore any types of values. In Go, underscore _ is the blank identifier.

Here is an example usage of blank identifier where the second value returned by the function is discarded. **x, _: = someFunc()**

Blank identifier can be used as import alias to invoke init function without using the package.

import (

"database/sql"

_ "github.com/lib/pq"

)

In the above example, the **pq** package has some code which need to be invoked to initialize the database driver provided by that package. And the exported functions within the above package is supposed to be not used.

We have already seen another example where blank identifier if used with iota to ignore certain constants.

4.3 Arrays

An array is an ordered container type with a fixed number of data. In fact, the arrays are the foundation where slice is built. We will study about slices in the next section. Most of the time, you can use slice instead of an array.

The number of values in the array is called the length of that array. The array type **[n]T** is an array of **n** values of type **T**. Here are two example arrays:

colors := [3]string{"Red", "Green", "Blue"} heights := [4]int{153, 146, 167, 170}

In the above example, the length of first array is **3** and the array values are string data. The second array contains **int** values. An array's length is part of its type, so arrays cannot be re-sized. So, if the length is different for two arrays, those are distinct incompatible types. The built-in **len** function gives the length of array.

Array values can be accessed using the index syntax, so the expression **s[n]** accesses the nth element, starting from zero.

An array values can be read like this:

colors := [3]string{"Red", "Green", "Blue"} i := colors[1] fmt.Println(i)

Similarly array values can be set using index syntax. Here is an example:

colors := [3]string{"Red", "Green", "Blue"} colors[1] = "Yellow"

Arrays need not be initialized explicitly. The zero value of an array is a usable array with all elements zeroed.

var colors [3]string colors[1] = "Yellow"

In this example, the values of colors will be empty strings (zero value). Later we can assign values using the index syntax.

There is a way to declare array literal without specifying the length. When using this syntax variant, the compiler will count and set the array length.

colors := [...]string{"Red", "Green", "Blue"}

In the chapter on control structures, we have seen how to use For loop for iterating over slices. In the same way, you can iterate over array.

Consider this complete example:

Listing: Array example

```go
package main

import "fmt"

func main() {

colors := [3]string{"Red", "Green", "Blue"}
```

```
fmt.Println("Length:", len(colors))

for i, v := range colors {

fmt.Println(i, v)

}

}
```

If you save the above program in a file named **colors.go** and run it, you will get output like this:

$ go run colors.go

Length: 3

Red

Green

Blue

In the above program, a string array is declared and initialized with three string values. In the 7th line, the length is printed and it gives 3. The **range** clause gives index and value, where the index starts from zero.

4.4 Slices

Slice is one of most important data structure in Go. Slice is more flexible than an array. It is possible to add and remove values from a slice. There will be a length for slice at any time. Though the length varies dynamically as the content value increase or decrease.

The number of values in the slice is called the length of that slice. The slice type **[]T** is a slice of type **T**. Here are two example slices:

colors := []string{"Red", "Green", "Blue"} heights := []int{153, 146, 167, 170}

The first one is a slice of strings and the second slice is a slice of integers. The syntax is similar to array except the length of slice is not explicitly specified. You can use built-in **len** function to see the length of slice.

Slice values can be accessed using the index syntax, so the expression **s[n]** accesses the nth element, starting from zero.

A slice values can be read like this:

colors := []string{"Red", "Green", "Blue"} i := colors[1] fmt.Println(i)

Similary slice values can be set using index syntax. Here is an example:

colors := []string{"Red", "Green", "Blue"} colors[1] = "Yellow"

Slices should be initialized with a length more than zero to access or set values. In the above examples, we used slice literal syntax for that. If you define a slice using **var** statement without providing default values, the slice will be having a special zero value called **nil**.

Consider this complete example:

Listing: Nil slice example

```
package main

import "fmt"

func main() {

var v []string

fmt.Printf("%#v, %#v\n", v, v == nil)

// Output: []string(nil), true

}
```

In the above example, the value of slice **v** is **nil**. Since the slice is nil, values cannot be accessed or set using the index. These operations are going to raise runtime error (index out of range).

Sometimes it may not be possible to initialize a slice with some value using the literal slice syntax given above. Go provides a built-in function named **make** to initialize a slice with a given length and zero values for all items. For example, if you want a slice with 3 items, the syntax is like this: **colors := make([]string, 3)**

In the above example, a slice will be initialized with 3 empty strings as the items. Now it is possible to set and get values using the index as given below:

colors[0] = "Red" colors[1] = "Green" colors[2] = "Blue" i := colors[1] fmt.Println(i)

If you try to set value at 3rd index (**colors[3]**), it's going to raise runtime error with a message like this: "index out of range". Go has a built-in function named **append** to add additional values. The append function will increase the length of the slice.

Consider this example:

Listing: Append to slice

```
1 package main

import (

"fmt" 5 )

func main() {

v := make([]string, 3)

fmt.Printf("%v\n", len(v))

v = append(v, "Yellow")

fmt.Printf("%v\n", len(v))

}
```

In the above example, the slice length is increased by one after append. It is possible to add more values using **append**. See this example:

Listing: Append more values to slice

```
package main

import (

"fmt" 5 )

func main() {

v := make([]string, 3)

fmt.Printf("%v\n", len(v))

v = append(v, "Yellow", "Black")

fmt.Printf("%v\n", len(v))

}
```

The above example appends two values. Though you can provide any number of values to append.

You can use the" ..." operator to expand a slice. This can be used to append one slice to another slice. See this example:

Listing: Append a slice to another

```
1 package main

import (

"fmt" 5 )

func main() {

v := make([]string, 3)

fmt.Printf("%v\n", len(v))

a := []string{"Yellow", "Black"}

v = append(v, a...)

fmt.Printf("%v\n", len(v))

}
```

In the above example, the first slice is appended by all items in another slice.

Slice Append Optimization

If you append too many values to a slice using a for loop, there is one optimization related that you need to be aware.

Consider this example:

Listing: Append to a slice inside a loop

```
1 package main
import (
"fmt" 5 )
func main() {
v := make([]string, 0)
for i := 0; i < 9000000; i++ {
v = append(v, "Yellow")
}
fmt.Printf("%v\n", len(v))
}
```

If you run the above program, it's going to take few seconds to execute. To explain this, some understanding of internal structure of slice is required. Slice is implemented as a struct and an array within. The elements in the slice will be stored in the underlying array. As you know, the length of array is part of the array type. So, when appending an item to a slice a new array will be created.

To optimize, the **append** function actually created an array with double length.

In the above example, the underlying array must be changed many times. This is the reason why it's taking few seconds to execute. The length of underlying array is called the capacity of the slice. Go provides a way to initialize the underlying array with a particular length. The **make** function has a fourth argument to specify the capacity.

In the above example, you can specify the capacity like this:

v := make([]string, 0, 9000000)

If you make this change and run the program again, you can see that it run much faster than the earlier code. The reason for faster code is that the slice capacity had already set with maximum required length.

4.5 Maps

Map is another important data structure in Go. We have briefly discussed about maps in the Quick Start chapter. As you know, map is an implementation of hash table. The hash table is available in many very high-level languages. The data in map is organized like key value pairs.

A variable of map can be declared like this:

var fruits map[string]int

To make use that variable, it needs to be initialized using make function.

fruits = make(map[string]int)

You can also initialize using the: = syntax:

fruits: = map[string]int{} or with var keywod:

var fruits = map[string]int{}

You can initialize map with values like this:

var fruits = map[string]int{

"Apple": 45,

"Mango": 24,

"Orange": 34, }

After initializing, you can add new key value pairs like this:

fruits["Grape"] = 15

If you try to add values to maps without initializing, you will get an error like this:

panic: assignment to entry in nil map

Here is an example that's going to produce panic error: **package main**

func main() { var m map[string]int

m["k"] = 7

}

To access a value corresponding to a key, you can use this syntax:

mangoCount := fruits["Mango"]

Here is an example: **package main import "fmt"**

func main() {

var fruits = map[string]int{

"Apple": 45,

"Mango": 24,

"Orange": 34,

}

fmt.Println(fruits["Apple"])

}

If the key doesn't exist, a zero value will be returned. For example, in the below example, value of **pineappleCount** is going be **0. package main import "fmt"**

```go
func main() {

var fruits = map[string]int{

"Apple": 45,

"Mango": 24,

"Orange": 34,

}

pineappleCount := fruits["Pineapple"] fmt.Println(pineappleCount)

}
```

If you need to check if the key exist, the above syntax can be modified to return two values. The first one would be the actual value or zero value and the second one would be a boolean indicating if the key exists.

```go
package main import "fmt"

func main() {

var fruits = map[string]int{

"Apple": 45,

"Mango": 24,

"Orange": 34,

}

_, ok := fruits["Pineapple"]

fmt.Println(ok)

}
```

In the above program, the first returned value is ignored using a blank identifier. And the value of **ok** variable is **false**. Normally, you can use if condition to check if the key exists like this:

```go
package main import "fmt"

func main() { var fruits = map[string]int{

"Apple": 45,

"Mango": 24,

"Orange": 34,

}

if _, ok := fruits["Pineapple"]; ok { fmt.Println("Key exists.")

} else {
```

```go
fmt.Println("Key doesn't exist.")

}

}
```

To see the number of key/value pairs, you can use the built-in len function.

```go
package main import "fmt"

func main() { var fruits = map[string]int{

"Apple": 45,

"Mango": 24,

"Orange": 34,

}

fmt.Println(len(fruits))

}
```

The above program should print **3** as the number of items in the map.

To remove an item from the map, use the built-in delete function.

```go
package main import "fmt"

func main() { var fruits = map[string]int{

"Apple": 45,

"Mango": 24,

"Orange": 34,

} delete(fruits, "Orange") fmt.Println(len(fruits))

}
```

The above program should print **2** as the number of items in the map after deleting one item.

4.6 Custom Data Types

Apart from the built-in data types, you can create your own custom data types. The type keyword can be used to create custom types. Here is an example.

```go
package main import "fmt" type age int

func main() { a := age(2)

fmt.Println(a)

fmt.Printf("Type: %T\n", a)

}
```

If you run the above program, the output will be like this:

$ go run age.go

2 Type: age

Structs

Struct is a composite type with multiple fields of different types within the struct. For example, if you want to represent a person with name and age, the **struct** type will be helpful. The **Person** struct definition will look like this:

type Person struct {

Name string

Age int

}

As you can see above, the **Person** struct is defined using **type** and **struct** keywords. Within the curly brace, attributes with other types are defined. If you avoid attributes, it will become an empty struct.

Here is an example empty struct:

type Empty struct { }

Alternatively, the curly brace can be in the same line.

type Empty struct {}

A struct can be initialized various ways. Using a **var** statement:

var p1 Person p1.Name = "Tom" p1.Age = 10

You can give a literal form with all attribute values:

p2 := Person{"Polly", 50}

You can also use named attributes. In the case of named attributes, if you miss any values, the default zero value will be initialized.

p3: = Person{Name: "Huck"} p4 := Person{Age: 10}

In the next, we are going to learn about functions and methods. That chapter expands the discussion about custom types behavior changes through functions associated with custom types called structs.

It is possible to embed structs inside other structs. Here is an example:

4.7. Pointers

type Person struct {Name string

}

type Member struct {

Person

ID int

}

When you are passing a variable as an argument to a function, Go creates a copy of the value and send it. In some situations, creating a copy will be expensive when the size of object is large. Another scenario where pass by value is not feasible is when you need to modify the original object inside the function. In the case of pass by value, you can modify it as you are getting a new object every time. Go supports another way to pass a reference to the original value using the memory location or address of the object.

To get address of a variable, you can use **&** as a prefix for the variable. Here in an example usage:

a: = 7

fmt.Printf("%v\n", &a)

To get the value back from the address, you can use * as a prefix for the variable. Here in an example usage:

: = 7

:= &a

fmt.Printf("%v\n", *b)

Here is a complete example:

Listing 4.13 : Pass by value vs reference

1 **package main**

import (

"fmt" 5 **)**

func value(a int) {

fmt.Printf("%v\n", &a)

}

func pointer(a *int) {

fmt.Printf("%v\n", a) 13 **}**

func main() {

a := 4

fmt.Printf("%v\n", &a)

value(a)

pointer(&a)

}

A typical output will be like this:

0xc42000a340

0xc42000a348

0xc42000a340

As you can see above, the second output is different from the first and third. This is because a value is passed instead of a pointer. And so, when we are printing the address, it's printing the address of the new variable.

In the functions chapter, the section about methods (section 5.6) explains the pointer receiver.

New

The built-in function new can be used to allocate memory. It allocates zero values and returns the address of the given data type.

Here is an example: **name := new(string)**

In this example, a string pointer value is allocated with zero value, in this case empty string, and assigned to a variable.

This above example is same as this:

var name *string name = new(string)

In this one string pointer variable is declared, but it's not allocated with zeror value. It will have nil value and so it cannot be dereferenced. If you try to reference, without allocating using the new function, you will get an error like this:

panic: runtime error: invalid memory address or nil pointer dereference

Here is another example using a custom type defined using a primitive type:

4.8. Exercises

type Temperature float64 name := new(Temperature)

Exercise1: Create a custom type for circle using float64 and define **Area** and **Perimeter**.

Solution: package main import "fmt" type Circle float64

func (r Circle) Area() float64 { return float64(3.14 * r * r)

}

func (r Circle) Perimeter() float64 { return float64(2 * 3.14 * r)

}

func main() { c := Circle(4.0) fmt.Println(c.Area()) fmt.Println(c.Perimeter())

}

The custom **Circle** type is created using the built-in **float64** type. It would be better if the circle is defined using a struct. Using struct helps to change the structure later with additional attributes. The struct will look like this:

type Circle struct { Radius float64

}

Exercise 2: Create a slice of structs where the struct represents a person with name and age.

Solution: package main import "fmt" type Person struct {

Name string

Age int }

func main() { persons := []Person{

Person{Name: "Huck", Age: 11},

Person{Name: "Tom", Age: 10},

Person{Name: "Polly", Age: 52},

}

fmt.Println(persons)

}

Conclusion: Mastering Data Structures in Go

Understanding and mastering data structures is essential for any developer who seeks to write efficient, scalable, and maintainable code. In Go, data structures play a significant role in enabling developers to store, organize, and manipulate data effectively. Throughout this exploration of Go's data structures, we have seen how various structures—ranging from basic arrays and slices to more complex trees and graphs—can be used to address different types of problems. This conclusion will recap key concepts, emphasize their importance, and discuss best practices for utilizing these structures to their full potential in Go.

Recap of Key Data Structures

1. **Arrays and Slices:** Arrays and slices are foundational data structures in Go. While arrays offer fixed-size collections, slices provide flexibility with dynamic resizing capabilities. Arrays are best used when you have a known and fixed number of elements, while slices allow for dynamic data management, making them suitable for cases where the size of the dataset may change. Slices, being backed by arrays, offer a blend of efficient indexing and flexible growth, which is why they are often preferred over arrays in practical programming scenarios.

2. **Maps:** Maps, or hash tables, provide an efficient way to store and retrieve data using key-value pairs. Their ability to perform constant time operations for insertions, deletions, and

lookups makes them a go-to choice for scenarios where quick data retrieval is essential. Whether managing user records by unique identifiers or maintaining a cache, maps are versatile tools that offer the efficiency needed for quick data access and management.

3. **Structs:** Structs are composite data types that enable developers to define custom structures, grouping different types of data together. They form the backbone of many more complex data structures and are essential for creating tailored solutions to specific problems. By using structs, developers can create clear and logical representations of real-world objects, such as users, products, and more. Structs also lay the groundwork for implementing more intricate data structures like linked lists and trees.

4. **Linked Lists:** Linked lists are linear data structures that are useful when elements need to be dynamically added or removed. Unlike arrays, linked lists do not require contiguous memory allocation, which provides flexibility in handling varying sizes of data. Their linear nature, with pointers linking nodes, allows for efficient insertion and deletion, although they lack the fast random access of arrays. Variations like doubly linked lists and circular linked lists further expand the possible use cases.

5. **Stacks and Queues:** Stacks and queues are linear data structures that control the order in which data is processed. Stacks operate on a Last In, First Out (LIFO) principle, while queues use a First In, First Out (FIFO) approach. Stacks are ideal for tasks involving nested operations, such as parsing or evaluating expressions, and managing undo functionality in applications. Queues are suitable for scenarios that require sequential processing, such as scheduling tasks, handling requests, and implementing breadth-first search in algorithms.

6. **Trees:** Trees, especially binary trees and their variants, are hierarchical data structures that are used for organizing data in a way that makes searching, insertion, and deletion efficient. Binary search trees (BSTs) are particularly useful for scenarios where data needs to be kept in a sorted order, as they allow for fast lookup, insertion, and deletion operations. Advanced trees, such as AVL trees or Red-Black trees, add balancing features to ensure efficiency remains high, even as data changes. Other specialized trees, like Tries, are used for string search and prefix matching, showcasing the adaptability of tree structures.

7. **Graphs:** Graphs represent interconnected data points and are used in various applications, from modeling relationships on social networks to finding the shortest paths in navigation systems. Unlike linear data structures, graphs can model complex, non-linear relationships, which makes them suitable for tasks like network routing, dependency resolution, and representing workflows. Understanding graphs opens up possibilities for solving intricate problems that require connections and path-finding.

Importance of Choosing the Right Data Structure

Choosing the appropriate data structure is crucial for writing effective software. The performance, maintainability, and scalability of an application can be significantly influenced by the choice of data structures. For instance, using a slice when a map would be more suitable could lead to inefficient lookups, while opting for a stack over a queue might not represent the problem's natural order of processing.

The key considerations when selecting a data structure include:

- **Performance Needs:** How frequently will the data be accessed, updated, or deleted? Structures like arrays and slices are suitable for scenarios requiring constant time access, while maps excel at quick lookups.

- **Data Size and Growth:** Will the data set grow dynamically? If so, structures like slices, linked lists, and maps offer the flexibility required.

- **Order of Processing:** Does the problem require sequential or hierarchical data processing? Stacks and queues help with sequential tasks, while trees and graphs can handle hierarchical relationships.

Go's Simplicity and Efficiency

One of the strengths of Go as a language is its simplicity. Go offers a minimalist approach to programming, focusing on straightforward and understandable code. This extends to how data structures are implemented and used. The language's standard library provides essential data structures that are easy to work with, and its syntax encourages developers to write clean, efficient code.For example, slices in Go are much more intuitive than the array handling seen in many other languages, with built-in functions like append, copy, and len making slice manipulation straightforward. Similarly, maps are designed to provide a simple yet powerful way to manage key-value pairs, abstracting away the complexity of underlying hash functions.

Moreover, Go's performance is impressive, thanks to its compiled nature and efficient memory management. Data structures implemented in Go are inherently fast, making Go an excellent choice for developing applications that require high performance, such as web servers, database systems, and real-time applications.

Best Practices for Using Data Structures in Go

1. **Understand the Problem Domain:** Before deciding on a data structure, thoroughly understand the problem you are trying to solve. Determine the nature of the data, how it will be processed, and what kind of operations will be most frequent. This understanding will guide you to select the most appropriate data structure.

2. **Leverage Go's Built-In Tools:** Make use of Go's built-in data structures whenever possible. They are optimized for performance and are easy to use. For example, slices are more flexible than arrays and should be preferred in most cases unless a fixed-size collection is required.

3. **Create Custom Structures When Necessary:** While built-in data structures suffice for many tasks, there are scenarios where custom structures might be needed. Structs can be used to build complex data models, and linked lists or trees can be implemented from scratch for specialized use cases. Go's support for pointers and structs makes it easy to define such custom structures.

4. **Focus on Code Readability:** One of Go's guiding principles is code readability. When working with data structures, ensure that the code remains clean and easy to understand. Use descriptive variable names, organize code into functions, and avoid overly complex operations that could make the code difficult to maintain.

5. **Consider Memory Management:** Memory management is an important aspect, especially when working with large data sets. Understanding how Go manages memory and knowing when to use pointers can help optimize the use of data structures. For example, using slices instead of copying entire arrays can save memory, and careful use of maps can help prevent memory leaks.

6. **Test for Edge Cases:** When implementing data structures, especially custom ones, always test for edge cases. Consider scenarios like empty collections, large data sets, or unusual data inputs. Go's simplicity in writing unit tests makes it easier to ensure your data structures are robust and handle all possible cases.

Future of Data Structures in Go Development

As Go continues to grow in popularity, especially in the fields of web development, cloud computing, and systems programming, the importance of efficient data structures will only increase. New libraries and tools are constantly being developed to extend Go's functionality, making it even easier for developers to implement sophisticated data structures. Emerging areas such as machine learning, data analysis, and big data processing also stand to benefit from Go's efficiency and simplicity. While languages like Python and Java have traditionally been the go-to choices for such fields, Go's performance and ease of concurrency provide a compelling case for its adoption in these areas. As more developers explore the potential of Go, it is likely that the language's ecosystem will grow to include even more powerful data structure implementations.

Conclusion

Mastering data structures in Go is not just about knowing how to use slices, maps, or trees—it's about understanding how to solve problems efficiently. Each data structure has its strengths and weaknesses, and the key to effective programming lies in choosing the right one for the job. By understanding the principles behind each structure and leveraging Go's simplicity, developers can write code that is not only efficient but also easy to maintain and scale.The future of Go looks promising, with its straightforward approach and robust standard library paving the way for efficient software development. Whether you're developing a high-performance web server, a database system, or a real-time analytics tool, understanding data structures in Go will enable you to build applications that are both fast and reliable. As you continue to work with Go, keep exploring, experimenting, and learning—your ability to choose and implement the right data structures will be the foundation of your success as a developer.

6. Go: Concurrency

Introduction

Concurrency is one of the core strengths of the Go programming language, designed to handle multiple tasks simultaneously. It is a programming concept that allows multiple operations to overlap, improving efficiency and responsiveness, especially in I/O-bound and high-performance computing applications. In Go, concurrency is elegantly implemented through Goroutines and Channels, providing a lightweight, easy-to-use mechanism for parallel execution.

Unlike traditional threads in many programming languages, which can be heavy and resource-intensive, Go offers a more efficient and scalable way of handling concurrent tasks. This introduction will explore key concurrency concepts in Go, including Goroutines, Channels, synchronization mechanisms like the Select statement, and the utilities provided by the sync package.

1. Goroutines: Creating and Managing

What are Goroutines?
Goroutines are lightweight threads managed by the Go runtime. They are much more efficient than traditional OS threads, allowing you to spawn thousands of them without exhausting system resources. When you create a Goroutine, you are essentially instructing the Go runtime to run a function concurrently.

Syntax:

go myFunction()

The keyword go initiates the function myFunction as a Goroutine. When this line is executed, myFunction runs concurrently with other code.

Creating Goroutines

Goroutines are straightforward to create. Here's a basic example:

```
package main

import (
    "fmt"
    "time"
)
func printMessage(message string) {
    for i := 0; i < 5; i++ {
        fmt.Println(message)
        time.Sleep(500 * time.Millisecond)
```

```
    }
}
func main() {

    go printMessage("Hello from Goroutine!") // Running as a Goroutine

    printMessage("Hello from main function!") // Running in the main thread

}
```

In this example, printMessage is called twice. The first time, it runs as a Goroutine and, the second time, it runs in the main thread. This illustrates how Goroutines can run concurrently with other code.

Managing Goroutines

Managing Goroutines effectively is crucial, especially when dealing with a large number of concurrent tasks. This can be achieved using techniques such as synchronization and coordination, which will be covered later.

2. Channels: Communication Between Goroutines

What are Channels?

Channels provide a way for Goroutines to communicate with each other and synchronize their execution. They can be thought of as pipes that connect Goroutines, allowing data to be sent from one to another. Channels are typed, meaning they can only carry values of a specific type.

Syntax:

ch := make(chan int)

Here, ch is a channel that can carry integer values.

Sending and Receiving Data

To send data to a channel, you use the <- operator:

ch <- 10 // Send the integer 10 to the channel

To receive data from a channel:

data := <- ch // Receive data from the channel

Example of Channel Usage:
package main

import (

    "fmt"

)

```go
func sum(a int, b int, ch chan int) {
    result := a + b
    ch <- result // Send the result to the channel
}
func main() {
    ch := make(chan int)
    go sum(3, 5, ch)
    result := <- ch // Receive the result from the channel
    fmt.Println("Sum:", result)
}
```

In this example, the sum function runs as a Goroutine and sends the result to the main function via the channel Ch.

Buffered vs. Unbuffered Channels

Channels in Go can be either buffered or unbuffered. Buffered channels allow sending multiple values without requiring a corresponding receive operation for each send. This can be useful for controlling the flow of data between Goroutines.

Buffered Channel Example:

```go
ch := make(chan int, 3) // Buffered channel with a capacity of 3
```

3. Select Statement and Synchronization

What is the Select Statement?
The select statement allows a Goroutine to wait on multiple communication operations. It is similar to a switch statement but operates on channels. The select statement will block until one of its cases can proceed, then it will execute that case.

Example:

```go
package main

import (
    "fmt"
    "time"
)
func main() {
    ch1 := make(chan string)
    ch2 := make(chan string)
```

```go
go func() {
    time.Sleep(1 * time.Second)
    ch1 <- "Channel 1"
}()
go func() {
    time.Sleep(2 * time.Second)
    ch2 <- "Channel 2"
}()
select {
case msg1 := <-ch1:
    fmt.Println(msg1)
case msg2 := <-ch2:
    fmt.Println(msg2)
}
}
```

In this example, select waits for either ch1 or ch2 to send a message. Once a message is received, it proceeds with that case.

4. Using the Sync Package

The sync package provides additional tools for Goroutine synchronization. These include:

4.1 WaitGroups

WaitGroup is a synchronization primitive that waits for a collection of Goroutines to finish. It blocks the main thread until all the Goroutines are completed.

Example:

```go
package main
import (
    "fmt"
    "sync"
)
func worker(id int, wg *sync.WaitGroup) {
    defer wg.Done()
```

```go
    fmt.Printf("Worker %d starting\n", id)
}
func main() {
    var wg sync.WaitGroup
    for i := 1; i <= 3; i++ {
        wg.Add(1)
        go worker(i, &wg)
    }
    wg.Wait()
}
```

4.2 Mutexes

Mutex is used to protect shared resources. It locks the resource when one Goroutine is accessing it, preventing other Goroutines from interfering until it is unlocked.

Example:

```go
package main
import (
    "fmt"
    "sync"
)
var (
    counter int
    mutex   sync.Mutex
)
func increment(wg *sync.WaitGroup) {
    defer wg.Done()
    mutex.Lock()
    counter++
    mutex.Unlock()
}
func main() {
```

```go
    var wg sync.WaitGroup
    for i := 0; i < 100; i++ {
        wg.Add(1)
        go increment(&wg)
    }
    wg.Wait()
    fmt.Println("Counter:", counter)
}
```

4.3 Other Synchronization Techniques

Other structures provided by the sync package include RWMutex, which allows multiple readers or one writer, and Cond, which is useful for signalling between Goroutines.

5. Best Practices for Concurrency in Go

While Go makes concurrency easy, it's important to follow best practices to avoid common pitfalls like race conditions, deadlocks, and resource leaks. Here are some recommended practices when working with concurrency in Go:

5.1 Use Goroutines Sparingly

Although Goroutines are lightweight, creating thousands without a clear purpose can lead to performance degradation. Carefully design your program to only use Goroutines where necessary, ensuring they serve a specific function. Unnecessary Goroutines can lead to excessive memory consumption and context switching.

5.2 Gracefully Shutdown Goroutines

A common issue with Goroutines is that they can continue to run even after the main function exits. To prevent this, it's important to have a mechanism to gracefully shut down Goroutines, especially in server applications. This can be achieved using a context package, which allows you to control the lifecycle of Goroutines.

Example Using context for Graceful Shutdown:

```go
package main
import (
    "context"
    "fmt"
    "time"
)
```

```go
func doWork(ctx context.Context) {
    for {
        select {
        case <-ctx.Done():
            fmt.Println("Goroutine exiting...")
            return
        default:
            fmt.Println("Working...")
            time.Sleep(500 * time.Millisecond)
        }
    }
}
func main() {
    ctx, cancel := context.WithTimeout(context.Background(), 2*time.Second)
    defer cancel()
    go doWork(ctx)
    time.Sleep(3 * time.Second)
    fmt.Println("Main function done")
}
```

In the above example, the Goroutine doWork will be stopped gracefully when the context ctx is cancelled.

5.3 Avoid Blocking Operations

When working with concurrency, it's crucial to avoid blocking operations, especially in critical sections of code. Blocking can lead to delays, resource starvation, and even deadlocks. Use non-blocking alternatives where possible and leverage select statements for timeout handling.

5.4 Properly Handle Channel Closing

Channels should be closed carefully to avoid panic conditions. Only the sender should close the channel, and never the receiver. Closing a channel that is still being written to can lead to runtime errors.

Example of Proper Channel Closure:

```go
package main
```

```go
import (

    "fmt"

)

func main() {

    ch := make(chan int)

    go func() {

        for i := 0; i < 5; i++ {

            ch <- i

        }

        close(ch) // Close the channel when done

    }()

    for value := range ch {

        fmt.Println(value)

    }

}
```

In this example, the sender is responsible for closing the channel, ensuring that the receiver knows when to stop receiving data.

6. Common Concurrency Patterns

Go supports several concurrency patterns that are commonly used to solve different kinds of problems. Here are a few:

6.1 Worker Pools

A worker pool is a group of Goroutines that perform a set of tasks concurrently. This pattern is beneficial when dealing with a large number of tasks that can be executed concurrently.

Example of a Worker Pool:

```go
package main

import (

    "fmt"

    "sync"

)

func worker(id int, jobs <-chan int, results chan<- int) {
```

```go
    for job := range jobs {
        fmt.Printf("Worker %d started job %d\n", id, job)
        results <- job * 2 // Process job
    }
}
func main() {
    const numJobs = 5
    jobs := make(chan int, numJobs)
    results := make(chan int, numJobs)
    var wg sync.WaitGroup
    for w := 1; w <= 3; w++ {
        wg.Add(1)
        go func(id int) {
            defer wg.Done()
            worker(id, jobs, results)
        }(w)
    }
    for j := 1; j <= numJobs; j++ {
        jobs <- j
    }
    close(jobs)
    wg.Wait()
    for r := 1; r <= numJobs; r++ {
        fmt.Println("Result:", <-results)
    }
}
```

In this example, three worker Goroutines process five jobs concurrently. This pattern allows for efficient resource utilization, especially when handling tasks that might otherwise block or take time.

6.2 Pipeline Pattern

The pipeline pattern involves chaining multiple stages of Goroutines, where each stage receives data, processes it, and passes it on to the next stage. This pattern is useful for data processing tasks, like parsing and transforming data streams.

Example:

```go
package main

import (
    "fmt"
)

func generator(nums ...int) <-chan int {
    out := make(chan int)
    go func() {
        for _, num := range nums {
            out <- num
        }
        close(out)
    }()
    return out
}

func square(in <-chan int) <-chan int {
    out := make(chan int)
    go func() {
        for num := range in {
            out <- num * num
        }
        close(out)
    }()
    return out
}

func main() {
    nums := generator(2, 3, 4)
    squares := square(nums)
```

```
    for sq := range squares {

        fmt.Println(sq)

    }

}
```

In this pipeline example, the generator Goroutine sends numbers to the square Goroutine, which processes and returns squared values.

7. Advanced Concurrency Concepts

7.1 Race Conditions and the race Detector

Race conditions occur when multiple Goroutines access shared resources concurrently, and at least one of the accesses is a write. This can lead to unpredictable behavior. Go provides a tool to detect race conditions called the race detector, which can be enabled during testing.

How to Use the race Detector:

```
go run -race main.go
```

7.2 Deadlocks

Deadlocks occur when two or more Goroutines are waiting for each other to release resources, leading to a standstill. Avoiding circular dependencies, careful planning of resource acquisition, and using timeouts with select statements are effective strategies to prevent deadlocks.

Common Deadlock Scenario:

```
var mutexA, mutexB sync.Mutex

func deadlock() {

    mutexA.Lock()

    defer mutexA.Unlock()

    mutexB.Lock() // Causes deadlock if another Goroutine holds mutexB and is waiting for mutexA

    defer mutexB.Unlock()

}
```

In the above scenario, if Goroutines acquire locks in inconsistent orders, a deadlock can happen. The key is to ensure consistent locking order.

If you observe, you could see many things happening around you at any given time. This is how the world function - the train is gently moving, passengers talking each other, farmers working in the field and many other things are happening simultaneously. We can say, the world we live in function concurrently.

Go has built-in concurrency features with syntax support. The Go concurrency is inspired by a paper published in 1978 by Tony Hoare. The paper title is Communicating sequential processes.

Go has some new terminologies and keywords related to concurrent programming. The two important words are goroutine and channel. This chapter will go through these concepts and walk through some examples to further explain concurrency in Go.

The Go runtime is part of the executable binary created when compiling any Go code. The Go runtime contains a garbage collector and a scheduler to manage lightweight threads called Goroutines. Goroutine is a fundamental abstraction to support concurrency. Goroutine is an independently executing part of the program. You can invoke any number of goroutines and all of them could run concurrently.

Goroutines can communicate to each other via typed conduits called channels. Channels can be used to send and receive data.

Goroutine

Goroutine is like a process running in the background. A function with go keyword as prefix starts the goroutine. Any function including anonymous function can be invoked with go keyword. In fact, the main function is a special goroutine invoked during the starup of any program by the Go runtime.

To understand the Goroutine better let's look at a simple program:

Listing: Goroutine with explicit sleep

```
package main

import (

"fmt"

"time" )

var msg string

func setMessage() {

msg = "Hello, World!" }

func main() {

go setMessage()

time.Sleep(1 * time.Millisecond)

fmt.Println(msg)

}
```

In the above program, setMessage function is invoked as a goroutine in line no 15 using the go keyword. If you run this program, you will get the hello world message printed. If you change the sleep time to Zero, the message will not be printed. This is because, the program exits when main function completes execution. And in this case, since setMessage is called as a goroutine, it goes to background and main goroutine execution continues. In the earlier case when the time sleep was 1 second, the goroutine gets some time to execute before main completed. That's why the msg value is set and printed.

Channels

Multiple goroutines can communicate using channels. Channels can be used to send and receive any type of values. You can send and receive values with this channel operator: **<-**

This is how to declare a channel of int values:

ch := make(chan int)

To send a value to ch channel:

ch <- 4

To receive a value from **ch** channel and assign to a variable:

v := <-ch

You can also receive value without really assigning:

<-ch

Sending and receiving values from channels becomes a blocking operation. So, if you try to receive value from a channel, there should be some other part of the code which sends a value this channel. Until a value sends to the channel, the receiving part of the code will block the execution.

Here is an example:

Listing: Goroutine with channels

```
1 package main
import (
"fmt" 5 )
var c = make(chan int)
var msg string
func setMessage() {
msg = "Hello, World!"
c <- 0
}
func main() {
go setMessage()
<-c
```

```
fmt.Println(msg)

}
```

In the above example, an int channel is assigned to a global variable named **c**. In line number 17, immediately after calling goroutines, channel is trying to receive a value. This becomes a blocking operation in the **main** goroutine. In line number 12, inside the **setMessage** function, after setting a value for **msg**, a value is sent to the **c** channel. This will make the operation to continue in the **main** goroutine.

Waitgroups

Go standard library has a sync package which provides few synchronization primitives. One of the mechanisms is Waitgroups which can be used to wait for multiple goroutines to complete. The **Add** function add the number of goroutines to wait for. At the end of these goroutines call **Done** function to indicate the task has completed. The **Wait** function call, block further operations until all goroutines are completed.

Here is a modified version of the previous example using Waitgroups.

Listing: Goroutine with Waitgroups

```
package main

import (

"fmt"

"sync" 6 )

var msg string

var wg sync.WaitGroup

func setMessage() {

msg = "Hello, World!"

wg.Done() 14 }

16 func main() { 17   wg.Add(1)

go setMessage()

wg.Wait()

fmt.Println(msg)

}
```

In the above example, the **Add** method at line number 17 make one item to wait for. The next line invoke the goroutine. The line number 19, the **Wait** method call blocks any further operations until goroutines are completed. The previous line made goroutine and inside the goroutine, at the end of that goroutine, there is a **Done** call at line number 13.

Here is another example:

Listing: Goroutine with Waitgroups

```go
package main

import (
"fmt"
"sync"
"time")
func someWork(i int) {
time.Sleep(time.Millisecond * 10)
fmt.Println(i) }
func main() {
var wg sync.WaitGroup
for i := 0; i < 5; i++ {
wg.Add(1)
go func(j int) {
defer wg.Done()
someWork(j)
}(i)
}
wg.Wait()
}
```

Select

The select is a statement with some similarity to switch, but used with channels and goroutines. The select statement lets a goroutine wait on multiple communication operations through channels.

Under a select statement, you can add multiple cases. A select statement blocks until one of its case is available for run – that is the channel has some value. If multiple channels used in cases has value readily available, select chooses one at random.

Here is an example:
```go
package main

import "time" import "fmt" func main() {

c1 := make(chan string) c2 := make(chan string)
```

```go
go func() { time.Sleep(time.Second * 1)
c1 <- "one"
}() go func() { time.Sleep(time.Second * 2)
c2 <- "two"
}()
for i := 0; i < 2; i++ { select { case msg1 := <-c1: fmt.Println("received", msg1)
case msg2 := <-c2:
fmt.Println("received", msg2)
}
}
}
```

Buffered Channels

Buffered channels are channels with a given capacity. The capacity is the size of channel in terms of number of elements. If the capacity is zero or absent, the channel is unbuffered. For a buffered channel communication succeeds only when both a sender and receiver are ready. Whereas for a buffered channel, communication succeeds without blocking if the buffer is not full (sends) or not empty (receives).

The capacity can be given as the third argument to make function: **make(chan int, 100)**

Consider the below example:

Listing: Buffered Channel

```go
package main
import "fmt"
func main() {
ch := make(chan string, 2)
ch <- "Hello"
ch <- "World"
fmt.Println(<-ch)
fmt.Println(<-ch)
}
```

The ch channel is a buffered channel, this makes it possible to send value without any receiver present.

Channel Direction

When declaring a function with channels as input parameters, you can also specify the direction of the channel. The direction of channel declares whether it can only receive or only send values. The channel direction helps to increases the type-safety of the program.

Here is an example:

Listing: Channel channel

```
package main

import "fmt"

func sendOnly(name chan<- string) {

name <- "Hi"}

func receiveOnly(name <-chan string) {

fmt.Println(<-name) 11 }

func main() {

n := make(chan string)

go func() {

fmt.Println(<-n)

}()
sendOnly(n)

go func() {

n <- "Hello"
}()

receiveOnly(n)

}
```

In the above example, the **send Only** function define a channel variable which can be only used for sending data. If you tried to read from that channel within that function, it's going to be compiled time error. Similary the **receive Only** function define a channel variable which can be only user for receive data. You cannot send any value to that channel from that function.

Lazy Initialization Using sync.Once

The sync package provides another struct called Once which is useful for lazy initialization.

Here is an example:

```
import (

"sync"
```

```go
) type DB struct{}

var db *DB var once sync.Once

func GetDB() *DB { once.Do(func() { db = &DB{}

}) return db

}
```

If the above GetDB function is called multiple times, only once the DB object will get constructed.

Exercises

Exercise 1: Write a program to download a list of web pages concurrently using Goroutines.

Hint: Use this tool for serving junk content for testing: **https:// github.com/baijum/lipsum**
Solution: package main

```go
import (

"io/ioutil"

"log"

"net/http"

"net/url"

"sync"

)

func main() { urls := []string{

"http://localhost:9999/1.txt",

"http://localhost:9999/2.txt",

"http://localhost:9999/3.txt",

"http://localhost:9999/4.txt",

} var wg sync.WaitGroup for _, u := range urls {

wg.Add(1) go func(u string) { defer wg.Done() ul, err := url.Parse(u) fn :=
ul.Path[1:len(ul.Path)]

res, err := http.Get(u) if err != nil {

log.Println(err, u)

} content, _ := ioutil.ReadAll(res.Body) ioutil.WriteFile(fn, content, 0644) res.Body.Close()

}(u)

} wg.Wait()
```

}

Conclusion: The Essence of Concurrency in Go

Concurrency in Go is a pivotal aspect that distinguishes it from other programming languages. It facilitates the development of efficient, scalable, and high-performance applications, making it ideal for modern computing needs. The language was designed with concurrency in mind, providing simple yet powerful tools to manage multiple tasks simultaneously. This makes Go particularly suited for building web servers, cloud-based applications, distributed systems, and other solutions where parallel task execution is crucial.

1. The Advantages of Goroutines

One of the most significant innovations in Go is the use of Goroutines. Unlike traditional threads, which are managed by the operating system and can be heavy in terms of memory and CPU usage, Goroutines are managed by the Go runtime. They are lightweight, efficient, and allow you to spawn thousands of concurrent tasks without significant overhead. This efficiency is achieved through the use of a segmented stack, which grows and shrinks as needed, reducing the amount of memory required.

Goroutines make concurrent programming more approachable by abstracting away much of the complexity associated with traditional threading models. For instance, developers don't need to worry about explicitly managing thread pools or handling the intricacies of thread lifecycle management. By using Goroutines, concurrency becomes more accessible, even for those new to parallel programming.

2. Communication and Synchronization with Channels

While Goroutines provide the means for concurrent execution, Channels facilitate communication between them. Channels allow Goroutines to send and receive messages, enabling them to synchronize their operations effectively. This communication model helps avoid the common pitfalls of shared memory concurrency, where multiple threads access the same data, often leading to race conditions and bugs that are difficult to debug.

Channels are integral to Go's concurrency model because they help coordinate the actions of Goroutines. Whether you're implementing a producer-consumer scenario, coordinating multiple workers in a pool, or building a pipeline to process data, Channels make it straightforward to pass information between concurrent tasks. Go's simplicity in this aspect reduces the likelihood of errors, making your code cleaner, more maintainable, and easier to understand.

3. Effective Use of the Select Statement

Another vital feature for managing concurrent tasks in Go is the select statement. It allows a Goroutine to wait for multiple channel operations, executing the first one that becomes available. This capability is particularly useful in scenarios where you need to handle multiple streams of data or want to implement timeouts and non-blocking operations.

For example, you might be processing input from multiple data sources or monitoring multiple servers. With the select statement, you can efficiently manage which channels to read from or write to without blocking your entire program. This feature enhances the responsiveness of applications, especially those that interact with external systems or rely on real-time data processing.

4. Synchronization with the Sync Package

While Channels handle many synchronization needs, there are cases where you need finer control over how Goroutines access shared resources. The sync package provides several synchronization primitives, including Mutexes, WaitGroups, and Cond. These tools help you manage shared state safely and efficiently, preventing data races and ensuring that your program behaves as expected even under concurrent loads.

- **Mutexes** allow you to lock shared data structures, ensuring that only one Goroutine can access them at a time. This is essential when working with critical sections of code that modify shared data.

- **WaitGroups** enable you to wait for a collection of Goroutines to complete before proceeding, which is helpful when orchestrating a set of concurrent tasks.

- **Cond** is a more advanced synchronization primitive that facilitates signaling between Goroutines, providing a way to coordinate tasks that need to be executed in a specific order.

These synchronization tools provide greater flexibility when building more complex concurrent systems, where coordination between Goroutines requires more than just message passing.

5. Common Concurrency Patterns in Go
Throughout the development process, several patterns have emerged that help structure concurrent code effectively:

- **Worker Pools:** This pattern allows you to manage a group of Goroutines that can process tasks concurrently. It is particularly useful when you need to handle many tasks that can be processed independently. By distributing tasks across multiple workers, you can maximize resource utilization and improve overall throughput.

- **Pipelines:** Pipelines help break down a complex task into smaller, manageable stages, each running as a separate Goroutine. This model is especially useful for data processing applications where data needs to be transformed through multiple steps.

- **Fan-Out/Fan-In:** In this pattern, a single Goroutine distributes work to multiple Goroutines (fan-out), which perform tasks concurrently. Once completed, the results are collected by another Goroutine (fan-in). This is efficient for tasks that can be processed independently and then aggregated.

By applying these patterns, developers can create scalable, efficient, and maintainable concurrent systems. The use of these patterns reduces the complexity of managing multiple Goroutines, making code easier to read and maintain.

6. Handling Challenges: Race Conditions, Deadlocks, and More

Despite the ease of writing concurrent code in Go, challenges still exist. Issues like race conditions, deadlocks, and resource leaks can arise if concurrency is not handled properly. These are classic problems in concurrent programming, but Go provides tools and strategies to mitigate them.

- **Race Conditions:** Go includes a built-in race detector, which can be activated during testing. This tool helps identify sections of your code where Goroutines are accessing shared resources unsafely. By detecting race conditions early, you can refactor your code to use proper synchronization mechanisms, ensuring that your program runs as expected.

- **Deadlocks:** Deadlocks occur when two or more Goroutines are stuck waiting for each other to release resources. To avoid this, it is important to establish consistent locking orders and utilize non-blocking synchronization techniques. Go's select statement, for example, can help implement timeouts, preventing deadlocks by ensuring that operations don't wait indefinitely.

- **Resource Leaks:** If Goroutines are not managed correctly, they can continue to run even when no longer needed, leading to memory and resource leaks. This is why it's important to have clear strategies for Goroutine lifecycle management. Using contexts and cancellation signals can help ensure that Goroutines terminate gracefully when their tasks are complete.

7. The Evolution of Concurrency in Go

Since its inception, Go has continued to evolve, making improvements to its concurrency model. Initially, the simplicity of Goroutines and Channels was a breakthrough, and as the language matured, more sophisticated features and patterns have been introduced to make concurrent programming even more robust. The introduction of better tools, optimizations in the Go scheduler, and the ongoing development of the language have solidified Go's place as a leading language for concurrent programming.

The efficiency of Go's concurrency model has been particularly beneficial in the era of cloud computing and microservices architecture, where handling multiple requests concurrently is essential. Go's ability to handle high-concurrency workloads has made it a preferred choice for many cloud-based and distributed applications.

8. Practical Applications of Concurrency in Go

Concurrency in Go is not just a theoretical concept; it has practical applications that have been proven across industries. From web servers to distributed systems, from networked applications to task schedulers, the ability to handle multiple tasks concurrently makes Go an ideal choice for various real-world scenarios.

For instance:

- **Web Servers:** Go's concurrency model enables the development of fast, scalable web servers that can handle thousands of requests per second. Popular frameworks like Gin and Echo leverage Go's concurrency features to provide performant web solutions.

- **Microservices:** The microservices architecture relies on the ability to process multiple requests in parallel. Go's lightweight Goroutines and efficient Channels make it easier to design microservices that are not only scalable but also easy to maintain.

- **Data Processing:** In applications that involve heavy data processing, such as big data analytics, Go's pipelines and worker pools provide efficient ways to handle data streams and process large datasets concurrently.

- **Real-Time Systems:** Real-time systems, such as financial trading platforms, game servers, and IoT applications, require fast, concurrent handling of data inputs. Go's concurrency mechanisms allow these systems to be highly responsive and efficient.

9. Future Directions for Concurrency in Go

The Go community continues to explore and push the boundaries of what can be achieved with concurrent programming. The language designers are constantly improving the Go runtime, focusing on performance optimizations and enhancing the scheduler to manage Goroutines more effectively. Upcoming versions of Go promise even better handling of concurrent workloads, with potential improvements to how Goroutines are scheduled across multiple CPU cores.

Additionally, the Go ecosystem continues to grow, with libraries and frameworks that help developers write concurrent code more easily. New tools and best practices are continually emerging, making it easier for developers to adopt and integrate concurrency into their projects.

As the demand for scalable, performant software continues to grow, the need for efficient concurrency models becomes even more critical. Go, with its straightforward yet powerful concurrency mechanisms, is well-positioned to meet these demands, ensuring that developers can build reliable, fast, and scalable applications for the future.

Final Thoughts

Concurrency is a complex topic, but Go manages to make it approachable without sacrificing power. Its concurrency model, centered around Goroutines and Channels, offers a simple yet effective way to write concurrent programs. By providing built-in tools for communication, synchronization, and coordination, Go enables developers to focus on solving problems without getting bogged down by the intricacies of traditional threading.

Mastering concurrency in Go requires understanding not only how to create and manage Goroutines but also how to communicate between them, synchronize their actions, and avoid common pitfalls. With the right knowledge and practices, developers can harness the full potential of Go's concurrency model to build robust, efficient, and scalable applications.

7. Go: Error Handling and Reflection

Introduction

Error Handling in Go

Go (Golang) has a unique approach to error handling compared to many other programming languages. Instead of relying on exceptions, it uses explicit error values that indicate when something has gone wrong. This design philosophy is built around simplicity, robustness, and clarity, allowing developers to handle errors in a straightforward manner.

1. **Error Handling Philosophy in Go**

   o Unlike languages that use exceptions to signal errors, Go's philosophy is to treat errors as values. This means that functions return error objects as a second return value, which can be checked directly. For instance:

```
file, err := os.Open("example.txt")

if err != nil {

  // handle error

  log.Fatal(err)

}
```

   o This approach encourages developers to deal with errors immediately, resulting in more reliable and predictable code.

2. **The error Interface**

   o In Go, errors are represented by the error interface:

```
type error interface {

  Error() string

}
```

   o Any type that implements this interface can be used as an error, giving developers the flexibility to create custom error types.

3. **Creating Custom Errors**

   o Sometimes, the default error messages are not sufficient, and developers might want to add more context. Go allows the creation of custom error types to include additional information.

```
type MyError struct {

  Msg string
```

```go
    Code int
}
```

```go
func (e *MyError) Error() string {
    return fmt.Sprintf("Error %d: %s", e.Code, e.Msg)
}
```

- o Using custom error types helps in distinguishing different kinds of errors and in making error messages more descriptive.

4. **Wrapping Errors**

   - o With Go 1.13, the language introduced error wrapping, allowing for easier error tracking and debugging.

```go
err := fmt.Errorf("failed to read file: %w", originalErr)
```

   - o Error wrapping retains the original error context and can be unwrapped using errors.Unwrap().

5. **Error Handling Best Practices**

   - o Check errors immediately: By handling errors right after a function call, developers ensure that the application does not continue in an erroneous state.

   - o Use descriptive error messages: This helps in diagnosing the issue more quickly when something goes wrong.

   - o Create custom error types: For better error handling, especially when returning more complex information.

Reflection in Go

Reflection allows a program to inspect and manipulate objects at runtime. In Go, the reflect package is used for this purpose. It provides the ability to explore the types and values of variables, making it possible to write more dynamic and generic code.

1. **The reflect Package**

   - o The reflect package provides tools to discover information about types, values, and structs at runtime. It is useful when you need to work with values without knowing their exact types beforehand.

```go
import "reflect"

func PrintTypeInfo(v interface{}) {
    t := reflect.TypeOf(v)
    fmt.Println("Type:", t)
```

```
fmt.Println("Kind:", t.Kind())
}
```

- o This code snippet retrieves the type and kind of the variable v, which can be of any type.

2. Types and Values

- o reflect.Type and reflect.Value are two central concepts in the reflect package.
  - Type represents the Go type (e.g., int, string, struct).
  - Value represents the actual value of a variable.

```
var x int = 42
t := reflect.TypeOf(x)
v := reflect.ValueOf(x)
fmt.Println("Type:", t)   // Output: int
fmt.Println("Value:", v)  // Output: 42
```

3. Modifying Values

- o Reflection also allows modifying values, but it must be done with caution. Only values that are settable (like those passed by reference) can be modified.

```
func SetValue(v interface{}) {
  rv := reflect.ValueOf(v)
  if rv.Kind() == reflect.Ptr && rv.Elem().CanSet() {
    rv.Elem().SetInt(100)
  }
}
var num int = 10
SetValue(&num)
fmt.Println(num) // Output: 100
```

4. Use Cases for Reflection

- o Generic functions: Functions that can handle different types of inputs without knowing their types in advance.
- o Testing frameworks: Reflection is often used in testing frameworks to inspect function signatures and dynamically invoke methods.

- o Serialization/Deserialization: Reflection can help when marshaling and unmarshaling JSON, XML, or other data formats, as it allows programs to map data to structs dynamically.

5. **Reflection Best Practices**

- o Use reflection sparingly: While reflection is powerful, it can make code less readable and harder to debug. It should only be used when necessary.

- o Type assertions for simple cases: In many cases, you can avoid using reflection by opting for type assertions or switches. This makes the code cleaner and more efficient.

- o Understand the cost: Reflection can have a performance impact, so it is important to assess whether it is the right tool for the job.

Combining Error Handling and Reflection

When working with Go, there are scenarios where error handling and reflection may come together. For example, a function might need to validate or process inputs of various types, and any invalid input should produce a meaningful error.

1. **Dynamic Validation**

- o Consider a case where a function receives a configuration object that can have multiple fields of different types. Using reflection, you can inspect each field and ensure that it meets specific conditions.

```go
func ValidateConfig(cfg interface{}) error {

  val := reflect.ValueOf(cfg)

  if val.Kind() != reflect.Struct {

    return fmt.Errorf("expected a struct, got %v", val.Kind())

  }

  for i := 0; i < val.NumField(); i++ {

    field := val.Field(i)

    if field.Kind() == reflect.Int && field.Int() < 0 {

      return fmt.Errorf("field %d is invalid: value must be non-negative", i)

    }

  }

  return nil

}
```

- o In this example, ValidateConfig checks the fields of a struct and returns an error if any integer field has a negative value.

2. **Custom Error Types with Reflection**

- o Sometimes, it might be necessary to return different types of errors based on the structure of input data. By combining reflection and custom error types, you can provide more granular control.

```go
type ValidationError struct {
    FieldName string
    Problem   string
}
func (e *ValidationError) Error() string {
    return fmt.Sprintf("Validation Error - %s: %s", e.FieldName, e.Problem)
}
func CheckStruct(v interface{}) error {
    val := reflect.ValueOf(v)
    if val.Kind() != reflect.Struct {
        return &ValidationError{"Struct", "Invalid Type"}
    }
    // More checks...
    return nil
}
```

Error handling is the process of detecting and handling an erroneous situation that can lead to the crash of a program.

Compile-time errors occur with the compilation of the program.

Errors that occur at the execution of the program are called runtime errors. Opening a file that doesn't exist in a directory is the best example of a runtime error. Error handling detects such runtime errors, represents and handles them as specified.

The Go language has a built-in error type to indicate an abnormal condition. The error type is used like other data types—store them in memory, pass them to any function, and many others. In other languages, we use try-catch or try-except for error handling but there is nothing like that here as the Go language doesn't have exceptions. In Go, errors are handled either by multiple return values or by panic. The following is an example of trying to open a file that doesn't exist which gives a runtime error.

We can open a file in the Go language with the following syntax: func Open(name string) (file *File, err error)

Example: package
main import
("fmt"
"os"

)

func main(){ file, err := os.Open("./example.json")
fmt.Println("file status:", file) fmt.Println("error status:",
err)
}

Output:

file status:

error status: open ./example.json: The system cannot find the file specified.

In the example given above, since the file doesn't exist in the current directory, it returns nil instead of the file handler and an error message that occurs while opening a file. Let's create a file named example.json in the current directory and run the program again. In this case, it finds the file and returns the file handler and nil to Here is the updated output after creating a specified file:

file status: &{0x1185c420}
error status:
To handle an error, we can compare the last return value err to If the value of err is not there is an error. If err is the operation has been done successfully.

Error type

Error is an interface type that contains a single method Error of return type string. The default value of the error type is The error type is defined as shown below:

type error interface{

Error() string

}

Any type that implements the error interface is considered as an error.

Example: package main import "fmt"
type My_error struct{} func
(error_object *My_error) Error() string{
return "Unexpected outcome"
} func main(){
fmt.Println(&My_error{}
)
}

Output:

Unexpected outcome

In the program given above, we create a struct My_error that has no field. Struct My_error is used to implement the Error method that returns an error message as a string. We can call an Error method directly in case of any error to find its output.

Example:
```
package
main import "fmt"
type My_error
struct{} func
(error_object
*My_error)
Error() string{
return
"Unexpected
outcome"
} func main(){ obj :=
My_error{}
fmt.Println(obj.Error()
)
}
```

Error package

Go has a built-in package called errors in the src directory. It implements various functions to manipulate errors. It has a function called New that is used to return an error of a specified format.

Example:
```
package
main import
("fmt"
"os"

"errors"

)

func main(){ file, err := os.Open("./example.json") if(err!=nil){
error_msg := errors.New("file operation failed")
fmt.Println(error_msg)
}

if(err==nil){ fmt.Println("file opened
successfully", file)
}

}
```

Output:

file operation failed

In the program given above, in the case of an error, we called the new function by passing an error message. This function accepts the error message as a string and returns it as an error type value. Here, the type of error_msg is which points to errors.errorString. error String is a struct type that has a string type of a field in the errors package. The struct type error String implements the Error method and returns a string type of value.

For a better understanding, you must have a look at the errors package in the src directory.

Defer statement

Execution of a specific code can be deferred until the surrounding function returns by using the defer statement. An expression in the defer statement must be a function call. The arguments passed in the defer statement are evaluated as the compiler finds a defer keyword, but the execution of the defer statement takes place at the end when the function returns. Multiple clean-up operations are performed in the defer statement such as closing the files if any file is open.

The defer statement works in the following ways: The defer statement pushes a function into the stack that is executed in Last in the first out order. When the surrounding function returns, all functions are called that are stored in the stack. The function that is stored at the end in the stack is executed first.

The values passed in the defer function arguments are evaluated as the compiler finds the defer statement.

In defer functions, both the read and write operations can be performed.

Return values can be modified in defer functions.

Example: package
main import
("fmt"
"os"

) func open_file(){ defer file.Close() file, err :=
os.Open("./example.txt") fmt.Println("file status:", file)
fmt.Println("error status:", err)
} func
main(){
open_file()
}

Output:

Error: undefined: file

The program given above has a function called open_file. When the compiler starts the execution of it gets a defer statement.

While evaluating the values, it doesn't get the file object, so it gives an error. We can resolve this issue as shown below. **Example:** package main

import ("fmt"

```go
"os"

) func open_file(){ file, err :=
os.Open("./example.txt") defer file.Close()
fmt.Println("file status:", file) fmt.Println("error
status:", err)
} func
main(){
open_file()
}
```

Output:

```
file status:
&{0x1186c420} error
status:
```

The following is an example that explains that defer function calls are executed in the LIFO order.
We can also execute the defer statement in a loop.

Example: package main
import "fmt" func
show_value(){ for itr:=0;
itr<=10; itr++{ defer
fmt.Println("value:", itr)
} } func
main(){
show_value()
}

Output:

```
value: 10
value: 9 value:
8 value: 7
value: 6 value:
5 value: 4
value: 3 value:
2 value: 1
value: 0
```

Here is another example in which defer is used to update the return value as shown below.

Example: package main import "fmt" func
update_return_value() (i int) { defer func() {i =
i+10}() return 1 } func main(){ fmt.Println("updated
return value:", update_return_value())
}

Output:

updated return value: 11

Panic

Panic is another way of error handling. It is used to check for unexpected errors throughout the program. It is somehow similar to exception as it also occurs during runtime. It skips the execution of a function if it returns an error that shows unexpected behavior. Whenever a Panic function is called in any function, it stops the execution of that function, executes the defer statement which is given to handle that panic, returns to caller statement, and continues with further execution.

In Go, a runtime error also causes panic in some cases like in out-of-bound accesses, divide by zero, and many others.

Syntax:
Panic (interface {})
Panic accepts any value as an argument because the empty interface can accept any type of value.

Example: package
main import "fmt"
var result int func
op(a, b int) int {
result = a / b return
result
} func main(){ result =
op(10, 0)
fmt.Println("Completed"
)
}

Output:

panic: runtime error: integer divide by zero

On executing the example shown above, it gives a panic that is caused by a runtime error on dividing a number by zero. When panic occurs, the program gets terminated immediately. We can call a panic function on a specific case when a program is showing unexpected behavior and set an error message as required.

Example: package main import
"fmt" var result int func op(a, b int)
int { if(b==0){ panic("Can't divide a
number by zero!")
}

result = a/b return
result
} func main(){ result =
op(10, 0)
fmt.Println("Completed"
)}

Output:

panic: Can't divide a number by zero!

Here, everything remains the same but it shows an error message which is what we required. In the same way, panic can be initiated by calling a panic function with any possible erroneous condition or a situation that can show unexpected behavior.

Example: package main

```
import "fmt" func
show_value(max int){ for
itr:=1; itr<=max; itr++{
if(itr==5){ panic("Not
acceptable")
}

fmt.Println(itr)

}} func main(){
show_value(10)
fmt.Println("Completed"
)
}
```

Output:

1

2

3

4

panic: Not acceptable

In the program given above, we do not want to show values more than 4. If a value greater than 4 is passed in a parameter, it prints the values up to 4; and when it comes to 5, it shows panic and stops further execution. In some cases, we might execute some clean-up or other necessary operation before the program terminates. The same can be done by using the defer function that executes after getting the panicking situation.

Example:

```
package main import "fmt" var result
int func op_defer(){ fmt.Println("op
defer function executed")
} func main_defer(){ fmt.Println("main
defer function executed")
}
```

```go
func op(a, b int) int { defer
op_defer() if(b==0){ panic("Can't
divide a number by zero!")
}
```

```go
result = a/b return
result
} func main(){ defer
main_defer() result =
op(10, 0)
fmt.Println("Completed"
)
}
```

Output:

op defer function executed main
defer function executed panic:
Can't divide a number by zero!

Recovery

Go provides a built-in function called Recover that controls the panicking situation. In the Go
language errors handling is done by using the recover function since try-catch, try-except, or other
similar methods are used in other languages. In the example given above, we saw that the execution
of a program terminates when a panic occurs. The Recover function is used inside the defer
functions because only defer statements are executed after panicking. The value passed to panic is
returned by the recover function. If there is no panic in the program, the recover function returns nil.

Example: package main import "fmt"
var result int func op_defer(){
fmt.Println("op defer function
executed")
} func main_defer(){ fmt.Println("main
defer function executed")
}

```go
func op(a, b int) int { defer
func() { if r := recover(); r !=
nil { fmt.Println("Panic
recovered", r) op_defer() }
}() if(b==0){ panic("Can't divide a
number by zero!")
}
```

```go
result = a/b return
result
} func main(){ defer
main_defer() result =
```

```
op(10, 0)
fmt.Println("Completed"
)
}
```

Output:

Panic recovered Can't divide a number by
zero! op defer function executed
Completed main defer function executed

In the program given above, we called the "op" method from the main Goroutine. When it gets
panicked, the program should terminate. However, before the termination, it executes the list of
defer calls. While executing the defer function, it gets the recover function that takes control of the
panic and returns the non-nil value passed in the panic. Here, the recover function resumes the
execution of the program and after executing op_defer function, it comes back to **function caller
statement** in main and continues the further execution. At the end, the defer function of the main
Goroutine is called and thus, the program executes smoothly.

Reflection

Reflection is a key feature of a programming language that can be defined as examining the program
execution and modifying it at runtime. Reflection plays an important role in object-oriented
programming languages.

Reflection allows the exploration of any data at runtime without knowing its name defined at
compile time. By using reflection, we can inspect the behavior of any method, interface, struct, or
any data. Inspecting the source code at runtime is called reflection.

By using reflection, we can get the type, field, and the value of any type. Although in the Go
language, every variable is declared with its type but still, there could be many cases where we may
need to know the type of a variable at runtime. Here, reflection comes in.

Example: func main(){ slice_val :=[]string {"one",
"two", "three", "four", "five", "six"} map_val := map
[string] int64{} for itr:=0; itritr++{
map_val[slice_val[itr]] = 0
}

}

In the example given above, we initialize a slice of string type. We need to use the items of the slice
like a key of a map. Here, we have declared a map that has the string type of keys. What if we need
to initialize that map at runtime or a slice is of any type?

In that case, we would need to find the type of slice at runtime.

For that, we could use reflection.

The reflect package

Go provides a built-in package called reflect that provides the functionality of reflection at runtime. We can get the

"reflect"

package in the src directory. The reflect package contains a few variables and methods to manipulate the object of various types.

It is used to return the dynamic type of a variable that is static of interface type. As an empty interface can accept any value, we can get the exact type of value that is accepted by an interface with the use of the reflect package. The reflect package is mainly used to get the type, value, and kind of a variable.

Type

The reflect package provides the method TypeOf to get the type of a variable. This function returns the value of the type The type has various methods to define the property of that type. The signature of this function is as follows: funcTypeOf(i interface{}) type

This function takes an interface as an argument. Any value is accepted by an interface and then analyzed by the TypeOf function.

Syntax:
variable_type := reflect.TypeOf(variable)

Example: package
main import
("fmt"
"reflect"

)

func main(){ type student
struct{ name string age int }
stu := student{"Akansha",
17} fmt.Println(stu) stu_type
:= reflect.TypeOf(stu)
fmt.Println("type of 'stu' variable:", stu_type) fmt.Println("type of 'stu_type' variable:", reflect.TypeOf(stu_ type)) fmt.Println("name of 'stu' variable type:", stu_type.Name())

}

Output:

{Akansha 17}

type of 'stu' variable: main.student
type of 'stu_type' variable:
*reflect.rtype name of 'stu' variable
type: student

Value

The reflect package has a method to evaluate the value of a variable.

Syntax:
value: =
reflect.ValueOf(variable)

Example:

```
package main
import ("fmt"
"reflect"

)

func main(){

type student struct{ name
string age int } stu :=
student{"Akansha", 17}
fmt.Println(stu) stu_type :=
reflect.TypeOf(stu)
fmt.Println("value of 'stu' variable:", reflect.ValueOf(stu)) fmt.Println("value of 'stu_type' variable:",
reflect.ValueOf(stu_ type))

}
```

Output:

```
{Akansha 17} value of 'stu' variable:
{Akansha 17} value of 'stu_type'
variable: main.student
```

Kind

Kind is quite a different method of the reflect package. The type defines the type of a variable while "kind" defines the source type of a variable type. This function is used with a type to get its source, not with variables.

Example: package
main import
("fmt"
"reflect"

)

```
func main(){ type student
struct{ name string age int }
stu := student{"Akansha",
17} fmt.Println(stu) stu_type
:= reflect.TypeOf(stu)
stu_kind := stu_type.Kind()
fmt.Println("type of 'stu'
variable:", stu_type.Name())
```

```
fmt.Println("kind of
'stu_type' variable:",
stu_kind) }
```

Output:

{Akansha 17}

type of 'stu' variable: student
kind of 'stu_type' variable:
struct

Here, we can see that student is a type of struct. So, the source type of the student type is a struct.

NumField()

This method is used to get the number of fields contained by a struct. As this function is defined in the reflect package, it only works with type or reflect.Type.

Example: package
main import
("fmt"
"reflect"

)

```
func main(){ type student struct{ name string age
int } stu := student{"Akansha", 17} stu_value :=
reflect.ValueOf(stu) num_fields :=
stu_value.NumField() fmt.Println("number of fields
in 'stu':", num_fields, reflect. TypeOf(stu_value))
stu_type := reflect.TypeOf(stu) fmt.Println("number
of fields in 'stu':", num_fields, reflect.
TypeOf(stu_type))

}
```

Output:

number of fields in 'stu': 2 reflect.Value

number of fields in 'stu': 2 *reflect.rtype

Field

This function is used to get the value of struct fields. It returns the value of type reflect.Value.

Example: package
main import
("fmt"
"reflect"

)

```go
func main(){ type student struct{ name string age int } stu := student{"Akansha", 17}
stu_value := reflect.ValueOf(stu) num_fields := stu_value.NumField() for itr:=0;
itritr++{ fmt.Printf("value of %dth field is:%v of type %T\n", itr+1,
stu_value.Field(itr), stu_value.Field(itr))
}

}
```

Output:

value of 1th field is:Akansha of type reflect.Value value of 2th field is:17 of type reflect.Value

String(), Int() & Float()

In the reflect package, the Value function returns the data of type We can convert such values to string or any other type as required.

Example: package
main import
("fmt"
"reflect"

)

func main(){

type student struct{
name string age int
income float32
} stu := student{"Akansha", 17, 40000.565} stu_value :=
reflect.ValueOf(stu) fmt.Printf("Type of name is %T and
value is %v\n", stu_value. Field(0), stu_value.Field(0))
fmt.Printf("Type of age is %T and value is %v\n",
stu_value. Field(1), stu_value.Field(1)) fmt.Printf("Type
of income is %T and value is %v\n", stu_value. Field(2),
stu_value.Field(2)) name :=
reflect.ValueOf(stu.name).String() age :=
reflect.ValueOf(stu.age).Int()
income := reflect.ValueOf(stu.income).Float() fmt.Printf("Type of name is %T and value is %v\n",
name, name) fmt.Printf("Type of age is %T and value is %v\n", age, age) fmt.Printf("Type of income
is %T and value is %v\n", income, income)

}

Output:

Type of name is reflect.Value and value is Akansha Type of age is reflect.Value and value is 17

Type of income is reflect.Value and value is 40000.566

Type of name is string and value is Akansha

Type of age is int64 and value is 17

Type of income is float64 and value is 40000.56640625

Laws of reflection

Go defines three laws of reflection that define how reflection works and the points that should be remembered while working with reflection. The three laws of reflection are as follows: **Reflection goes from interface value to reflection object** Since an empty interface accepts any value, it makes it quite hard to understand what type of value is stored by an interface. Here, reflection works to get the type and value contained by an interface. The type and value of a variable are evaluated by using the functions TypeOf and ValueOf as we have already seen in the previous example. The first law of reflection is all about extracting a reflection object from an interface.

Example:

```
package main
import ("fmt"
"reflect"

) func show_value(i interface{}){ value_type := reflect.TypeOf(i)
value := reflect.ValueOf(i) fmt.Printf("Passed value is %v of type
%v\n", value, value_type.Kind())
fmt.Println(reflect.TypeOf(value))
fmt.Println(reflect.TypeOf(value_type))
} func main(){ type
student struct{
name string age int
income float32
} stu := student{"Akansha", 17,
40000.565} show_value(stu)
}
```

Output:

passed value is {Akansha 17 40000.566} of type struct reflect.Value

*reflect.rtype

The second law is the inverse of the first law. The second law says the type reflect.Value and reflect.Type can be converted to interface value. The following is an example of reflection's second law.

Example: package
main import
("fmt"
"reflect"

```
) func show_value(i
interface{}){ value_type :=
reflect.TypeOf(i) value :=
```

```
reflect.ValueOf(i)
fmt.Println(reflect.TypeOf(val
ue))
fmt.Println(reflect.TypeOf(val
ue_type)) interface_val :=
value.Interface()
fmt.Println("Interface value
is:", interface_val)
fmt.Println("Interface value
type is:", reflect.
TypeOf(interface_val).Kind())
} func main(){ type
student struct{
name string age int
income float32
} stu := student{"Akansha", 17,
40000.565} show_value(stu)
}
```

Output:

reflect.Value

*reflect.rtype

Interface value is: {Akansha 17 40000.566}

Interface value type is: struct **To modify a reflection object, the value must be settable** On getting the value of a variable with the use of the ValueOf function, it returns the value of type The third law says that to assign a value to reflect.Value type variable, the value must be of reflect.Value type. If it is not of the same type, it will show panic.

Example: package
```
main import
("fmt"
"reflect"

)

func main(){ var str
string = "Hello" val :=
reflect.ValueOf(str)
fmt.Println(val)
val.SetString("World
") // will throw panic
}
```

Output:

panic: reflect: reflect.Value.SetString using unaddressable value.

In the example given above, we cannot set the value for type reflect.Value as World is not addressable. To get rid of such issues, we can first check if a variable is settable or not by using the function

Example: package
main import
("fmt"
"reflect"

)

```
func main(){ var str
string = "Hello" val :=
reflect.ValueOf(str)
fmt.Println(val)
fmt.Println(val.CanSet())
}
```

Output:
Hello false

Conclusion: Mastering Error Handling and Reflection in Go

Error handling and reflection are essential concepts that distinguish Go from many other programming languages, playing a crucial role in creating reliable, maintainable, and flexible software. Both of these mechanisms help developers write clean, robust code, but they approach their goals from different angles.

1. Error Handling: A Paradigm of Simplicity and Explicitness

Go's approach to error handling emphasizes simplicity, clarity, and explicit control over how errors are managed. By avoiding the use of exceptions, which are common in many languages like Java, Python, and C++, Go encourages developers to handle errors as they occur. This means that every function call has the potential to return an error, which must be explicitly checked and addressed by the developer. This design choice has several advantages:

- **Enhanced Code Clarity**: Since errors are treated as regular values, it's clear when and where errors may occur, and how they should be handled. Developers can see the possible failure points and make decisions on error recovery right away.

- **Encouragement of Robust Code**: The practice of checking errors immediately after they are returned helps ensure that developers don't inadvertently ignore potential issues. This habit results in more reliable and stable software because problems are identified and managed proactively.

- **Improved Debugging and Maintenance**: Handling errors close to their source simplifies debugging. Error messages are created where errors happen, so the context is fresh, and the issue can be pinpointed quickly. This helps reduce the time spent troubleshooting unexpected crashes or failures.

- **Error Wrapping for Better Context**: With the introduction of error wrapping, Go made it easier to keep track of errors across multiple function calls. When errors propagate through a series of function calls, wrapping them preserves the original context, providing better insight into the root cause of the problem.

However, while Go's approach promotes a culture of explicit error handling, it also comes with some trade-offs. For example, it can lead to verbose code, especially when functions need to handle multiple potential errors. Developers must strike a balance between verbosity and simplicity, often using helper functions or structuring their code in a way that reduces repetitive error-checking patterns.

2. Reflection: Empowering Flexibility and Dynamism

Reflection in Go is a powerful tool that enables developers to write more generic and dynamic code. Through the reflect package, developers can inspect and modify variables, discover types, and even interact with unknown data structures. This capability opens the door to several advanced programming patterns:

- **Dynamic Data Processing**: Reflection makes it possible to write functions that can handle multiple data types without knowing their specifics at compile time. This is particularly useful for frameworks, libraries, or applications that need to interact with data from various sources or handle user-defined types.

- **Custom Serialization/Deserialization**: Reflection enables the dynamic marshaling and unmarshaling of data structures, allowing developers to convert objects to and from formats like JSON, XML, or custom protocols. This makes it easier to integrate Go applications with external systems and APIs.

- **Testing and Automation**: Testing frameworks often use reflection to examine function signatures, validate parameters, and call methods. This allows developers to write more comprehensive tests that adapt to changes in the codebase without extensive manual rework.

- **Developing Frameworks and Middleware**: Reflection is crucial when building reusable frameworks or middleware that need to operate on user-provided data structures or invoke user-defined functions. This flexibility makes Go a solid choice for building modular, extensible software.

Despite its power, reflection comes with its own set of challenges. The use of reflection can lead to code that is harder to read, debug, and maintain. Additionally, reflection incurs a performance cost because it bypasses some of the optimizations available when types are known at compile time. Therefore, it is recommended to use reflection only when there is no alternative that can achieve the same result more simply.

3. Best Practices for Error Handling and Reflection

To make the most of Go's error handling and reflection capabilities, developers should follow certain best practices:

- **For Error Handling**:

- **Handle errors immediately**: Check for errors as soon as they occur, and don't ignore them. If necessary, log the error or return it to the caller for further handling.

- **Use descriptive error messages**: Ensure that error messages are informative and provide enough context to diagnose the problem quickly.

- **Create custom error types**: When building more complex applications, use custom error types to provide additional context about errors. This makes it easier to handle specific errors differently and helps in debugging.

- **Take advantage of error wrapping**: Use error wrapping to propagate errors with context, allowing the original error message to be preserved while adding more detail.

- **For Reflection**:

  - **Use reflection sparingly**: Only resort to reflection when absolutely necessary, as it can make code harder to understand and maintain.

  - **Prefer concrete types**: Whenever possible, work with concrete types instead of relying on reflection. This allows Go's compiler to optimize the code and makes it easier to follow.

  - **Be mindful of performance**: Reflection is generally slower than working with known types because it involves extra checks and lookups. Measure the performance impact of reflection-based solutions to ensure they are acceptable.

  - **Document reflective code**: Since reflective code can be challenging to understand, always provide clear documentation to explain how and why reflection is being used. This will help other developers (and your future self) understand the intent and maintain the code more easily.

4. The Future of Error Handling and Reflection in Go

Go has evolved significantly since its inception, and error handling and reflection are two areas that have seen important updates. With the language's commitment to backward compatibility, changes are introduced thoughtfully, without disrupting existing codebases. Future versions of Go may continue to refine these areas, making error handling even more robust and reflection more efficient and user-friendly.

- **Potential Enhancements in Error Handling**: Future versions of Go could introduce more sophisticated error-handling mechanisms, such as built-in helpers for common error patterns, improved error propagation, or even new language features that simplify the verbosity often associated with error checking.

- **Evolving Reflection Mechanisms**: Reflection could also see improvements, such as optimizations to reduce performance overhead or new features that make it easier to work with generics. The recent addition of generics in Go 1.18 might open new avenues for reducing the reliance on reflection, providing type-safe solutions that achieve similar flexibility.

5. Bridging Error Handling and Reflection: Real-World Use Cases

In real-world applications, error handling and reflection often intersect. Consider scenarios like data validation, where an application processes inputs from multiple sources. Using reflection, a program can dynamically inspect the inputs and check for validity, but each validation step might result in an error that needs to be captured and managed. By combining Go's robust error-handling capabilities with reflection, developers can write generic functions that adapt to different data structures, handle errors gracefully, and provide useful feedback.

Another example is in building libraries that work with external plugins or modules. Such libraries might not know the structure of the plugins they interact with until runtime. Reflection allows the library to inspect and interact with the plugins, while detailed error handling ensures that any issues encountered during interaction are caught and reported, providing a smooth user experience.

6. Conclusion: A Language for the Pragmatic Developer

Go's emphasis on pragmatic, straightforward programming is reflected in its error-handling model and support for reflection. By treating errors as first-class values, Go encourages developers to write clean, maintainable code that handles failures gracefully. Meanwhile, the flexibility offered by reflection enables the creation of dynamic, reusable components that can adapt to a variety of scenarios.

However, the true mastery of these concepts lies in understanding when and how to use them effectively. For error handling, this means writing clear, informative error messages and thinking carefully about the flow of error propagation. For reflection, it involves striking a balance between flexibility and simplicity, ensuring that code remains performant and easy to understand.

Go's approach to error handling and reflection serves as a testament to its design philosophy: simplicity, clarity, and efficiency. As the language continues to grow and evolve, developers who grasp these core principles will be well-equipped to build robust, scalable, and high-performance software. The combination of these tools provides Go developers with the ability to write code that is not only functional but also resilient, maintainable, and capable of gracefully handling the complexities of real-world applications.

8. Go: Structs and Interfaces

Introduction

Go, also known as Golang, is a statically typed, compiled programming language known for its simplicity, concurrency, and efficiency. Among its core features, structs and interfaces are pivotal for understanding data structures and polymorphic behavior. This introduction will delve into what structs and interfaces are, how they work, and their practical uses in Go.

Structs in Go

What is a Struct?

A struct in Go is a composite data type that groups together variables under a single name. Each variable in a struct is called a field, and these fields can be of different data types. Structs allow you to create complex data structures by combining simpler ones.

For instance, you can represent a Person struct with fields for name, age, and address:

```
type Person struct {
    Name    string
    Age     int
    Address string
}
```

Creating and Initializing Structs

To use a struct, you must declare a variable of the struct type and initialize it. Structs can be initialized in multiple ways:

Named Fields Initialization:

```
p1 := Person{Name: "Alice", Age: 30, Address: "123 Go Lane"}
```

Order-Based Initialization:

```
p2 := Person{"Bob", 25, "456 Gopher Street"}
```

Zero Value Initialization:

```
var p3 Person // All fields will be set to their zero values
```

Accessing and Modifying Struct Fields

You can access or modify struct fields using the dot (.) notation:

```
p1.Age = 31 // Modify field
```

```
fmt.Println(p1.Name) // Access field
```

Embedded Structs

Go supports embedding, allowing one struct to be included within another. This provides a way to compose structs, and the embedded struct's fields and methods can be accessed directly:

```go
type Employee struct {

    Person // Embedded struct

    JobTitle string

    Salary   float64

}

e := Employee{

    Person: Person{Name: "Charlie", Age: 28, Address: "789 Go Blvd"},

    JobTitle: "Software Engineer",

    Salary:   75000,

}

fmt.Println(e.Name) // Direct access to embedded fields
```

Struct Methods

Methods can be associated with structs. In Go, methods are functions with a receiver. The receiver can be a value or a pointer of the struct type:

```go
func (p Person) Greet() string {

    return "Hello, my name is " + p.Name

}
```

Pointers to Structs

Using pointers to structs is crucial for modifying struct data without copying it. When you pass a struct to a function, it is copied by value. If you want to modify the original struct, pass a pointer:

```go
func UpdateAddress(p *Person, newAddress string) {

    p.Address = newAddress

}

p := Person{Name: "Dana", Age: 40}

UpdateAddress(&p, "999 Gopher Avenue")
```

```
fmt.Println(p.Address) // Output: 999 Gopher Avenue
```

Summary of Structs

Structs in Go provide a flexible and efficient way to organize data. They support nesting, pointers, and methods, making them essential for building robust applications.

Interfaces in Go

What is an Interface?

An interface in Go is a type that defines a set of method signatures. Unlike structs, interfaces do not hold data themselves. Instead, they specify a set of methods that a type must implement to be considered as satisfying the interface.

For example, consider the following interface:

```
type Greeter interface {

    Greet() string

}
```

Any type that implements the Greet() method automatically satisfies the Greeter interface.

Defining and Implementing Interfaces

Let's define a struct that implements the Greeter interface:

```
type Robot struct {

    ID   int

    Name string

}
func (r Robot) Greet() string {

    return "Beep boop, I am " + r.Name

}
```

Now, a Robot can be used wherever a Greeter is expected:

```
var g Greeter

g = Robot{ID: 101, Name: "Robo"}

fmt.Println(g.Greet()) // Output: Beep boop, I am Robo
```

Interfaces as Contracts

Interfaces in Go act as contracts. When a type satisfies an interface, it guarantees that it has implemented all the methods declared by the interface. This promotes loose coupling and polymorphism.

For instance, consider the following example:

```
type Notifier interface {

    Notify() string

}

type Email struct {

    Address string

}

func (e Email) Notify() string {

    return "Sending email to " + e.Address

}

type SMS struct {

    Number string

}

func (s SMS) Notify() string {

    return "Sending SMS to " + s.Number

}

func SendNotification(n Notifier) {

    fmt.Println(n.Notify())

}

SendNotification(Email{Address: "example@mail.com"})

SendNotification(SMS{Number: "+1234567890"})
```

This demonstrates how different types (Email and SMS) can implement the same interface, allowing the SendNotification function to accept both types.

Empty Interfaces

The empty interface (interface {}) is a special type of interface that has no methods. Since all types implement at least zero methods, all types satisfy the empty interface. This can be used to write generic code:

```
func PrintAnything(val interface{}) {

    fmt.Println(val)
```

```
}
PrintAnything(42)

PrintAnything("Hello, Go!")
```

While this provides flexibility, it does not have type safety, so use it carefully.

Structs and Interfaces Together

Combining structs and interfaces opens up powerful design patterns. For example, consider a program that logs different types of messages:

```go
type Logger interface {
    Log(message string)
}
type ConsoleLogger struct{}
func (c ConsoleLogger) Log(message string) {
    fmt.Println("Console:", message)
}
type FileLogger struct {
    FilePath string
}
func (f FileLogger) Log(message string) {
    // Code to write to a file at f.FilePath
    fmt.Println("File:", message)
}
func main() {
    var logger Logger
    logger = ConsoleLogger{}
    logger.Log("This is a console log.")
    logger = FileLogger{FilePath: "/var/log/app.log"}
    logger.Log("This is a file log.")
}
```

Practical Uses of Structs and Interfaces

Structs for Data Modeling

Structs are ideal for data modeling, representing complex entities in your application. For example, structuring responses from web APIs, handling user information, or organizing configurations.

Interfaces for Abstraction

Interfaces abstract behavior, allowing your application to swap out concrete implementations. For instance, if you need to change a logging mechanism from console logging to file logging, you can do this without altering the core application logic.

Dependency Injection with Interfaces

Interfaces enable dependency injection, a technique for achieving decoupled, testable code. By passing interface types as parameters, you can inject different implementations during runtime or testing:

```go
type Database interface {

    Connect() error

}

type MySQL struct{}

type PostgreSQL struct{}

func (db MySQL) Connect() error {

    fmt.Println("Connected to MySQL")

    return nil

}

func (db PostgreSQL) Connect() error {

    fmt.Println("Connected to PostgreSQL")

    return nil

}

func SetupDatabase(db Database) {

    db.Connect()

}

func main() {

    SetupDatabase(MySQL{})

    SetupDatabase(PostgreSQL{})

}
```

This example showcases how different databases can be swapped out seamlessly by satisfying the Database interface.

GoLang Structures

In GoLang, a structure or struct is a user-defined type that allows us to group/combine elements of possibly diverse kinds into a single type. A struct can represent any real-world thing with a collection of properties/ fields. In general, this idea is related to classes in object-oriented programming. It is a lightweight class that does not support inheritance but supports composition.

An address, for example, includes a name, street, city, state, and Pin code. As seen below, it makes logical to combine all three characteristics into a single structure address.

Declaring a structure:

type Address struct {name string   street no string   city string

state string Pin-code int

}

The type keyword adds a new type in the preceding code. It is followed by the type name (Address) and the keyword struct, indicating that we define a struct. Within the curly braces, the struct has a list of several fields. Each field has a name as well as a kind.

Nota bene: We may also make them more compact by combining many fields of the same kind, as demonstrated in the following example:

type Address struct {
    name, streetno, city, state string
    Pin-code int
}

To define a structure:

The syntax for declaring a structure is stated below:

var x Address

The above code creates a variable of type Address, which is initially initialized to zero. Zero indicates that all fields have been set to their corresponding zero value for a struct. So, the fields name, street no., city, and state are all set to " " and the field Pin-code is set to 0.

We may also use a struct literal to initialize a variable of a struct type, as illustrated below:

var x = Address{"Abishek", "PritamNagar", "Delhi", "Noida", 293616}

Note:

- Remember to pass the field values in the same order specified in the struct. Furthermore, it is difficult to use the approach above to initialize only a subset of fields.

- Go also provides the name: value syntax (the order of fields is irrelevant when using this syntax). As a result, we can only initialize a subset of the fields. All uninitialized fields are set to their default value of zero.

Example:

```
var x = Address{Name:"Abhishek", streetno:"PritamNagar", state:"Delhi", Pin-code:
293616} //city:""
// Program to show how to
// declare and define struct
package main import "fmt"
// Defining struct type type Address struct {    Name    string
city    string    Pin-code int
}
func main() {
   // Declaring variable of a 'struct' type
   // All the struct fields are initialized with
their zero value    var x Address    fmt.Println(x)
   // Declaring and initializing a
   // struct using struct literal    x1 := Address{"Anisha", "Delhi", 3663272}
   fmt.Println("Address1: ", x1)
   // Naming fields while
   // initializing a struct
 x2 := Address{Name: "Abhishek", city: "Balli", Pincode: 287011}
   fmt.Println("Address2: ", x2)
   // Uninitialized fields are set to
   // their corresponding zerovalue    x3 := Address{Name: "Amritsar"}
fmt.Println("Address3: ", x3) }
```

How Can We Get to Struct Fields?

We must use the dot (.) operator to access specific fields of a struct.

Example:

```
// program to show how to
// access fields of struct
package main import "fmt"
  // defining struct type Car struct {
   Name, Modelno, Color string
   WeightinKg       float64
}
// the main Function func main() {
   x := Car{Name: "BMW", Modelno: "BTC2",
       Color: "Black", WeightinKg: 1720}
   // Accessing the struct fields
```

```
   // using dot operator     fmt.Println("Car Name: ", x.Name)
fmt.Println("Car Color: ", x.Color)
   // Assigning a new value
   // to a struct field
   x.Color = "White"
   // Displaying result     fmt.Println("Car: ", x) }
```

Pointers to a Struct

Pointers are variables in the Go programming language, or GoLang used to hold the memory address of another variable. As seen in the following example, we can also build a reference to a struct:

```
// Program to illustrate // pointer to the struct
package main import "fmt"
// defining structure type Employee struct {     first-name, last-name
string
   age, salary int
}
func main() {
   // passing address of the struct variable
   // empy is a pointer to the Employee struct     empy := &Employee{"Samrit", "Anders",
35, 7000}     // (*empy).first-name is the syntax to access     // the first-name field of the
empy struct     fmt.Println("First Name:", (*empy).first-name)
   fmt.Println("Age:", (*empy).age) }
```

We may use empy.first-name instead of the explicit dereference (*empy) in GoLang. To access the first-name field, type first-name. The following is an example to demonstrate this:

```
// Program to illustrate the
// pointer to the struct
package main
 import "fmt"
// Defining structure type Employee struct {     first-name, last-name
string     age, salary   int
}
// the main Function func main() {
   // taking pointer to the struct
   empy := &Employee{"Samrit", "Anders", 59, 7000}
   // empy.first-name is used to access
   // the field first-name
   fmt.Println("First Name: ", empy.first-name)
   fmt.Println("Age: ", empy.age) }
```

GoLang's Nested Structure

A structure, also known as a struct in GoLang, is a user-defined type that allows us to group items of multiple kinds into a single unit. A struct can represent any real-world thing with various attributes or fields. The Go programming language supports nested structures. A nested structure is a structure that is the field of another structure. A nested structure is a structure that is enclosed within another structure.

Syntax:

type structname1 struct{
// Fields }
type structname2 struct{ variablename structname1 }

Let's look at a few instances to assist us to understand this concept:

First example:

```
// Program to illustrate the
// nested structure package main import "fmt"
// Creating the structure type Author struct {    name   string
branchno  string    year  int
}
// Creating the nested structure
type HR struct {
   // structure as field     details Author
}
func main() {
   // Initializing fields
   // of the structure     results := HR{
      details: Author{"Sonali", "EDE", 2014},
   }
   // Display values
   fmt.Println("\nDetails of the Author")
   fmt.Println(results) }
```

Second example:

```
// Program to illustrate the
// nested structure package main import "fmt"
// Creating the structure type Students struct {    name   string
branchno  string    year  int
   }
   // Creating the nested structure type Teachers struct {    name
   string    subject string    expr   int    details Students
   }
   func main() {
```

```go
    // Initializing fields
    // of the structure     results := Teachers{        name:
"Sunita",      subject: "PHP",      expr:    2,
      details: Student{"Rahil", "CDE", 4},
    }
    // Display the values
    fmt.Println("Details of the Teachers")    fmt.Println("Teacher's name: ", results.name)
    fmt.Println("Subject: ", results.subject)    fmt.Println("Experience: ", results.exp)
    fmt.Println("\nDetails of Students")    fmt.Println("Student's name: ", results.
    details.name)
      fmt.Println("Student's branch name: ",
    results.details.branch)
      fmt.Println("Year: ", results.details.year) }
```

GoLang's Anonymous Structure and Field

A structure, also known as a struct in GoLang, is a user-defined type that allows us to organize items of multiple kinds into a single unit. A struct can represent any real-world thing with a collection of attributes or fields.

Anonymous Structure

In the Go programming language, we may build an anonymous structure. An anonymous building does not have a name. It is useful to create a structure that will only use once. Use the following syntax to create an anonymous structure:

```go
variablename := struct{
// fields
}{// Fieldvalues}
```

Let us illustrate this notion with an example:

```go
// Program to illustrate
// the concept of anonymous structure
package main import "fmt"
// the main function func main() {
  // Creating, initializing
  // anonymous structure
  Elements := struct {        name    string        branch    string
language  string
    Particles int
  }{
    name: "Pihu", branch: "ECE", language:  "C#", Particles: 298,
  }
  // Display anonymous structure    fmt.Println(Element) }
```

Anonymous Fields

We may build anonymous fields in a Go structure. Anonymous fields do not have a name; instead, we specify the field type, and Go will use the type as the field's name. The structure's anonymous fields may be created using the following syntax:

```
type structname struct{
    int    bool    float64
}
```

Important Notes:

• It is not permitted to create two or more fields of the same type in a structure, as seen below:

```
type students struct{
int int }
```

If we attempt to do so, the compiler will generate an error.

• It is permissible to combine anonymous and named fields, as demonstrated below:

```
type students struct{
 name int  prices int  string }
```

Below is an example to explain the anonymous field concept:

```
// Program to illustrate
// the concept of anonymous structure
package main import "fmt"
// Creating structure
// with the anonymous fields type students struct {
    int    string    float64
}
// the main function func main() {
    // Assigning the values to anonymous
    // fields of the students structure    value := students{143, "Sud", 8200.21}
    // Display values of the fields
    fmt.Println("Enrollment number : ", value.int)    fmt.Println("Student name : ",
value.string)    fmt.Println("Package price : ", value.float64)
}
```

GoLang Methods

Methods for Go language support Go methods are identical to Go functions with one exception: the method includes a receiver parameter. The method can access the receiver's properties with the aid of the receiver argument. The receiver can be of either struct or non-struct type in this case. When we write code, the receiver and receiver type must be in the same package. Furthermore, we are not permitted to write a method whose receiver type is already specified in another package, including inbuilt types such as int, string, and so on. If we attempt to do so, the compiler will generate an error.

Syntax:

```
func(receiver-name Type) method-name(parameter-
list)(return-type){
// Code }
```

Within the method, the receiver may access.

Method with the Struct Type Receiver

We may construct a method whose receiver is of the struct type in the Go programming language. This receiver is available within the method, as seen in the following example:

```
// Program to illustrate
// the method with struct type receiver
package main import "fmt"
// the author structure type author struct {     name
string    branch    string    particles int    salary    int
}
// Method with a receiver of author type
func (x author) show() {
    fmt.Println("Author's Name: ", x.name)    fmt.Println("Branch Name: ", x.branch)
fmt.Println("Published articles: ", x.particles)    fmt.Println("Salary: ", x.salary)
}
// the main function func main() {
    // Initializing values
    // of the author structure
    rest := author{     name:    "Monika",    branch:
"CDE",    particles: 204,    salary:   37000,
    }
    // Calling method    rest.show() }
```

Method with the Non-Struct Type Receiver

In Go, we may define a method with a non-struct type receiver as long as the type and method declarations are in the same package. If they are present in many packages, such as int, string, and so on, the compiler will generate an error because they are defined in multiple packages.

Example:

```
// Program to illustrate method
// with the non-struct type receiver
package main import "fmt"
// Type definition type data int
// Defining method with
// the non-struct type receiver func (c1 data) multiply(c2 data) data {
    return c1 * c2
```

```
}
/*
// if you try to run this code,
// then compiler will throw an error func(c1 int)multiply(c2 int)int{
return c1 * c2
}
*/
```
// Main function func main() {   value1 := data(43)   value2 := data(26)   rest :=
value1.multiply(value2)   fmt.Println("Final result: ", rest) }

Methods with the Pointer Receiver

A method with a pointer recipient is permitted in the Go programming language. If a modification is made to the method using a pointer receiver, it will be reflected in the caller, which is not feasible with value receiver methods.

Syntax:

```
func (p *Type) method-name(...Type) Type {
// Code }
```

Example:

```
// Program to illustrate pointer receiver
package main import "fmt"
// the author structure type author struct {    name
string    branch   string    particles int
}
// Method with a receiver of the author type func (x *author) show(abranch string) {
   (*x).branch = abranch }
// the main function func main() {
   // Initializing values
   // of the author structure
   rest := author{
      name:  "Shona",       branch: "CDE",
   }
   fmt.Println("Author's name: ", rest.name)    fmt.Println("Branch Name(Before): ", rest.
branch)
   // Creating pointer    p := &rest
   // Calling show method
   p.show("ERE")
   fmt.Println("Author's name: ", rest.name)    fmt.Println("Branch Name(After): ", rest.
branch) }
```

Method Can Accept Both the Pointer and the Value

As we all know, when a function has a value argument, it will only take the values of the parameter, and if we try to give a pointer to a value function, it will reject it, and vice versa. On the other hand, a Go method can accept both a value and a pointer, depending on whether it is specified with a pointer or a value receiver. As illustrated in the following example:

```
// Program to illustrate how
// the method can accept pointer and value
package main  import "fmt"
// Author structure type author struct {     name   string
branch string
}
// Method with pointer
// receiver of author type
func (x *author) show_1(abranch string) {
   (*x).branch = abranch }
 // Method with a value
// receiver of author type func (x author) show_2() {
   x.name = "Gautam"
   fmt.Println("Author's name(Before) : ", x.name)
}
// the main function func main() {

   // Initializing values
   // of the author structure
   rest := author{     name: "Sonika",      branch: "CSA",    }
fmt.Println("Branch Name(Before): ", rest. branch)
   // Calling show_1 method
   // (pointer method) with the value
   res.show_1("ECE")    fmt.Println("Branch Name(After): ", rest. branch)
   // Calling show_2 method
   // (value method) with a pointer
   (&rest).show_2()
   fmt.Println("Author's name(After): ", res.namet) }
```

Difference between the Method and the Function

Method	Function
It includes a receiver.	It does not include a receiver.
In the program, methods with the same name but various kinds might define.	The program does not define functions with the same name but distinct types.
It cannot use to create a first-order object.	It may be used as a first-order object and can be passed.

Interfaces

The interfaces of the Go language differ from those of other languages. The interface is a special type in Go used to express a set of one or more method signatures. The interface is abstract, thus we cannot make an instance of it. However, we are permitted to establish an interface type variable that may be assigned with a concrete type value that has the methods required by the interface. In other words, the interface is both a set of methods and a custom type.

How Do We Make an Interface?
In the Go programming language, we can define an interface with the following syntax:

type interfacename interface{
// Method-signatures }

   Example:
   // Creating interface type myinterface interface{

   // Methods func1() int func2() float64 }

The interface name is enclosed by the type and interface keywords, while curly brackets enclose the method signatures.

How to Implement Interfaces

In order to implement an interface in the Go language, all of the methods specified in the interface must implement. The interfaces for the Go programming language are implemented implicitly. And, unlike other languages, it lacks a specific term for implementing an interface. As illustrated in the following   example.

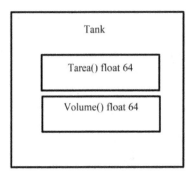

   Example:
   // Program illustrates how
   // to implement interface
   package main
   import "fmt"
   // Creating interface type tank interface {
      // Methods

```go
    Tarea() float64
    Volume() float64
}
type myvalue struct {    radius float64    height float64
}
// Implementing methods of t
ank interface
func (m myvalue) Tarea() float64
{
    return 2*m.radius*m.height +        2*3.14*m.radius*m.radius
}
func (m myvalue) Volume() float64
{
    return 3.14 * m.radius * m.radius * m.height
}
// the main Method func main() {

    // Accessing elements of the
    // tank interface    var tk tank    tk = myvalue{10, 14}
    fmt.Println("The Area of tank :", tk.Tarea())    fmt.Println("The Volume of tank:",
tk.Volume()) }
```

Important Notes:

- The interface's zero value is nil.

- When an interface includes no methods, it is referred to as an empty interface. As a result, all types implement the empty interface.

  Syntax:

  interface{}

- **Interface Types:** There are two types of interfaces: static interfaces and dynamic interfaces. The static type is the interface itself, such as tank in the example below. However, because the interface lacks a static value, it always points to the dynamic values.

  A variable of the interface type contains the value of the type that implements the interface; hence, the value of that type is known as dynamic value, and the type is the dynamic type. It's also referred to as concrete value and concrete type.

Example:

```go
// Program to illustrate concept
// of the dynamic values and types package main import "fmt"
// Creating interface type tank interface {

    // Methods
    Tarea() float64
```

```
    Volume() float64
} func main() {    var tk tank
    fmt.Println("The Value of the tank interface
is: ", tk)    fmt.Printf("The Type of the tank interface is:
%T ", tk) }
```

In the example, we have an interface called a tank. In this example, fmt.Println("The Value of the tank interface is: ", tk) returns the interface's dynamic value, whereas fmt.Printf("The Type of the tank interface is: percent T ", tk) returns the dynamic type, which is nil because the interface does not know who is implementing it.

- **Type Assertions:** A type assertion in Go is an operation performed on the value of an interface. In other words, type assertion is a procedure for extracting the interface's values.

Syntax:

a.(T)

In this case, a is the interface's value or expression, and T is the type, sometimes known as the asserted type. The type assertion is used to determine whether or not the dynamic type of its operand matches the claimed type. If the T is of concrete type, the type assertion verifies that the specified dynamic type of a is equal to the T; if the verification is successful, the type assertion returns the dynamic value of a. If the checking fails, the operation will fail. If T is an interface type, the type assertion tests if the supplied dynamic type of a satisfies T; if the checking succeeds, the dynamic value is not extracted.

Example:

// Program to illustrate the

// type assertion package main import "fmt"

func myfun(a interface{}) {

    // Extracting the value of a   vals := a.(string)   fmt.Println("Value: ", vals)

} func main() {   var val interface {   } = "Helloeveryone"   myfun(vals) }

If we alter the val:= a.(string) command in the above example to val:= a.(int), the program panics. To address this issue, we apply the following syntax:

value, ok := a.(T)

If the type of the a is T, then the value includes the dynamic value of the a, and ok is set to true. And if the type of the a is not equal to T, then ok is set to false, and value contains a value of zero, and the program does not panic. As shown in the following program:

```
// Program to illustrate the type assertion
package main import "fmt" func myfun(a interface{}) {    value,
ok := a.(float64)    fmt.Println(value, ok)
```

```
} func main() {    var a1 interface {
   } = 97.09    myfun(a1)    var a2 interface { } =
"Helloeveryone"    myfun(a2) }
```

- **Type Switch:** A type switch in a Go interface compares the concrete type of an interface to the numerous types provided in the case statements. It is identical to type assertion with one exception: case specifies types rather than values. A type can also compare to an interface type. As illustrated in the following example:

```
// Program to illustrate the type switch
package main import "fmt"
func myfun(a interface{}) {    // Using the type switch    switch
a.(type) {    case int:
    fmt.Println("Type: int, Value:", a.(int))    case string:
    fmt.Println("\nType: string, Value: ",
a.(string))    case float64:
    fmt.Println("\nType: float64, Value: ",
a.(float64))    default:
    fmt.Println("\nType not found")
  }
}
// the main method func main() {    myfun("Helloeveryone")
   myfun(59.9)    myfun(true)
}
```

- **Use of Interface:** We may use interface when we want to pass multiple sorts of arguments to methods or functions such as the Println () function. When many types implement the same interface, we may also use interface.

Why Go Interfaces Are Great

An "interface" in object-oriented programming describes what an object can accomplish. Typically, this takes the form of a list of methods that an object to have is required. C #, Java supports interfaces, and the Go programming language, although Go's interfaces are notably simple to use.

We don't have to declare that a Go type (which functions similarly to a "class" in other languages) implements an interface, as we would in C# or Java. We just declare the interface, and then any type that has those methods may be used anywhere that interface is required.

Redundant Functions

Assume we have a pet package (a "package" is equivalent to a "library" in other languages) containing Dogs and Cats types. A Dogs has the Fetch technique, a Cats has the Purr method, and both dogs and cats have the Walk and Sit methods.

```go
package pets import "fmt" type Dogs struct {
Name  string
    Breed string
}
func (d Dogs) Walk() {
    fmt.Println(d.Name, "walks across room")
}
func (d Dogs) Sit() {
    fmt.Println(d.Name, "sits down")
}
func (d Dogs) Fetch() {
    fmt.Println(d.Name, "fetches toy")
}
type Cats struct {    Name  string
    Breed string
}
func (c Cats) Walk() {
    fmt.Println(c.Name, "walks across room")
}
func (c Cats) Sit() {
    fmt.Println(c.Name, "sits down")
}
func (c Cats) Purr() {    fmt.Println(c.Name, "purrs") }
```

Now, let's create an example. Go program that demonstrates what the Dog and Cat types are capable of. We'll create a DemoDog function that takes a Dog and calls the Walk and Sit methods on it. Then, we'll create a DemoCat function that accomplishes the same thing for cats.

```go
package main import "pets"
func DemoDogs(dog pets.Dogs) {
    dog.Walk()    dog.Sit()
}
func DemoCat(cat pets.Cats) {
    cat.Walk()    cat.Sit()
} func main() {
    dog := pets.Dogs{"Fido", "Terrier"}    cat := pets.Cats{"Fluffy",
"Siamese"}    DemoDogs(dog)    // call outputs:
    // Fido walks across room
    // Fido sit down    DemoCat(cat)    // call outputs:
    // Fluffy walks across room
    // Fluffy sit down }
```

Unfortunately, the DemoDogs and DemoCats routines are identical, except that one takes a Dogs and the other takes Cats. Because we could alter one function but fail to update the other, repeating code like that increases the risk of inconsistency. It would be perfect if we could get rid of DemoCats and only give Cats to DemoDogs; however, this would lead to an error:

```
DemoDogs(cat)
// ./demo.go:19: cannot use cat (type pets.Cats)
// as type pets.Dogs in argument to DemoDogs
```

Enter Interface

But we don't have to keep two almost identical functions simply because they take different types. This is precisely the problem that interfaces are created to fulfill.

We'll create a FourLegged interface with Walk and Sit methods for all kinds. Then, instead of the DemoDogs and DemoCats functions, we'll replace them with a single Demo function that accepts any FourLegged value (whether it's a Dogs or a Cats).

```
package main import "pets" // This interface represents any type that has Walk and Sit
methods. type FourLegged interface {
    Walk()
    Sit()
}
// We can replace DemoDogs and DemoCats
// with this single function. func Demo(animal FourLegged) {
    animal.Walk()    animal.Sit()
} func main() {
    dog := pets.Dogs{"Rido", "Ferrier"}    cat := pets.Cats{"Pluffy",
"Diames"}    Demo(dog)    // Above call (again) outputs:
    // Fido walks across room
    // Fido sit down    Demo(cat)    // The above call (again) outputs:
    // Fluffy walks across room
    // Fluffy sit down }
```

Embedding Interfaces

The interface in Go is a collection of method signatures and a type, which means you may construct a variable of an interface type. Although the Go language does not enable inheritance, the Go interface does. In embedding, an interface can embed other interfaces or their method signatures, with the same results as seen in first and second examples. We may embed an unlimited number of interfaces in a single interface. And when we embed other interfaces in an interface, if we alter the methods of the interfaces, the changes will be reflected in the embedded interface as well, as illustrated in Example 3.

Syntax:

```
type interfacename1 interface {
    Method1()
}
type interfacename2 interface {
    Method2()
}
type finalinterfacename interface {
```

interfacename1   interfacename2 }

First example:

```
// Program to illustrate the concept
// of embedding interfaces
package main import "fmt" // Interface 1
type AuthorDetail interface {
   details()
}
// Interface 2
type AuthorArticle interface {
   articles()
}
// Interface 3 embedded with the interface 1 and 2
type FinalDetail interface {
   AuthorDetail
AuthorArticle
}


// Structure type author struct {    a_name    string
branch   string   college string   year    int   salary
int    particles int    tarticles int
}

// Implementing the method of
// the interface 1 func (a author) details() {
   fmt.Printf("The Author Name: %s", a.a_name)     fmt.Printf("\nThe Branch: %s and
passing year:
%d",
                       a.branch, a.year)    fmt.Printf("\nThe College Name: %s", a.college)
fmt.Printf("\nThe Salary: %d", a.salary)    fmt.Printf("\nThe Published articles: %d",
a.particle)
}
// Implementing method of the interface 2
func (a author) articles() {
   pendingarticle := a.tarticle - a.particle         fmt.Printf("\nPending  articles:  %d",
pendingarticle)
}
// the main value func main() {
   // Assigning values to the structure
   values := author{       a_name:   "Ricky",       branch:
"Accounts",      college:  "XYZ",       year:    2019,      salary:
40000,      particle: 107,      tarticle: 206,
     }
     // Accessing methods of the interface 1 and 2
```

```go
// Using the FinalDetail interface    var f FinalDetail = values
f.details()
f.articles() }
```

Explanation: As seen in the preceding example, we have three interfaces. Interfaces 1 and 2 are basic interfaces, but interface 3 is an embedded interface containing interfaces 1 and 2. As a result, any changes made in interfaces 1 and 2 will be reflected in interface 3. And interface 3 has access to all of the methods available in interfaces 1 and 2.

Second example:

```go
// Program to illustrate concept of embedding
interfaces package main import "fmt" //
Interface 1
type AuthorDetail interface {
    details()
}
// Interface 2
type AuthorArticle interface {
    article()
}
// Interface 3 embedded with the interface 1 and
2's methods
type FinalDetail interface {
    detail()    article()
}
// Structure type author struct {    a_name    string
branch    string    college    string    year    int
salary    int    particle int    tarticle int
}
  // Implementing method of the interface 1
func (a author) details() {
    fmt.Printf("The Author Name: %s", a.a_name)    fmt.Printf("\nThe Branch: %s and
passing year:
%d", a.branch, a.year)
    fmt.Printf("\nThe College Name: %s",
a.college)
    fmt.Printf("\nThe Salary: %d", a.salary)    fmt.Printf("\nThe Published articles: %d",
a.particle)
}
// Implementing method of the interface 2
func (a author) articles() {
    pendingarticle := a.tarticle - a.particle    fmt.Printf("\nThe Pending articles: %d",
pendingarticle)
}
// the main value func main() {
```

```go
    // Assigning the values to structure
values := author{     a_name:  "Ricky",      branch:
"Accounts",      college: "XYZ",      year:     2019,
salary:   40000,      particle: 107,       tarticle: 206,
    }
    // Accessing the methods
    // of the interface 1 and 2
    // Using the FinalDetail interface    var f FinalDetail = values
    f.detail()
    f.article() }
```

Explanation: As seen in the preceding example, we have three interfaces. Interfaces 1 and 2 are basic interfaces, whereas interface 3 is an embedded interface containing method signatures for interfaces 1 and 2. As a consequence, any modifications made to interfaces 1 and 2's methods will be reflected in interface 3. And interface 3 has access to all of the methods available in interfaces 1 and 2.

Third example:

```go
    // Program to illustrate concept of embedding
    interfaces package main import "fmt" //
    Interface 1
    type AuthorDetail interface {
        detail()
    }
    // Interface 2
    type AuthorArticle interface {
        article()    picked()
    }
    // Interface 3
    // Interface 3 embedded with interface 1's method
    and interface 2
    // And also contain its own method type FinalDetail interface {
        detail()
        AuthorArticle    cdeatil()
    }
    // Structure type author struct {    a_name    string
    branch    string    college string    year      int
    salary    int    particle int    tarticle int    cid      int
    post      string    pick      int
    }
    // Implementing method of the interface 1
func (a author) detail() {
    fmt.Printf("The Author Name: %s", a.a_name)    fmt.Printf("\nThe Branch: %s and
passing year:
%d", a.branch, a.year)
```

```go
    fmt.Printf("\nThe College Name: %s",
a.college)
    fmt.Printf("\nThe Salary: %d", a.salary)    fmt.Printf("\nThe Published articles: %d",
a.particle)
}
// Implementing methods of the interface 2
func (a author) article() {

    pendingarticle := a.tarticle - a.particle    fmt.Printf("\nPending articles: %d",
pendingarticle)
}
func (a author) picked() {
    fmt.Printf("\nThe Total number of picked
articles: %d", a.pick)
}
// Implementing the method of the embedded
interface
func (a author) cdeatil() {    fmt.Printf("\nAuthor Id: %d", a.cid)    fmt.Printf("\nPost:
%s", a.post)
}
// the main value func main() {
    // Assigning values to structure
    values := author{    a_name:  "Ricky",    branch:  "Accounts",
college: "XYZ",    year:  2019,    salary:  40000,    particle: 107,
tarticle: 206,    cid:    3097,    post:    "Content writer",
    pick:    38,
    }
    // Accessing methods
      // of the interface 1 and 2
      // Using the FinalDetails interface    var f FinalDetails = values
      f.detail()
      f.article()
      f.picked()
      f.cdeatil() }
```

Explanation: As seen in the preceding example, we have three interfaces. Interfaces 1 and 2 are basic interfaces, whereas interface 3 is an embedded interface that contains the method signatures of interfaces 1 and 2 and its own method. As an outcome, any modifications made to the methods of interfaces 1 and 2 will be reflected in interface 3. And interface 3 has access to all of the methods in it, including those in interfaces 1, 2, and its own.

Inheritance

One of the most fundamental ideas in object-oriented programming is inheritance, which involves inheriting the properties of the superclass into the base class. Because GoLang does not provide classes, inheritance is accomplished through struct embedding. We cannot directly expand structs, but must instead employ a notion known as composition, in which the struct is used to create additional objects. As a result, there is no inheritance concept in GoLang.

In composition, base structs can be embedded in a child struct, and the base struct's methods can be called directly on the child struct, as demonstrated in the following examples.

First example:

```
// Program to illustrate
// the concept of inheritance
package main import (    "fmt" )
// declaring struct type Comic struct{
    // declaring the struct variable
    Universe string
}
// function to return
// universe of comic
func (comic Comic) ComicUniverse() string {
    // returns the comic universe    return comic.Universe
}
// declaring struct type Marvel struct{       // anonymous field,
    // this is composition where the
    // struct is embedded
    Comic
}
// declaring struct type DC struct{
    // anonymous field
    Comic
}
// the main function func main() {

    // creating instance    cs1 := Marvel{
        // child struct can directly access base
struct variables         Comic{
            Universe: "MCU",
        },    }
    // child struct can directly access base
struct methods    // printing base method using child        fmt.Println("The Universe
is:", cs1.
ComicUniverse())            cs2 := DC{
        Comic{
            Universe : "DC",
        },   }
    // printing base method using the child     fmt.Println("The Universe is:", cs2.
ComicUniverse())
}
```

Multiple inheritance occurs when a child struct has access to various attributes, fields, and methods of more than one base struct. As seen by the following code, the child struct embeds all of the base structs:

Second example:

```go
// Program to illustrate
// the concept of multiple inheritances
package main
 import (    "fmt" )
// declaring first base struct
type first struct{
   // declaring the struct variable
   base_one string
}
// declaring the second base struct
type second struct{
   // declaring the struct variable
   base_two string
}
// function to return first struct variable func (f first) printBase1() string{
   // returns string of first struct
   return f.base_one
}
// function to return second struct variable func (s second) printBase2() string{    //
returns string of first struct
   return s.base_two
}
// child struct which embeds both base structs
type child struct{
   // anonymous fields, struct embedding
   // of multiple structs
   first    second
}
// the main function func main() {
   // declaring instance
   // of child struct    cs1 := child{
      // child struct can directly access base
struct variables       first{
         base_one: "In base struct 1.",
      },      second{
         base_two: "\nIn base struct 2.\n",
      },   }
   // child struct can directly access base
struct methods
   // printing the base method
```

Polymorphism Using Interfaces

The term polymorphism refers to presence of many forms. Polymorphism, in other words, is the ability of a message to be displayed in more than one form. In technical terms, polymorphism refers to the usage of the same method name (but distinct signatures) for multiple types. A lady, for example, might have many characteristics at the same time, for example, a mother, wife, sister, employee, and so forth. As a result, the same individual exhibits diverse behavior in different settings. This is known as polymorphism.

We cannot create polymorphism in Go using classes since Go does not allow classes, but we can achieve it using interfaces. As previously stated, interfaces are implicitly implemented in Go. So, when we establish an interface and other kinds want to implement it, those types utilize the interface with the aid of the interface's methods without knowing the type. A variable of an interface type in an interface can hold any value that implements the interface. In the Go programming language, this characteristic aids interfaces in achieving polymorphism. Let us use an example.

```
// Program to illustrate the
// concept of polymorphism using the interfaces
package main import "fmt" // Interface type
employee interface {    develop() int    name()
string
}
// Structure1 type team1 struct {     totalapp_1 int
name_1    string
}
// Methods of employee interface
// are implemented by team1 structure func (tm1 team1) develop() int {
return tm1.totalapp_1
}
func (tm1 team1) name() string {
   return tm1.name_1
}
// Structure 2 type team2 struct {     totalapp_2 int
name_2    string
}
// Methods of the employee interface are
// implemented by team2 structure func (tm2 team2) develop() int {
return tm2.totalapp_2
}
func (tm2 team2) name() string {
   return tm2.name_2
}
func finaldevelop(i []employee) {
```

```
    totalproject := 0     for _, ele := range i {
        fmt.Printf("\nThe Project environment = %s\n
", ele.name())
        fmt.Printf("The Total number of project %d\n
", ele.develop())
        totalproject += ele.develop()
    }
    fmt.Printf("\nThe Total projects completed by "+
        "the company = %d", totalproject) }
 // The main function func main() {
    res1 := team1{totalapp_1: 20,
        name_1: "IOS"}     res2 := team2{totalapp_2: 35,        name_2:
"Android"}     final := []employee{res1, res2}
    finaldevelop(final) }
```

Explanation: In the above example, an interface name is used as an employee. This interface has two methods: develop() and name(). The develop() method returns the total number of projects, while the name() method returns the name of environment in which they are created.

We now have two structures, team1 and team2. totalapp_1 int, name_1 string, totalapp_2 int, and name_2 string are the fields in both structures. These structures (team1 and team2) are now implementing the employee interface methods.

Following that, we write a finaldevelop() method that returns the total number of projects created by the organization. It takes an argument of a slice of employee interfaces. It estimates the total number of projects generated by the firm by iterating through the slice and calling the develop() function on each of its members. It also shows the project's environment by invoking the name() function. Different develop() and name() methods will be invoked depending on the concrete type of the employee interface. So, we accomplished polymorphism in the finaldevelop() method.

If you add another team to this program that implements an employee interface, the finaldevelop() function will determine the total number of projects created by the firm without regard for polymorphism.
This chapter covered structs definition, declaration of struct, nested and anonymous structure. We also covered method with the struct and non-type receiver. Moreover, we learned about interfaces, polymorphism, and inheritance.

Conclusion

Structs and interfaces are two of the most essential components of Go, providing a solid foundation for building scalable, efficient, and maintainable software. Their simplicity and flexibility make them the perfect tools for structuring data and implementing polymorphic behavior, offering developers the ability to create clean and modular code that adheres to the principles of software design.

Why Structs Matter

Structs in Go are not just simple containers for grouping data; they embody the principles of encapsulation and modularity. By allowing different types of data to be grouped together under a single name, structs make it possible to model real-world entities in a straightforward yet flexible manner. Whether you are working on web applications, system tools, or networking programs, structs help keep code organized by clearly defining how data should be structured.

For instance, if you are building a web application, a struct can model a user profile, encapsulating details like name, email, and address. When developing system tools, structs might be used to store configurations, making it easy to read, modify, and pass configuration data throughout the application. This structured approach is a significant step up from more primitive ways of handling data, such as using multiple variables or arrays, which can lead to convoluted and hard-to-maintain code.

Moreover, by combining structs with methods, Go provides a simple yet powerful mechanism for creating objects. While Go does not follow the classical object-oriented programming paradigm, its approach allows methods to be associated with structs, making it possible to define behaviors related to the data they encapsulate. This results in more readable, understandable, and reusable code.

Benefits of Interfaces

Interfaces, on the other hand, bring another layer of power by enabling polymorphic behavior. In traditional programming languages, polymorphism is often achieved through class inheritance. However, Go takes a different approach. Instead of requiring a strict inheritance hierarchy, it allows types to satisfy interfaces simply by implementing the necessary methods. This enables Go to avoid many of the pitfalls of deep inheritance chains, which can lead to code that is difficult to understand and maintain.

Go's interfaces act as contracts, ensuring that any type implementing an interface must have all the required methods. This makes it easier to reason about code and understand how different parts of a program interact. By programming to an interface rather than a specific implementation, developers can write flexible and adaptable code that can be easily extended.

For example, in a system that processes payments, an interface called Payment Processor could be defined. Any struct that implements the methods defined in Payment Processor—such as Process Payment—can be used as a payment processor. This means that you can have different implementations for credit cards, PayPal, and cryptocurrency payments, all under a unified interface. If a new payment method needs to be added, it is as simple as writing a new struct that implements the Payment Processor interface, without altering existing code.

The Power of Combining Structs and Interfaces

The real strength of Go emerges when combining structs and interfaces, allowing developers to build software that is decoupled, modular, and easy to test. Structs provide a way to manage and encapsulate data, while interfaces define behavior. This combination is especially powerful in creating systems where behavior needs to vary based on the data being processed or external factors.

In a practical scenario, consider building a logging system. Structs can define different logging mechanisms, such as Console Logger, File Logger, or Database Logger. By implementing a Logger interface, which specifies methods like Log Info or Log Error, these structs can provide different ways to handle logging, but the rest of the application does not need to know or care about the specifics. This approach makes it easy to switch from logging to a console output to writing logs to a file or even storing logs in a database, without rewriting the core logic of the application.

This decoupling also makes unit testing more straightforward. By using interfaces, developers can create mock implementations for testing. For instance, if your code depends on a Database interface, you can write a Mock Database that mimics the behavior of the actual database, allowing you to test how your code interacts with a database without needing an actual connection. This kind of flexibility is invaluable in a robust software development process.

Real-World Use Cases and Patterns

In real-world applications, structs and interfaces are used in various design patterns that enhance code structure and reusability:

1. **Adapter Pattern:** This pattern is used to translate one interface to another. For example, if you have an old API that outputs data in a specific format, but your new system expects a different format, you can write an adapter struct that implements the expected interface and translates between the old and new formats. This allows you to integrate older systems without altering their code.

2. **Decorator Pattern:** By defining an interface and implementing various decorator structs, you can dynamically add behaviors to objects. For example, you might have a basic Notificator interface and then add structs like Email Decorator or SMS Decorator that wrap the original notifier and extend its functionality.

3. **Strategy Pattern:** Interfaces enable you to define a family of algorithms, encapsulate each one, and make them interchangeable. For example, different algorithms for sorting or calculating discounts can be implemented as structs that satisfy a common interface. The application can switch between strategies at runtime based on user input or configuration.

Simplicity and Clarity

One of the reasons Go has been widely adopted is its focus on simplicity. Its handling of structs and interfaces aligns with this philosophy, providing just enough features to enable powerful data modeling and abstraction without overcomplicating the language. This simplicity translates to readability and ease of use, making Go an excellent choice for teams that prioritize maintainability and rapid development.

Developers coming from other languages might initially find Go's approach to be less feature-rich, especially if they are accustomed to classical inheritance and object-oriented design. However, the simplicity and clarity of Go's model often result in fewer bugs and less technical debt, as there is a smaller surface area for things to go wrong. This makes Go particularly well-suited for systems programming, microservices, and cloud-native applications, where stability and performance are crucial.

Performance Considerations

Structs in Go are efficient. Since structs are composed of fields that directly store data, there is minimal overhead when creating or accessing struct instances. This is particularly important for high-performance systems, such as servers handling numerous concurrent requests or real-time data processing systems. By controlling data layout with structs, developers can optimize for cache locality and reduce memory allocations, leading to faster and more predictable performance.

Interfaces also play a role in efficient program design. While they introduce a slight overhead because of the way Go handles type assertions and interface values, they are still efficient enough to be used extensively without a significant performance penalty. Additionally, the flexibility they provide can lead to a more modular codebase, which often offsets the minor cost of their use.

Best Practices

When working with structs and interfaces in Go, consider the following best practices:

1. **Use Pointers with Structs When Necessary:** Passing structs by value copies the entire struct, which can be inefficient if the struct is large. Using pointers allows you to pass references instead of making copies, saving memory and improving performance.

2. **Keep Interfaces Small:** Define interfaces with as few methods as possible. This follows the **Interface Segregation Principle** (ISP), which states that no client should be forced to depend on methods it does not use. Small interfaces are more flexible and easier to implement.

3. **Design for Dependency Injection:** By passing interface types to functions instead of concrete implementations, you enable easy swapping of dependencies. This improves testability and reduces coupling.

4. **Document Your Structs and Interfaces:** Proper documentation helps other developers (and your future self) understand the purpose and usage of your types. This is especially important when using interfaces, as their purpose may not always be immediately clear.

5. **Avoid Overuse of Empty Interfaces:** While empty interfaces (interface{}) provide flexibility, they sacrifice type safety. Use them sparingly and prefer more specific interfaces whenever possible.

Conclusion: Structs and Interfaces as Cornerstones of Go

Structs and interfaces form the backbone of Go's type system. While Go does not have the class-based inheritance model found in many object-oriented languages, its use of structs and interfaces enables developers to write clean, modular, and maintainable code. By understanding how to effectively use these features, developers can create flexible applications that are easy to scale and adapt to changing requirements.

Whether you are building a simple command-line tool or a distributed system, mastering the use of structs and interfaces will help you write code that is robust, performant, and easy to understand. These constructs reflect Go's philosophy of simplicity and efficiency, allowing you to focus on writing clear and effective software without getting bogged down by unnecessary complexity.

In conclusion, as you continue your journey with Go, make structuring your data with **structs** and abstracting behavior with **interfaces** a key part of your design strategy. Doing so will open up a world of possibilities, making your code more flexible, reusable, and elegant, while adhering to the clean, minimalist style that Go champions.

9. Go: Packages and Core Packages

Introduction to Packages in Go

Go is a statically typed, compiled programming language that emphasizes simplicity, efficiency, and ease of use. One of the key features that contribute to its simplicity and modularity is the concept of **packages**. Packages enable developers to organize their code effectively, promote code reuse, and simplify dependency management. This introduction will provide an overview of packages in Go, how to create and use them, and explore the core packages that are fundamental to Go development.

What Are Packages?

In Go, a package is essentially a directory that contains Go source files. Every Go program is made up of packages, which act as building blocks for code organization. Each file within a package can contain several functions, types, variables, and constants that can be accessed by other files within the same package or external packages, depending on their visibility.

Packages help in:

1. **Code Organization**: Grouping related code together.

2. **Reusability**: Making it easier to use the same code across different projects.

3. **Encapsulation**: Controlling what is exposed to other parts of the program.

Structure of a Go Package

A package is defined by a **package statement** at the beginning of the Go file. For example:

```
package main

import "fmt"

func main() {

    fmt.Println("Hello, World!")

}
```

In the example above:

- The package main statement declares that this file belongs to the main package.

- The main package is a special package in Go, signifying that the file will be compiled into an executable program. Every Go program must have a main package with a main function.

If the package is not named main, it is considered a library package and can be imported by other packages.

Creating and Using Packages

Creating a Package

To create a package, create a directory and add Go files to it. For instance, you might have a package named calculator:

Directory Structure:

calculator/

   add.go

   subtract.go

add.go:

```
package calculator

func Add(a, b int) int {

    return a + b

}
```

subtract.go:

```
package calculator

func Subtract(a, b int) int {

    return a - b

}
```

Using a Package

To use a package, it must be imported into your Go file:

```
package main

import (

    "fmt"

    "calculator"

)

func main() {

    sum := calculator.Add(5, 3)

    fmt.Println("Sum:", sum)

}
```

Visibility and Exported Identifiers

In Go, visibility of functions, types, and variables within a package is controlled by the **case** of the first letter. If an identifier starts with an uppercase letter, it is **exported** (public) and can be accessed from other packages. If it starts with a lowercase letter, it is **unexported** (private) and only available within the package.

For example:

package example

// Exported function

func ExportedFunc() {}

// Unexported function

func unexportedFunc() {}

Importing Packages

Go provides a flexible import system. You can:

- Import specific packages.

- Rename imported packages for convenience.

- Use blank imports to import packages solely for their side effects (like initialization).

Examples:

import "fmt"   // Import fmt package

import calc "calculator"   // Import with alias

import _ "net/http/pprof" // Import for side effects only

Core Packages in Go

Go comes with an extensive standard library that covers a wide range of functionalities. Here are some of the essential core packages:

1. **fmt**

   o Provides input and output functionalities, such as printing to the console or reading input.

   o Functions like Print, Printf, Println, Scan, and Sscanf are commonly used.

Example:

fmt.Println("Hello, Go!")

2. **os**

   o Offers platform-independent interface for operating system functionality.

   o Includes functions for handling files, environment variables, and system commands.

Example:

```
file, err := os.Open("example.txt")
if err != nil {
    fmt.Println("Error:", err)
}
defer file.Close()
```

3. **io and ioutil**
   - Provide basic interfaces for I/O primitives. While io contains interfaces like Reader, Writer, Closer, ioutil has convenient utilities like reading a whole file into memory.
   - **Note**: ioutil has been deprecated in favor of os and io for new code.

4. **net/http**
   - Enables the building of HTTP servers and clients. It is a powerful package for web development and communication over HTTP.

Example:

```
http.HandleFunc("/", func(w http.ResponseWriter, r *http.Request) {
    fmt.Fprintf(w, "Hello, World!")
})
http.ListenAndServe(":8080", nil)
```

5. **strings**
   - Provides functions for manipulating UTF-8 encoded strings.
   - Includes useful functions like Contains, HasPrefix, ToLower, Replace, and Split.

Example:

```
result := strings.ToUpper("hello")
fmt.Println(result) // Output: HELLO
```

6. **strconv**
   - Used for conversions to and from string representations of basic data types (integers, floats, booleans).

Example:

```
num, err := strconv.Atoi("123")
if err != nil {
    fmt.Println(err)
}
```

```
fmt.Println(num)
```

7. **math**

   o Provides basic constants and mathematical functions, including Abs, Pow, Sin, Sqrt, and more.

8. **time**

   o Essential for handling date and time operations.

   o Functions like Now, Parse, Format, After, Sleep provide comprehensive time management.

Example:

```
now := time.Now()

fmt.Println("Current Time:", now)
```

9. **encoding/json**

   o Helps in encoding and decoding JSON. This package is widely used for web services and data exchange.

Example:

```
type User struct {
  Name string `json:"name"`
  Age  int    `json:"age"`
}

jsonStr := `{"name":"Alice","age":25}`

var user User

json.Unmarshal([]byte(jsonStr), &user)

fmt.Println(user)
```

10. **sync**

   o Provides synchronization primitives like Mutex, WaitGroup, Once, etc.

   o Critical for concurrent programming to manage shared resources.

Example:

```
var wg sync.WaitGroup

wg.Add(1)

go func() {
  defer wg.Done()
```

```
    fmt.Println("Goroutine")
}()
wg.Wait()
```

Go was designed to be a language that encourages good software engineering practices. An important part of high-quality software is code reuse – embodied in the principle "Don't Repeat Yourself."

As we saw in chapter 7 functions are the first layer we turn to allow code reuse. Go also provides another mechanism for code reuse: packages. Nearly every program we've seen so far included this line:

import "fmt"

fmt is the name of a package that includes a variety of functions related to formatting and output to the screen. Bundling code in this way serves 3 purposes:

1.   It reduces the chance of having overlapping names. This keeps our function names short and succinct

2.   It organizes code so that it's easier to find code you want to reuse.

3.   It speeds up the compiler by only requiring recompilation of smaller chunks of a program. Although we use the package fmt, we don't have to recompile it every time we change our program.

Creating Packages

Packages only really make sense in the context of a separate program which uses them. Without this separate program we have no way of using the package we create. Let's create an application that will use a package we will write. Inside that folder create a file called main.go which contains this:

```
package main

import "fmt"

import "golang-book/chapter 9/math"

func main() { xs := []float64{1,2,3,4} avg := math.Average(xs) fmt.Println(avg)

}
```

Now create another folder inside of the chapter11 folder called math. Inside of this folder create a file called math.go that contains this:

```
package math

func Average(xs []float64) float64 { total := float64(0) for _, x := range xs { total += x

}

return total / float64(len(xs)) }
```

Using a terminal in the math folder you just created run go install. This will compile the math.go program and create a linkable object file.

Now go back to the chapter9 folder and run go run main.go. Some things to note:

1.   math is the name of a package that is part of Go's standard distribution, but since Go packages can be hierarchical, we are safe to use the same name for our package.

2.   When we import our math library we use its full name (import "golang-book/chapter9/math"), but inside of the math.go file we only use the last part of the name (package math).

3.   We also only use the short name math when we reference functions from our library. If we wanted to use both libraries in the same program Go allows us to use an alias:

```go
import m "golang-book/chapter9/math"

func main() {
    xs := []float64{1,2,3,4}    avg := m.Average(xs)    fmt.Println(avg)
}
```

m is the alias.

4.   You may have noticed that every function in the packages we've seen start with a capital letter. In Go if something starts with a capital letter that means other packages (and programs) are able to see it. If we had named the function average instead of Average our main program would not have been able to see it.

It's a good practice to only expose the parts of our package that we want other packages using and hide everything else. This allows us to freely change those parts later without having to worry about breaking other programs, and it makes our package easier to use.

5.   Package names match the folders they fall in. There are ways around this, but it's a lot easier if you stay within this pattern.

Documentation

Go has the ability to automatically generate documentation for packages we write in a similar way to the standard package documentation. In a terminal run this command:

```
godoc golang-book/chapter9/math Average
```

You should see information displayed for the function we just wrote. We can improve this documentation by adding a comment before the function:

```go
// Finds the average of a series of numbers func Average(xs []float64) float64 {
```

If you run go install in the math folder, then re-run the godoc command you should see our comment below the function definition. This documentation is also available in web form by running this command:

```
godoc -http=":6060"
```

and entering this URL into your browser:

http://localhost:6060/pkg/

You should be able to browse through all of the packages installed on your system.

Testing

Programming is not easy; even the best programmers are incapable of writing programs that work exactly as intended every time. Therefore, an important part of the software development process is testing. Writing tests for our code is a good way to ensure quality and improve reliability.

Go includes a special program that makes writing tests easier, so let's create some tests for the package we made in the last chapter. In the math folder from chapter11 create a new file called math_test.go that contains this:

```
package math import "testing"

func TestAverage(t *testing.T) { var v float64

v = Average([]float64{1,2}) if v != 1.5 {

t.Error("Expected 1.5, got ", v) }

}
```

Now run this command:

```
go test
```

You should see this:

```
$ go test PASS

ok      golang-book/chapter11/math      0.032s
```

The go test command will look for any tests in any of the files in the current folder and run them. Tests are identified by starting a function with the word Test and taking one argument of type *testing.T. In our case since we're testing the Average function, we name the test function TestAverage.

Once we have the testing function setup, we write tests that use the code we're testing. In this case we know the average of [1,2] should be 1.5 so that's what we check. It's probably a good idea to test many different combinations of numbers so let's change our test program a little:

```
package math import "testing"

type testpair struct {values []float64 average float64

}

var tests = []testpair{

  { []float64{1,2}, 1.5 },

  { []float64{1,1,1,1,1,1}, 1 },
```

```
    { []float64{-1,1}, 0 },

}

func TestAverage(t *testing.T) { for _, pair := range tests { v := Average(pair.values) if v !=
pair.average {

t.Error(

"For", pair.values,

"expected", pair.average,

"got", v,

)

}

}

}
```

This is a very common way to setup tests (abundant examples can be found in the source code for the packages included with Go). We create a struct to represent the inputs and outputs for the function. Then we create a list of these structs (pairs). Then we loop through each one and run the function.

Problems

1.   Writing a good suite of tests is not always easy, but the process of writings tests often reveals more about a problem then you may at first realize. For example, with our Average function what happens if you pass in an empty list

([]float64{})? How could we modify the function to return 0 in this case?

2.   Write a series of tests for the Min and Max functions you wrote in the previous chapter.

The Core Packages

Instead of writing everything from scratch, most real-world programming depends on our ability to interface with existing libraries. This chapter will take a look at some of the most commonly used packages included with Go.

First a word of warning: although some of these libraries are fairly obvious (or have been explained in previous chapters), many of the libraries included with Go require specialized domain specific knowledge (for example: cryptography). It is beyond the scope of this book to explain these underlying technologies.

Strings

Go includes a large number of functions to work with strings in the strings package:

```
package main
```

```go
import (

"fmt"

"strings"

)

func main() { fmt.Println( // true

strings.Contains("test", "es"),

// 2

strings.Count("test", "t"),

// true

strings.HasPrefix("test", "te"),

// true

strings.HasSuffix("test", "st"),

// 1

strings.Index("test", "e"),

// "a-b"

strings.Join([]string{"a","b"}, "-"),

// == "aaaaa"

strings.Repeat("a", 5),

// "bbaa"

strings.Replace("aaaa", "a", "b", 2),

// []string{"a","b","c","d","e"} strings.Split("a-b-c-d-e", "-"),

// "test"

strings.ToLower("TEST"),

// "TEST"

strings.ToUpper("test"),

)

}
```

Sometimes we need to work with strings as binary data. To convert a string to a slice of bytes (and viceversa) do this:

```go
arr := []byte("test")
```

```go
str := string([]byte{'t','e','s','t'})
```

Input / Output

Before we look at files, we need to understand Go's io package. The io package consists of a few functions, but mostly interfaces used in other packages. The two main interfaces are Reader and Writer. Reader's support reading via the Read method. Writers support writing via the Write method. Many functions in Go take Readers or Writers as arguments. For example, the io package has a Copy function which copies data from a Reader to a Writer:

```go
func Copy(dst Writer, src Reader) (written int64, err error)
```

To read or write to a []byte or a string you can use the Buffer struct found in the bytes package:

```go
var buf bytes.Buffer buf.Write([]byte("test"))
```

A Buffer doesn't have to be initialized and supports both the Reader and Writer interfaces. You can convert it into a []byte by calling buf.Bytes(). If you only need to read from a string you can also use the strings.NewReader function which is more efficient than using a buffer.

Files & Folders

To open a file in Go use the Open function from the os package. Here is an example of how to read the contents of a file and display them on the terminal:

```go
package main

import (

"fmt"

"os"

)

func main() { file, err := os.Open("test.txt") if err != nil {

// handle the error here return

}

defer file.Close()

// get the file size stat, err := file.Stat() if err != nil { return

}

// read the file

bs := make([]byte, stat.Size())

_, err = file.Read(bs) if err != nil { return

}

str := string(bs) fmt.Println(str)
```

```
}
```

We use defer file.Close() right after opening the file to make sure the file is closed as soon as the function completes. Reading files is very common, so there's a shorter way to do this:

```go
package main

import (

"fmt"

"io/ioutil"

)

func main() { bs, err := ioutil.ReadFile("test.txt") if err != nil { return

}

str := string(bs) fmt.Println(str)

}
```

Here is how we can create a file:

```go
package main

import (

"os"

)

func main() { file, err := os.Create("test.txt") if err != nil {

// handle the error here return

}

defer file.Close()

file.WriteString("test") }
```

To get the contents of a directory we use the same os.Open function but give it a directory path instead of a file name. Then we call the Readdir method:

```go
package main

import (

"fmt"

"os"

)

func main() { dir, err := os.Open(".") if err != nil { return
```

```
}

defer dir.Close()

fileInfos, err := dir.Readdir(-1) if err != nil { return

}

for _, fi := range fileInfos { fmt.Println(fi.Name())

}

}
```

Often, we want to recursively walk a folder (read the folder's contents, all the sub-folders, all the sub-subfolders, …). To make this easier there's a Walk function provided in the path/filepath package:

```
package main

import (

"fmt"

"os"

"path/filepath"

)

func main() { filepath.Walk(".", func(path string, info

os.FileInfo, err error) error {

fmt.Println(path) return nil

}) }
```

The function you pass to Walk is called for every file and folder in the root folder. (in this case.)

Errors

Go has a built-in type for errors that we have already seen (the error type). We can create our own errors by using the new function in the errors package:

```
package main import "errors"

func main() { err := errors.New("error message") }
```

Containers & Sort

In addition to lists and maps Go has several more collections available underneath the container package. We'll take a look at the container/list package as an example.

List

The container/list package implements a doubly-linked list. A linked list is a type of data structure that looks like this:

Each node of the list contains a value (1, 2, or 3 in this case) and a pointer to the next node. Since this is a doubly-linked list each node will also have pointers to the previous node. This list could be created by this program:

```
package main import ("fmt" ; "container/list")

func main() { var x list.List

x.PushBack(1)

x.PushBack(2)

x.PushBack(3)

for e := x.Front(); e != nil; e=e.Next() { fmt.Println(e.Value.(int)) }

}
```

The zero value for a List is an empty list (a *List can also be created using list.New). Values are appended to the list using PushBack. We loop over each item in the list by getting the first element, and following all the links until we reach nil.

Sort

The sort package contains functions for sorting arbitrary data. There are several predefined sorting functions (for slices of ints and floats) Here's an example for how to sort your own data:

```
package main import ("fmt"; "sort")

type Person struct {

Name string

Age int

} type ByName []Person

func (this ByName) Len() int { return len(this)

}

func (this ByName) Less(i, j int) bool { return this[i].Name < this[j].Name

}

func (this ByName) Swap(i, j int) { this[i], this[j] = this[j], this[i]

}

func main() { kids := []Person{

{"Jill",9},

{"Jack",10},
```

```
}
```

```
sort.Sort(ByName(kids)) fmt.Println(kids)
```

```
}
```

The Sort function in sort takes a sort.Interface and sorts it. The sort.Interface requires 3 methods: Len, Less and Swap. To define our own sort, we create a new type (ByName) and make it equivalent to a slice of what we want to sort. We then define the 3 methods.

Sorting our list of people is then as easy as casting the list into our new type. We could also sort by age by doing this:

```
type ByAge []Person func (this ByAge) Len() int { return len(this)
```

```
}
```

```
func (this ByAge) Less(i, j int) bool { return this[i].Age < this[j].Age
```

```
}
```

```
func (this ByAge) Swap(i, j int) { this[i], this[j] = this[j], this[i] }
```

Hashes & Cryptography

A hash function takes a set of data and reduces it to a smaller fixed size. Hashes are frequently used in programming for everything from looking up data to easily detecting changes. Hash functions in Go are broken into two categories: cryptographic and non-cryptographic.

The non-cryptographic hash functions can be found underneath the hash package and include adler32, crc32, crc64 and fnv. Here's an example using crc32:

```
package main
```

```
import (
```

```
"fmt"
```

```
"hash/crc32"
```

```
)
```

```
func main() { h := crc32.NewIEEE()
```

```
h.Write([]byte("test")) v := h.Sum32() fmt.Println(v)
```

```
}
```

The crc32 hash object implements the Writer interface, so we can write bytes to it like any other Writer. Once we've written everything, we want we call Sum32() to return a uint32. A common use for crc32 is to compare two files. If the Sum32 value for both files is the same, it's highly likely (though not 100% certain) that the files are the same. If the values are different then the files are definitely not the same:

```
package main
```

```go
import (

"fmt"

"hash/crc32"

"io/ioutil"

)

func getHash(filename string) (uint32, error) { bs, err := ioutil.ReadFile(filename) if err != nil {
return 0, err

}

h := crc32.NewIEEE()

h.Write(bs)

return h.Sum32(), nil

}

func main() { h1, err := getHash("test1.txt") if err != nil { return

}

h2, err := getHash("test2.txt") if err != nil { return

}

fmt.Println(h1, h2, h1 == h2)
}
```

Cryptographic hash functions are similar to their noncryptographic counterparts, but they have the added property of being hard to reverse. Given the cryptographic hash of a set of data, it's extremely difficult to determine what made the hash. These hashes are often used in security applications.

One common cryptographic hash function is known as SHA-1. Here's how it is used:

```go
package main

import (

"fmt"

"crypto/sha1"

)

func main() { h := sha1.New()

h.Write([]byte("test")) bs := h.Sum([]byte{}) fmt.Println(bs)

}
```

This example is very similar to the crc32 one, because both crc32 and sha1 implement the hash.Hash interface. The main difference is that whereas crc32 computes a 32-bit hash, sha1 computes a 160-bit hash. There is no native type to represent a 160-bit number, so we use a slice of 20 bytes instead.

Servers

Writing network servers in Go is very easy. We will first take a look at how to create a TCP server:

```
package main

import (

"encoding/gob"

"fmt"

"net"

)

func server() {

// listen on a port

ln, err := net.Listen("tcp", ":9999") if err != nil { fmt.Println(err) return

} for {

// accept a connection c, err := ln.Accept() if err != nil { fmt.Println(err) continue

}

// handle the connection go handleServerConnection(c) }

}

func handleServerConnection(c net.Conn) {

// receive the message var msg string

err := gob.NewDecoder(c).Decode(&msg) if err != nil { fmt.Println(err)

} else { fmt.Println("Received", msg)

}

c.Close() }

func client() {

// connect to the server

c, err := net.Dial("tcp", "127.0.0.1:9999") if err != nil { fmt.Println(err) return

}

// send the message msg := "Hello World" fmt.Println("Sending", msg) err = gob.NewEncoder(c).Encode(msg) if err != nil { fmt.Println(err)
```

```go
}
c.Close()
}
func main() { go server() go client()

var input string fmt.Scanln(&input)

}
```

This example uses the encoding/gob package which makes it easy to encode Go values so that other Go programs (or the same Go program in this case) can read them. Additional encodings are available in packages underneath encoding (like encoding/json) as well as in 3rd party packages.

HTTP

HTTP servers are even easier to setup and use:

```go
package main import ("net/http" ; "io")

func hello(res http.ResponseWriter, req

*http.Request) { res.Header().Set(

"Content-Type",

"text/html",

)

io.WriteString( res,

`<doctype html>

<html>

<head>

<title>Hello World</title>

</head>

<body>

Hello World!

</body>

</html>`, )

}
func main() { http.HandleFunc("/hello", hello) http.ListenAndServe(":9000", nil) }
```

HandleFunc handles a URL route (/hello) by calling the given function. We can also handle static files by using FileServer:

http.Handle(

"/assets/", http.StripPrefix("/assets/",

http.FileServer(http.Dir("assets")),),)

RPC

The net/rpc (remote procedure call) and net/rpc/jsonrpc packages provide an easy way to expose methods so they can be invoked over a network. (rather than just in the program running them)

```go
package main

import (

"fmt"

"net"

"net/rpc"

)

type Server struct {}

func (this *Server) Negate(i int64, reply

*int64) error { *reply = -i return nil

}

func server() { rpc.Register(new(Server))

ln, err := net.Listen("tcp", ":9999") if err != nil { fmt.Println(err) return

} for { c, err := ln.Accept() if err != nil { continue

}

go rpc.ServeConn(c)

}

}

func client() { c, err := rpc.Dial("tcp", "127.0.0.1:9999") if err != nil { fmt.Println(err) return

}

var result int64

err = c.Call("Server.Negate", int64(999),

&result) if err != nil { fmt.Println(err)
```

```
} else { fmt.Println("Server.Negate(999) =",

result) }

}

func main() { go server() go client()

var input string fmt.Scanln(&input)

}
```

This program is similar to the TCP example, except now we created an object to hold all the methods we want to expose and we call the Negate method from the client. See the documentation in net/rpc for more details.

Parsing Command Line Arguments

When we invoke a command on the terminal it's possible to pass that command arguments. We've seen this with the go command:

```
go run myfile.go
```

run and myfile.go are arguments. We can also pass flags to a command:

```
go run -v myfile.go
```

The flag package allows us to parse arguments and flags sent to our program. Here's an example program that generates a number between 0 and 6. We can change the max value by sending a flag (-max=100) to the program:

```
package main import ("fmt";"flag";"math/rand")

func main() { // Define flags

maxp := flag.Int("max", 6, "the max value")

// Parse flag.Parse()

// Generate a number between 0 and max fmt.Println(rand.Intn(*maxp)) }
```

Any additional non-flag arguments can be retrieved with flag.Args() which returns a []string.

Synchronization Primitives

The preferred way to handle concurrency and synchronization in Go is through goroutines and channels as discussed. However, Go does provide more traditional multithreading routines in the sync and sync/atomic packages.

Mutexes

A mutex (mutal exclusive lock) locks a section of code to a single thread at a time and is used to protect shared resources from non-atomic operations. Here is an example of a mutex:

```
package main

import (
```

```go
    "fmt"

    "sync"

    "time"

)

func main() { m := new(sync.Mutex)

for i := 0; i < 10; i++ { go func(i int) {

m.Lock()

fmt.Println(i, "start") time.Sleep(time.Second) fmt.Println(i, "end") m.Unlock()

}(i)

}

var input string fmt.Scanln(&input)

}
```

When the mutex (m) is locked any other attempt to lock it will block until it is unlocked. Great care should be taken when using mutexes or the synchronization primitives provided in the sync/atomic package.

Traditional multithreaded programming is difficult; it's easy to make mistakes and those mistakes are hard to find, since they may depend on a very specific, relatively rare, and difficult to reproduce set of circumstances. One of Go's biggest strengths is that the concurrency features it provides are much easier to understand and use properly than threads and locks.

Conclusion: The Power of Packages in Go

The concept of packages in Go is more than just a means of organizing code; it is a fundamental part of how Go encourages developers to write clean, efficient, and modular software. Packages enable a consistent structure across projects, promote code reuse, simplify dependency management, and foster collaboration across development teams. In this conclusion, we will delve deeper into why packages are essential in Go, discuss best practices for using them, and highlight the importance of core packages in building robust and scalable applications.

Modular Design and Code Reusability

One of the primary benefits of packages is the ability to modularize code. In software development, modular design refers to dividing a program into separate, independent modules that can function together cohesively. This approach helps in maintaining code, improving readability, and reducing errors.

By splitting code into different packages, developers can isolate functionalities and limit the scope of changes. For example, a package dedicated to database interactions can be developed, tested, and debugged independently of the rest of the application. This modularity is especially useful for large projects, where changes in one part of the program are less likely to have unintended effects on other parts.

Moreover, packages make it easy to reuse code. Functions, types, and constants defined in one package can be imported and used across multiple projects, reducing the need for rewriting code. This reuse leads to less redundancy, lower maintenance costs, and a more consistent implementation of commonly used features.

Encapsulation and Access Control

Encapsulation is another crucial concept facilitated by packages in Go. When developers create packages, they can decide which parts of the code should be publicly accessible and which parts should remain internal to the package. Go achieves this through the convention of capitalizing identifiers that should be exported and starting internal identifiers with a lowercase letter.

This control over access ensures that developers can expose only the necessary components of a package while keeping implementation details hidden. This "black box" approach allows developers to change internal implementations without affecting other parts of the program that depend on the package, as long as the public interface remains consistent.

Simplified Dependency Management

In traditional software development, managing dependencies across multiple projects can become a challenging task, especially when dealing with external libraries or complex projects. Go's package system simplifies this process. Developers only need to specify the packages they want to import, and the Go tools automatically fetch and integrate those packages into the project.

Furthermore, Go introduced the concept of modules, a higher-level dependency management system that builds on packages. Modules allow developers to specify dependencies in a go.mod file, making it easy to track and update external packages, manage versioning, and ensure consistent builds across different environments. This streamlined approach to dependency management reduces conflicts and helps teams work together more efficiently.

The Role of Core Packages

Go's standard library, consisting of numerous core packages, is one of the language's most valuable assets. It covers a broad range of functionalities that allow developers to handle common programming tasks without relying on third-party libraries. This not only simplifies development but also ensures that applications are built on a solid foundation maintained by the Go team.

Let's revisit why core packages are so essential:

1. **Reliability and Efficiency**: Core packages in Go are rigorously tested and optimized for performance. When you use the net/http package to build a web server, you can be confident that it is secure, efficient, and reliable. This robustness allows developers to focus on writing application-specific logic instead of worrying about low-level details.

2. **Consistency Across Projects**: By using standard packages, developers can maintain consistency across different projects. For example, handling JSON data using the encoding/json package ensures that similar data processing logic is applied across multiple services. This leads to easier maintenance and debugging.

3. **Comprehensive Coverage**: The standard library's packages cover a wide array of programming needs, from basic I/O operations (os, io) to more complex tasks like encryption (crypto), web server creation (net/http), and concurrent programming (sync). This extensive

coverage reduces the need for third-party libraries, minimizing security risks and dependency bloat.

Best Practices for Using Packages in Go

To make the most of packages in Go, developers should follow certain best practices:

1. **Organize by Functionality, Not Layers**: Instead of creating packages based on traditional software layers (e.g., controllers, services, models), group related functionalities together. For example, create a package named authentication that handles all authentication-related tasks instead of spreading this code across different layers.

2. **Keep Packages Small and Focused**: Each package should have a clear, single responsibility. If a package becomes too large or does too many things, consider splitting it into smaller packages. This approach improves maintainability and readability.

3. **Use Meaningful Names**: Package names should be short, descriptive, and convey the purpose of the package. Names should be lowercase and avoid underscores or other special characters. For example, a package named config clearly indicates that it handles configuration settings.

4. **Avoid Circular Dependencies**: Circular dependencies occur when two packages depend on each other, directly or indirectly. This situation can lead to compile-time errors and complex code structures. By organizing packages carefully and avoiding tight coupling, you can prevent these issues.

5. **Use Aliases Judiciously**: Aliases can be useful for shortening long package names or avoiding name conflicts, but they can also make the code less readable if overused. Always prioritize clarity when deciding to use aliases.

Future of Packages in Go

The evolution of Go has brought about significant enhancements to how packages and modules are managed. With the introduction of modules, Go addressed many issues that arose with traditional dependency management, such as versioning conflicts and the difficulty of managing transitive dependencies.

The future of Go packages seems promising, with ongoing improvements aimed at further simplifying the development process. As the language continues to evolve, we can expect enhancements that provide even better dependency resolution, improved package security through features like vulnerability scanning, and more intuitive ways to work with modules.

Moreover, the Go community plays an essential role in maintaining and expanding the ecosystem around packages. Open-source contributors develop a myriad of libraries that supplement the core packages, providing solutions to niche problems while adhering to the simplicity and efficiency that Go promotes. Developers are encouraged to contribute to the community by sharing their packages, ensuring that the ecosystem remains vibrant and diverse.

Packages and Concurrency

Go's concurrency model is one of its standout features, and packages play a critical role in its implementation. The sync and sync/atomic packages, for instance, provide essential primitives for managing concurrency, such as mutexes, atomic counters, and wait groups. This enables developers to write concurrent applications without the complexity often associated with multithreading.

The modularity provided by packages allows developers to isolate concurrent code into specific packages, making it easier to understand, test, and maintain. For example, a package that handles worker pools can encapsulate all concurrency-related logic, providing a simple API for other parts of the application to use without needing to understand the underlying complexity.

The Go Standard Library: A Trusted Toolbox

In summary, the Go standard library can be thought of as a trusted toolbox. When you start a new project, you have a set of reliable, pre-tested tools at your disposal that cover a wide array of common programming tasks. By relying on core packages, you reduce the overhead of needing to evaluate, test, and maintain third-party dependencies. You also gain the benefit of using code that is consistent across multiple projects, making it easier for teams to onboard new members and collaborate.

For any developer getting started with Go, it's essential to familiarize yourself with the core packages, as they provide a strong foundation for writing efficient, secure, and maintainable software. Experienced developers can leverage the advanced features of core packages to optimize performance, manage concurrency, and build robust web services, among other things.

Final Thoughts

The design philosophy behind Go — simplicity, clarity, and performance — is deeply integrated into how packages are implemented. Whether you are working on a small project or a large, complex system, packages help you keep your codebase manageable, scalable, and consistent. By understanding how to use packages effectively, you can write Go code that is not only easy to read and maintain but also modular and reusable.

As the language and its ecosystem continue to grow, developers should keep up with the best practices and new features related to packages. Learning to navigate the nuances of package management in Go will help you build better software, faster, and with fewer bugs. Whether you are writing a command-line utility, a web service, or a distributed system, packages will be at the core of your Go journey, guiding you to organize, modularize, and optimize your code effectively.

In essence, the simplicity and power of Go's package system allow developers to focus on solving real-world problems without getting bogged down by the complexities of the underlying infrastructure. Embracing the philosophy of packages and understanding the core packages provided by the Go standard library will be key to mastering the language and developing robust, efficient applications in 2024 and beyond.

10. Go: Harness Time, Manage Data, and Handle Input

Introduction

The Go programming language, often referred to as Golang, is well-known for its simplicity, performance, and efficiency, making it a popular choice for building scalable, concurrent, and fast applications. One of the language's strengths lies in its well-designed standard library, which provides developers with tools to efficiently manage various aspects of programming, including time manipulation, data handling, and input processing.

In "Harness Time, Manage Data, and Handle Input in Go 2024," we will explore essential concepts and features of Go that empower developers to handle time-based operations, manage various forms of data, and efficiently handle user and system input. This chapter provides a comprehensive guide, delving into the intricacies of these essential aspects, ensuring that you are well-equipped to develop robust Go applications.

1. Harness Time in Go

Time is an essential aspect of software development. Whether you are scheduling tasks, measuring performance, or logging events, working with time effectively is crucial. Go provides the time package, which offers a variety of functionalities to manage and manipulate time, including:

- **Creating and Formatting Time:** Learn how to create time.Time objects and format them according to different time zones and locales.

- **Measuring Time Intervals:** Understand how to measure the duration of operations using the time.Duration type.

- **Parsing Time Strings:** Discover how to convert string representations of time into time.Time objects, making it easy to work with dates from user input.

- **Working with Time Zones:** Understand how to handle time zones, convert between time zones, and make your application work seamlessly across different regions.

- **Timers and Tickers:** Utilize timers and tickers to schedule tasks, implement delays, or set up periodic operations.

Key Concepts

1. **Working with the time Package:**

   o Creating current and custom time instances.

   o Formatting time using predefined layouts and custom formats.

   o Parsing time strings for robust input handling.

2. **Time Zones and Offsets:**

   o Setting and converting time zones.

- Handling Daylight Saving Time (DST) changes.
- Using Location objects to manage regional time differences.

3. **Timers and Scheduling:**
   - Using the time.After and time.Tick functions.
   - Implementing periodic tasks with time.NewTicker.
   - Practical examples of scheduling and delayed execution.

2. Manage Data Efficiently in Go

Efficient data handling is at the core of building effective software applications. Go offers powerful and versatile data structures that make it easy to store, process, and manipulate data. From primitive types to more complex structures, Go's simplicity makes data handling straightforward and efficient. In this section, we will cover:

- **Primitive Data Types:** Overview of integer, float, string, and boolean data types and their usage.
- **Complex Data Structures:** Detailed explanations of arrays, slices, maps, and structs. Learn how to choose the right data structure for your needs.
- **Pointers and Memory Management:** Understand pointers in Go and how they are used to manage memory efficiently.
- **Data Serialization and Deserialization:** Explore methods to convert data to and from formats such as JSON, XML, and CSV for easy storage and transmission.
- **Working with Files:** Learn how to read from and write to files in Go, enabling persistent data storage and retrieval.

Key Concepts

1. **Understanding Go's Data Types:**
   - Detailed overview of Go's primitive and complex data types.
   - Practical examples of using these types to manage data effectively.

2. **Handling Collections:**
   - Arrays, slices, and maps for structured data management.
   - Techniques for sorting, searching, and filtering collections.
   - Tips for optimizing data processing tasks using Go's data structures.

3. **Data Interchange Formats:**
   - JSON and XML parsing and generation.
   - Reading and writing CSV files.
   - Serialization and deserialization practices for robust data handling.

4. **File Handling:**

   o   Opening, reading, writing, and closing files.

   o   Best practices for error handling while working with files.

   o   Managing file permissions and concurrent file access.

3. Handle Input in Go

Handling user and system input is a fundamental aspect of any interactive application. Go's robust I/O packages make it easy to read input from a variety of sources, including the console, files, and even network connections. This section focuses on:

- **Reading Input from the Console:** Capture user input using fmt.Scan, bufio, and os.Stdin.

- **Handling Command-Line Arguments:** Learn how to read and process command-line arguments, enabling users to provide input when running your application.

- **Reading and Writing Files:** Detailed examples of how to read data from and write data to files, with emphasis on efficient file operations.

- **Working with Buffers:** Discover how to use buffers to process data streams efficiently, a key skill for handling large volumes of data or managing network input.

- **Network I/O:** Basic introduction to reading and writing data over network connections, enabling the development of networked applications.

Key Concepts

1. **Capturing Console Input:**

   o   Utilizing fmt.Scan, bufio.NewReader, and os.Stdin for efficient input handling.

   o   Examples demonstrating interactive user input scenarios.

2. **Command-Line Arguments and Flags:**

   o   Accessing command-line arguments via os.Args.

   o   Parsing options and flags using the flag package.

   o   Best practices for building command-line tools in Go.

3. **Efficient File I/O:**

   o   Reading and writing text and binary files.

   o   Working with large files efficiently.

   o   Managing concurrent file access in multi-threaded programs.

4. **Introduction to Network I/O:**

   o   Basics of reading from and writing to network sockets.

   o   Using the net package to build simple client-server applications.

This chapter demonstrates how to manipulate dates and time using the Go standard library time package.

Get Dates

The Go standard library time package provides functionality to extract specific fields from a Time data type that describe a particular point in time. These can be made available to a program by importing the time package.

A date/time instance of a new Time data type can be created with fields describing the current date and time using a time.Now( ) function. The fields are initialized from the system clock on your device for the current locale.

The value within an individual field can be retrieved using an appropriate method of the Time data type. For example, the value of the year field can be retrieved using its Year( ) method. Similarly, there are Month( ), Day( ), and Weekday( ) methods that retrieve other individual fields of a Time data type.

Method	Returns
Now( )	A time.Time data type comprising current date, time, and time zone fields
Year( )	Year with 4 digits (YYYY)
Month( )	Month name of the year
Day( )	Day number of the month
Weekday( )	Day name of the week

There are also these three methods whose returned Time data type values can usefully be assigned to variables:

Method	Returns
Date( )	Year with 4 digits (YYYY), month name of the year, and day number of the month
ISOWeek( )	Week number of the year (1-53) and year with 4 digits (YYYY)
YearDay( )	Day number of the year (1-365/366)

It is important to recognize that a Time data type contains individual fields and so is not a string. You can, however, convert it to a string using its String () method:

The values returned by the Time data type methods are not strings.

Begin by importing the Go standard library time package into a program

import ("fmt"

"time"

)

src\date\main.go

Next, create a date/time instance of the Time data type, initialized with the current date and time dt := time.Now( )

Add statements to output all fields of the date/time instance and to confirm its data type

fmt.Printf("DateTime: %v \n", dt) fmt.Printf("DateTime Type: %T \n", dt)

Next, add a statement to output today's day name fmt.Printf("Today is: %v \n", dt.Weekday( ))

Now, add statements to display today's date, current week, and day number of the year

y, m, d := dt.Date( )

fmt.Printf("Date: %v %v, %v \n", m, d, y)

yr, wk := dt.ISOWeek( )

fmt.Printf("Week No.: %v in %v \n", wk, yr)

dy := dt.YearDay( ) fmt.Printf("Day No.: %v \n", dy)

Save the program file in a "date" directory, then run the program to see the date field values

The time zone values specify the offset from the UTC (Universal Time Clock) and a time zone abbreviation – see here for more on time zones.

Get Times

The time values within individual fields of a Time data type can be retrieved using appropriate methods. For example, the value of the hour field can be retrieved using its Hour( ) method. Similarly, there are Minute( ), Second( ), and Nanosecond( ) methods that retrieve other individual fields of a Time data type.

Method	Returns
Hour( )	Hour number of the day (0-23)
Minute( )	Minute number of the hour (0-59)
Second( )	Second number of the minute (0-59)
Nanosecond( )	Nanosecond of the second (0-999999999)

Unlike other programming languages, the time package in Go does not provide a method to return a millisecond value from a Time data type. You can, however, divide the nanosecond value by one million to produce its millisecond equivalent.

There are also these three methods whose returned Time data type values can usefully be assigned to variables:

Method	Returns
Clock( )	Hour, minute, and second within the day
Unix( )	The number of seconds elapsed since the epoch (January 1, 1970 00:00:00 UTC)

UnixNano( )   The number of nanoseconds elapsed since the epoch (January 1, 1970 00:00:00 UTC)

Begin by importing the Go standard library time package into a program

import ("fmt"

"time"

)

src\times\main.go

Next, create a date/time instance of the Time data type, initialized with the current date and time dt := time.Now( )

The UnixNano () method is useful to seed the Go random number generator – see the example here.

 Add statements to output all fields of the date/time instance and to confirm its data type fmt.Printf("DateTime: %v \n", dt)

fmt.Printf("DateTime Type: %T \n\n", dt)

Next, add statements to evaluate the current hour and display an appropriate greeting

hr := dt.Hour( )

switch { case hr < 12 : fmt.Println("Good Morning!")

case hr < 18 :

fmt.Println("Good Afternoon!")

default :

fmt.Println("Good Evening!") }

Now, add statements to display the current time

h, mn, s := dt.Clock( ) fmt.Printf ("Time: %v:%v,:%v \n", h, mn, s)

Finally, add statements to display the current time field for nanoseconds and its equivalent millisecond value

ns := dt.UnixNano( ) ms := ns / 1000000

fmt.Println("Nanoseconds:", ns) fmt.Println("Milliseconds:", ms)

Save the program file in a "times" directory, then run the program to see the time field values

Single-digit hour, minute, and second values are not returned with a leading zero by default.

Format Date and Time

The date and time values within individual fields of a Time data type can be formatted in a variety of ways using its Format () method. This takes a single argument that is a "layout" string, which specifies how to format a date/time value. The format must only be specified by exactly using elements of this reference string:

Mon Jan 2 15:04:05 2006 MST

Since MST (Mountain Standard Time) is 7 hours behind UTC (Universal Time Coordinated), the reference string can alternatively be considered numerically to look like this:

01 02 03:04:05PM '06 -0700

If you want the Format( ) method to return only the day, month, and time in hh:mm format, the layout can be specified as:

"Mon Jan 2 15:04" or numerically as:

"01/02 03:04"

You can have the day name and month name returned as full names by specifying the long name versions in the layout:

"Monday January 2 15:04"

The time package includes predefined UnixDate, ANSIC, and RFC3339 constants that you can use as date/time layout formats.

A custom layout can specify the components in any order to suit different locales – for example, for appropriate date formatting.

The time package also includes a predefined Kitchen constant that you can use as a time layout format. This will display the time in a 12-hour format and append "AM" or "PM" as appropriate.

Additionally, the time components can be formatted to be displayed in a 24-hour format that will automatically prefix single-digit hours with a zero by specifying "15:04".

Both 12-hour format and 24-hour format will automatically prefix single-digit minutes with a zero.

ANSIC refers to the American National Standards Institute standard date/time format for the C programming language. RFC 3339 refers to the Request For Comment date/time document of the Internet Engineering Taskforce (IETF).

Begin by importing the Go standard library time package into a program

```
import ( "fmt"

"time"

)
```

src\format\main.go

Next, create a date/time instance of the Time data type, initialized with the current date and time, then display its components in various formats dt := time.Now( )

```
fmt.Println( "\nDefault Format:", dt ) fmt.Println( "Unix Format:", dt.Format( time.UnixDate ) )
fmt.Println( "ANSIC Format:", dt.Format( time.ANSIC ) ) fmt.Println( "RFC3339 Format:",
dt.Format( time.RFC3339 ) ) fmt.Println( "Custom Format:", dt.Format( "January 2, 2006
[Monday]" ) )
```

Now, display only date components formatted to be appropriate in two locales

fmt.Println("\nUS Format:", dt.Format("January 2, 2006")) fmt.Println("UK Format:", dt.Format("2 January, 2006"))

Then, display only time components in a 12-hour format and in a 24-hour format

fmt.Println("\nTime 12-Hour:", dt.Format(time.Kitchen)) fmt.Println("Time 24-Hour:", dt.Format("15:04"))

Save the program file in a "format" directory, then run the program to see the formatted date and time field values.

The time.Kitchen constant is equivalent to specifying a layout format of "15:04PM".

Set Date and Time

You can create your own Time data types using the Date( ) function of the Go standard library time package. This requires eight arguments to specify (in this order) a year, a month, a day number, an hour, a minute, a second, a nanosecond, and a location.

All arguments are specified as integer values except for the month and location.

The month can be specified using one of the time package predefined full-name month constants for JanuaryDecember, for example, time.January.

The location can be specified using one of the time package predefined location constants atime.UTC, for Universal Time Coordinated or time.Local, for your system clock.

The date fields in any Time data type can be modified using the AddDate( ) method of the Go standard library time package to specify three arguments for year, month, and day. Positive values will advance the date, and negative values will retard the date. For example, time.AddDate(1, 0, 0) will advance the date one year.

Similarly, the time package's Add( ) method can be used to specify a single duration argument by which to modify a date/time. This value can be an int64 value representing a number of nanoseconds by which to modify the date/time. More conveniently, you can use constants time.Hour, time.Minute, time.Second, or time.Millisecond to modify individual time fields of a Time data type. For example, time.Add(10 * time.Hour) will advance the time 10 hours.

You can also create your own Time data types from a string using the Parse( ) function of the Go standard library time package. This requires two arguments to specify a layout and a date/time string. Usefully, this function returns two values, which are a Time data type and an error. If the function returns a Time data type, the error value will be nil, otherwise it will be an error message.

The layout should only use values from the Go reference string:

Mon Jan 2 15:04:05 2006 MST

Unless a time zone offset value is specified in the date/time string (e.g. -0500), the resulting Time data type will assume UTC time.

The Time data types can be formatted using the Format( ) method described here.

Begin by importing the Go standard library time package into a program

import ("fmt"

"time"

)

src\setdate\main.go

Next, create and display a date/time instance of the Time data type, initialized for noon on New Year's day

dt := time.Date(2025, time.January, 1, 12, 0, 0, time.Local) fmt.Printf("\nDateTime: %v \n\n", dt)

Advance the date two years to U.S. Independence Day, then display the modified date

dt = dt.AddDate(2, 6, 3) fmt.Printf("DateTime: %v \n\n", dt)

Now, initialize a layout string and a date/time string

layout := "2006-Jan-02 03:04PM" str := "2030-Dec-25 12:30AM"

Finally, attempt to create and display the fields of a Time data type, or display an error message if the attempt fails

t, err := time.Parse(layout, str)

if err != nil { fmt.Println(err)

} else { fmt.Printf("Parsed DateTime:" %v \n", t)

}

Save the program file in a "setdate" directory, then run the program to see the date and time field values

The layout string and date/time string must be in the same format when parsing a string to a Time data type.

The modified Time fields automatically recognize the change from Eastern Standard Time to Eastern Daylight Time.

Recognize Zones

All Time data types in Go programming are associated with a time zone. Typically, this will be UTC time, or the local time based upon the location of the system running the program. You can, however, specify an alternative location as an argument to a time.LoadLocation( ) function. The location name must correspond to a file in the Internet Assigned Numbers Authority (IANA) time zone database, such as "America/New_York", "Asia/Seoul", or "Europe/London". The time.LoadLocation( ) function returns two values, which are a Location type and an error. If the function successfully returns a Location type, the error value will be nil, otherwise it will be an error message.

You can create a Time data type of the current time in another time zone by appending a call to an In () function after its Now () function, in which the location is specified as an argument to the In( ) function.

You can ascertain the time zone associated with a Time data type by calling its Zone( ) method. This method returns two values, which are a three-letter TZ time zone abbreviation, such as "EST" (Eastern Standard Time) or "EDT" (Eastern Daylight Time), and a numerical value representing the seconds offset of that time zone from UTC. It is important to note that time zone abbreviations are not unique, so you should not rely solely upon these to recognize particular time zones. Some time zones change their time for Daylight Saving, so you might evaluate both the TZ abbreviation and offset to correctly recognize the time zone.

A list of IANA location names and TZ abbreviations is included with this book's download files – see here.

Daylight Saving in the USA reduces the offset from UTC by one hour. For example, Eastern Daylight Time (EDT) is UTC - 4 hours, Central Daylight Time (CDT) is UTC - 5 hours, etc.

Begin by importing the Go standard library time package into a program

import ("fmt"

"time"

)

src\zone\main.go Next, create and initialize variables with a default string value and a Time data type in a specified location

zone := "All"

loc, _ := time.LoadLocation("America/New_York") dt := time.Now( ).In(loc)

Ascertain the time zone abbreviation and offset seconds, then convert the offset to a positive minute number

abbr, offset := dt.Zone( ) if offset < 1 { offset = offset * -1

} offset /= 60

Now, evaluate the abbreviation and offset values

switch { case abbr == "EST" && offset == 300 : zone = "East Coast"

case abbr == "EDT" && offset == 240 :

zone = "East Coast"

}

Display the time zone details and an appropriate message

fmt.Printf("\nTZ: %v Offset Minutes: %v \n", abbr, offset) fmt.Println("Welcome to", zone, "Visitors!")

Save the program file in a "zone" directory, then run the program to see the time zone values.

A _ blank identifier is used here to ignore the returned error value due to space constraints, but you should ideally include an error-handler.

Delay Time

The Go standard library time package provides a Sleep( ) function that allows you to delay progress of a program by a specified duration period. The duration is supplied as an argument to the Sleep( ) function, and can be expressed as a multiplication of a time package constant. For example, 5 * time.Second expresses a duration of five seconds.

The Go standard library time package also provides three methods that compare an instance of the Time data type with another time specified as their argument. These methods will each return a boolean true or false value according to the result of the time comparison:

Method   Returns

Before(time) A boolean true value if the instance time is earlier than its argument time

After(time)   A boolean true value if the instance time is later than its argument time

Equal(time)   A boolean true value if the instance time and argument time represent the same instant – even in different time zones

If you would like to see the difference between two instances of the Time data type, you can use a Sub( ) method of a time instance to specify another time instance as its argument. This method will return the elapsed duration between the two instants as an int64 data type value of nanosecond precision.

It is often preferable to present duration periods with less than nanosecond precision, so the Go standard library time package includes a Round( ) method to specify more concise precision. This method requires one argument to determine your preferred rounding behavior. Typically, the argument is supplied as one of the time package constants. For example, calling the method with Round(time.Millisecond) will round a nanosecond precision duration to the nearest millisecond, Round(time.Second) will round a nanosecond precision duration to the nearest second, and so on.

Begin by importing the Go standard library time package into a program

```
import ( "fmt"

"time"

)
```

src\delay\main.go

Next, create and display components of a Time data type

```
start := time.Now( ) fmt.Println( "\nStarted At:", start.Format( "03:04:05" ) )
```

Now, delay the program's progress for five seconds time.Sleep(5 * time.Second)

Then, create and display a second Time data type

finish := time.Now( ) fmt.Println("Finished At:", finish.Format("03:04:05"))

> Compare the start and finish times

fmt.Println("\nStart First?:", start.Before(finish)) fmt.Println("Finish First?:", finish.Before(start))

> Finally, display the length of the delay

diff := finish.Sub(start) fmt.Println("\nTime Elapsed:", diff.Round(time.Second))

Save the program file in a "delay" directory, then run the program to see the time delay

The ability to delay execution is particularly useful in pausing individual "goroutines" – see the example here for more details.

Manage Data

This chapter demonstrates how to manipulate text and numbers using the Go standard library math, string, and strconv packages.

Unite Strings Split Strings Find Characters Convert Strings Calculate Areas Evaluate Numbers Round Decimals Generate Randoms Summary

Unite Strings

In Go programming, a string is zero or more characters enclosed within double quote marks. So, these are all valid string values: s1 := "My First String" s2 := "" s3 := "2" s4 = "nil"

The empty quotes of s2 initialize the variable as an empty string value. The numeric value assigned to s3 is a string representation of the number. The Go nil zero value, which normally represents the absence of any value, is simply a string literal when it is enclosed within quotes.

Essentially, a string is a collection of characters; each character containing its own data – just like elements in a defined array. It is, therefore, logical to regard a string as an array of characters and apply array characteristics when dealing with string values. The built-in len( ) function will return the number of characters in a string, much like it returns the number of elements in an array.

The + operator, which can be used to add numeric values, doubles as a concatenation operator for joining string values together to create a single united string.

The Go standard library strings package contains useful functions for string manipulation. Its Join( ) function joins (concatenates) all elements of a string array to create a single united string. This function requires two arguments to specify the name of a string array and a separator value to be placed between each string element in the united string. Typically, you will specify a single space as the separator to create a space-separated united string.

The fmt.Printf( ) and fmt.Println( ) functions that write to standard output can add spaces and newline characters to output, but do not change the actual strings. They do, however, both return two values, which are the number of bytes written and any write error. If no error is encountered, the error value will be nil as usual. With the English language, the number of bytes written will normally represent the number of characters output – including nonprinting characters contained within the string.

The ASCII code number for a non-printing \t tab character is 9, and for a non-printing \n newline character is 10.

Begin by importing the Go standard library strings package into a program

import ("fmt"

"strings"

)

src\join\main.go

Initialize two string variables and a concatenated string

s1, s2 := "The Truth is rarely Pure ", "and never Simple." str := s1 + s2

Next, output the concatenated string and its length

chars, err plitAfterSplitAfterlass="blue1">:= fmt.Printf("\n%v \n", str) if err != nil { fmt.Println(err)

} else { fmt.Println("Bytes Written: ", chars) fmt.Println("String Length:", len(str)) }

Initialize a string array and a joined string

arr := [ ]string { "\n\tStrive", "For", "Greatness!" } ast := strings.Join(arr, " ")

Now, output the joined string and first two characters

fmt.Println(ast)

if ast[0] == 10 && ast[1] == 9 { fmt.Printf("1st Char: ASCII %v Newline\n", ast[0]) fmt.Printf("2nd Char: ASCII %v Tab\n", ast[1]) }

Save the program file in a "join" directory, then run the program to see the united strings.

The number of bytes written here exceeds the string length because the fmt.Printf( ) method adds two newline characters and one space character.

Split Strings

The Go standard library strings package provides several functions that allow a specified string to be separated into substrings. These functions treat the string like an array in which each element contains a character or a space.

Frequently, you may want to separate a space-separated sentence into an array of substrings that are each individual words. The strings package conveniently provides a Fields( ) function that will perform that very task. This function requires the string sentence as its sole argument, and will return an array of substrings containing each individual word from that string.

The strings package has a Split( ) function that requires two arguments to specify a string and a separator. This function will return an array of substrings that exist between occurrences of the specified separator. For example, when the string is a space-separated sentence and the separator is a space character, the Split( ) function will return an array of words within that sentence.

The strings package also has a SplitN( ) function that works just like the Split( ) function, but accepts a third argument to specify how many substrings to return. Subsequent occurrences of the specified separator will simply be returned in the final substring if the specified number of substrings exceeds the number of separators. For example, when the string is a space-separated sentence, the separator is a space character, and only two substrings are specified, the SplitN( ) function will return a substring containing the first word in the sentence and a substring containing the entire remainder of that sentence including spaces.

It is important to recognize that the Fields( ), the Split( ), and the SplitN( ) functions discard the specified separator and only include the characters around the separator in the returned substrings. There are, however, two further functions that allow you to also include the separators in the returned substrings.

The strings package's SplitAfter( ) function works like the Split( ) function, but includes the separator in the returned substrings. Similarly, the strings package's SplitAfterN( ) function works like the SplitN( ) function, but includes the separator in the returned substrings.

Data is often stored as Comma-Separated Values in CSV files, which can be usefully split into individual values.

Begin by importing the Go standard library strings package into a program

```
import ( "fmt" " strings"

)
```

src\split\main.go

Start the main function by initializing a string variable

```
str := "I can, and, I will."
```

Next, add statements to pass a description and substrings of the variable string to a listing function

```
list( "Fields", strings.Fields( str ) )

list( "Split", strings.Split( str, "," ) ) list( "SplitN", strings.SplitN( str, ",", 2 ) )

list( "SplitAfter", strings.SplitAfter( str, "," ) ) list( "SplitAfterN", strings.SplitAfterN( str, ",", 2 ) )
```

After the main function, add the function to list the description and all substrings upon each call

```
func list( desc string, subs [ ]string ) { fmt.Print( "\n", desc, ": " ) for _, v := range subs { fmt.Print( "[", v, "] " )

}

fmt.Print( "\n" ) }
```

Save the program file in a "split" directory, then run the program to see the substrings

Only split methods that contain the word "After" in their name will retain the separators.

Find Characters

The Go standard library strings package provides several functions that allow a specified string to be searched to find a specified character or substring (pattern). These functions treat the string as an array in which each element contains a character or a space.

The strings package has a Contains( ) function that requires two arguments to specify a string and a pattern to find. This function will simply return true or false to indicate the result of a (case-sensitive) search. For example, to search for a "Pro" pattern: strings.Contains("Go Programming in easy steps", "Pro")

The strings package also has an Index( ) function that requires two arguments to specify a string and a pattern to find. This function will return an integer that is the index position of the first instance of the pattern in the searched string if the search succeeds, otherwise it will return -1 when the search fails.

The strings package's Count( ) function requires two arguments to specify a string and a pattern to find. You can use this function to discover how many non-overlapping instances of a pattern occur in a searched string. If the pattern is an empty string, this function will normally return 1 plus the number of characters in the searched string. This allows you to determine the number of characters in a searched string by deducting 1 from the returned integer.

The strings package's HasPrefix( ) function requires two arguments to specify a string and a pattern to find. This function will return true or false to indicate whether the searched string begins with the specified pattern.

Similarly, the strings package's HasSuffix( ) function requires two arguments to specify a string and a pattern to find, and will return true or false to indicate whether the searched string ends with the specified pattern.

You can modify a searched string by replacing a specified pattern with a replacement substring using the strings package's Replace( ) function. This function requires four arguments to specify the string to search, the pattern to find, the replacement substring, and an integer denoting the number of instances to be replaced. If you want to replace all instances of the pattern within the searched string, simply specify -1 as the number of replacements.

The strings.Index( ) function stops searching when it finds the first instance of the pattern in the searched string.

Begin by importing the Go standard library strings package into a program

import ("fmt"

"strings"

)

src\find\main.go

Start the main function by initializing a string variable str := "I can resist everything except temptation"

Next, test whether a substring exists within the string, then find the index position of the first instance

fmt.Printf("\nFound 'an': %v \n", strings.Contains(str, "an")) fmt.Printf("Found 'an' at: %v \n", strings.Index(str, "an"))

Now, count how many instances of a particular letter appear in the string

fmt.Printf("Count of 'e': %v \n", strings.Count(str, "e"))

Then, test whether the string begins or ends with a particular substring

fmt.Printf("Prefix 'ion': %v \n", strings.HasPrefix(str, "ion")) fmt.Printf("Suffix 'ion': %v \n", strings.HasSuffix(str, "ion"))

Finally, replace a substring within the string fmt.Println(strings.Replace(str, "temptation", "chocolate", 1))

Save the program file in a "find" directory, then run the program to see the search results.

Convert Strings

The Go standard library strings package provides functions to convert the character case of strings.

The strings package has a ToUpper( ) function that requires a single string argument. This function will simply return a copy of the string with all its characters converted to uppercase letters.

Similarly, the strings package's ToLower( ) function requires a single string argument, and will return a copy of the string with all its characters converted to lowercase letters.

The strings package also has a ToTitle( ) function that requires a single string argument. This function will return a copy of the string with the first character of each word converted to an uppercase letter – but only when the string argument is all lowercase. If you want to convert a string of mixed-case letters to title case you must first convert it to lowercase using the strings package's ToLower( ) function.

When a program receives user input following a request for a numeric value, the input might be of a string data type and may include spaces that the user has inadvertently entered. You can remove spaces from the beginning and end of a string using the strings package's Trim( ) function. This requires two arguments to specify the string and character to be removed. To remove all leading and trailing spaces, the second argument will be " " to specify a single space character.

Once unnecessary spaces have been removed from a string containing an input number, the data type must be converted to a numeric type before the program can use the input in arithmetical operations. This can be achieved by importing the Go standard library strconv package. This package contains an Atoi( ) function (ASCII to Integer) that requires a single string argument, and will return an integer and any error. If no error is encountered, the error value will be nil or it will contain a descriptive error message if the method cannot return an integer data type.

Similarly, the strconv package contains an Itoa( ) function that can convert an integer to a string data type. This method simply requires an integer argument, and will return a string copy.

A strconv.ParseInt( ) method can also be used to convert a string data type to an integer. The strconv.Atoi( ) method is equivalent to calling strconv.ParseInt(str, 10, 0).

Begin by importing the Go standard library strings package and strconv package into a program

```
import ( "fmt"

"strings" "strconv"

)
```

src\conv\main.go

Start the main function by initializing a string variable, then display the string with different character cases str := "I have Nothing to declare except My Genius"

```
fmt.Println( strings.ToUpper( str ) ) fmt.Println( strings.ToLower( str ) ) fmt.Println( strings.Title( strings.ToLower( str ) ) )
```

Now, assign a number and spaces to the variable

```
str = " 42 " fmt.Printf( "\n%v Type: %T, Length: %v \n", str, str, len( str ) )
```

Then, remove leading and trailing spaces from the string

```
str = strings.Trim( str, " " ) fmt.Printf( "\n%v Type: %T, Length: %v \n", str, str, len( str ) )
```

Finally, attempt to change the data type to an integer

```
num, err := strconv.Atoi( str ) if err != nil { fmt.Println( err )

} else { fmt.Printf( "%v Type: %T \n", num, num ) }
```

Save the program file in a "conv" directory, then run the program to see the string conversions.

Change the string assignment to " $42 " in Step 3, then save and run the program to see a parsing error message appear as the conversion to an integer fails.

Calculate Areas

The Go standard library math package provides a number of useful functions and constant mathematical values. The constants are listed in the table below together with their approximate value:

Constant	Description
math.E	Constant e, base of the natural logarithm, with an approximate value of 2.71828
math.Pi	The constant Pi, with an approximate value of 3.14159
math.Phi	The constant Phi (the "Golden Ratio"), with an approximate value of 1.61803
math.Sqrt2	The square root of 2, with an approximate value of 1.41421
math.SqrtE	The square root of constant e, with an approximate value of 1.64872

math.SqrtPi	The square root of constant Pi, with an approximate value of 1.77246
math.SqrtPhi	The square root of constant Phi, with an approximate value of 1.27202
math.Ln2	The natural logarithm of 2, with an approximate value of 0.69315
math.Log2E	The base-2 logarithm of constant e, with an approximate value of 1.44269
math.Ln10	The natural logarithm of 10, with an approximate value of 2.30259
math.Log10E	The base-10 logarithm of constant e, with an approximate value of 0.43429

The math constants are mostly used in Go programs that have a particular mathematical purpose, but all the math package constants are listed above for completeness.

The Golden Ratio appears many times in geometry and art. It is the ratio of a line segment cut into two pieces of different lengths, where the length ratio of the long piece to the short piece is equal to the length ratio of the whole segment to the long piece.

Begin by importing the Go standard library math package into a program

import ("fmt"

"math"

)

src\area\main.go

Declare three floating-point variables var rad, area, perim float64

Next, initialize the first variable and display its value to two decimal places

rad = 4 fmt.Printf("\nRadius of Circle: %.2f \n", rad)

Now, calculate the area of a circle based on the given radius, then display the area to two decimal places

area = math.Pi * (rad * rad) fmt.Printf("\nArea of Circle: %.2f \n", area)

Then, calculate the perimeter of a circle based on the given radius, and display the perimeter to two decimal places

perim = 2 * (math.Pi * rad) fmt.Printf("\nPerimeter of Circle: %.2f \n", perim)

Save the program file in an "area" directory, then run the program to see the calculated values.

Evaluate Numbers

The Go math package provides these useful functions that can be used to evaluate float64 arguments:

Function	Returns
math.Abs( )	An absolute value
math.Acos( )	An arc cosine value

math.Asin( )	An arc sine value
math.Atan( )	An arc tangent value
math.Atan2( )	An angle from an X-axis point
math.Ceil( )	A rounded-up value
math.Cos( )	A cosine value
math.Exp( )	An exponent of constant e
math.Floor( )	A rounded-down value
math.IsNaN( )	A boolean true or false value
math.Log( )	A natural logarithm value
math.Max( )	The larger of two numbers
math.Min( )	The smaller of two numbers
math.Pow( )	A power value
math.Round( )	The nearest integer value
math.Sin( )	A sine value
math.Sqrt( )	A square root value
math.Tan( )	A tangent value

The math.IsNan( ) function (Is-Not-a-number) is useful to discover whether a value cast to the float64 data type is indeed a number.

The math package contains lots more functions but those listed here are useful for many mathematical operations. Discover more in the Go documentation at golang.org/pkg/math

Begin by importing the Go standard library math package into a program

```
import ( "fmt"

"math"

)
```

src\maxmin\main.go

Next, initialize two variables

```
square := math.Pow( 5, 2 )    // 5 to power 2 ( 5 x 5 ). cube := math.Pow( 4, 3 )    // 4 to power 3 ( 4 x 4 x 4 ).
```

Now, compare the positive value of the variables and display the largest and smallest numbers

```
fmt.Println( "\nLargest Positive:", math.Max( square, cube ) ) fmt.Println( "\nSmallest Positive:", math.Min( square, cube ) )
```

Then, add statements to reverse the numerical polarity of each variable – making positive values into negative values square *= -1 cube *= -1

Finally, compare the negative value of the variables and display the largest and smallest numbers

fmt.Println("\nLargest Negative:", math.Max(square, cube)) fmt.Println("\nSmallest Negative:", math.Min(square, cube))

Save the program file in a "maxmin" directory, then run the program to see the compared values.

The largest negative value is the one closest to zero.

Round Decimals

The Go standard library math package provides a number of useful functions for rounding a decimal value to a near integer. These functions are listed in the table below, together with a brief description of each one:

Function	Returns
math.Floor(x)	The greatest integer less than x
math.Ceil(x)	The least integer greater than x
math.Round(x)	The nearest integer to x
math.Trunc(x)	The integer part of x

If you want to reduce a long floating-point value to just two decimal places, first multiply the floating-point value by 100, then use math.Round( ) to remove any remaining decimal places, then divide by 100 to return two decimal places.

Procedures that multiply, operate, then divide can be written as individual steps, or parentheses can be used to determine the order in a single succinct expression. For example, commuting a long floating point value in a variable named "num" can be written as:

num = num * 100 num = math.Round(num) num = num / 100 or alternatively as: num = math.Round(num * 100) / 100

The Go programming language has a strong type system that unlike other programming languages, does not support type conversion (a.k.a. "casting") implicitly. You can, however, perform explicit type conversion between compatible data types, such as float64 and int types using the syntax dataType(value) to convert a value to another data type. In converting a floating-point value to an integer, the value is truncated, losing the decimal places.

The math.Round( ) function will round up from the mid-point, so math.Round(7.5) returns 8, not 7.

Begin by importing the Go standard library math package into a program

import ("fmt"

"math"

)

src\round\main.go

Initialize a floating-point variable and display its value var pi float64 = math.Pi fmt.Println("Pi:", pi)

Next, display nearest integers to the floating-point value

fmt.Println("\nFloor:", math.Floor(pi)) fmt.Println("Ceiling:", math.Ceil(pi)) fmt.Println("Round:", math.Round(pi)) fmt.Println("Truncated:", math.Trunc(pi))

Now, reduce the floating-point value to two places

fmt.Println("\nShort Pi:", math.Round(pi * 100) / 100)

Finally, initialize another floating-point variable and cast its value to an integer variable

var e1 float64 = math.E fmt.Printf("\nE: %v %T \n", e1, e1) var e2 int = int(e1) fmt.Printf("Cast: %v %T \n", e2, e2)

Save the program file in a "round" directory, then run the program to see the rounded decimals.

Generate Randoms

The Go standard library math package contains a rand package that provides functions to generate pseudo-random numbers. You can make this available to your program by importing math/rand.

The rand.Intn( ) function returns a random number from zero up to the number specified as its argument. The rand.Perm( ) function returns a sequence of integers, from zero up to the number specified as its argument, in a pseudo-random order.

The randomizing pattern is based upon a default "seed" that will return the same pseudo-random order each time the program runs. This may be what you want, but often it is preferable to generate a different order each time the program runs. To make this happen, you must specify a custom seed as an integer argument to a rand.Seed( ) function that will be unique each time the program runs. It is convenient to use the current system time for this purpose by calling the time.Now( ) function and extracting the integer count of elapsed nanoseconds since the Epoch using the Time data type's UnixNano( ) method. This value will be different each time the program runs, so specifying this integer as the argument to the rand.Seed( ) function will ensure a different pseudo-random order is generated each time the program runs.

Import the Go standard library math/rand package into a program, along with the time package to set a random seed and the strconv package to convert random numbers import ("fmt"

"math/rand" "strconv "time"

)

src\lotto\main.go

Next, specify a unique seed for the random generator rand.Seed(time.Now( ).UnixNano( ))

Now, generate a slice of integers from zero to 58 nums := rand.Perm(59)

Then, increment the range to become 1-59 inclusive

```
for i := 0 ; i < len( nums ) ; i++ { nums[ i ]++
}
```

In computing, the Epoch is the time at midnight on January 1, 1970.

Assign the first six numbers in pseudo-random order around hyphen characters in a formatted string

```
str := "\nYour Six Lucky Numbers: "
for i := 0 ; i < 6 ; i++ {
str += strconv.Itoa( nums[ i ] ) if i != 5 { str += " - "
}
}
```

Finally, display the formatted string

```
fmt.Println( str )
```

Save the program file in a "lotto" directory, then run the program repeatedly to see different random numbers.

Here the random numbers are in the range 1 to 59 – to play the UK Lotto game or the US New York Lotto game.

The int numbers must be converted to the string data type for concatenation.

Handle Input

This chapter demonstrates how to handle user input, and how to read and write text files using the Go standard library os, bufio, and io/ioutil packages.

Get User Input

The previous examples have illustrated how variables can be used to store text string values, numeric integer and floating-point decimal values, and boolean truth values in your programs. Now, they can be used to create a Guessing Game program by storing a generated random integer whose value the user will have to guess, a boolean truth value that will end the game when the user guesses correctly, and a variable containing the user's guess.

The familiar Go standard library fmt package provides Scan( ), Scanln( ), and Scanf( ) functions to read from standard input:

•   fmt.Scan( ) stores successive space-separated values into successive interface variables, and regards newlines as spaces.

•   fmt.Scanln( ) stores successive space-separated values into successive interface variables until it meets a newline.

•   fmt.Scanf( ) stores successive space-separated values into successive interface variables using a specified format.

Each of these functions returns two values, which are the number of items scanned and any read error. If no error is encountered, the error value will be nil as usual. Each function also requires one or more arguments to specify the address of interface variables.

The Guessing Game program can use the fmt.Scan( ) function to assign an input integer guess to an interface variable and compare its value against a generated random integer.

Begin by importing the Go standard library math/rand and time packages into a program, to provide a custom seeded random number generator

import ("fmt"

"math/rand" "time"

)

src\scan\main.go

Now, begin the main function by seeding the random number generator with the current time rand.Seed(time.Now( ).UnixNano( ))

Next, declare and initialize three variables

var num int = rand.Intn(20) + 1 var guess int = 0 var flag bool = true

Then, request the user enter an integer fmt.Print("\nGuess My Number 1-20: ")

Finally, add a loop to repeatedly compare the input against the random number until they match

for flag {

_, err := fmt.Scan(&guess)

if err != nil { fmt.Println(err)

} else if guess > num { fmt.Print("Too High, Try Again: ")

} else if guess < num {

fmt.Print("Too Low, Try Again: ")

} else if guess == num { fmt.Println("Correct - My Number Is", num) flag = false

}

}

Notice that the _ blank identifier is used to ignore the returned number of items scanned, and remember to use the & address of operator when assigning the input values to the interface variables.

Save the program file in a "scan" directory, then run the program to guess the randomly generated number.

Buffer Input

When you want to gather larger items of data into your program it is often preferable to store the data stream in a memory buffer. The Go standard library bufio (buffered input/output) package provides a Scanner type, which is a memory buffer with several useful methods to handle data streams. You can make this available to your program by importing the bufio package.

A Scanner instance is first created by specifying a source from which to read data as an argument to the bufio package's NewScanner( ) function. When the source is to be user input, you can import the Go standard library os package and specify os.Stdin (standard input) as the argument to NewScanner( ).

The Scanner instance has a Scan( ) method that reads all the user input and a Text( ) method that returns the input that has been read as a single string value.

The Scanner instance also has an Err( ) method that will return any read error. If no error is encountered, the error value will be nil as usual. It is useful to check for errors after calling the Scan( ) method and Text( ) method.

If you want to separate the input into individual string items, you can import the Go standard library strings package and specify the input to its Fields( ) function, to split the string into words.

Begin by importing the Go standard library bufio, os, and strings packages into a program, to handle input

import ("fmt"

"bufio" "os" "strings"

)

src\buffer\main.go

Next, request user input fmt.Print("\nEnter Text:")

Now, create a Scanner instance to store the user input in a memory buffer, then read the user input

scanner := bufio.NewScanner(os.Stdin) scanner.Scan( )

Then, output an error if one occurred or the stored data

if scanner.Err( ) != nil { fmt.Println(scanner.Err( ))

} else { fmt.Println(scanner.Text( )) }

Next, create a new Scanner instance to store other user input in a memory buffer

fmt.Print("\nEnter Text:") scanner = bufio.NewScanner(os.Stdin) scanner.Scan( )

Then, store individual items of the user input in individual elements of a slice words := strings.Fields(scanner.Text( ))

Finally, output an error if one occurred, or list the individual items of user input

if scanner.Err( ) != nil { fmt.Println(scanner.Err( ))

} else { for i, v := range words { fmt.Printf("%v: %v \n", i, v) }

}

Save the program file in a "buffer" directory, then run the program to see the user input.

The if conditional test is made as the Scan( ) method returns a boolean true value while reading input, but returns false when it reaches the end on input.

Command Flags

The command to run your program can recognize any number of parameters, so you can pass a space-separated list of argument values to the program when you run it. The Go standard library os (operating system) package provides an Args slice, which stores these argument values in individual elements. You can make this available to your program by importing the os package.

It is important to note that the very first element in os.Args will always contain the path to your program – argument values are then stored sequentially in subsequent elements. You can reference the argument values using [ ] square brackets as you would with any other slice – for example, the first argument value as os.Args[1].

Begin by importing the Go standard library os package into a program, to store command-line arguments.

import ("fmt"

"os"

)

src\params\main.go

Next, add a loop to display the program's default location on your system, together with any passed-in arguments

for i, v: = range os.Args { fmt.Printf("Argument %v: %v \n", i, v) }

Now, display the final passed-in argument

fmt.Println("\nLast Argument:", os.Args[len(os.Args)-1])

Save the program file in a "params" directory, then run the program with command-line arguments to see the output.

Run go build params to compile the program, then run it with the command params a b c to see the local program path instead of its default system location.

The Go standard library flag package provides functions for more advanced command-line processing. You can make these available to your program by importing the flag package.

You define flags using the flag package's String( ), Int( ), or Bool( ) functions. These each require three arguments to specify a flag name, default value, and a help message for that flag. They return the address of an appropriate variable data type to store the value. The user can optionally specify an alternative value for each flag at the command-line, prefixing the flag name with a hyphen. The flag package's Parse( ) function applies the user's values to the flag.

Begin by importing the Go standard library flag package into a program, to parse command-line flags

```
import ( "fmt"

"flag"

)
```

src\flags\main.go

Next, define three command-line flags

```
txt := flag.String( "txt", "C#", "A string" ) num := flag.Int( "num", 8, "An integer" ) sta := flag.Bool( "sta", false, "A boolean" )
```

Now, process the flags and display their values

```
flag.Parse( )

fmt.Println ( "\nText:", *txt ) fmt.Println( "Number:", *num, " Status:", *sta )
```

Save the program file in a "flags" directory, then run the program without and with input to see the flag values.

You need to use the * dereference operator to reference the value stored at the address of each defined flag.

Read Files

The Go standard library io package contains an ioutil (input/ output utility) package that provides functions to read text files. You make this available to your program by importing io/ioutil.

The ioutil package's ReadFile( ) function takes the path to a text file as its argument, and returns the entire text file content and any read error. If no error is encountered, the error value will be nil. It is good practice to check for errors after each file operation.

For finer control when reading text files, you can specify the path to a text file as an argument to the os package's Open( ) function. This simply opens the text file, for reading only, and returns an os.File type and any read error. The file type has Read( ), Seek( ), and Close( ) methods that allow you to process the text file's content.

The Seek( ) method determines the position at which to begin reading from the opened file. It requires two arguments to specify an offset position number and a zero (0) if this is relative to the start of the file, or one (1) if it is relative to the current position.

The Read( ) method requires a byte slice argument whose length will determine the number of bytes (characters) to read from the specified position. This method returns the number of bytes read and any read error.

The Close( ) method needs no arguments but must be called after completing other operations on an opened file. So that this requirement is not forgotten, you can call the Close( ) method with the defer keyword immediately after opening a file. This will then automatically close the file at the end of the enclosing function.

Begin by importing the Go standard library ioutil and os packages into a program, to read a text file.

```
import (

"fmt" "io/ioutil" "os"

)
```

src\read\main.go

Next, add a function to check for read errors

```
func check( err error ) { if err != nil { fmt.Println( err )

}

}
```

Now, in the main function, read an entire text file, then check for errors and display the text content

```
txt, err := ioutil.ReadFile( "C:/Textfiles/Oscar.txt" ) check( err ) fmt.Println( string( txt ) )
```

Next, open the same text file, then check for errors and remember to close the file after other operations complete

```
file, err := os.Open( "C:/Textfiles/Oscar.txt" ) check( err ) defer file.Close( )
```

Then, specify a starting position and check for errors

```
pos, err := file.Seek( 42, 0 ) check( err )
```

Now, read 15 characters and check for errors

```
slice := make( [ ]byte, 15 ) nb, err := file.Read( slice ) check( err )
```

Finally, display the starting position, the number of characters read, and the text that has been read

```
fmt.Printf( "\n%v bytes @ %v: ", nb, pos ) fmt.Printf( "%v\n", string( slice[ : nb ] ) )
```

Save the program file in a "read" directory, then run the program to see the text read from the specified file.

The text file Oscar.txt is included in the download archive of examples in this book (see here), but you will need to adjust the path in these steps to suit its location on your system.

You have to use the string( ) function to translate the byte slice character code numbers into their respective alphabetic characters.

Write Files

The Go standard library io package contains an ioutil (input/ output utility) package that provides functions to write text files. You make this available to your program by importing io/ioutil.

The ioutil package's WriteFile( ) function takes three arguments to specify the path to the file to be written, a byte slice of text characters to be written, and the numerical file permissions of that file.

This function returns an error message if the attempt to write fails, or an error value of nil if the file gets successfully written.

For finer control when writing text files, you can use the os package's OpenFile( ) function. This requires three arguments to specify the path of the file to be written, a flag specifying the operation type, and the numerical file permissions of that file. The flags specifying the operation type are os package constants. For example: os.O_RDWR to read and write, os.O_APPEND to append text, or os.O_CREATE to create a new file if none exists.

The OpenFile( ) function returns an os.File type and any read error. The file type has Write( ) and Close( ) methods that allow you to process the text file's content.

The Write( ) method requires a byte slice argument containing the text to be written. This method returns the number of bytes read and any read error.

The Close( ) method can be called with the defer keyword immediately after opening a file, to close the file at the end of the enclosing function after the file operations complete.

Begin by importing the Go standard library ioutil and os packages into a program, to write a text file.

import (

"fmt" "io/ioutil" "os"

)

src\write\main.go

Next, add a function to check for write errors

func check(err error) { if err != nil { fmt.Println(err)

}

}

There are several operation type flags, and multiple flags can be specified to the OpenFile( ) function. For more details, refer to the documentation at golang.org/pkg/os/#OpenFile

Now, in the main function, write an entire text file, then check for errors

txt := [ ]byte("\nA thousand suns will stream on thee, \nA thousand moons will quiver.\n")

err := ioutil.WriteFile("C:/Textfiles/Farewell.txt", txt, 0644)

check(err)

Next, open the same text file for an append operation, then check for errors and remember to close the file

file, err := os.OpenFile("C:/Textfiles/Farewell.txt",

os.O_APPEND, 0644)

check(err) defer file.Close( )

Now, append text to the existing file content and check for errors

slice := [ ]byte("by Alfred Lord Tennyson.\n")

nb, err := file.Write(slice) check(err)

Finally, display the number of characters written, and the text that has been written

fmt.Printf("\nAppended: %v bytes - %v", nb, string(slice[: nb]))

Save the program file in a "write" directory and run the program to write the text, then display the file contents.

The last three digits in the permission represent Owner, Group, and other users respectively. Each may have file permission to execute (1 point), write (2 points), and read (4 points). Totalling these points with 0644 allows the Owner to read and write to the file, but Group and Other users may only read the file. This protects the file from unauthorized changes.

A file type also has a WriteString( ) method that works just like the Write( ) method but accepts a string argument, rather than a byte slice argument.

Use Temporary Files

It is sometimes useful to create a temporary file on the user's system in which to store data during the execution of a Go program. The Go standard library io package has the ioutil package containing a TempFile( ) function for this purpose.

The TempFile( ) function returns an os.File type, and an error message or nil if the file gets created. This function requires two arguments to specify the directory in which to create the file and a filename pattern. You can specify the directory as a path, or as an ""empty string if you are happy to create the temporary file in the system's default directory for temporary files. You specify the file name pattern simply as a name string to which a generated random string will be appended. If the pattern includes a * wildcard character, the generated string will replace that character.

When the TempFile( ) function successfully creates a temporary file, it automatically opens that file ready to write and read. The returned file type has a Name( ) method with which to reference its path, including the pattern and random string file name. You can employ its Write( ) and WriteString( ) methods to add text content, and use its Close( ) method when processing is complete. As with other text files, the temporary file's content can be read using the ioutil.ReadFile( ) function.

You can delete a temporary file when it is no longer required by specifying its file name as the argument to an os.Remove( ) function. You can also examine the temporary file (and other files) by specifying a file name as the argument to the os.Stat( ) function. This returns an info type, plus an error message or nil.

Begin by importing the Go standard library ioutil and os packages into a program, to process a temporary file

import (

"fmt" "io/ioutil" "os"

)

src\temp\main.go

Next, add a function to check for errors

```
func check( err error ) { if err != nil { fmt.Println( err )

}

}
```

Now, in the main function, create a temporary text file, then check for errors and confirm the file exists

```
tmpFile, err := ioutil.TempFile( "", "Data-*" ) check( err ) fmt.Printf( "\nCreated File:\n%v \n",
tmpFile.Name( ) )
```

Write text into the temporary file, then check for errors

```
nb, err := tmpFile.WriteString( "Go Programming Fun!\n" ) check(err)
```

Next, read text from the temporary file and check for errors, then display the number of characters read

```
txt, err := ioutil.ReadFile( tmpFile.Name( ) ) check( err )
```

```
fmt.Printf( "\nRead: %v bytes - %v \n", nb, string( txt ) )
```

Remember to close the file after processing completes tmpFile.Close( )

Then, delete the temporary file os.Remove(tmpFile.Name( ))

Finally, attempt to examine the (now removed) temporary file and check for errors

```
_, err = os.Stat( tmpFile.Name( ) ) check( err )
```

Save the program file in a "temp" directory, and run the program to create, write, read, and delete a temporary file

The _ blank identifier represents the info type that is not used in this program.

Conclusion: Mastering Time, Data, and Input Management in Go

Throughout this chapter, we have delved into three fundamental aspects of software development in Go: harnessing time, managing data, and handling input. These elements play a vital role in creating robust, efficient, and reliable applications. As Go continues to gain traction in the software development community, having a deep understanding of these core areas is essential for developers who want to leverage the language to its full potential. In this conclusion, we will summarize key takeaways, provide insights into best practices, and explore how these concepts can be applied in real-world scenarios.

1. Harnessing Time in Go

Time management is a critical component in many applications, from scheduling tasks and triggering events to measuring execution times and handling time-based data. Go's time package is designed to make these operations straightforward and intuitive. Here are some key takeaways:

- **Ease of Use:** The time package provides a simple yet powerful API for handling time-related tasks. With functions for creating, formatting, and parsing time, developers can easily work with different time zones and locales. This makes it possible to build applications that are not only efficient but also globally adaptable.

- **Timers and Scheduling:** Using timers and tickers, you can schedule tasks, create delays, and implement periodic actions without the need for complex third-party libraries. Whether you are developing a web server that needs to refresh data periodically or building an automated system that triggers tasks at specific intervals, Go's native support for timers ensures that your application is responsive and reliable.

- **Measuring Execution Time:** Understanding how long a task takes to execute is essential for performance optimization. The time package makes it easy to measure time intervals, which can be particularly useful for profiling and debugging code.

Best Practices for Time Management in Go:

- Always be mindful of time zones when handling time data. Use the time.Location type to ensure your application behaves consistently across different regions.

- When working with timers and tickers, be sure to stop them when they are no longer needed to avoid resource leaks.

- Take advantage of time.Parse and time.Format to ensure consistent date and time representations, especially when dealing with user input or data from external sources.

Practical Application: Imagine you are building a global e-commerce platform that handles transactions from different time zones. Using Go's time manipulation capabilities, you can ensure that order timestamps are consistent across regions, handle time zone conversions for delivery schedules, and measure how long it takes to process transactions, giving you valuable insights into the performance of your system.

2. Managing Data Efficiently

Effective data management is at the heart of all software applications. Whether you are handling user input, processing files, or interacting with databases, understanding how to work with different data types and structures is crucial. Go offers a range of tools and data structures that make it easy to manage and manipulate data.

- **Versatile Data Structures:** Go provides a variety of data structures, including arrays, slices, maps, and structs. Each of these has its own strengths, and knowing when to use each type is key to writing efficient code. For instance, slices are ideal for dynamic data storage, while maps provide quick lookup capabilities.

- **Memory Management with Pointers:** Go's use of pointers allows for efficient memory management without the complexity seen in languages like C and C++. By passing pointers to functions, you can avoid copying large data structures, making your applications faster and more memory-efficient.

- **Data Serialization:** In today's interconnected world, data often needs to be transferred between systems. Go's support for JSON, XML, and other serialization formats makes it easy to convert data into a format that can be easily shared and understood by other applications, regardless of the language they are written in.

Best Practices for Data Management in Go:

- Use the right data structure for the task. For instance, use slices when dealing with dynamic arrays and maps for key-value storage. This can significantly improve the performance of your application.

- Always handle errors when reading from or writing to files. Go's error handling mechanism ensures that you can catch and address issues before they become critical problems.

- When dealing with large data sets, consider using channels and goroutines for concurrent data processing. This will help you take advantage of multi-core systems and improve the overall efficiency of your program.

Practical Application: Suppose you are developing a data analytics tool that processes large CSV files. Using Go's encoding/csv package, you can easily read and write CSV files. By leveraging slices and maps, you can efficiently store and manipulate data. Additionally, using goroutines allows you to process multiple files concurrently, significantly reducing the time required to analyze large data sets.

3. Handling Input in Go

Input handling is a fundamental aspect of any interactive application. Whether your program is a command-line tool, a web service, or a desktop application, it needs to be able to process user input and external data sources effectively.

- **Console Input:** Go provides straightforward methods to capture user input from the console. Functions like fmt.Scan, bufio.NewReader, and os.Stdin make it easy to read input, parse it, and use it within your application. This is particularly useful when building command-line tools that need to be interactive.

- **File I/O:** Reading from and writing to files is an essential skill in software development. Go's os, io, and bufio packages provide everything you need to handle files efficiently, from reading and writing text files to managing binary data. By understanding how to work with files, you can build applications that can store data persistently, read configurations, and generate reports.

- **Command-Line Arguments:** Many applications need to accept input via command-line arguments. Go's flag package allows you to easily parse command-line options and flags, making it simple to build customizable and flexible tools that users can control without modifying the code.

Best Practices for Input Handling in Go:

- Always validate and sanitize user input to prevent security vulnerabilities, such as injection attacks. This is especially important when dealing with inputs that are used to generate commands or query databases.

- Use buffered input when reading large files or streams to improve performance. The bufio package can significantly speed up reading and writing by reducing the number of I/O operations.

- When designing command-line tools, consider using third-party libraries like cobra to simplify the creation of complex command-line interfaces.

Practical Application: Imagine you are building a tool that automates server maintenance tasks. Users can run the tool with different command-line arguments to specify which tasks to perform, such as checking disk space, updating software, or restarting services. By using the flag package, you can easily parse these arguments, execute the appropriate tasks, and even allow users to schedule tasks to run at specific intervals using Go's time management features.

Bringing It All Together: The Power of Go's Simplicity

One of Go's greatest strengths is its simplicity. The language was designed to be easy to understand and use, and this philosophy extends to its standard library. By providing well-thought-out packages for time, data management, and input handling, Go allows developers to build powerful applications without relying heavily on external libraries. This not only reduces the complexity of your codebase but also makes your applications easier to maintain and deploy.

In modern software development, speed, scalability, and reliability are more important than ever. Go's efficient runtime, coupled with its powerful tools for managing time, data, and input, enables developers to meet these demands head-on. Whether you are building a high-performance web server, a real-time data processing system, or a simple command-line utility, the concepts covered in this chapter will form the backbone of your development efforts.

Real-World Scenarios:

- **Web Applications:** Handling user sessions, managing timeouts, and processing input from forms are common tasks in web development. Go's capabilities make it easy to build fast, secure, and reliable web services.

- **Automation Tools:** Automate repetitive tasks by scheduling jobs, reading configuration files, and handling various inputs. This is useful for DevOps tasks, data migration, and system monitoring.

- **Data Processing Pipelines:** Efficiently read, process, and store data from multiple sources, such as files, databases, and APIs. Go's concurrent programming model can be used to build scalable data pipelines that handle large volumes of data.

Final Thoughts

Mastering time management, data handling, and input processing in Go is crucial for any developer looking to build robust and efficient software. These skills will not only improve your ability to write clean, maintainable code but also enable you to tackle complex problems with confidence. By understanding the intricacies of Go's standard library and best practices for time, data, and input handling, you can develop applications that are both powerful and user-friendly.

As you continue your journey with Go, remember that the language's strength lies in its simplicity. Focus on writing clear, concise, and efficient code, and use the tools provided by Go's standard library to build scalable and maintainable applications. The knowledge and practices you've gained in this chapter will serve as a solid foundation for further exploration of Go's many features and capabilities, helping you become a proficient and confident Go developer.

11. Go: Reflection, Mutex and Channels

Introduction

1. Reflection in Go

Reflection in Go is a mechanism that allows a program to inspect its own structure, types, and values at runtime. It is essential for creating dynamic applications, particularly in scenarios where you don't know the types of objects at compile-time.

1.1. What is Reflection?

Reflection is about examining and manipulating objects at runtime. It allows you to:

- Inspect the type of a variable.

- Read and set the values of variables, even if they are private.

- Invoke methods on an object dynamically.

1.2. Go's reflect Package

The reflect package in Go provides the necessary tools for reflection. It has two core types: Type and Value.

- Type provides information about the kind and structure of a value (e.g., whether it is a struct, int, slice, etc.).

- Value allows you to access and modify the underlying data.

1.3. How to Use Reflection

Here's a basic example of using reflection in Go:

```
package main

import (

"fmt"

"reflect"

)

func main() {

var number int = 42

fmt.Println("Type:", reflect.TypeOf(number))     // Output: int

fmt.Println("Value:", reflect.ValueOf(number))   // Output: 42

}
```

1.4. Use Cases of Reflection

- **Serialization/Deserialization:** Converting data structures to and from formats like JSON.
- **Dynamic Function Calls:** Creating more flexible and dynamic code, such as dependency injection frameworks.
- **Testing Frameworks:** Allowing for dynamic creation of tests.

1.5. Pros and Cons

- **Pros:** Flexibility, dynamic code generation, runtime inspection.
- **Cons:** Reflective code is slower and can be harder to understand and maintain.

2. Mutex in Go

Mutexes (mutual exclusions) are used to prevent race conditions in concurrent programs by ensuring that only one Goroutine can access a shared resource at a time.

2.1. What is a Mutex?

A Mutex allows only one Goroutine to hold the lock at a time, ensuring safe access to shared resources. It prevents concurrent writes, which can lead to unpredictable behavior and bugs.

2.2. Types of Mutex in Go

Go provides two main types of mutexes:

- **sync.Mutex:** Basic lock with methods Lock and Unlock.
- **sync.RWMutex:** Allows multiple readers but only one writer.

2.3. Example Usage of sync.Mutex

```
package main

import (

"fmt"

"sync"

)

var (

counter int

mu      sync.Mutex

)

func increment(wg *sync.WaitGroup) {

defer wg.Done()

mu.Lock()

counter++
```

```go
        mu.Unlock()
}
func main() {
var wg sync.WaitGroup
for i := 0; i < 1000; i++ {
        wg.Add(1)
        go increment(&wg)
}
wg.Wait()
fmt.Println("Counter:", counter)
}
```

2.4. Best Practices

- **Always Unlock:** Always call Unlock after Lock, even if an error occurs. Consider using defer to ensure Unlock is called.
- **Minimize Lock Scope:** Keep the code between Lock and Unlock as short as possible to reduce contention.

3. Channels in Go

Channels are a powerful feature in Go that allow Goroutines to communicate with each other safely and efficiently. They are the backbone of concurrency in Go.

3.1. What are Channels?

Channels provide a way for Goroutines to synchronize execution and exchange data. They act as conduits, allowing one Goroutine to send data to another.

3.2. Creating and Using Channels

Channels can be created using the make function:

```go
package main
import "fmt"
func main() {
  ch := make(chan int)
  go func() {
    ch <- 42
  }()
```

```go
    fmt.Println(<-ch) // Output: 42
}
```

3.3. Types of Channels

- **Unbuffered Channels:** Block the sending Goroutine until the receiving Goroutine receives the data.
- **Buffered Channels:** Do not block the sending Goroutine until the buffer is full.

3.4. Channel Synchronization

Channels can be used for synchronization without sharing variables:

```go
package main

import "fmt"

func worker(done chan bool) {

    fmt.Println("Working...")

    done <- true

}

func main() {

    done := make(chan bool)

    go worker(done)

    <-done

    fmt.Println("Done!")

}
```

3.5. Select Statement

The select statement in Go allows a Goroutine to wait on multiple communication operations, making it more flexible.

```go
select {

case msg := <-ch1:

    fmt.Println("Received from ch1:", msg)

case msg := <-ch2:

    fmt.Println("Received from ch2:", msg)

default:

    fmt.Println("No messages received")
```

```
}
```

Reflection is a key feature of a programming language that can be defined as examining the program execution and modifying it at runtime. Reflection plays an important role in object-oriented programming languages.

Reflection allows the exploration of any data at runtime without knowing its name defined at compile time. By using reflection, we can inspect the behavior of any method, interface, struct, or any data. Inspecting the source code at runtime is called reflection.

By using reflection, we can get the type, field, and the value of any type. Although in the Go language, every variable is declared with its type but still, there could be many cases where we may need to know the type of a variable at runtime. Here, reflection comes in.

Example:
```
func main(){ slice_val :=[]string {"one", "two", "three",
"four", "five", "six"} map_val := map [string] int64{}
for itr:=0; itritr++{ map_val[slice_val[itr]] = 0
}

}
```

In the example given above, we initialize a slice of string type. We need to use the items of the slice like a key of a map. Here, we have declared a map that has the string type of keys. What if we need to initialize that map at runtime or a slice is of any type?

In that case, we would need to find the type of slice at runtime.

For that, we could use reflection.

The reflect package

Go provides a built-in package called reflect that provides the functionality of reflection at runtime. We can get the
"reflect"

package in the src directory. The reflect package contains a few variables and methods to manipulate the object of various types.

It is used to return the dynamic type of a variable that is static of interface type. As an empty interface can accept any value, we can get the exact type of value that is accepted by an interface with the use of the reflect package. The reflect package is mainly used to get the type, value, and kind of a variable.

Type

The reflect package provides the method TypeOf to get the type of a variable. This function returns the value of the type The type has various methods to define the property of that type. The signature of this function is as follows: funcTypeOf(i interface{}) type

This function takes an interface as an argument. Any value is accepted by an interface and then analyzed by the TypeOf function.

Syntax:

variable_type := reflect.TypeOf(variable)

Example: package
main import
("fmt"
"reflect"

)

```
func main(){ type student
struct{ name string age int }
stu := student{"Akansha",
17} fmt.Println(stu) stu_type
:= reflect.TypeOf(stu)
fmt.Println("type of 'stu' variable:", stu_type) fmt.Println("type of 'stu_type' variable:",
reflect.TypeOf(stu_ type)) fmt.Println("name of 'stu' variable type:", stu_type.Name())

}
```

Output:

{Akansha 17}

type of 'stu' variable: main.student
type of 'stu_type' variable:
*reflect.rtype name of 'stu' variable
type: student

Value

The reflect package has a method to evaluate the value of a variable.

Syntax: value :=
reflect.ValueOf(variable)
Example: package
main import
("fmt"
"reflect"

)

```
func main(){

type student struct{ name
string age int } stu :=
student{"Akansha", 17}
fmt.Println(stu) stu_type :=
reflect.TypeOf(stu)
fmt.Println("value of 'stu' variable:", reflect.ValueOf(stu)) fmt.Println("value of 'stu_type' variable:",
reflect.ValueOf(stu_ type))
```

}

Output:

{Akansha 17} value of 'stu' variable:
{Akansha 17} value of 'stu_type'
variable: main.student

Kind

Kind is quite a different method of the reflect package. The type defines the type of a variable while "kind" defines the source type of a variable type. This function is used with a type to get its source, not with variables.

Example: package
main import
("fmt"
"reflect"

)

func main(){ type student
struct{ name string age int }
stu := student{"Akansha",
17} fmt.Println(stu) stu_type
:= reflect.TypeOf(stu)
stu_kind := stu_type.Kind()
fmt.Println("type of 'stu'
variable:", stu_type.Name())
fmt.Println("kind of
'stu_type' variable:",
stu_kind) }

Output:

{Akansha 17}

type of 'stu' variable: student
kind of 'stu_type' variable:
struct

Here, we can see that student is a type of struct. So, the source type of the student type is a struct.

NumField()

This method is used to get the number of fields contained by a struct. As this function is defined in the reflect package, it only works with type or reflect.Type.

Example: package
main import
("fmt"
"reflect"

)

```go
func main(){ type student struct{ name string age
int } stu := student{"Akansha", 17} stu_value :=
reflect.ValueOf(stu) num_fields :=
stu_value.NumField() fmt.Println("number of fields
in 'stu':", num_fields, reflect. TypeOf(stu_value))
stu_type := reflect.TypeOf(stu) fmt.Println("number
of fields in 'stu':", num_fields, reflect.
TypeOf(stu_type))

}
```

Output:

number of fields in 'stu': 2 reflect.Value

number of fields in 'stu': 2 *reflect.rtype

Field

This function is used to get the value of struct fields. It returns the value of type reflect.Value.

Example: package
main import
("fmt"
"reflect"

)

```go
func main(){ type student struct{ name string age int } stu := student{"Akansha", 17}
stu_value := reflect.ValueOf(stu) num_fields := stu_value.NumField() for itr:=0;
itritr++{ fmt.Printf("value of %dth field is:%v of type %T\n", itr+1,
stu_value.Field(itr), stu_value.Field(itr))
}

}
```

Output:

value of 1th field is:Akansha of type reflect.Value value of 2th field is:17 of type reflect.Value

String(), Int() & Float()

In the reflect package, the Value function returns the data of type We can convert such values to string or any other type as required.

Example: package
main import
("fmt"
"reflect"

)

func main(){

type student struct{
name string age int
income float32
} stu := student{"Akansha", 17, 40000.565} stu_value :=
reflect.ValueOf(stu) fmt.Printf("Type of name is %T and
value is %v\n", stu_value. Field(0), stu_value.Field(0))
fmt.Printf("Type of age is %T and value is %v\n",
stu_value. Field(1), stu_value.Field(1)) fmt.Printf("Type
of income is %T and value is %v\n", stu_value. Field(2),
stu_value.Field(2)) name :=
reflect.ValueOf(stu.name).String() age :=
reflect.ValueOf(stu.age).Int()
income := reflect.ValueOf(stu.income).Float() fmt.Printf("Type of name is %T and value is %v\n",
name, name) fmt.Printf("Type of age is %T and value is %v\n", age, age) fmt.Printf("Type of income
is %T and value is %v\n", income, income)

}

Output:

Type of name is reflect.Value and value is Akansha Type of age is reflect.Value and value is 17

Type of income is reflect.Value and value is 40000.566

Type of name is string and value is Akansha

Type of age is int64 and value is 17

Type of income is float64 and value is 40000.56640625

Laws of reflection

Go defines three laws of reflection that define how reflection works and the points that should be remembered while working with reflection. The three laws of reflection are as follows: **Reflection goes from interface value to reflection object** Since an empty interface accepts any value, it makes it quite hard to understand what type of value is stored by an interface. Here, reflection works to get the type and value contained by an interface. The type and value of a variable are evaluated by using the functions TypeOf and ValueOf as we have already seen in the previous example. The first law of reflection is all about extracting a reflection object from an interface.

Example:

```go
package main
import ("fmt"
"reflect"

) func show_value(i interface{}){ value_type := reflect.TypeOf(i)
value := reflect.ValueOf(i) fmt.Printf("Passed value is %v of type
%v\n", value, value_type.Kind())
fmt.Println(reflect.TypeOf(value))
fmt.Println(reflect.TypeOf(value_type))
} func main(){ type
student struct{
name string age int
income float32
} stu := student{"Akansha", 17,
40000.565} show_value(stu)
}
```

Output:

passed value is {Akansha 17 40000.566} of type struct reflect.Value

*reflect.rtype

Reflection goes from reflection object to interface value

The second law is the inverse of the first law. The second law says the type reflect.Value and reflect.Type can be converted to interface value. The following is an example of reflection's second law.

Example:
```go
package
main import
("fmt"
"reflect"

) func show_value(i
interface{}){ value_type :=
reflect.TypeOf(i) value :=
reflect.ValueOf(i)
fmt.Println(reflect.TypeOf(value))
fmt.Println(reflect.TypeOf(value_type)) interface_val :=
value.Interface()
fmt.Println("Interface value
is:", interface_val)
fmt.Println("Interface value
type is:", reflect.
TypeOf(interface_val).Kind())
```

```
} func main(){ type
student struct{
name string age int
income float32
} stu := student{"Akansha", 17,
40000.565} show_value(stu)
}
```

Output:

reflect.Value

*reflect.rtype

Interface value is: {Akansha 17 40000.566}

Interface value type is: struct

To modify a reflection object, the value must be settable

On getting the value of a variable with the use of the ValueOf function, it returns the value of type
The third law says that to assign a value to reflect.Value type variable, the value must be of
reflect.Value type. If it is not of the same type, it will show panic.

Example: package
main import
("fmt"
"reflect"

)

```
func main(){ var str
string = "Hello" val :=
reflect.ValueOf(str)
fmt.Println(val)
val.SetString("World
") // will throw panic
}
```

Output:

panic: reflect: reflect.Value.SetString using unaddressable value.

In the example given above, we cannot set the value for type reflect.Value as World is not
addressable. To get rid of such issues, we can first check if a variable is settable or not by using the
function

Example: package
main import
("fmt"
"reflect"

)

```go
func main(){ var str
string = "Hello" val :=
reflect.ValueOf(str)
fmt.Println(val)
fmt.Println(val.CanSet())
}
```

Output:
Hello false

Mutex and Channels

Channels are like pipelines that connect to concurrently running Goroutines. In the language, a channel has a specific type and that type of values it can transport from one Goroutine to another. Go provides a channel operator through which we can send and receive the data through channels. A channel operator is used to sending and receive the data between two channels.

Get an understanding of deadlock

Understand the idea of select keyword with channels Understanding Golang lock/unlock concept through a mutex Declaring channels

In the Go language, we can declare a channel in two ways, using var or make method. The var keyword reserves the memory for the named variables of a specified type and initializes them with the type's default value. If we declare a channel variable using the var keyword, it creates a nil channel. Declaring a channel with the make method also reserves space in storage, initializes memory, and creates an underlying header of a specific type.

Syntax:

var name_of_channel chan type_of_channel

Or

Name_of_channel := make(chan type_of_channel)

Example: func main(){ var ch1 chan int fmt.Println("channel with 'var' keyword:", ch1) ch2 := make(chan string) fmt.Println("channel with 'make' method:", ch2)

}

Output:

channel with 'var' keyword:

channel with 'make' method: 0x1180e180

In the example given above, channel ch1 and ch2 transport integer and string type of data between channels. ch1 is declared with var keyword that initializes it with the default value nil. We cannot transfer the data using nil channels. Therefore, in Go language, channels are mostly declared with the make method. The "make" method provides easy to use channels and returns a value of a specified type. By default, channels are pointers but there is no need to dereference them to access the data.

Channel operations

Golang facilitates various channel operations as given below: Send operation with channels

The send operation sends the data of a specified type to a channel variable. The send operation blocks the channels until no channel is ready to receive the data. While sending data, it first checks for a channel that is ready to receive the data.

Example: func main(){ ch := make(chan int) ch<- 8 fmt.Println(ch)

}

The example given above will show an error. Statement ch<- 8 blocks the channel as no channel is ready to receive the data.

Receive operation in channel

By performing the receive operation, we can get the data from a channel to a variable. While receiving the data from channels, we

get two values. The first is the data that a channel sends and the other one indicates the status that whether an operation is successful or not. The idiom for the second value is ok. The value of ok variable is true if the data is received successfully from the channel and false if the channel is closed or empty.

Example: package main import "fmt" func show_value(c chan int){ c <- 8 } func main(){ c := make(chan int) go show_value(c) a, ok := <-c fmt.Println("value received from channel:", a) fmt.Println("status of operation is:", ok) }

Output:

value received from channel: 8 status of operation is: true

In the example given above, we are using the Goroutine show_value that sends a value to a channel. After calling the Goroutine, a channel is sending the data and on the next line,

the channel is ready to receive the data in the main function. As the operation is successful, true is assigned to an ok variable. The sending and receiving channel should be of the same type otherwise the compiler will show an error.

If we execute the same program with the channels declared using the var keyword, it will give an error.

Example:

func show_value(c chan int){ c <- 8 } func main(){ var c chan int go show_value(c) a, ok := <-c fmt.Println("value received from channel:", a) fmt.Println("status of operation is:", ok) }

Output:

error " [chan send chan>] "

We have observed that the send operation blocks a channel if no channel is ready to receive the data. So, we perform the receive operation to avoid such an issue. To overcome such scenarios, we can use buffered channels in Go programs. The following describes buffered and unbuffered channels briefly.

Unbuffered channel

By default, channels are unbuffered in the Go language. Such channels accept the send operation if there is a channel ready to receive the data. We saw in the previous examples that on sending data without any corresponding receiver, the compiler gives an error.

Buffered channel

Buffered channels can send specified number of values without any corresponding receiver. They store the values sent by a channel in a buffer and return when a corresponding channel is ready to receive the data. The number of values that is allowed to send without any receiver is called the capacity of a channel. The following is the syntax to create buffered channels in the Go language.

Syntax:

name_of_channel := make(chan type_of_channel, capacity_of_channel)

Example: func main(){ ch := make(chan int, 2) ch<- 8 a := <-ch fmt.Println(ch, a)

}

Output:

0x1183c0c0 8

In the example given above, the capacity of the buffered channel is 2 which indicates that it can send maximum 2 values without waiting for a receiver channel. We can send the second value as shown below:

Example: func main(){ ch := make(chan int, 2) ch<- 8 ch<- 99 a := <-ch b := <- ch fmt.Println(a, b)

}

Output:

8 99

In the example given above, it stores the values in a buffer and returns to the corresponding receiver when the channel is ready to receive the data. We can receive the data from two or multiple channels in the same line as shown below: a, b := <-ch, <-ch

In the above program, on sending the third value without a corresponding receiver channel, it will give an error as the capacity of the channel is 2.

Find the capacity of the channel

Golang provides a function cap to get the capacity of a channel.

The following example illustrates the use of the cap function with channels.

Example: func main(){ ch := make(chan int, 2) cap_ch := cap(ch) fmt.Println("Capacity of channel is:", cap_ch) for itr := 1; itr<=cap_ch; itr++{ ch<- itr*2 fmt.Println("value received from channel is:", <-ch)

}

}

Output:

Capacity of channel is: 2 value received from channel is: 2 value received from channel is: 4

Deadlock

In the previous examples, we saw that on sending data, it waits for a channel that is ready to receive the data. If it doesn't find any receiver channel, it blocks that Goroutine and passes the control to other Goroutines to run. When it finds the receiver channel in another Goroutine, it unblocks the send operation and runs that Goroutine.

In such cases, if we don't get any receiver channel in another Goroutins or there is no other Goroutine available in the program, the compiler imagines that all the Goroutines are asleep. The send operation remains blocked until the end of the program.

Such a situation is called a deadlock.

The deadlock can occur in two ways depending on the operation that is being blocked.

On sending the data to a channel, it blocks the current Goroutine and schedules other Goroutines with the hope of getting a receiver channel. Here, the "sending operation is getting blocked."

On receiving the data from a channel, it checks for an existing value in a channel. If a channel contains no value, it blocks the receive operation until it doesn't get any value in that channel. So here, the "receive operation is getting blocked." In the Go language, a deadlock occurs if we have at least one blocked operation and no other Goroutine is available to schedule in a

program. In such a case, the program crashes and the compiler shows an error. The following example explains a deadlock. Example: package main import "fmt" func show(){ fmt.Println("Hello")

} func main(){ str_ch := make(chan string) go show() str_ch<- "Hello world" fmt.Println("Send operation is getting blocked")

}

Output: Hello fatal error: all goroutines are asleep – deadlock!

goroutine 1 [chan send]

In the example given above, we are calling Goroutines then trying to send a value to a channel. It blocks the send operations as there is no other channel to receive the data. After blocking the main Goroutines, there is no other Goroutine to schedule. Hence, the deadlock occurs.

Example: package main import "fmt" func show(){ fmt.Println("Hello world")

```
} func main(){ str_ch := make(chan string) go show() a := <- str_ch fmt.Println("Receive operation
is getting blocked", a)

}
```

Output: Hello fatal error: all goroutines are asleep – deadlock!

goroutine 1 [chan receive]

In the example given above, after calling we are trying to receive a value from the channel but no value has been assigned to a channel till now. So, it blocks the current main Goroutine. As it continues, it finds that there is no other Goroutine to schedule.

In such a case, a deadlock occurs and the compiler gives a fatal error.

Using multiple Goroutines

A Go program can have multiple Goroutines with sharing values.

Go defines the concept as "Do not communicate by sharing memory. Instead, share memory by communicating."

```
Example: package main import "fmt" func square(num_ch chan int){ value := <-num_ch sqr_val :=
value*value num_ch<- sqr_val

} func cube(num_ch chan int){ value := <-num_ch cube_val := value*value*value num_ch<-
cube_val

} func main(){ num := make(chan int) // 1 go square(num) // 2 num<- 3 // 3 sqr_val := <-num // 4 go
cube(num) // 5 num<- 3 // 6 cube_val := <-num // 7 fmt.Println("Square of value:", sqr_val) // 8
fmt.Println("Cube of value:", cube_val) // 9

}
```

Output:

Square of value: 9

Cube of value: 27

First, we are creating a channel called "num" that passes an integer type of value.

In the second line, we call the "square" goroutine. In this Goroutine, we are trying to get the value from a channel. But since no value has been assigned to a channel till now, it blocks the receive operation and control is passed to the "main"

Goroutine.

In the third line, we pass "3" to a channel that further executes the receive operation in the square Goroutine. Then, the final value is passed to a channel called 'num_ch' in the Goroutine.

In the fourth line, the channel is ready to receive a value that is sent by the "square" goroutine. Thus, we get a square of 3.

In the same way, we get a cube of value in line 5, 6, and 7.

Closing a channel

While programming, there may be an instance where after creating a channel, we do not want to use it further in our Go program.

In such a case, Go provides a method to close a channel that indicates that no value will be sent through a channel. The close function is used to close a channel.

While receiving the value from a channel, we can get the status of a channel. It will return true if a channel is open and the receive operation is successful; otherwise, it will return false if a channel is closed.

Example: package main import "fmt" func cube(value chan int){ fmt.Println("In cube goroutine") val := <-value value <- val*val*val

} func square(value chan int){ fmt.Println("In square goroutine") val := <-value fmt.Println(val) value <- val*val

} func main(){ num := make(chan int) go square(num)

num<- 3 sqr_val := <-num go cube(num) num<- 3 close(num) cube_val, ok := <-num fmt.Println("Square of value:", sqr_val) fmt.Println("Cube of value:", cube_val, ok)

}

Output:

In square Goroutine

3

In cube goroutine

Square of value: 9

Cube of value: 0

Panic: send on closed channel

In the example given above, after calling the cube Goroutine we passed a value to the num channel. Before we received the final value from the channel sent by the cube Goroutine, we closed that channel. This situation lead to a runtime panic. On receiving a value from a closed channel, it returns zero without any error and assigns false to an ok variable.

The direction of a channel

In the previous examples, we have seen that we can perform, read and write both operations on a channel. By default, Go provides a bidirectional nature of channels.

We can also create unidirectional channels in the Go language that either allow the read operation or receive operation.

The syntax of declaring the unidirectional channel is as follows: Receive only channel name_of_channel := make(<- chanint) Send only channel name_of_channel := make(chan -

Here is an example of send only channel below:

Example: package main import ("fmt" "sync"

)

```
var wg sync.WaitGroup func square(value chan<- int){ fmt.Println("defining send only goroutine")
val := value fmt.Println(val) wg.Done() } func main(){ send_ch := make(chan<- int, 1) wg.Add(1)
go square(send_ch) send_ch<- 3 wg.Wait()
```

}

Output:

defining send only Goroutine

0x1183c0c0

In the example given above, we have defined a send only unidirectional channel send_ch that only sends a value to a channel. We cannot receive value from such channels. On receiving value from such channels, the compiler gives an error as shown below:

Example: package main import ("fmt"

"sync"

)

```
var wg sync.WaitGroup func square(value chan<- int){ fmt.Println("defining send only goroutine")
val := value fmt.Println(val) val<- value
```

```
wg.Done() } func main(){ send_ch := make(chan<- int, 1) wg.Add(1) go square(send_ch) send_ch<-
3 wg.Wait()
```

}

Output:

Cannot use value chan<- int> as type int in send

In the same way, we can declare receive only channels in the Go language. An example of receiving only channels is shown below: Example:

package main import ("fmt"

"sync"

)

```
var wg sync.WaitGroup func square(value <-chan int){ fmt.Println("defining receive only
goroutine") val := <-value fmt.Println(val) wg.Done() } func main(){ receive_ch := make(<-chan int)
wg.Add(1) go square(receive_ch) wg.Wait()
```

}

In the example given above, we created a receive only channel receive_ch and called squareGoroutine. Here, we are trying to receive a value from a channel. As there is no value in the channel, it blocks the receive operation and the compiler gives an error "deadlock." We can see the solution to this issue in the next

program. We can convert a bidirectional channel to unidirectional for a specific Goroutine.

Example: package main import "fmt" func receive(receive_ch chan<- int, val int) { receive_ch<- val

} func square(receive_ch<-chan int, send_ch chan<- int){ fmt.Println("defining send only goroutine") val := <- receive_ch send_ch<- val

} func main(){ send_ch := make(chan int, 1) receive_ch := make(chan int,1) receive(receive_ch, 6) square(receive_ch, send_ch) fmt.Println(<-send_ch)

}

Output:

defining send only Goroutine

6

The select keyword

Select is used for network communication or to wait for multiple channel operations. The select statement is like a switch that works with multiple cases. With the select statement, the case refers to the channel's send/receive operation. Select waits for a specific case until it to ready to perform the operation specified in a particular case statement. If no case is defined within a select statement, then it will lead to a deadlock since it didn't get any case for channel communication. The select statement gets blocked if no case statement is ready to execute. In the case of blocking, it waits for a case that is ready to perform a channel operation. To avoid select blocking, it can have a default case like a switch statement. If no case statement is ready to perform the communication, it proceeds with the default case. If the select statement has multiple cases that are ready to perform the specified channel operation, it selects any random case statement and executes it.

The syntax of the select statement is the same as the switch statement except for the case statement. Here, the case statement defines a channel operation.

Syntax:

select{ case send_receive_operation1: // body of case statement 1 case send_receive_operation2:

// body of case statement 2

......

......

}

Multiple examples of the select statement that describe the use of the select statement in different ways are as given below. Example: package main import ("fmt" "time"

)

```go
func square(num_ch chan int){ value := <-num_ch sqr_val := value*value
time.Sleep(5*time.Second) num_ch<- sqr_val

} func cube(num_ch chan int){ value := <-num_ch cube_val := value*value*value
time.Sleep(10*time.Second) num_ch<- cube_val

} func main(){ sqr_ch := make(chan int) go square(sqr_ch) sqr_ch<- 3

cube_ch := make(chan int) go cube(cube_ch) cube_ch<- 5 select{ case sqr_val := <-sqr_ch:
fmt.Println("square of a value is:", sqr_val) case cube_val := <-cube_ch:

fmt.Println("Cube of a value is:", cube_val)

}

}
```

Output:

square of a value is: 9

In the example given above, we have two Goroutines, square and We are calling both of them by passing a channel value from the main Goroutine. The select statement has two cases. In the first case, receive the value from the channel sqr_ch that is sent by the square goroutine. In the second case, we receive the value from channel cube_ch that is sent by the cube goroutine. In the square goroutine, we have given sleep time for 5 seconds and 10

seconds for the cube goroutine so that the square goroutines will finish its execution first. As the square Goroutine finishes its execution, it will send the value to a channel and case1 would be ready to execute in the select statement. The select statement executes that case and comes out of its block.

In the example given above, we saw that only one case was ready to execute at a time. The following is an example where both cases are ready to execute at the same time.

Example: package main import ("fmt"

"time"

)

```go
func square(num_ch chan int){ value := <-num_ch sqr_val := value*value
time.Sleep(1*time.Second) num_ch<- sqr_val

} func cube(num_ch chan int){ value := <-num_ch

cube_val := value*value*value time.Sleep(1*time.Second) num_ch<- cube_val

} func main(){ sqr_ch := make(chan int) go square(sqr_ch) sqr_ch<- 3 cube_ch := make(chan int) go
cube(cube_ch) cube_ch<- 5 select{ case sqr_val := <-sqr_ch: fmt.Println("square of a value is:",
sqr_val) case cube_val := <-cube_ch:
```

```
    fmt.Println("Cube of a value is:", cube_val)

    }

}
```

Output:

Cube of a value is: 125

Or square of a value is: 9

Here, the sleep time for both the Goroutines is the same (1 second). So, both the cases would be ready to execute at the same time. In such a case, the select statement randomly picks the case and executes it. The output of this program varies on executing it again and again.

Now, it could be possible that the select statement didn't find any case statement to execute.

Example: package main import ("fmt"

"time"

)

func square(num_ch chan int){

 _ = <-num_ch

time.Sleep(1*time.Second)

} func cube(num_ch chan int){

 _ = <-num_ch time.Sleep(1*time.Second)

} func main(){ sqr_ch := make(chan int) go square(sqr_ch) sqr_ch<- 3 cube_ch := make(chan int) go cube(cube_ch) cube_ch<- 5 select{ case sqr_val := <-sqr_ch: fmt.Println("square of a value is:", sqr_val) case cube_val := <-cube_ch:

fmt.Println("Cube of a value is:", cube_val)

}

}

Output:

Fatal error: all goroutines are asleep – deadlock!

goroutine 1 [select]

In this case, we sent the value to channels that are received by Goroutines. Now, in both the case statements, we are trying to receive the value from a channel, but the channel doesn't have any value. As the select statement doesn't find any ready case statement here, it blocks the select statement and also leads to a deadlock.

To avoid a deadlock, we can add the default statement in select that proceeds the execution if select doesn't find any ready case statement.

Example: package main import ("fmt"

"time"

)

```go
func square(num_ch chan int){

    _ = <-num_ch time.Sleep(1*time.Second)

} func cube(num_ch chan int){

    _ = <-num_ch time.Sleep(1*time.Second)

} func main(){ sqr_ch := make(chan int) go square(sqr_ch) sqr_ch<- 3 cube_ch := make(chan int) go cube(cube_ch) cube_ch<- 5 select{ case sqr_val := <-sqr_ch: fmt.Println("square of a value is:", sqr_val) case cube_val := <-cube_ch: fmt.Println("Cube of a value is:", cube_val) default: fmt.Println("No case statement is ready to execute!")

    }

}
```

Output:

No case statement is ready to execute!

Here is an example where the select statement doesn't have any case for channel communication.

Example: func main(){ select{

```go
    }

}
```

Output:

Fatal error: all goroutines are asleep – deadlock! goroutine 1 [select cases>]

With this blank select statement, the compiler will give a fatal error and lead to a deadlock.

We saw that a maximum of one case is executed with a select statement at a time. We can execute multiple cases by repeatedly checking if a case is ready to execute.

Example: package main import ("fmt"

"time"

)

```go
func square(num_ch chan int){ value := <-num_ch sqr_val := value*value
time.Sleep(5*time.Second) num_ch<- sqr_val

} func cube(num_ch chan int){ value := <-num_ch cube_val := value*value*value
time.Sleep(10*time.Second) num_ch<- cube_val
```

```
} func main(){ sqr_ch := make(chan int) go square(sqr_ch) sqr_ch<- 3 cube_ch := make(chan int) go
cube(cube_ch) cube_ch<- 5

for itr := 1; itr<= 2; itr++{

select{ case sqr_val := <-sqr_ch: fmt.Println("square of a value is:", sqr_val) case cube_val := <-
cube_ch:

fmt.Println("Cube of a value is:", cube_val)

}

}

}
```

Output:

square of a value is: 9

Cube of a value is: 125

Here, we are executing the select statement two times as we have two cases in the select statement. Since the square Goroutine has less sleep time, it will finish its execution first and case1 would be ready to execute. So, a select statement first executes On the second time, it finds case2 that is ready to execute. In this way, the select statement waits for the Goroutine to finish its execution and proceeds with the specified case.

Golang provides the facility to build concurrent programs that sometimes lead to unexpected behavior. Concurrency comes with multiple bugs that are quite hard to debug. The following defines some possible unexpected situations and how to detect and solve them.

Data race in Go

Data race can be defined by a situation where two or multiple threads concurrently access the same memory location and perform at least one write operation. It occurs with the execution of multi-threading programming. The following example defines data race in Go language.

```
Example: package main import "fmt" var value = 45 func update_value(){ if(value==45){ value++ }
fmt.Println(value)

} func main(){ go update_value() //gr1 go update_value() //gr2

}
```

In the example given above, we have two Goroutines, and and both are accessing the same variable value to update its value.

There could be three cases with this program. It depends on the order of execution of the Goroutines gr1 and gr2.

Case 1: gr1 first reads the data and then updates the value according to a specific condition. After the execution of gr2 reads the data checks for the conditions and updates the data. Here, the order of the Goroutines is synchronized. No concurrent process is running here; the program will provide an accurate result. result.

Case 2: Here, gr1 first reads the data and then gr2 reads the data. So, both the Goroutines will read the value 45 in this case.

After that gr1 and gr2 write a value as the condition is satisfied with both the Goroutines. Here, the the execution goes wrong and gets an unexpected result. result.

Case 3: Here, gr1 first reads the data and then gr2 reads the data. So, both the Goroutines will read the value 45 in this case.

After that, gr2 and gr1 write a value as the condition gets satisfied with both the Goroutines. Here, the execution goes wrong and there is an unexpected result.

result.

Race condition

A race condition is a feature of a program or system that can lead to an unexpected result. A race condition occurs when two or multiple operations are performed at the same time in a program or system. Due to incorrect timing or ordering of operation, it leads to the crash of a program. A race condition is different from a data race. It is not necessary that if a program has a race condition, it must be because of a data race. A program can have a race condition but not a data race.

The following is an example where a data race doesn't exist but it defines a race condition.

Example:

Thread 1 Thread2 lock(1) lock(1) value = 1 value = 2 unlock(1) unlock(1)

In the example given above, we used a lock before updating the value of a variable to synchronize the process. There would never be any concurrent process, so data race doesn't exist here.

We can get race condition with such examples. As we don't know the order of execution for these threads, it's hard to determine which process updates the value of a variable. The final value of a variable can be 1 or 2.

Check for data race

While working with multi-threading, it becomes necessary to protect a program from abnormal behavior to make the program reliable and scalable. Go language provides a "data race detector"

tool that tracks all the operations related to static/dynamic memory access and how and when the memory is accessed in a program. Dynamic tracking is done for unsynchronized access to shared variables. This tool looks for a race condition. If a program has a race condition because of a data race, it prints a warning message. The Go race detector tool was introduced with the v1.1

version of Go, integrated with the Go toolchain. This tool supports Linux/amd64, Linux/ppc64le, linuxarm64, FreeBSD/amd64, NetBSD/amd64, Darwin/amd64, and windows/amd64.

To enable the race detector in a program, -race flag is raised while executing a program. We can raise the race flag in the following ways:

go test –race package_name go run –race program_name go build –race command_name go install –race package_name

It is advisable to use a race detector if it is necessary as it consumes the CPU and memory ten times more. Also, we can say that with concurrency, data sharing between Goroutines must be properly synchronized to avoid such erroneous conditions.

Mutex

In the Go language, Mutex provides a mechanism to synchronize the data access between multiple goroutines. Mutex follows the concept of a mutual exclusion lock that allows only one Goroutine to access the memory at a time by the locking and unlocking mechanism.

Till now, we have used channels for synchronized communication between Goroutines. Although channels are also good as they have the built-in property of thread safety and prevent a race condition, it is advisable not to use channels in every situation.

With a large application, a channel allows single thread access to memory but the performance penalty occurs with channels if less number of resources is shared between them. Channels and Mutex both have their pros and cons depending on the requirement and the way of programming.

Here, we are going to use the concept of mutual exclusion provided by a data structure Mutex. Mutex is defined in the sync package available in the src directory. It has an interface locker that encapsulates the functionally of locking and unlocking by declaring two methods, Lock and These two methods are implemented by the mutex struct type. Mutex defines these two methods to lock and unlock a block of code that is executed by only one Goroutine at a time. Data access is synchronized with Mutex by keeping a lock when a shared resource is being used so that no other Goroutine can use it. After using that shared

resource, the lock is removed. It prevents race condition between multiple Goroutines if they are accessing the same memory space at a time.

Here is an example that shows how Mutex locks and unlocks a block of code and enables synchronized data access.

Example: package main import ("fmt"

"sync"

) type initial_amount struct{ amount int sync.Mutex } func (ia *initial_amount) withdraw_amount(withdraw_val int){ ia.Lock() ia.amount = ia.amount - withdraw_val ia.Unlock() } func (ia *initial_amount) deposit_amount(deposit_val int){ ia.Lock() ia.amount = ia.amount + deposit_val ia.Unlock() }

func (ia *initial_amount) get_balance() int { val :=ia.amount return val } func main(){ ia := initial_amount{amount: 2000} for itr:= 1; itr<=10; itr++{ go ia.deposit_amount(500) go ia.withdraw_amount(300)

} final_amount := ia.get_balance() fmt.Println("Final balance is:",final_amount)

}

Output:

Final balance is: 4100

In the program given above, we create a struct initial_amount that has two fields, amount and The amount variable is shared between two Goroutines, withdraw_amount and deposit_amount.

Here, Mutex is defined as a struct field that locks and unlocks the access to amount variable. withdraw_amount withdraws an amount and updates amount variable. Similarly, deposit_amount deposits an amount as specified and updates the same amount variable. Both Goroutines are called from the main Goroutine; they will run concurrently. In the deposit_amount goroutine, before updating the value of the "amount" variable, we use the lock method so that any other goroutine won't be able to access the amount variable at the same time. When deposit_amount updates the value, it unlocks the resources to make them available for other Goroutines. In such a way, the access to the amount variable is synchronized.

When we run the above program with the race detector, it prints the output message with a data race warning that indicates the data race exists in the above program. In the get_balace method, we are accessing the same shared variable amount to read its value. While accessing this variable, the lock is being acquired either by deposit_amount or withdraw_amount method. We can prevent this warning by acquiring a lock before reading the value in get_balance method.

func (ia *initial_amount) get_balance() int { ia.Lock() val := ia.amount ia.Unlock() return val

}

Now run the program with the same race detector tool.

Output:

Final balance is: 3800

This time, the is quite different as it waits for some time to acquire a lock for the shared variable.

Also, it didn't get any data race warning here. Now the question is of not getting the correct result.

The get_balance method is being called before the termination of all Goroutines, so it returns the intermediate value of a variable.

We can resolve this issue by using WaitGroup as shown below: Example:

package main import ("fmt"

"sync"

)

var wg sync.WaitGroup type initial_amount struct{ amount int sync.Mutex } func (ia *initial_amount) withdraw_amount(withdraw_val int){ ia.Lock() ia.amount = ia.amount - withdraw_val ia.Unlock() wg.Done() } func (ia *initial_amount) deposit_amount(deposit_val int){ ia.Lock() ia.amount = ia.amount + deposit_val ia.Unlock() wg.Done() }

func (ia *initial_amount) get_balance() int { ia.Lock() val := ia.amount ia.Unlock() return val } func main(){ ia := initial_amount{amount: 2000} for itr:= 1; itr<=10; itr++{

wg.Add(1) go ia.deposit_amount(500) wg.Add(1) go ia.withdraw_amount(300)

```
} wg.Wait() final_amount := ia.get_balance() fmt.Println("final balance is:", final_amount)
}
```

Output:

final balance is: 4000

RWMutex

Any thread either reads the data or modifies it. On performing a write operation, data sharing is not allowed with multiple Goroutines, whereas with a read operation, multiple Goroutines can read the data from the same memory space without any issue. Based on several operations, Golang provides a specific reader/writer Mutex that multiple readers and writers can behold.

Like Mutex, RWMutex is also available in a sync package.

RWMutex is a struct that contains various fields to track the memory access by multiple threads. RWMutex implements multiple methods that provide a specific type of lock/unlocking service.

RLock()

It is used to acquire a lock rw for reading purpose. Multiple readers can acquire this lock in a single program. RLock is not bound with a specific thread.

RUnlock()

This method releases the acquired lock for a single RLock call that doesn't affect another running read operation. In the Go language, one thread may RLockrw another thread and it can release that.

Lock()

It locks rw for writing purpose. This type of lock is acquired by only one thread at a time. If another thread acquires a lock for the reading/writing purpose, Lock blocks until the lock is available to acquire.

Unlock()

This method unblocks rw to make it available for another writer thread. On executing Unlock without acquiring the lock, the compiler will give an error at runtime.

There is a point to remember which is that we cannot contain Mutex and RWMutex both as struct field in a single program. In such a case, the compiler will give the error "ambiguous selector."

The following example defines thread-safe maps with the use of RWMutex.

Example: package main import ("fmt"

"sync"

"time"

)

```
type Map_struct struct{ map_val map[int] int sync.RWMutex } func (map_data *Map_struct)
update_map(keyval int){ map_data.Lock() map_data.map_val[keyval] = keyval * 10
```

```
map_data.Unlock() } func (map_data *Map_struct) read_map(){ map_data.RLock() val :=
map_data.map_val map_data.RUnlock() fmt.Println(val) } func main(){ ia :=
Map_struct{map_val:make(map[int]int)} for itr:= 1; itr<10; itr++{ go ia.update_map(itr) go
ia.read_map() } time.Sleep(5 * time.Second)

}
```

Output:
map[1:10 2:20] map[1:10 2:20] map[1:10 2:20 3:30] map[1:10 2:20 3:30 4:40] map[1:10 2:20 3:30
4:40 5:50] map[1:10 2:20 3:30 4:40 5:50 6:60] map[1:10 2:20 3:30 4:40 5:50 6:60 7:70] map[1:10
2:20 3:30 4:40 5:50 6:60 7:70 8:80] map[1:10 2:20 3:30 4:40 5:50 6:60 7:70 8:80 9:90]

In the program given above, we create a struct Map_struct that has two fields, map_val and
RWMutex object. Embedding of RWMutex object allows accessing multiple methods for In the
main Goroutine, we initialize the struct and call Goroutines in a loop. Here, we have two Goroutines.
read_map reads the map values and update_map modifies the map. read_map goroutine puts RLock
to perform read operation, and after reading a map, it releases the lock using the Goroutine
update_map acquires the lock for a write operation and after updating the map, it releases the lock
using the Unlock method. We give time sleep for 5 seconds at the end of the main Goroutine so that
all the running Goroutines can finish their execution till that time.

Conclusion: The Role of Reflection, Mutex, and Channels in Go's Concurrency Model

Reflection in Go: Flexibility and Dynamic Programming

Reflection is a powerful tool that allows Go developers to write flexible, dynamic code. By
leveraging the reflect package, developers can inspect the type and value of variables at runtime,
manipulate fields and methods, and interact with data structures in a way that would otherwise
require hardcoding or static analysis. This capability is especially beneficial in scenarios where
applications need to handle varying types of data structures or require dynamic behavior. Examples
include building serialization frameworks, implementing generic data processing pipelines, or
creating plug-in architectures where new functionality can be added without recompiling the core
codebase.

However, the use of reflection comes with trade-offs. Reflective code can be more challenging to
read and debug, as it relies on runtime information that may not be evident when looking at the
source code. Additionally, reflection is generally slower than direct method calls or accessing fields
directly, as the type information is inspected at runtime. This can lead to performance overhead,
especially in performance-critical applications. Therefore, developers should use reflection
judiciously, opting for it only when dynamic behavior is truly needed and when no other simpler
solutions are available.

Reflection shines in scenarios like creating automated testing frameworks, where it can dynamically
identify test cases based on naming conventions or tags, or in data marshaling/unmarshaling, where
it can convert data structures to JSON or XML without requiring explicit definitions for every data
type. By understanding how to use reflection effectively, Go developers can create more robust and
adaptable software systems that can accommodate future changes with ease.

Mutex in Go: Ensuring Safe Concurrency

Concurrency is one of Go's hallmark features, making it possible to build programs that can handle multiple tasks at the same time. However, with concurrency comes the challenge of managing shared resources. Without proper coordination, multiple Goroutines could attempt to read and write to the same variable simultaneously, leading to race conditions and unpredictable behavior. This is where Mutexes come into play.

A Mutex ensures that only one Goroutine can access a shared resource at a time. When a Goroutine locks a Mutex, it gains exclusive access to the resource, preventing other Goroutines from modifying it until the lock is released. This guarantees the integrity of the data, as it prevents concurrent writes or simultaneous reads and writes that could lead to inconsistent states.

Mutexes are simple yet effective tools for handling concurrency, but they require careful management. For instance, if a Goroutine fails to release a Mutex, it can lead to a deadlock where other Goroutines are indefinitely blocked from accessing the resource. Developers should always use defer to unlock Mutexes as soon as the critical section of code is completed. Additionally, the scope of the lock should be kept as small as possible to minimize the time a resource is locked, reducing the chance of contention between Goroutines.

Beyond the standard sync.Mutex, Go also provides sync.RWMutex, which distinguishes between read and write locks. This is useful in scenarios where multiple Goroutines need to read the same resource but only one Goroutine should be allowed to modify it at a time. Using RWMutex, multiple read locks can be held concurrently, but write locks are exclusive. This fine-grained control can improve performance by allowing concurrent reads while still maintaining data integrity.

Real-world examples of Mutex usage include building thread-safe caches, managing shared resources in web servers, and coordinating access to files or databases. By understanding how to effectively use Mutexes, developers can write robust concurrent programs that are both safe and efficient.

Channels in Go: Seamless Communication Between Goroutines

Channels are Go's idiomatic way of handling concurrency. Unlike Mutexes, which prevent race conditions by enforcing exclusive access, Channels provide a way for Goroutines to communicate and synchronize their actions. They enable the passing of data between Goroutines, which can simplify the design of concurrent programs by avoiding the need for explicit locking mechanisms.

An unbuffered channel blocks the sending Goroutine until another Goroutine is ready to receive the data, ensuring synchronization between the two. This blocking behavior can be used to coordinate actions between Goroutines, such as signaling when a task is completed or distributing work among a set of worker Goroutines. Buffered channels, on the other hand, allow data to be sent without an immediate receiver, providing a way to decouple the sending and receiving operations. This can be useful in scenarios where bursts of data need to be processed asynchronously, such as in task queues or data pipelines.

One of the most powerful features of channels is the select statement, which allows a Goroutine to wait on multiple channel operations. This makes it possible to write non-blocking concurrent code that can handle multiple tasks simultaneously, such as reading from multiple sources or responding to timeouts. The select statement can be used to implement sophisticated concurrency patterns, including fan-in, where multiple sources send data to a single channel, and fan-out, where a single source distributes data to multiple Goroutines for parallel processing.

Channels make it easy to write clean, efficient concurrent code, but they also come with their own set of challenges. Deadlocks can occur if a channel operation is left unhandled, and buffered channels can lead to memory issues if data is produced faster than it can be consumed. It's essential to design systems that properly manage the flow of data, ensuring that producers and consumers are balanced, and that there are mechanisms in place to handle timeouts and errors gracefully.

Real-world applications of channels include building concurrent web servers, handling distributed processing tasks, and creating real-time systems that need to process streams of data, such as live video or messaging applications. The elegance of Go's concurrency model lies in the ability to compose these simple constructs—Goroutines, Mutexes, and Channels—into complex systems that are both scalable and maintainable.

Best Practices for Using Reflection, Mutex, and Channels Together

Understanding how to use Reflection, Mutexes, and Channels effectively can greatly enhance the robustness and performance of Go applications. Here are some best practices to consider when working with these tools:

1. **Minimize the Use of Reflection:** Reflection should be used sparingly due to its performance overhead and potential complexity. Use it only when dynamic behavior is required, and prefer type-safe alternatives whenever possible. If reflection must be used, encapsulate it in well-documented helper functions to hide the complexity from the rest of the codebase.

2. **Optimize Mutex Locking:** Keep the code between Lock and Unlock as short as possible to reduce contention. Always use defer to ensure that a locked Mutex is properly unlocked, even if an error occurs. For read-heavy workloads, consider using sync.RWMutex to allow concurrent reads while ensuring exclusive access for writes.

3. **Design Efficient Channel Communication:** Use channels to simplify communication between Goroutines, but be mindful of potential deadlocks and race conditions. Ensure that channels are properly closed to avoid unexpected blocking, and use the select statement to handle multiple channel operations, timeouts, and error conditions gracefully.

4. **Combine Channels and Mutexes Carefully:** There are situations where both channels and Mutexes are needed—such as when managing shared state across multiple Goroutines while also coordinating tasks. Be careful to avoid situations where a Mutex is held while waiting on a channel, as this can lead to deadlocks. Instead, structure the code so that the critical sections are kept separate from communication logic.

5. **Use Concurrency Patterns Effectively:** Go's concurrency primitives make it possible to implement a variety of patterns, such as worker pools, pipelines, and event-driven architectures. By understanding how to leverage these patterns, developers can create systems that are scalable and maintainable. For instance, a worker pool can be implemented using channels to distribute tasks to a fixed set of workers, while Mutexes can ensure that shared resources are safely managed.

Conclusion: Building Robust Concurrent Applications in Go

Reflection, Mutexes, and Channels form the backbone of Go's approach to concurrency, enabling developers to build efficient, scalable, and safe applications. Reflection allows for dynamic behavior, making it easier to create flexible systems that can adapt to varying data types and runtime conditions. Mutexes provide a straightforward way to manage shared resources, ensuring data integrity even in complex concurrent programs. Channels offer an elegant means of communication and synchronization between Goroutines, facilitating the design of concurrent systems without the need for explicit locking.

Together, these tools empower developers to write concurrent programs that are not only performant but also easy to reason about and maintain. Understanding the nuances of each feature and how they can be combined effectively is key to mastering concurrency in Go. By following best practices and learning from real-world scenarios, developers can harness the full power of Go's concurrency model to build robust, high-performance applications that meet the demands of modern software development.

As Go continues to evolve, the language's focus on simplicity and efficiency ensures that its concurrency model remains a critical feature. For those looking to delve deeper into concurrent programming, understanding these foundational concepts is an essential step towards mastering Go and building scalable systems that can handle the challenges of today's computing landscape.

12. Go: Testing and Tooling

Introduction

Testing is an integral part of software development, and Go (Golang) provides a robust, built-in testing framework. The language's simplicity, performance, and scalability are enhanced by its comprehensive tooling suite, allowing developers to write, test, and deploy code efficiently. In "Testing and Tooling in Go 2024," we'll explore Go's native testing tools, along with third-party options that enhance the testing experience, and a variety of tools that facilitate effective development, debugging, and code analysis.

Go's testing ecosystem has been evolving, and recent versions have introduced new features and improvements, making it easier for developers to write unit tests, benchmark their code, and manage dependencies. This content will guide you through best practices and advanced tooling for testing Go applications, ensuring that you can build reliable, maintainable, and high-quality software.

Importance of Testing in Software Development

Before diving into the specifics of Go, it's essential to understand why testing is crucial:

1. **Reliability**: Testing ensures that your code works as intended, reducing bugs in production.

2. **Maintainability**: Well-tested code can be refactored with confidence, knowing that tests will catch any unintended changes.

3. **Performance**: Benchmarking helps identify bottlenecks and optimize the performance of your applications.

4. **Collaboration**: Clear test coverage allows teams to understand code behavior without needing to go through the entire codebase.

Go's Approach to Testing

Go's testing framework is simple yet powerful. It follows a philosophy of minimalism and efficiency, with everything needed for basic testing included in the testing package. There is no need to install additional frameworks, and setting up tests is straightforward. Go's go test command makes it easy to run tests, benchmark code, and even generate code coverage reports.

The testing Package

The testing package is the cornerstone of testing in Go. It allows developers to write unit tests, integration tests, and benchmarks. Here's a brief overview of its features:

- **Unit Tests**: These are used to test individual components of code. They are written as functions that follow a naming convention starting with Test (e.g., TestAddFunction).

- **Benchmarking**: Performance testing is as essential as functionality testing. Go's testing framework allows developers to benchmark code easily using functions that begin with Benchmark.

- **Table-Driven Tests**: Go encourages writing clean, maintainable test cases by using table-driven tests, where inputs and expected outputs are defined in a table format. This makes it easy to add new test cases without changing the test logic.

Running Tests

The command go test is used to run all tests in the current directory. It's simple, yet packed with options:

- go test ./... runs tests in the current directory and all subdirectories.

- go test -v runs tests in verbose mode, showing detailed output.

- go test -cover generates a coverage report, indicating which parts of the code are covered by tests.

Best Practices for Writing Tests

1. **Test Independently**: Each test should be independent and should not rely on other tests.

2. **Avoid External Dependencies**: When possible, mock external dependencies to ensure that tests can be run without requiring access to external systems.

3. **Use Table-Driven Tests**: This makes it easier to expand test cases and ensures cleaner code.

4. **Maintain Readability**: Test cases should be easy to read and understand, making it easier to diagnose failures.

5. **Leverage Subtests**: Use subtests to run variations of tests, especially when running the same logic with different inputs.

Benchmarking in Go

Go makes benchmarking simple and efficient. Benchmarking functions are defined similarly to test functions but start with Benchmark (e.g., BenchmarkSort). The benchmarking framework measures the performance of your code under different conditions, helping identify performance bottlenecks.

Example of a benchmark function:

```go
func BenchmarkAdd(b *testing.B) {

  for i := 0; i < b.N; i++ {

    Add(1, 2)

  }

}
```

You can run benchmarks using the go test -bench command.

Advanced Testing Tools

Mocking with gomock and testify

While Go's built-in testing framework is powerful, some scenarios require more advanced tooling. Libraries like gomock and testify help with mocking and assertions, making it easier to write tests for complex interactions and external dependencies.

1. **gomock**: This is a popular mocking library that helps simulate interfaces, allowing developers to test components without relying on actual implementations.

2. **testify**: This provides helpful utilities for writing cleaner, more expressive tests. It includes easy-to-use assertion methods, which make test results easier to interpret.

Fuzz Testing

Go introduced fuzz testing support in version 1.18. Fuzz testing, or fuzzing, is an automated testing technique that provides random inputs to functions and checks for unexpected behaviors. It is particularly useful for uncovering edge cases and security vulnerabilities.

Code Coverage Analysis

Go's -cover flag provides a basic but effective way to analyze how much of your codebase is covered by tests. It can be used to generate detailed reports, helping developers identify untested parts of their code.

go test -coverprofile=coverage.out

go tool cover -html=coverage.out

Continuous Integration with Go

Automating testing using Continuous Integration (CI) is crucial in modern software development. CI tools like GitHub Actions, Travis CI, and CircleCI can be configured to automatically run tests whenever code is committed, ensuring that new changes don't introduce bugs.

Example CI Configuration:

A typical .github/workflows/go.yml file for GitHub Actions might look like:

name: Go

on: [push, pull_request]

jobs:

  test:

    runs-on: ubuntu-latest

    steps:

    - uses: actions/checkout@v2

    - name: Set up Go

      uses: actions/setup-go@v3

      with:

```
go-version: '^1.19'
```

```
- name: Run Tests
```

```
run: go test -v ./...
```

Go's Tooling Ecosystem

Beyond testing, Go's tooling ecosystem provides numerous utilities that streamline the development process.

Code Formatting and Linting

1. **gofmt**: This tool formats Go code according to a consistent style, making it easy to read and maintain.

2. **golint**: This is a linter that identifies stylistic errors and offers suggestions for improvement.

Dependency Management with go mod

Dependency management is essential for building modular, maintainable software. Go Modules (go mod) provide a robust system to manage dependencies, pin versions, and ensure reproducibility.

1. **go mod init**: Initializes a new Go module.

2. **go mod tidy**: Removes unnecessary dependencies and adds missing ones.

3. **go mod vendor**: Copies dependencies to the vendor directory, useful for ensuring builds use specific versions.

Debugging with dlv (Delve)

dlv (Delve) is a Go debugger that helps developers step through code, inspect variables, and identify bugs. Debugging is essential for resolving complex issues, and Delve integrates well with popular IDEs like VS Code and GoLand.

Profiling and Performance Analysis

Performance profiling is crucial for understanding how your code behaves under different conditions. Go provides built-in tools for profiling CPU, memory, and blocking operations. Use pprof to capture and analyze performance profiles.

Example:

```
go test -bench . -cpuprofile=cpu.prof
```

```
go tool pprof cpu.prof
```

Writing automated tests helps you to improve the quality and reliability of software. This chapter is about writing automated tests in Go. The standard library contains a package named testing to write tests. Also, the built-in Go tool has a test runner to run tests.

Consider this test for a Hello function which takes a string as input and returns another string. The expected output string should start with "Hello," and ends with the input value followed by an exclamation.

Test for Hello

package hello

import "testing"

func TestHello(t *testing.T) {

out := Hello("Tom")

if out != "Hello, Tom!" {

t.Fail()

}

}

In the first line, the package name is hello which is the same as the package where the function is going to be defined. Since both test and actual code is in the same package, the test can access any name within that package irrespective whether it is an exported name or not. At the same, when the actual problem is compiled using the go build command, the test files are ignored. The build ignores all files with the name ending _test.go. Sometimes these kinds of tests are called white-box test as it is accessing both exported and unexported names within the package. If you only want to access exported names within the test, you can declare the name of the test package with _test suffix. In this case, that would be hello_test, which should work in this case as we are only testing the exported function directly. However, to access those exported names – in this case, a function – the package should import explicitly.

The line no. 5 starts the test function declaration. As per the test framework, the function name should start with Test prefix. The prefix is what helps the test runner to identify the tests that should be running.

The input parameter t is a pointer of type testing.T. The testing.T type provides functions to make the test pass or fail. It also gives functions to log messages.

In the line no. 6 the Hello function is called with "Tom" as the input string. The return value is assigning to a variable named out.

In line no. 7 the actual output value is checked against the expected output value. If the values are not matching, the Fail function is getting called. The particular function state is going to be marked as a failure when the Fail function is getting called.

The test is going to pass or fail based on the implementation of the Hello function. Here is an implementation of the function to satisfy the test:

Hello function

package hello

```
import "fmt"

// Hello says "Hello" with name

func Hello(name string) string {

return fmt.Sprintf("Hello, %s!", name)

}
```

As you can see in the above function definition, it takes a string as an input argument. A new string is getting constructed as per the requirement, and it returns that value.

Now you can run the test like this:

```
$ go test

PASS

ok_/home/baiju/hello  0.001
```

If you want to see the verbose output, use the -v option:

```
$ go test -v

=== RUN TestHello

--- PASS: TestHello (0.00s)

PASS

ok_/home/baiju/hello  0.001s
```

Failing a Test

To fail a test, you need to explicitly call Fail function provided by the value of testing.T type. As we have seen before, every test function has access to a testing.T object. Usually, the name of that value is going to write as t. To fail a test, you can call the Fail function like this:

t.Fail()

The test is going be a failure when the Fail function is getting called. However, the remaining code in the same test function continue to execute. If you want to stop executing the further lines immediately, you can call FailNow function.

t.FailNow()

Alternatively, there are other convenient functions which give similar behavior along with logging message. The next section discusses logging messages.

Logging Message

The testing.T has two functions for logging, one with default formatting and the other with the user-specified format. Both functions accept an arbitrary number of arguments.

The Log function formats its arguments using the default formats available for any type. The behavior is similar to fmt.Println function. So, you can change the formatted value by implementing the fmt.Stringer interface:

type Stringer interface { String() string }

Failing with Log Message

You need to create a method named String which returns a string for your custom types.

Here is an example calling Log with two arguments:

t.Log("Some message", someValue)

In the above function call, there are only two arguments given, but you can pass any number of arguments.

The log message going to print if the test is failing. The verbose mode, the -v command-line option, also log the message irrespective of whether a test fails or not.
The Logf function takes a string format followed by arguments expected by the given string format. Here is an example:

t.Logf("%d no. of lines: %s", 34, "More number of lines")

The Logf formats the values based on the given format. The Logf is similar to fmt.Printf function.

Usually, logging and marking a test as failure happens simultaneously. The testing.T has two functions for logging with failing, one with default formatting and the other with the user-specified format. Both functions accept an arbitrary number of arguments.

The Error function is equivalent to calling Log followed by Fail. The function signature is similar to Log function. Here is an example calling Error with two arguments:

t.Error("Some message", someValue)

Similar to Error function, the Errorf function is equivalent to calling Logf followed by Fail. The function signature is similar to Logf function.

The Errorf function takes a string format followed by arguments expected by the given string format. Here is an example:

t.Errorf("%d no. of lines: %s", 34, "More number of lines") The Errorf formats the values based on the given format.

Skipping Test

When writing tests, there are situations where particular tests need not run. Some tests might have written for a specific environment. The criteria for running tests could be CPU architecture, operating system or any other parameter. The testing package has functions to mark test for skipping.

The SkipNow function call marks the test as having been skipped. It stops the current test execution. If the test has marked as failed before skipping, that particular test is yet considered to have failed. The SkipNow function doesn't accept any argument. Here is a simple example:

```go
package hello
import ("runtime"

"testing" 6 )

func TestHello(t *testing.T) {

if runtime.GOOS == "linux" {

t.SkipNow()

}

out := Hello("Tom")

if out != "Hello, Tom!" {

t.Fail()

}

}
```

If you run the above code on a Linux system, you can see the test has skipped. The output is going to be something like this:

```
$ go test . -v

=== RUN TestHello

--- SKIP: TestHello (0.00s)

PASS

ok_/home/baiju/skip   0.001s
```

As you can see from the output, the test has skipped execution.

There are two more convenient functions similar to Error and Errorf. Those functions are Skip and Skipf. These functions help you to log a message before skipping. The message could be the reason for skipping the test.

Parallel Running

t.Skip("Some reason message", someValue)

The Skipf function takes a string format followed by arguments expected by the given string format. Here is an example:

t.Skipf("%d no. of lines: %s", 34, "More number of lines") The Skipf formats the values based on the given format.

You can mark a test to run in parallel. To do so, you can call the t.Parallel function. The test is going to run in parallel to other tests marked parallel.

Sub Tests

The Go testing package allows you to group related tests together in a hierarchical form. You can define multiple related tests under a single-parent test using the 'Run' method.

To create a subtest, you use the t.Run() method. The t.Run() method takes two arguments: the name of the subtest and the body of the subtest. The body of the subtest is a regular Go function.

For example, the following code creates a subtest called foo:

```go
func TestBar(t *testing.T) {

t.Run("foo", func(t *testing.T) {

// This is the body of the subtest.

})

}
```

Subtests are reported separately from each other. This means that if a subtest fails, the test runner will report the failure for that subtest only. The parent test will still be considered to have passed.

Subtests can be used to test different aspects of a function or method. For example, you could use subtests to test different input values, different output values, or different error conditions.

Subtests can also be used to test different implementations of a function or method. For example, you could use subtests to test a function that is implemented in Go and a function that is implemented in C.

Subtests are a powerful feature of the Go testing package. They can be used to organize your tests, make them easier to read and maintain, and test different aspects of your code.

Exercises

Exercise 1: Create a package with a function to return the sum of two integers and write a test for the same.

Solution: sum.go: package sum

```go
// Add adds to integers func Add(first, second int) int { return first + second

} sum_test.go: package sum import "testing"

func TestAdd(t *testing.T) { out := Add(2, 3)

if out != 5 {

t.Error("Sum of 2 and 3:", out)

}

}
```

Tooling

Good support for lots of useful tools is another strength of Go. Apart from the built-in tools, there any many other community-built tools. This chapter covers the built-in Go tools and few other external tools.

The built-in Go tools can access through the go command. When you install the Go compiler (gc); the go tool is available in the path. The go tool has many commands. You can use the go tool to compile Go programs, run test cases, and format source files among other things.

Getting Help

The go tool is self-documented. You can get help about any commands easily. To see the list of all commands, you can run the "help" command. For example, to see help for build command, you can run like this: go help build

The help command also provides help for specific topics like" buildmode"," cache"," filetype", and" environment" among other topics. To see help for a specific topic, you can run the command like this: go help environment

Basic Information

Version

When reporting bugs, it is essential to specify the Go version number and environment details. The Go tool gives access to this information through the following commands. To get version information, run this command:

go version

The output should look something like this: go version go1.20.4 linux/amd64

As you can see, it shows the version number followed by operating system and CPU architecture.

Environment

To get environment variables, you can run this command: go env

The output should display all the environment variables used by the Go tool when running different commands.

A typical output will look like this:

GO111MODULE=""

GOARCH="amd64"

GOBIN=""

GOCACHE="/home/baiju/.cache/go-build"

GOENV="/home/baiju/.config/go/env"

GOEXE=""

GOEXPERIMENT=""

```
GOFLAGS=""
GOHOSTARCH="amd64"
GOHOSTOS="linux"
GOINSECURE=""
GOMODCACHE="/home/baiju/go/pkg/mod"
GONOPROXY=""
GONOSUMDB=""
GOOS="linux"
GOPATH="/home/baiju/go"
GOPRIVATE=""
GOPROXY="https://proxy.golang.org,direct"
GOROOT="/usr/local/go"
GOSUMDB="sum.golang.org"
GOTMPDIR=""
GOTOOLDIR="/usr/local/go/pkg/tool/linux_amd64"
GOVCS=""
GOVERSION="go1.20.4"
GCCGO="gccgo"
GOAMD64="v1"
AR="ar"
CC="gcc"
CXX="g++"
CGO_ENABLED="1"
GOMOD="/dev/null"
GOWORK=""
CGO_CFLAGS="-O2 -g"
CGO_CPPFLAGS=""
CGO_CXXFLAGS="-O2 -g"
CGO_FFLAGS="-O2 -g"
CGO_LDFLAGS="-O2 -g"
```

PKG_CONFIG="pkg-config"

GOGCCFLAGS="-fPIC -m64 -pthread -Wl,--no-gc-sections -fmessage-length=0

-fdebug-prefix-map=/tmp/go-build1378738152=/tmp/go-build

-gno-record-gcc-switches"

List

The list command provides meta information about packages. Running without any arguments shows the current packages import path. The -f helps to extract more information, and it can specify a format. The text/template package syntax can be used to specify the format.

The struct used to format has many attributes, here is a subset:

Dir – directory containing package sources

ImportPath – import path of package in dir

ImportComment – path in import comment on package statement

Name – package name

Doc – package documentation string

Target – install path

GoFiles – list of .go source files

Building and Running

Here is an example usage:

$ go list -f '{{.GoFiles}}' text/template

[doc.go exec.go funcs.go helper.go option.go template.go]

To compile a program, you can use the build command. To compile a package, first change to the directory where the program is located and run the build command: go build

You can also compile Go programs without changing the directory. To do that, you are required to specify the package location in the command line. For example, to compile github.com/baijum/introduction package run the command given below: go build github.com/baijum/introduction

If you want to set the executable binary file name, use the -o option: go build -o myprog

If you want to build and run at once, you can use the "run" command: go run program.go

You can specify more that one Go source file in the command line arguments: go run file1.go file2.go file3.go

Of course, when you specify more than one file names, only one "main" function should be defined among all of the files.

Conditional Compilation

Sometimes you need to write code specific to a particular operating system. In some other case the code for a particular CPU architecture. It could be code optimized for that particular combination. The Go build tool supports conditional compilation using build constraints. The Build constraint is also known as build tag. There is another approach for conditional compilation using a naming convention for files names. This section is going to discuss both these approaches.

The build tag should be given as comments at the top of the source code. The build tag comment should start like this:

// +build

The comment should be before package documentation and there should be a line in between.

The space is OR and comma is AND. The exclamation character is stands for negation. Here is an example:

// +build linux,386

In the above example, the file will compile on 32-bit x86 Linux system.

// +build linux darwin

The above one compiles on Linux or Darwin (Mac OS).

// +build !linux

The above runs on anything that is not Linux.

The other approach uses file naming convention for conditional compilation. The files are ignore if it doesn't match the target OS and CPU architecture, if any.

This compiles only on Linux:

stat_linux.go

This one on 64 bit ARM linux:

os_linux_arm64.go

Running Test

The Go tool has a built-in test runner. To run tests for the current package, run this command: go test

To demonstrate the remaining commands, consider packages organized like this:

|-- hello.go

|-- hello_test.go

|-- sub1

| |-- sub1.go

| `-- sub1_test.go

`-- sub2

|-- sub2.go

`-- sub2_test.go

If you run go test from the top-level directory, it's going to run tests in that directory, and not any sub directories. You can specify directories as command line arguments to go test command to run tests under multiple packages simultaneously. In the above listed case, you can run all tests like this:

go test . ./sub1 ./sub2

Instead of listing each packages separates, you can use the ellipsis syntax:

go test ./...

The above command run tests under current directory and its child directories.

By default go test shows very few details about the tests.

$ go test ./... ok_/home/baiju/code/mypkg 0.001s ok_/home/baiju/code/mypkg/sub10.001s

--- FAIL: TestSub (0.00s)

FAIL

FAIL_/home/baiju/code/mypkg/sub2 0.003s

In the above results, it shows the name of failed test. But details about other passing tests are not available. If you want to see verbose results, use the -v option.

$ go test ./... -v

=== RUN   TestHello

--- PASS: TestHello (0.00s)

PASS

ok   _/home/baiju/code/mypkg   0.001s

=== RUN   TestSub

--- PASS: TestSub (0.00s)

PASS

ok_/home/baiju/code/mypkg/sub1   0.001s

=== RUN   TestSub

--- FAIL: TestSub (0.00s)

FAIL

FAIL   _/home/baiju/code/mypkg/sub2   0.002s

If you need to filter tests based on the name, you can use the -run option.

```
$ go test ./... -v -run Sub testing: warning: no tests to run PASS

ok      _/home/baiju/code/mypkg      0.001s [no tests to run]

=== RUN      TestSub

--- PASS: TestSub (0.00s)

PASS

ok      _/home/baiju/code/mypkg/sub1          0.001s

=== RUN      TestSub

--- FAIL: TestSub (0.00s)

FAIL

FAIL   _/home/baiju/code/mypkg/sub2          0.002s
```

As you can see above, the TestHello test was skipped as it doesn't match" Sub" pattern.

The chapter on testing has more details about writing test cases.

golangci-lint is a handy program to run various lint tools and normalize their output. This program is useful to run through continuous integration. You can download the program from here: https://github.com/golangci/golangci-lint

The supported lint tools include Vet, Golint, Varcheck, Errcheck, Deadcode, Gocyclo among others. golangci-lint allows to enable/disable the lint tools through a configuration file.

Formatting Code

Go has a recommended source code formatting. To format any Go source file to conform to that format, it's just a matter of running one command. Normally you can integrate this command with your text editor or IDE. But if you really want to invoke this program from command line, this is how you do it: go fmt myprogram.go

In the above command, the source file name is explicitly specified. You can also give package name: go fmt github.com/baijum/introduction

The command will format source files and write it back to the same file. Also it will list the files that is formatted.

Generating Code

If you have use case to generate Go code from a grammar, you may consider the go generate. In fact, you can add any command to be run before compiling the code. You can add a special comment in your Go code with this syntax:

//go:generate command arguments

For example, if you want to use peg (https://github. com/pointlander/peg), a Parsing Expression Grammar implementation, you can add the command like this:

```
//go:generate peg -output=parser.peg.go grammar.peg
```

When you build the program, the parser will be generated and will be part of the code that compiles.

Embedding Code

Go programs are normally distributed as a single binary. What if your program needs some files to run. Go has a feature to embed files in the binary. You can embed any type of files, including text files and binary files. Some of the commonly embedded files are SQL, HTML, CSS, JavaScript, and images. You can embed individual files or directories including nested sub-directories.

You need to import the embed package and use the //go:embed compiler directive to embed. Here is an example to embed an SQL file:

```
import _ "embed"
```

```
//go:embed database-schema.sql var dbSchema string
```

As you can see, the "embed" package is imported with a blank identifier as it is not directly used in the code. This is required to initialize the package to embed files. The variable must be at package level and not at function or method level.

The variable could be slice of bytes. This is useful for binary files. Here is an example: import _ "embed"

```
//go:embed logo.jpg var logo []byte
```

If you need an entire directory, you can use the embed.FS as the type: import "embed"

```
//go:embed static var content embed.FS
```

Displaying Documentation

Go has good support for writing documentation along with source code. You can write documentation for packages, functions and custom defined types. The Go tool can be used to display those documentation.

To see the documentation for the current packages, run this command: go doc

To see documentation for a specific package:

```
go doc strings
```

The above command shows documentation for the "strings" package.

```
go doc strings
```

If you want to see documentation for a particular function within that package:

```
go doc strings.ToLower or a type:
```

```
go doc strings.Reader
```

Or a method:

go doc strings.Reader.Size

Find Suspicious Code Using Vet

There is a handy tool named vet to find suspicious code in your program. Your program might compile and run. But some of the results may not be desired output.

Consider this program:

Exercises

Listing: Suspicious code

```
package main

import (

"fmt" 5 )

func main() {

v := 1

fmt.Printf("%#v %s\n", v)

}
```

If you compile and run it. It's going to be give some output. But if you observe the code, there is an unnecessary %s format string.

If you run vet command, you can see the issue:

```
$ go vet susp.go

# command-line-arguments

./susp.go:9: Printf format %s reads arg #2, but call has only 1 arg
```

Exercise 1: Create a program with function to return "Hello, world!" and write test and run it. hello.go:

```
package hello

// SayHello returns a "Hello word!" message func SayHello() string { return "Hello, world!"

} hello_test.go: package hello import "testing"

func TestSayHello(t *testing.T) { out := SayHello() if out != "Hello, world!" {

t.Error("Incorrect message", out)

}
}
```
To run the test: go test . -v

Conclusion

The world of software development demands that applications be reliable, performant, and maintainable. Achieving this level of quality and robustness requires a solid testing strategy and a versatile set of development tools. Go (Golang), as a language, excels in offering developers a simple yet powerful suite of built-in testing tools, alongside a growing ecosystem of third-party utilities, libraries, and best practices.

As we have explored throughout "Testing and Tooling in Go 2024," the Go language's design philosophy centered around simplicity, performance, and ease of use—extends to its testing framework and development tools. This alignment has enabled Go developers to write clean, testable code without needing to learn complex configurations or additional frameworks.

Recap of Key Concepts

1. The Go Testing Framework

Go's testing package is the core of its testing suite, providing straightforward, easy-to-write tests for unit testing, integration testing, and benchmarking. The go test command simplifies the process of running tests, analyzing code coverage, and managing performance benchmarks. This minimalistic approach makes it easy for developers to adopt testing as a regular part of their development workflow.

Key takeaways from Go's built-in testing include:

- **Ease of Use**: No additional setup or installation is required. The testing package is included in the standard library.

- **Consistency**: Go's standard library provides consistency in how tests are written and executed, encouraging best practices across projects.

- **Performance Testing**: Benchmarking capabilities are built-in, allowing developers to easily measure and optimize performance.

2. Best Practices for Writing Effective Tests

Writing effective tests in Go involves more than just checking if your code runs correctly. It's about ensuring your code behaves as expected across a wide range of scenarios, and that it can be refactored or extended without breaking. The introduction of table-driven tests, subtests, and mocking frameworks like gomock and testify has made it easier to write maintainable, reusable, and readable tests.

Some key principles include:

- **Independent Tests**: Each test should be isolated, ensuring it can run independently of others.

- **Mocking and Stubbing**: Use mocks and stubs to isolate the functionality being tested and avoid reliance on external dependencies.

- **Readable Tests**: Writing clear, concise, and self-explanatory test cases helps teams maintain and extend codebases more effectively.

3. Advanced Testing with Fuzzing

Fuzz testing is one of the newer additions to Go's testing toolkit. It helps find unexpected behavior by feeding random data to your functions, allowing developers to discover edge cases and potential vulnerabilities that may not be easily identified through regular unit tests. Fuzzing is particularly effective in scenarios where input validation is critical, such as parsing user input or handling network requests.

4. Code Coverage Analysis

Code coverage is a critical aspect of understanding how well your code is tested. Go provides built-in tools for generating coverage reports, allowing developers to identify untested parts of their applications and improve test coverage. Running go test -cover and analyzing reports with go tool cover gives teams a clear view of where to focus their testing efforts.

The Role of Tooling in Go Development

Beyond testing, effective development relies on a broad ecosystem of tools that streamline tasks such as formatting, debugging, dependency management, and continuous integration. Go has evolved significantly in these areas, and the following are crucial tools that every Go developer should be familiar with:

1. Code Formatting and Linting

Go's go fmt tool ensures that code adheres to a standard style, making it more readable and maintainable. Code consistency reduces the cognitive load on developers, allowing them to focus on logic rather than syntax. Linters, like go lint and static check, go a step further by identifying potential issues in code and suggesting improvements. They help catch bugs, enforce style guidelines, and ensure that best practices are followed.

2. Dependency Management

Go Modules (go mod) has revolutionized how dependencies are managed in Go projects. Developers can now pin specific versions, handle transitive dependencies, and ensure consistency across different environments. The go mod tools (go mod init, go mod tidy, go mod vendor) provide an effective way to manage dependencies without the complexities seen in other languages.

Key benefits include:

- **Version Control**: Locking dependencies to specific versions prevents unexpected changes from breaking code.

- **Simplicity**: Go Modules are easy to set up and manage, reducing the friction associated with dependency management.

3. Debugging with Delve (dlv)

Delve (dlv) is the go-to debugging tool for Go developers. Its ability to set breakpoints, inspect variables, and step through code execution helps identify issues that are not easily caught by tests alone. Integrated support with popular editors and IDEs like VS Code and GoLand makes it easy to debug directly within the development environment.

4. Continuous Integration and Deployment

In modern development, automated testing and deployment pipelines are a necessity. Go integrates well with CI/CD tools such as GitHub Actions, Travis CI, Jenkins, and CircleCI, allowing developers to automate the testing, building, and deployment process. By setting up CI pipelines, teams can ensure that code is always tested before it is merged, reducing the risk of introducing bugs into the main codebase.

Future of Testing and Tooling in Go

The Go community is continuously evolving, and with it, the ecosystem of tools and best practices. Go's recent updates, including support for fuzz testing and improvements in modules, indicate a bright future where testing and tooling will continue to become more robust, easier to use, and more integrated into the language.

Upcoming Trends and Developments:

1. **Better Integration with IDEs**: As the Go language grows, there's been a push towards better integration with development environments, enhancing features like auto-completion, refactoring, and debugging.

2. **Cloud-Native Testing**: With the rise of cloud-native applications, there's an increasing need for testing tools that work seamlessly with cloud platforms. Developers can expect more integrations with container orchestration tools like Kubernetes for seamless testing of distributed applications.

3. **Enhanced Static Analysis**: Tools that provide deeper insights into code behavior and quality, like go vet and static check, will continue to evolve, catching more complex bugs and suggesting performance optimizations.

Practical Takeaways

For developers looking to improve their testing and development workflows in Go, consider the following practical tips:

1. **Adopt a Test-Driven Development (TDD) Approach**: Writing tests before implementing code can help clarify requirements and produce more reliable, bug-free code.

2. **Automate Everything**: From running tests to building and deploying code, automate repetitive tasks using CI/CD pipelines to ensure consistency and efficiency.

3. **Leverage the Ecosystem**: While Go's built-in tools are powerful, the ecosystem offers numerous libraries that can simplify complex tasks (e.g., mockery for generating mocks, assert for assertions).

Final Thoughts

The essence of Go's success lies in its simplicity, and this extends to its testing and tooling framework. By reducing the need for external dependencies and providing intuitive, easy-to-use tools, Go empowers developers to focus on writing clean, efficient, and reliable code. The language's comprehensive testing capabilities, along with its seamless integration into CI/CD pipelines, ensure that developers can maintain high standards of quality throughout the development lifecycle.

"Testing and Tooling in Go 2024" has provided an in-depth exploration of Go's testing framework, practical tooling, and strategies to enhance software development. The knowledge gained will help developers build robust, maintainable, and performant applications that can stand the test of time. As the ecosystem continues to grow, embracing new tools, libraries, and best practices will be key to harnessing the full potential of the Go language.

13. Go: The Art of Testing Technical Requirements

Introduction

In the world of software development, testing is an essential practice that ensures the reliability, robustness, and overall quality of an application. For a programming language like Go (or Golang), which is known for its efficiency, simplicity, and strong concurrency features, testing plays a vital role in building high-performance, scalable, and maintainable systems. The art of testing in Go goes beyond simply writing test cases; it involves understanding the nuances of Go's testing ecosystem, adhering to best practices, and mastering various testing strategies that align with the technical requirements of modern software systems.

With the release of Go 2024, several new features and enhancements have been introduced to the language, offering improved support for writing, executing, and maintaining tests. This chapter will guide you through the fundamentals of testing in Go, exploring the tools, frameworks, and techniques that help developers build resilient software. We will discuss various testing paradigms, delve into best practices, and provide real-world examples to illustrate how to effectively test technical requirements in Go.

The Importance of Testing in Go

Testing is a critical step in the software development lifecycle (SDLC) that helps ensure that the code meets the functional and non-functional requirements. It allows developers to identify bugs early in the development process, leading to fewer errors in production and ultimately reducing costs. In Go, testing is baked into the language, making it easy to write and run tests. Go's built-in testing tools and the simplicity of the language syntax encourage developers to adopt a test-driven development (TDD) approach, ensuring that code is well-tested and reliable.

Understanding Go's Testing Framework

One of the key strengths of Go is its simplicity, and this extends to its testing framework. The testing package in Go provides the fundamental tools for writing unit tests, integration tests, and benchmarks. Let's break down the components of Go's testing ecosystem:

1. **The testing Package:** The testing package is included in Go's standard library and is the foundation for writing test cases. It offers a simple way to write tests using the TestXxx naming convention, where Xxx can be any descriptive name. Tests are written as functions that take a *testing.T parameter, which is used to report errors and log information during the test run.

2. **Test Files and Naming Conventions:** Test files in Go follow a specific naming pattern. A file containing tests should end with _test.go. This naming convention ensures that the Go toolchain can recognize and execute these files as test files. Inside these files, you can write functions that test specific parts of your code, verify outputs, and validate expected behaviors.

3. **Running Tests:** Running tests in Go is straightforward. Simply use the go test command, and Go will automatically identify the test files and execute the tests. The command can be customized with various flags to control verbosity, run benchmarks, and more.

4. **Subtests:** Subtests allow you to group related test cases under a single test function, making it easier to organize and run specific parts of your tests. You can create subtests using the t.Run method, which also supports parallel execution to speed up the testing process.

5. **Benchmarks:** Performance testing is crucial in systems where efficiency is a priority. Go's testing package includes built-in support for benchmarks, enabling developers to measure the performance of their code. Benchmark functions are defined using the BenchmarkXxx naming convention and accept a *testing.B parameter to control the execution of the benchmarking loop.

Testing Types in Go

Testing in Go can be classified into several types, each serving a different purpose:

1. **Unit Testing:** Unit tests are designed to test individual functions or components in isolation. They are the most common type of tests and help verify that a specific piece of code works as expected. Unit tests are typically fast to run and provide quick feedback to developers.

2. **Integration Testing:** Integration tests validate the interaction between different parts of an application. Unlike unit tests, they check how components work together and often involve external dependencies such as databases, APIs, and third-party services. In Go, integration tests can be placed in the same _test.go files but are usually more complex and may require setup and teardown procedures.

3. **End-to-End (E2E) Testing:** E2E tests simulate real-world user interactions and test the entire application flow from start to finish. They are less common in Go projects but can be implemented using tools like ginkgo and godog for behavior-driven development (BDD). E2E tests ensure that the application behaves as expected under different scenarios and edge cases.

4. **Benchmark Testing:** Benchmarking is essential for applications where performance is critical. In Go, benchmarks allow you to measure the speed and efficiency of your code. The *testing.B parameter lets you control the number of iterations and gather performance metrics.

Testing Best Practices in Go

1. **Write Clear and Descriptive Test Cases:** Each test should have a clear purpose and description, making it easy to understand what is being tested. Use meaningful test names that describe the behavior being tested, and avoid writing large, monolithic test functions. Smaller, focused tests are easier to maintain and debug.

2. **Use Table-Driven Tests:** Table-driven tests are a popular testing pattern in Go that makes it easier to write and manage multiple test cases for the same function. This pattern involves creating a slice of test cases, where each entry in the slice represents a different input and expected output. This approach simplifies the process of adding new test scenarios and improves readability.

3. **Leverage Subtests and Parallel Testing:** Subtests help organize your tests, while parallel testing speeds up execution time. Use the t.Run function to create subtests, and call t.Parallel() inside each subtest to run them concurrently. Parallel testing is particularly useful when testing functions that do not have dependencies on shared resources.

4. **Mocking and Dependency Injection:** To effectively test components that rely on external services, such as databases or APIs, you can use mocking and dependency injection. Mocking allows you to simulate the behavior of an external service, ensuring that your tests run in isolation without requiring the actual service. Dependency injection makes it easier to replace real dependencies with mocks during testing.

5. **Continuous Integration and Automated Testing:** Automating the testing process ensures that your tests are run every time new code is committed to the repository. Continuous Integration (CI) tools like Jenkins, CircleCI, and GitHub Actions can be used to automate testing, providing immediate feedback to developers and ensuring that new changes do not break existing functionality.

New Features in Go for Testing

With Go 2024, several new features have been introduced that enhance the testing experience:

1. **Improved Test Coverage Reporting:** Go 2024 has enhanced support for test coverage, making it easier to visualize which parts of the code are covered by tests. Developers can use the -cover flag with the go test command to generate coverage reports, and additional tools can convert these reports into visual representations.

2. **Native Support for Test Fixtures:** Test fixtures, which are reusable pieces of data or setup code, are now more straightforward to implement with Go 2024's enhancements. This feature simplifies the setup and teardown of integration tests, reducing boilerplate code and making tests more maintainable.

3. **Enhanced Benchmarking Tools:** Benchmarking has been further improved, with additional flags and options to fine-tune the performance testing process. Developers can now gather more detailed metrics, analyze memory usage, and identify performance bottlenecks more efficiently.

4. **Better Support for Mocking Libraries:** While Go's standard library does not include built-in mocking tools, Go 2024 offers improved compatibility with popular mocking libraries like gomock and testify. These enhancements streamline the process of setting up and managing mocks, making it easier to write comprehensive tests.

Example: Writing a Simple Unit Test in Go

```go
package mathutil

import "testing"

func TestAdd(t *testing.T) {
    result := Add(2, 3)
    expected := 5
```

```
    if result != expected {

        t.Errorf("Add(2, 3) = %d; want %d", result, expected)

    }

}
```

In this example, the TestAdd function tests the Add function. The t.Errorf method is used to report a test failure if the result does not match the expected value. Running go test will automatically execute this test.

Software systems are destined to grow and evolve over time. Open or closed source software projects have one thing in common: their complexity seems to follow an upward curve as the number of engineers working on the code base increases. To this end, having a comprehensive set of tests for the code base is of paramount importance. This chapter performs a deep dive into the different types of testing that can be applied to Go projects.

Technical requirements

To get you up and running as quickly as possible, each example project includes a makefile that defines the following set of targets:

target	Description
deps	Install any required dependencies
test	Run all the tests and report coverage
lint	Check for lint errors

Unit testing

By definition, a unit is the smallest possible bit of code that we can test. In the context of Go programming, this would typically be a single function. However, according to the SOLID design principles that we explored in the previous chapters, each Go package could also be construed as an independent unit and tested as such.

The term unit testing refers to the process of testing each unit of an application in isolation to verify that its behavior conforms to a particular set of specifications.

In this section, we will dive into the different methodologies of unit testing at our disposal (black- versus white-box testing). We will also examine strategies for making our code easier to unit test and cover the built-in Go testing packages, as well as third-party packages, that are designed to make writing tests more streamlined.

Mocks, stubs, fakes, and spies – commonalities and differences

Before digging deeper into the concepts behind unit testing, we need to discuss and disambiguate some of the terms that we will be using in the upcoming sections. While these terms have been out there for years, software engineers tend to occasionally conflate them when writing tests. A great example of such confusion becomes evident when you hear engineers use the terms mock and stub interchangeably.

To establish some common ground for a fruitful discussion and to clear any confusion around this terminology, let's examine the definition of each term, as outlined by Gerard Meszaros [5] in his XUnit Test Patterns: Refactoring Test Code book on test patterns.

Stubs and spies!

A stub is the simplest test pattern that we can use in our tests. Stubs typically implement a particular interface and don't contain any real logic; they just provide fixed answers to calls that are performed through the course of a test.

CAPTCHA is a fairly straightforward way to determine whether a system is interacting with a human user or another program. This is achieved by displaying a random, often noisy, image containing a distorted sequence of letters and numbers and then prompting the user to type the text content of the image.

As a big fan of the SOLID principles, I opted to define two interfaces, Challenger and Prompter, to abstract the CAPTCHA image generation and the user-prompting implementation. After all, there is a plethora of different approaches out there for generating CAPTCHA images: we could pick a random image from a fixed set of images, generate them using a neural network, or perhaps even call out to a third-party image generation service. The same could be said about the way we actually prompt our users for an answer. This is how the two interfaces are defined:

```go
// Challenger is implemented by objects that can generate CAPTCHA image

// challenges. type Challenger interface {

    Challenge() (img image.Image, imgText string)

}

// Prompter is implemented by objects that display a CAPTCHA image to the

// user, ask them to type their contents and return back their response. type Prompter interface {

    Prompt(img image.Image) string

}
```

At the end of the day, the actual business logic doesn't really care how the CAPTCHA images or the users' answers were obtained. All we need to do is fetch a challenge, prompt the user, and then perform a simple string comparison operation, as follows:

```go
func ChallengeUser(c Challenger, p Prompter) bool {

    img, expAnswer := c.Challenge()    userAnswer := p.Prompt(img)

    if subtle.ConstantTimeEq(int32(len(expAnswer)), int32(len(userAnswer)))

     == 0 {        return false    }

    return subtle.ConstantTimeCompare([]byte(userAnswer),

[]byte(expAnswer)) == 1

}
```

One interesting, at least in my opinion, aspect of the preceding code is that it uses constant time string comparisons instead of using the built-in equality operator for comparing the expected answer and the user's response.

Constant-time comparison checks are a common pattern in security related code as it prevents information leaks, which can be exploited by adversaries to perform a timing side-channel attack. When executing a timing attack, the attacker provides variable-length inputs to a system and then employs statistical analysis to collect additional information about the system's implementation based on the time it takes to execute a particular action.

Imagine if, in the preceding CAPTCHA scenario we had used a simple string comparison that essentially compares each character and returns false on the first mismatch. Here's how an attacker could slowly brute-force the answer via a timing attack:

Start by providing answers following the $a pattern and measuring the time it takes to get a response. The $ symbol is a placeholder for all possible alphanumeric characters. In essence, we try combinations such as aa, ba, and so on.

Once we have identified an operation that takes longer than the rest, we can assume that that particular value of $ (say, 4) is the expected first character of the CAPTCHA answer! The reason this takes longer is that the string comparison code matched the first character and then tried matching the next character instead of immediately returning it, like it would if there was a mismatch.

Continue the same process of providing answers but this time using the 4$a pattern and keep extending the pattern until the expected CAPTCHA answer can be recovered.

In order to test the Challenge User function, we need to create a stub for each of its arguments. This would provide us with complete control over the inputs to the comparison business logic. Here's what the stubs might look like:

```
type stubChallenger string

func (c stubChallenger) Challenge() (image.Image, string) {    return
image.NewRGBA(image.Rect(0, 0, 100, 100)), string(c)

}

type stubPrompter string

func (p stubPrompter) Prompt(_ image.Image) string {

    return string(p)

}
```

Pretty simple, right? As you can see, the stubs are devoid of any logic; they just return a canned answer. With the two stubs in place, we can write two test functions that exercise the match/non-match code paths:

```
func TestChallengeUserSuccess(t *testing.T) {

    got := captcha.ChallengeUser(stubChallenger("42"), stubPrompter("42"))

    if got != true {
```

```
            t.Fatal("expected ChallengeUser to return true")

    }

}

func TestChallengeUserFail(t *testing.T) {

    got := captcha.ChallengeUser(stubChallenger("lorem ipsum"),

stubPrompter("42"))    if got != false {

        t.Fatal("expected ChallengeUser to return false")

    }

}
```

Now that we have a general understanding of how stubs work, let's look at another useful test pattern: spies! A spy is nothing more than a stub that keeps a detailed log of all the methods that are invoked on it. For each method invocation, the spy records the arguments that were provided by the caller and makes them available for inspection by the test code.

Surely, when it comes to Go, the most popular spy implementation is the venerable Response Recorder type, which is provided by the net/http/httptest package. Response Recorder implements the http.ResponseWriter interface and can be used for testing HTTP request handling code without the need to spin up an actual HTTP server. However, HTTP server testing is not that interesting; let's take a look at a slightly more engaging example.

The package contains a simple chatroom implementation that is perfect for applying the spy test pattern. The following is the definition of the Room type and its constructor:

```
// Publisher is implemented by objects that can send a message to a user. type Publisher interface {

    Publish(userID, message string) error

}

type Room struct {    pub Publisher    mu    sync.RWMutex    users []string }

// NewRoom creates a new chat root instance that used pub to broadcast

// messages. func NewRoom(pub Publisher) *Room {    return &Room{pub: pub} }
```

As you can see, Room contains a Publisher instance that gets initialized by the value that's passed to the NewRoom constructor. The other interesting public methods that are exposed by the Room type (not shown here but available in this book's GitHub repo) are AddUser and Broadcast. The first method adds new users to the room, while the latter can be used to broadcast a particular message to all the users currently in the room.

Before we write our actual testing code, let's create a spy instance that implements the Publisher interface and records any published messages:

```
type entry struct {    user    string    message string }
```

```go
type spyPublisher struct {    published []entry }

func (p *spyPublisher) Publish(user, message string) error {

    p.published = append(p.published, entry{user: user, message: message})

    return nil }
```

In the preceding spy implementation, each time the Publish method is invoked, the stub will append a {user, message} tuple to the published slice. With our spy ready to be used, writing the actual test is a piece of cake:

```go
func TestChatRoomBroadcast(t *testing.T) {

    pub := new(spyPublisher)    room := chat.NewRoom(pub)    room.AddUser("bob")
room.AddUser("alice")

    _ = room.Broadcast("hi")    exp := []entry{

        {user: "bob", message: "hi"},

        {user: "alice", message: "hi"},

    }

    if got := pub.published; !reflect.DeepEqual(got, exp) {

        t.Fatalf("expected the following messages:\n%#+v\ngot:\n%#+v", exp,

got)    }

}
```

This test scenario involves creating a new room, adding some users to it, and broadcasting a message to everyone who has joined the room. The test runner's task is to verify that the call to Broadcast did in fact broadcast the message to all the users. We can achieve this by examining the list of messages that have been recorded by our injected spy.

Mocks

You can think of mocks as stubs on steroids! Contrary to the fixed behavior exhibited by stubs, mocks allow us to specify, in a declarative way, not only the list of calls that the mock is expected to receive but also their order and expected argument values. In addition, mocks allow us to specify different return values for each method invocation, depending on the argument tuple provided by the method caller.

All things considered; mocks are a very powerful primitive at our disposal for writing advanced tests. However, building mocks from scratch for every single object we want to substitute as part of our tests is quite a tedious task. This is why it's often better to use an external tool and code generation to automate the creation of the mocks that are needed for our tests.

Introducing gomock

In this section, we will be introducing gomock [4], a very popular mocking framework for Go that leverages reflection and code generation to automatically create mocks based on Go interface definitions.

The framework and its supporting tools can be installed by running the following commands:

$ go get github.com/golang/mock/gomock

$ go install github.com/golang/mock/mockgen

The mockgen tool is responsible for analyzing either individual Go files or entire packages and generating mocks for all (or specific) interfaces that are defined within them. It supports two modes of operation:

Source code scanning: We pass a Gi file to mockgen, which is then parsed in order to detect interface definitions.

Reflection-assisted mode: We pass a package and a list of interfaces to mockgen.

The tool uses the Go reflection package to analyze the structure of each interface.

gomock provides a simple and concise API for specifying the expected behavior of mock instances that are created via the mockgen tool. To access this API, you need to create a new instance of the mock and invoke its oddly-cased EXPECT method. EXPECT returns a special object (a recorder, in gomock terminology) that provides the means for us to declare the behavior of the method calls that are performed against the mock.

To register a new expectation, we need to do the following:

1.   Declare the name of the method that we expect to be called, along with its arguments.

2.   Specify the return value (or values) that the mock should return to the caller when it invokes the method with the specified set of arguments.

3.   Optionally, we need to specify the number of times that the caller is expected to invoke the method.

To further streamline the creation of tests, mockgen populates the returned recorder instances with methods whose names match the interfaces that we are trying to mock. All we need to do is invoke those methods on the recorder object and specify the arguments that the mock expects to receive from the caller as a variadic list of interface{} values. When defining the expected set of arguments, you basically have two options:

  Specify a value whose type matches the one from the method signature (for example, foo if the argument is of the string type). gomock will only match a call to an expectation if the input argument, value, is strictly equal to the value that's specified as part of the expectation.

  Provide a value that implements the gomock.Matcher interface. In this case, gomock will delegate the comparison to the matcher itself. This powerful feature gives us the flexibility to model any custom test predicate that we can think of. gomock already defines a few handy built-in matchers that we can use in our tests: Any, AssignableToTypeOf, Nil, and Not.

After specifying the expected method call and its arguments, gomock will return an expectation object that provides auxiliary methods so that we can configure the expected behavior further. For instance, we can use the expectation object's Return method to define the set of values to be returned to the caller once the expectation is matched. It is also important to note that unless we explicitly specify the expected number of calls to the mocked method, gomock will assume that the method can only be invoked once and will trigger a test failure if the method is not invoked at all or is invoked multiple times. If you require more fine-grained control over the number of expected invocations, the returned expectation object provides the following set of helper methods: Times, MinTimes, and MaxTimes.

In the next two sections, we will analyze an example project and go through all the individual steps for writing a complete, mock-based unit test for it.

For the purpose of demonstrating the creation and use of mocks in our code, we will be working with the example code from the Chapter/dependency package. This package defines a Collector type whose purpose is to assemble a set of direct and indirect (transitive) dependencies for a given project ID. To make things a bit more interesting, let's assume that each dependency can belong to one of the following two categories:

A resource that we need to include (for example, an image file) or reserve (for example, a block of memory or an amount of disk space) Another project with its own set of dependencies

To obtain the list of direct dependencies and their respective types, the collector dependency will be performing a series of calls to an external service. To ensure that the implementation lends itself to easier testing, we will not be working with a concrete client instance for the external service. Instead, we will define an interface with the set of required methods for accessing the service and have our test code inject a mock that satisfies that interface. Consider the following definition for the API interface:

```
type API interface {

    // ListDependencies returns the list of direct dependency IDs for a

    // particular project ID or an error if a non-project ID argument is    // provided.

    ListDependencies(projectID string) ([]string, error)

    // DependencyType returns the type of a particular dependency.

    DependencyType(dependencyID string) (DepType, error)

}
```

To create a new Collector instance, we need to invoke the New Collector constructor (not shown) and provide an API instance as an argument. Then, the unique set of dependencies for a particular project ID can be obtained via a call to the All-Dependencies method. It's a pretty short method whose full implementation is as follows:

```
func (c *Collector) AllDependencies(projectID string) ([]string, error) {

    ctx := newDepContext(projectID)    for ctx.HasUncheckedDeps() {        projectID =
ctx.NextUncheckedDep()
```

```
    projectDeps, err := c.api.ListDependencies(projectID)
    if err != nil {
        return nil, xerrors.Errorf("unable to list dependencies for
project %q: %w", projectID, err)
    }
    if err = c.scanProjectDependencies(ctx, projectDeps); err != nil {
        return nil, err
    }
  }
  return ctx.depList, nil }
```

The preceding block of code is nothing more than a breadth-first search (BFS) algorithm in disguise! The ctx variable stores an auxiliary structure that contains the following:

A queue whose entries correspond to the set of dependencies (resources or projects) that we haven't visited yet. As we visit the nodes of the project dependency graph, any newly discovered dependencies will be appended to the tail of the queue so that they can be visited in a future search loop iteration.

The unique set of discovered dependency IDs that are returned to the caller once all the entries in the queue have been processed.

To seed the search, initially, we populate the queue with the projectID value that was passed in as an argument to the method. With each loop iteration, we dequeue an unchecked dependency ID and invoke the ListDependencies API call to get a list of all its direct dependencies. The obtained list of dependency IDs is then passed as input to the scanProjectDependencies method, whose role is to examine the dependency list and update the contents of the ctx variable. The method's implementation is pretty straightforward:

```
func (c *Collector) scanProjectDependencies(ctx *depCtx, depList []string)
error {
    for _, depID := range depList {        if ctx.AlreadyChecked(depID) {
            continue
        }
        ctx.AddToDepList(depID)
        depType, err := c.api.DependencyType(depID)
        if err != nil {            return xerrors.Errorf("unable to get dependency type for id %q:
%w", depID, err)
```

```
        }
    if depType == DepTypeProject {          ctx.AddToUncheckedList(depID)

    }
  }    return nil

}
```

While iterating the dependency list, the implementation automatically skips any dependency that has already been visited. On the other hand, new dependency IDs are appended to the set of unique dependencies that have been tracked by the ctx variable via a call to the AddToDepList method.

As we mentioned previously, if the dependency corresponds to another project, we need to recursively visit its own dependencies and add them to our set as transitive dependencies. The DependencyType method from the API interface provides us with the means for querying the type of a dependency by its ID. If the dependency does in fact point to a project, we append it to the tail of the unvisited dependencies queue via a call to the AddToUncheckedList method. The last step guarantees that the dependency will eventually be processed by the search loop inside the AllDependencies method.

Leveraging gomock to write a unit test for our application

Now that we are aware of the implementation details of our example project, we can go ahead and write a simple, mock-based unit test for it. Before we begin, we need to create a mock for the API interface. This can be achieved by invoking the mockgen tool with the following options:

$ mockgen \

  -destination mock/dependency.go \

  github.com/PacktPublishing/Hands-On-Software-Engineering-with-

Golang/Chapter/dependency \API

The preceding command does the following:

Creates a mock folder in the dependency package

Generates a file called dependency.go with the appropriate code for mocking the API interface and places it in the mock folder

To save you the trouble of having to manually type in the preceding command, the Makefile in the dependency folder includes a predefined target for rebuilding the mocks that were used in this example. All you need to do is switch to the folder with the example code in it and run make mocks.

So far, so good. How can we use the mock in our tests though? The first thing we need to do is create a gomock controller and associate it with the testing.T instance that gets passed to our test function by the Go standard library. The controller instance defines a Finish method that our code must always run before returning from the test (for example, via a defer statement). This method checks the expectations that were registered on each mock object and automatically fails the test if they were not met. Here's what the preamble of our test function would look like:

```
// Create a controller to manage all our mock objects and make sure

// that all expectations were met before completing the test

ctrl := gomock.NewController(t) defer ctrl.Finish()
```

```
// Obtain a mock instance that implements API and associate it with the controller. api :=
mock_dependency.NewMockAPI(ctrl)
```

The purpose of this particular unit test is to verify that a call to the AllDependencies method with a specific input yields an expected list of dependency IDs. As we saw in the previous section, the implementation of the AllDependencies method uses an externallyprovided API instance to retrieve information about each dependency. Given that our test will inject a mocked API instance into the Collector dependency, our test code must declare the expected set of calls to the mock. Consider the following block of code:

```
gomock.InOrder(    api.EXPECT().       ListDependencies("proj0").Return([]string{"proj1",
"res1"}, nil),     api.EXPECT().       DependencyType("proj1").Return(dependency.DepTypeProject,
nil),     api.EXPECT().      DependencyType("res1").Return(dependency.DepTypeResource, nil),
api.EXPECT().        ListDependencies("proj1").Return([]string{"res1", "res2"}, nil),
api.EXPECT().

        DependencyType("res2").Return(dependency.DepTypeResource, nil),

)
```

Under normal circumstances, gomock would just check that the method call expectations are met, regardless of the order that they were invoked in. However, if a test relies on a sequence of method calls being performed in a particular order, it can specify this to gomock by invoking the gomock.InOrder helper function with an ordered list of expectations as arguments. This particular pattern can be seen in the preceding code snippet.

With the mock expectations in place, we can complete our unit by introducing the necessary logic to wire everything together, invoke the AllDependencies method with the input (proj0) that our mock expects, and validate that the returned output matches a predefined value ("proj1", "res1", "res2"):

```
collector := dependency.NewCollector(api) depList, err := collector.AllDependencies("proj0")

if err != nil {

   t.Fatal(err) }

if exp := []string{"proj1", "res1", "res2"}; !reflect.DeepEqual(depList,

exp) {

   t.Fatalf("expected dependency list to be:\n%v\ngot:\n%v", exp, depList) }
```

This concludes our short example about using gomock to accelerate the authoring of mock based tests. As a fun learning activity, you can experiment with changing the expected output for the preceding test so that the test fails. Then, you can work backward and try to figure out how to tweak the mock expectations to make the test pass again.

Fake objects

In a similar fashion to the other test patterns that we have discussed so far, fake objects also adhere to a specific interface, which allows us to inject them into the subject under test. The main difference is that fake objects do, in fact, contain a fully working implementation whose behavior matches the objects that they are meant to substitute.

So, what's the catch? Fake object implementations are typically optimized for running tests and, as such, they are not meant to be used in production. For example, we could provide an in-memory key-value store implementation for our tests, but our production deployments would require something with better availability guarantees.

To achieve a better understanding of how fake objects work, let's take a look at the content of the package. This package exports a function called SumOfSquares, which operates on a slice of 32-bit floating-point values. The function squares each element of the slice, adds the results together, and returns their sum. Note that we are using a single function purely for demonstration purposes; in a real-world scenario, we would compose this function with other similar functions to form a compute graph that our implementation would then proceed to evaluate.

To purposefully add a bit of extra complexity to this particular scenario, let's assume that the input slices that are passed to this function typically contain a very large number of values. It is still possible, of course, to use the CPU to calculate the result. Unfortunately, the production service that depends on this functionality has a pretty strict time budget, so using the CPU is not an option. To this end, we have decided to implement a vectorized solution by offloading the work to a GPU.

The Device interface describes the set of operations that can be offloaded to the GPU:

```
type Device interface {

    Square([]float32) []float32

    Sum([]float32) float32

}
```

Given an object instance that implements Device, we can define the SumOfSquares function as follows:

```
func SumOfSquares(c Device, in []float32) float32 {

    sq := c.Square(in)    return c.Sum(sq) }
```

Nothing too complicated here... Alas, it wasn't until we started working on our tests that we realized that while the compute nodes where we normally run our production code do provide beefy GPUs, the same could not be said for each one of the machines that's used locally by our engineers or the CI environment that runs our tests each time we create a new pull request.

Obviously, even though our real workload deals with lengthy inputs, there is no strict requirement to do the same within our tests; as we will see in the following sections, this is a job for an end-to-end test. Therefore, we can fall back to a CPU implementation if a GPU is not available when our tests are running. This is an excellent example of where a fake object could help us out. So, let's start by defining a Device implementation that uses the CPU for all its calculations:

```
type cpuComputeDevice struct{}
```

```go
func (d cpuComputeDevice) Square(in []float32) []float32 {
    for i := 0; i < len(in); i++ {
        in[i] *= in[i]
    }   return in }
func (d cpuComputeDevice) Sum(in []float32) (sum float32) {
    for _, v := range in {
        sum += v
    }   return sum }
```

Our test code can then switch between the GPU- or the CPU-based implementation on the fly, perhaps by inspecting the value of an environment variable or some command-line flag that gets passed as an argument to the test:

```go
func TestSumOfSquares(t *testing.T) {
    var dev compute.Device    if os.Getenv("USE_GPU") != "" {
        t.Log("using GPU device")        dev = gpu.NewDevice()
    } else {
        t.Log("using CPU device")        dev = cpuComputeDevice{}
    }
    // Generate deterministic sample data and return the expected sum
    in, expSum := genTestData(1024)
    if gotSum := compute.SumOfSquares(dev, in); gotSum != expSum {
        t.Fatalf("expected SumOfSquares to return %f; got %f", expSum,
gotSum)    }
}
```

With the help of a fake object, we can always run our tests while still offering this ability to engineers who do have local access to GPUs to run the tests using the GPU-based implementation. Success!

Black-box versus white-box testing for Go packages – an example

Black- and white-box testing are two different approaches to authoring unit tests. Each approach has its own set of merits and goals. Consequently, we shouldn't treat them as competing approaches but rather as one complementing the other. So, what is the major difference between these two types of tests?

Black-box testing works under the assumption that the underlying implementation details of the package that we test, also known as the subject under test (SUT), are totally opaque (hence the name blackbox) to us, the tester. As a result, we can only test the public interface or behavior of a particular package and make sure it adheres to its advertised contract.

On the other hand, white-box testing assumes that we have prior knowledge of the implementation details of a particular package. This allows the tester to either craft each test so that it exercises a particular code path within the package or to directly test the package's internal implementation.

To understand the difference between these two approaches, let's take a look at a short example. The package implements a facade called PriceCalculator.

A facade is a software design pattern that abstracts the complexity of one or more software components behind a simple interface.

In the context of microservice-based design, the facade pattern allows us to transparently compose or aggregate data across multiple, specialized microservices while providing a simple API for the facade clients to access it.

In this particular scenario, the facade receives a UUID representing an item and a date representing the period we are interested in as input. Then, it communicates with two backend microservices to retrieve information about the item's price and the VAT rate that was applied on that particular date. Finally, it returns the VAT-inclusive price for the item to the facade's client.

The services behind the facade

Before we dive deeper into the inner workings of the price calculator, let's spend a bit of time examining how the two microservice dependencies work; after all, we will need this information to write our tests.

The price microservice provides a REST endpoint for retrieving an item's published price on a particular date. The service responds with a JSON payload that looks like this:

```
{

   "price": 10.0,

   "currency": "GBP"

}
```

The second microservice in this example is called vat and is also RESTful. It exposes an endpoint for retrieving the VAT rate that was applicable on a particular date. The service responds with a JSON payload as follows:

```
{

   "vat_rate": 0.29

}
```

As you can see, the returned JSON payload is quite simple and it would be trivial for our test code to mock it.

Writing black-box tests

For the purpose of writing our black-box tests, we will start by examining the public interface of the retail package. A quick browse of the retail.go file reveals a NewPriceCalculator function that receives the URLs to the price and vat services as arguments and returns a PriceCalculator instance. The calculator instance can be used to obtain an item's VAT-inclusive price by invoking the PriceForItem method and passing the item's UUID as an argument. On the other hand, if we are interested in obtaining a VAT-inclusive item price for a particular date in the past, we can invoke the PriceForItemAtDate method, which also accepts a time period argument.

The black-box tests will live in a separate package with the name retail_test.

The $PACKAGE_test naming convention is, more or less, the standard way for doing blackbox testing as the name itself alludes to the package being tested while at the same time preventing our test code from accessing the internals of the package under test.

One caveat of black-box testing is that we need to mock/stub any external objects and/or services that the tested code depends on. In this particular case, we need to provide stubs for the price and vat services. Fortunately, the net/http/httptest package, which ships with the Go standard library provides a convenient helper for spinning up a local HTTPS server using random, unused ports. Since we need to spin up two servers for our tests, let's create a small helper function to do exactly that:

```go
func spinUpTestServer(t *testing.T, res map[string]interface{})
*httptest.Server {
    encResponse, err := json.Marshal(res)
    if err != nil {
        t.Fatal(err)    }
    return httptest.NewServer(http.HandlerFunc(func(w http.ResponseWriter,
req *http.Request) {
        w.Header().Set("Content-Type", "application/json")        if _, wErr := w.Write(encResponse);
wErr != nil {
            t.Fatal(wErr)
        }
    }))
}
```

Nothing too complicated here; the spinUpTestServer function receives a map with the expected response's content and returns a server (which our test code needs to explicitly close) that always responds with the response payload formatted in JSON. With this helper function in place, setting up the stubs for our services becomes really easy:

```go
// t is a testing.T instance

priceSvc := spinUpTestServer(t, map[string]interface{}{
```

```
    "price": 10.0,
})
defer priceSvc.Close()
vatSvc := spinUpTestServer(t, map[string]interface{} {
    "vat_rate": 0.29,
}) defer vatSvc.Close()
```

So, all we need to do now is call the NewPriceCalculator constructor and pass the addresses of the two fake servers. Hold on a minute! If those servers always listen on a random port, how do we know which addresses to pass to the constructor? One particularly convenient feature of the Server implementation that's provided by the httptest package is that it exposes the endpoint where the server is listening for incoming connections via a public attribute called URL. Here's what the rest of our blackbox test would look like:

```
pc := retail.NewPriceCalculator(priceSvc.URL, vatSvc.URL) got, err := pc.PriceForItem("1b6f8e0f-bbda-4f4e-ade5-aa1abcc99586")
if err != nil {
    t.Fatal(err) }
if exp := 12.9; got != exp {
    t.Fatalf("expected calculated retail price to be %f; got %f", exp, got) }
```

As we mentioned previously, the preceding code snippet lives in a different package, so our tests must import the package under test and access its public contents using the retail selector.

We could add a few more tests, for example, to validate the PriceForItem behavior when one or both of the services return an error, but that's as far as we can test using black-box testing alone! Let's run our test and see what sort of coverage we can get:

Not bad at all! However, if we need to boost our test coverage metrics further, we'll need to invest some time and come up with some white-box tests.

Boosting code coverage via white-box tests

One major difference compared to the tests we wrote in the previous section is that the new set of tests will live in the same package as the package we are testing. To differentiate from the black-box tests that we authored previously and hint to other engineers perusing the test code that these are internal tests, we will place the new tests in a file named retail_internal_test.go.

Now, it's time to pull the curtain back and examine the implementation details of the retail package! The public API of the package is always a good place to begin our exploratory work. An effective strategy would be to identify each exported function and then (mentally) follow its call-graph to locate other candidate functions/methods that we can exercise via our white-box tests. In the unlikely case that the package does not export any functions, we can shift our attention to other exported symbols, such as structs or interfaces. For instance, here is the definition of the PriceCalculator struct from the retail package:

```go
type PriceCalculator struct {
    priceSvc svcCaller
    vatSvc   svcCaller
}
```

As we can see, the struct contains two private fields of the svcCaller type whose names clearly indicate they are somehow linked to the two services that the facade needs to call out to. If we keep browsing through the code, we will discover that svcCaller is actually an interface:

```go
type svcCaller interface {
    Call(req map[string]interface{}) (io.ReadCloser, error)
}
```

The Call method receives a map of request parameters and returns a response stream as an io.ReadCloser. From the perspective of a test writer, the use of such an abstraction should make us quite happy since it provides us with an easy avenue for mocking the actual calls to the two services!

As we saw in the previous section, the public API exposed by the PriceCalculator type is composed of two methods:

PriceForItem, which returns the price of an item at this point in time PriceForItemAtDate, which returns the price of an item at a particular point intime.

Since the PriceForItem method is a simple wrapper that calls PriceForItemAtDate with the current date/time as an argument, we will focus our analysis on the latter. The implementation of PriceForItemAtDate is presented as follows:

```go
func (pc *PriceCalculator) PriceForItemAtDate(itemUUID string, date
time.Time) (float64, error) {
    priceRes := struct {
        Price float64 `json:"price"`
    }{}
    vatRes := struct {
        Rate float64 `json:"vat_rate"`
    }{}
    req := map[string]interface{}{"item": itemUUID, "period": date}
    if err :=
pc.callService(pc.priceSvc, req, &priceRes); err != nil {
        return 0, xerrors.Errorf("unable to
retrieve item price: %w", err)
    }
    req = map[string]interface{}{"period": date}
    if err := pc.callService(pc.vatSvc, req, &vatRes); err != nil {
        return 0, xerrors.Errorf("unable
to retrieve vat percent: %w", err)
    }
    return vatInclusivePrice(priceRes.Price, vatRes.Rate), nil
```

```
}
```

The preceding code block makes use of a helper called callService to send out a request to the price and vat services and unpack their responses into the priceRes and vatRes variables. To gain a clearer understanding of what happens under the hood, let's take a quick peek into the implementation of callService:

```go
func (pc *PriceCalculator) callService(svc svcCaller, req map[string]interface{}, res interface{}) error {

    svcRes, err := svc.Call(req)

    if err != nil {

        return xerrors.Errorf("call to remote service failed: %w", err)

    }

    defer drainAndClose(svcRes)

    if err = json.NewDecoder(svcRes).Decode(res); err != nil {        return xerrors.Errorf("unable to decode remote service response:

%w", err)

    } return nil }
```

The callService method implementation is pretty straightforward. All it does is invoke the Call method on the provided svcCaller instance, treats the returned output as a JSON stream, and attempts to unmarshal it into the res argument that's provided by the caller.

Now, let's go back to the implementation of the PriceForItemAtDate method. Assuming that no error occurred while contacting the remote services, their individual responses are passed as arguments to the vatInclusivePrice helper function.

As you can probably tell by its name, it implements the business logic of applying VAT rates to prices. Keeping the business logic separate from the code that is responsible for talking to other services is not only a good indicator of a well-thought-out design but it also makes our test-writing job easier. Let's add a small table-driven test to validate the business logic:

```go
func TestVatInclusivePrice(t *testing.T) {

    specs := []struct {        price float64        vatRate float64        exp    float64

    }{

        {42.0, 0.1, 46.2},

        {10.0, 0, 10.0},

    }

    for specIndex, spec := range specs {

        if got := vatInclusivePrice(spec.price, spec.vatRate); got !=
```

```
    spec.exp {
            t.Errorf("[spec %d] expected to get: %f; got: %f", specIndex,
spec.exp, got)
        }
    }
}
```

With that test in place, the next thing we want to test is PriceForItem. To do that, we need to somehow control access to the external services. Although we will be using stubs for simplicity, we could also use any of the other test patterns that we discussed in the previous section. Here is a stub that implements the same approach as the test server from our black-box tests but without the need to actually spin up a server!

```
type stubSvcCaller map[string]interface{}

func (c stubSvcCaller) Call(map[string]interface{}) (io.ReadCloser, error)
{
    data, err := json.Marshal(c)
    if err != nil {       return nil, err   }
    return ioutil.NopCloser(bytes.NewReader(data)), nil }
```

Using the preceding stub definition, let's add a test for the PriceForItem method's happy path:

```
func TestPriceForItem(t *testing.T) {
    pc := &PriceCalculator{
        priceSvc: stubSvcCaller{ "price": 42.0, },        vatSvc: stubSvcCaller{ "vat_rate": 0.10, },    }
    got, err := pc.PriceForItem("foo")
    if err != nil {
        t.Fatal(err)   }
    if exp := 46.2; got != exp {
        t.Fatalf("expected calculated retail price to be %f; got %f", exp,
got)   }
}
```

Of course, our tests wouldn't really be complete without explicitly testing what happens when a required dependency fails! For this, we need yet another stub, which always returns an error:

```
type stubErrCaller struct {
```

```
    err error }
```

```go
func (c stubErrCaller) Call(map[string]interface{}) (io.ReadCloser, error)
{
    return nil, c.err }
```

With this stub implementation, we can test how the PriceCalculator method behaves when particular classes of errors occur. For example, here is a test that simulates a 404 response from the vat service to indicate to the caller that no VAT rate data is available for the specified time period:

```go
func TestVatSvcErrorHandling(t *testing.T) {
    pc := &PriceCalculator{
        priceSvc: stubSvcCaller{ "price": 42.0, },
        vatSvc: stubErrCaller{
            err: errors.New("unexpected response status code: 404"),
        },
    }
    expErr := "unable to retrieve vat percent: call to remote service
failed: unexpected response status code: 404"
    _, err := pc.PriceForItem("foo")    if err == nil || err.Error() != expErr {
        t.Fatalf("expected to get error:\n %s\ngot:\n %v", expErr, err)
    }
}
```

Let's run the black- and white-box tests together to check how the total coverage has changed now that we've introduced the new tests:

While the ratio of white-box and black-box tests in the Go standard library's sources seems to strongly favor white-box testing, this should not be construed as a hint that you shouldn't be writing black-box tests! Black-box tests certainly have their place and are very useful when you're attempting to replicate the exact set of conditions and inputs that trigger the particular bug that you are trying to track down. What's more, as we will see in the upcoming sections, black-box tests can often serve as templates for constructing another class of tests, commonly referred to as integration tests.

Table-driven tests versus subtests

In this section, we will be comparing two slightly different approaches when it comes to grouping and executing multiple test cases together. These two approaches, namely tabledriven tests and subtests, can easily be implemented using the basic primitives provided by Go's built-in testing package. For each approach, we will discuss the pros and cons and eventually outline a strategy to fuse the two approaches together so that we can get the best of both worlds.

Table-driven tests

Table-driven tests are a quite compact and rather terse way to efficiently test the behavior of a particular piece of code in a host of different scenarios. The format of a typical table-driven test consists of two distinct parts: the test case definitions and the test-runner code.

To demonstrate this, let's examine a possible implementation of the infamous FizzBuzz test: given a number, N, the FizzBuzz implementation is expected to return Fizz if the number is evenly divisible by 3, Buzz if the number is evenly divisible by 5, FizzBuzz if the number is evenly divisible by both 3 and 5, or the number itself in all other cases. Here is a listing from the Chapter04/table-driven/fizzbuzz.go file, which contains the implementation we will be working with:

```go
func Evaluate(n int) string {
    if n != 0 {       switch {       case n%3 == 0 && n%5 == 0:

        return "FizzBuzz"       case n%3 == 0:       return "Fizz"       case n%5 == 0:
return "Buzz"

    }

}

    return fmt.Sprint(n) }
```

In the majority of cases, test scenarios will only be accessed by a single test function. With that in mind, a good strategy would be to encapsulate the scenario list inside the test function with the help of a pretty nifty Go feature: anonymous structs. Here is how you would go about defining the struct that contains the scenarios and a scenario list using a single block of code:

```go
specs := []struct {    descr string    input int    exp  string

}{

    {descr: "evenly divisible by 3", input: 9, exp: "Fizz"},

    {descr: "evenly divisible by 5", input: 25, exp: "Buzz"},

    {descr: "evenly divisible by 3 and 5", input: 15, exp: "FizzBuzz"},    // The following case is
intentionally wrong to trigger a test failure!

    {descr: "example of incorrect expectation", input: 0, exp: "FizzBuzz"},

    {descr: "edge case", input: 0, exp: "0"},

}
```

In the preceding code snippet, you may have noticed that I included a description for each test case. This is more of a personal preference, but in my opinion, it makes the test code more pleasant to the eyes and, more importantly, helps us easily locate the specs for failing test cases as opposed to visually scanning the entire list looking for the Nth scenario that corresponds to a failed test.

Granted, either approach would be efficient for the preceding example where every test case is neatly laid out in a single line, but think how much more difficult things would be if each spec block contained nested objects and thus each spec was defined using a variable number of lines.

Once we have written down our specs, making sure that we have also included any edge cases that we can think of, it is time to run the test. This is actually the easy part! All we need to do is iterate the list of specs, invoke the subject under test with the input(s) provided by each spec, and verify that the outputs conform to the expected values:

```
for specIndex, spec := range specs {

    if got := fizzbuzz.Evaluate(spec.input); got != spec.exp {

        t.Errorf("[spec %d: %s] expected to get %q; got %q", specIndex,

spec.descr, spec.exp, got)

    }

}
```

One important aspect of the preceding test-runner implementation is that even when a test case fails, we don't immediately abort the test by invoking any of the t.Fail/FailNow or t.Fatal/f helpers, but rather exhaust our list of test cases. This is intentional as it allows us to see an overview of all the failing cases in one go. If we were to run the preceding code, we would get the following output:

Figure: Example of a failing case in a table-driven test

One unfortunate caveat of this approach is that we cannot request for the go

test command to explicitly target a specific test case. We can always ask go test to only run a specific test function in isolation (for example, go test -run

TestFizzBuzzTableDriven), but not to only run the failing test case number 3 within that test function; we need to sequentially test all the cases every single time! Being able to target specific test cases would be a time-saver if our test-runner code was complex and each test case took quite a bit of time to execute.

Subtests

With the release of Go 1.7, the built-in testing package gained support for running subtests.

Subtests are nothing more than a hierarchy of test functions that are executed sequentially. This hierarchical structuring of the test code is akin to the notion of a test suite that you may have been exposed to in other programming languages.

So, how does it work? The testing.T type has been augmented with a new method called Run that has the following signature:

```
Run(description string, func(t *testing.T))
```

This new method provides a new mechanism for spawning subtests that will run in isolation while still retaining the ability to use the parent test function to perform any required setup and teardown steps.

As you might expect, since each subtest function receives its own testing.T instance argument, it can, in turn, spawn additional subtests that are nested underneath it. Here's what a typical test would look like when following this approach:

```go
func TestXYZ(t *testing.T){     // Run suite setup code...

    t.Run("test1", func(t *testing.T){

        // test1 code

    })

    t.Run("test2", func(t *testing.T){

        // test2 code

    })

    // Run suite tear-down code...

}
```

What's more, each subtest gets its own unique name, which is generated by concatenating the names of all its ancestor test functions and the description string that gets passed to the invocation of Run. This makes it easy to target any subtest in a particular hierarchy tree by specifying its name to the -run argument when invoking go test. For example, in the preceding code snippet, we can target test2 by running go test -run TestXYZ/test2.

One disadvantage of subtests compared to their test-driven brethren is that they are defined in a much more verbose way. This could prove to be a bit of a challenge if we need to define a large number of test scenarios.

The best of both worlds

At the end of the day, nothing precludes us from combining these two approaches into a hybrid approach that gives us the best of both worlds: the terseness of table-driven tests and the selective targeting of subtests.

To achieve this, we need to define our table-driven specs, just like we did before. Following that, we iterate the spec list and spawn a subtest for each test case. Here's how we could adapt our FizzBuzz tests so that they follow this pattern:

```go
func TestFizzBuzzTableDrivenSubtests(t *testing.T) {

    specs := []struct {       descr, exp string       input     int

    }{

        {descr: "evenly divisible by 3", input: 9, exp: "Fizz"},

        {descr: "evenly divisible by 3 and 5", input: 15, exp: "FizzBuzz"},

        {descr: "edge case", input: 0, exp: "0"},

    }
```

```
    for specIndex, spec := range specs {

        t.Run(spec.descr, func(t *testing.T) {

            if got := fizzbuzz.Evaluate(spec.input); got != spec.exp {

                t.Errorf("[spec %d: %s] expected to get %q; got %q",
specIndex, spec.descr, spec.exp, got)

            }

        })

    }

}
```

Let's say we wanted to only run the second test case. We can easily achieve this by passing its fully qualified name as the value of the -run flag when running go test:

```
go test -run TestFizzBuzzTableDrivenSubtests/evenly_divisible_by_3_and_5
```

Using third-party testing frameworks

One great thing about testing Go code is that the language itself comes with batteries included: it ships with a built-in, albeit minimalistic, framework for authoring and running tests.

From a purist's perspective, that's all that you need to be up and running! The builtin testing package provides all the required mechanisms for running, skipping, or failing tests. All the software engineer needs to do is set up the required test dependencies and write the appropriate predicates for each test. One caveat of using the testing package is that it does not provide any of the more sophisticated test primitives, such as assertions or mocks, that you may be used to if you've come from a Java, Ruby, or Python background. Of course, nothing prevents you from implementing these yourself!

Alternatively, if importing additional test dependencies is something you don't object to, you can make use of one of the several readily available third-party packages that provide all these missing features. Since a full, detailed listing of all third-party test packages is outside of the scope of this book, we will focus our attention on one of the most popular test framework packages out there: gocheck.

The gocheck package [3] can be installed by running go get gopkg.in/check.v1. It builds on top of the standard Go testing package and provides support for organizing tests into test suites. Each suite is defined using a regular Go struct that you can also exploit so that it stores any additional bits of information that might be needed by your tests.

In order to run each test suite as part of your tests, you need to register it with gocheck and hook gocheck to the Go testing package. The following is a short example of how to do that:

```
import (    "testing"

    "gopkg.in/check.v1"

) type MySuite struct{}
```

```
// Register suite with go check var _ = check.Suite(new(MySuite))
```

```
// Hook up gocheck into the "go test" runner. func Test(t *testing.T) { check.TestingT(t) }
```

As you would expect of any framework that supports test suites, gocheck allows you to optionally specify setup and teardown methods for both the suite and each test by defining any of the following methods on the suite type:

SetUpSuite(c *check.C)

SetUpTest(c *check.C)

TearDownTest(c *check.C)

TearDownSuite(c *check.C)

Likewise, any suite method matching the TestXYZ(c *check.C) pattern will be treated as a test and executed when the suit runs. The check.C type gives you access to some useful methods, such as the following:

Log/Logf: Prints a message to the test log

MkDir: Creates a temporary folder that is automatically removed after the suite finishes running

Succeed/SucceedNow/Fail/FailNow/Fatal/Fatalf: Controls the outcome of a running test

Assert: Fails the test if the specified predicate condition isn't met

By default, gocheck buffers all its output and only emits it when a test fails. While this helps cut down the noise and speeds up the execution of chatty tests, you might prefer to see all the output. Fortunately, gocheck supports two levels of verbosity that can be controlled via command-line flags that are passed to the go test invocation.

To force gocheck to output its buffered debug log for all tests, regardless of their pass/fail status, you can run go test with the -check.v argument. The fact that gocheck prefers to buffer all the logging output is less than ideal when you're trying to figure out why one of your tests hangs. For such situations, you can dial up the verbosity and disable buffering by running gocheck with the -check.vv argument. Finally, if you wish to run a particular test from a test suite (akin to go test -run XYZ), you can run gocheck with -check.f

XYZ, where XYZ is a regular expression matching the names of the test(s) you wish to run.

While we mentioned that the check.C object provides an Assert method, we haven't really gone into any detail on how it works or how the assertion predicates are defined. The signature of Assert is as follows:

Assert(obtained interface{}, checker Checker, args ...interface{})

The following table contains a list of useful Checker implementations provided by gocheck that you can use to write your test assertions.

Checker	Description	Example
Equals	Check for equality	c.Assert(res, check.Equals, 42)

DeepEquals	Check interfaces, slices, and others for equality	c.Assert(res, check.DeepEquals, []string{"hello", "world"})
IsNil	Check if the value is nil	c.Assert(err, check.IsNil)
HasLen	Check the length of the slice/map/channel/strings	c.Assert(list, check.HasLen, 2)
Matches	Check that the string matches the regex	c.Assert(val, check.Matches, ".*hi.*")
ErrorMatches	Check that the error message matches the regex	c.Assert(err, check.Matches, ".*not found")
FitsTypeOf	Check that the argument is assigned to a variable with the given type	c.Assert(impl, check.FitsTypeOf,os.Error(nil))
Not	Invert the check result	c.Assert(val, check.Not(check.Equals)), 42)

Of course, if your tests require more sophisticated predicates than the ones built into gocheck, you can always roll your own by implementing the Checker interface.

This concludes our tour of gocheck. If you are interested in using it in your projects, I would definitely recommend visiting the package home [3] and reading its excellent documentation. If you already use gocheck but want to explore other popular testing frameworks for Go, I would suggest taking a look at the stretchr/testify package [7], which offers similar functionality (test suites, assertions, and so on) to gocheck but also includes support for more advanced test primitives such as mocks.

Integration versus functional testing

In this section, we will attempt to dispel any confusion between the definitions of two very important and useful types of testing: integration tests and functional tests.

Integration tests

Integration tests pick up from where unit testing left off. Whereas unit testing ensures that each individual unit of a system works correctly in isolation, integration testing ensures that different units (or services, in a microservice architecture) interoperate correctly.

Let's consider a hypothetical scenario where we are building an e-shop application. Following the SOLID design principles, we have split our backend implementation into a bunch of microservices. Each microservice comes with its own set of unit tests and, by design, exposes an API that adheres to a contract agreed on by all engineering teams. For the purpose of this demonstration, and to keep things simple, we want to focus our efforts on authoring an integration test for the following two microservices:

The product microservice performs the following functions:

It exposes a mechanism for manipulating and querying product metadata; for example, to add or remove products, return information about item prices, descriptions, and so on

The basket microservice stores the list of items that have been selected by the customer. When a new item is inserted into a customer's basket, the basket service queries the product service for the item metadata and updates the price summary for the basket. At the same time, it subscribes to the product service change stream and updates the basket's contents if the product metadata is updated.

One important implementation aspect to be aware of is that each microservice uses its own dedicated data store. Keep in mind though that this approach does not necessarily mean that the data stores are physically separated. Perhaps we are using a single database server and each microservice gets its own database on that server.

The integration test for these two services would live in a separate Go test file, perhaps with an _integration_test.go suffix so that we can immediately tell its purpose just by looking at the filename. The setup phase of the tests expects that the DB instance(s) that are required by the services have already been externally prepared. As we will see later in this chapter, a simple way to provide DB connection settings to our tests is via the use of environment variables. The tests would proceed to spin up the services that we want to test and then run the following integration scenarios:

Invoke the product service API to insert a new product into the catalog. Then, it would use the basket service API to add the product to a customer basket and verify that the DB that's used by the basket service contains an entry with the correct product metadata.

Add a product to a customer basket. Then, it would use the product service API to mutate the item description and verify that the relevant basket DB entry is updated correctly.

One caveat of integration tests is that we need to maintain strict isolation between individual tests. Consequently, before running each test scenario, we must ensure that the internal state of each service is reset properly. Typically, this means that we need to flush the database that's used by each service and perhaps also restart the services in case they also maintain any additional in-memory state.

Evidently, the effort that's required to set up, wire together, and prime the various components that are needed for each integration test makes writing such tests quite a tedious process. Not to diminish the significance of integration testing, it is my belief that engineers can make better use of their time by writing a large number of unit tests and just a handful of integration tests.

Functional tests

Functional or end-to-end tests take system testing to a whole new level. The primary purpose of functional testing is to ensure that the complete system is working as expected. To this end, functional tests are designed to model complex interaction scenarios that involve multiple system components. A very common use case for functional tests is to verify end-to-end correctness by simulating a user's journey through the system.

For instance, a functional test for an online music streaming service would act as a new user who would subscribe to the service, search for a particular song, add it to their playlist, and perhaps submit a rating for the song once it's done playing.

It is important to clarify that all the preceding interactions are meant to occur via the web browser. This is a clear-cut case where we need to resort to a scriptable browser automation framework such as Selenium [6] in order to accurately model all the required button clicks that we expect a real user to perform while using the system.

While you could probably find a package that provides Go bindings for Selenium, the truth of the matter is that Go is not the best tool for writing functional tests. Contrary to unit and integration tests, which live within Go files, functional tests are normally written in languages such as Python, JavaScript, or Ruby. Another important distinction is that, due to their increased complexity, functional tests take a significantly longer time to run.

While it's not uncommon for software engineers working on a particular feature to also provide functional test suites, in the majority of cases, the task of authoring functional tests is one of the primary responsibilities of the quality assurance (QA) team. As a matter of fact, functional tests are the front and center part of the pre-release workflow that's followed by QA engineers before they can give the green light for a new release.

Functional tests don't usually target production systems; you wouldn't want to fill up your production DB with dummy user accounts, right? Instead, functional tests target staging environments, which are isolated and often downsized sandboxes that mirror the setup of the actual production environment. This includes all the services and resources (databases, message queues, and so on) that are needed for the system to operate. One exception is that access to external third-party services such as payment gateways or email providers is typically mocked unless a particular functional test requests otherwise.

Functional tests part deux – testing in production!

That's not to say that you cannot actually run your functional tests in a live production environment! Surely whether that's a good or bad idea is a debatable point, but if you do decide to go down that route, there are a few patterns that you can apply to achieve this in a safe and controlled way.

To get the ball rolling, you can begin by revising your DB schemas so that they include a field that indicates whether each row contains real data or is part of a test run. Each service could then silently ignore any test records when it handles live traffic.

If you are working with a microservice architecture, you can engineer your services so that they do not talk to other services directly but rather to do so via a local proxy that is deployed in tandem with each service as a sidecar process. This pattern is known as the ambassador pattern and opens up the possibility of implementing a wide range of really cool tricks, as we will see later in this chapter.

Since all the proxies are initially configured to talk to the already deployed services, nothing prevents us from deploying a newer version of a particular service and have it run side-by-side with the existing version. Since no traffic can reach the newly deployed service, it is common to use the term dark launch to refer to this kind of deployment.

Once the new versions of the services that we need to test against have been successfully deployed, each functional test can reconfigure the local proxies to divert test traffic (identified perhaps by an HTTP header or another type of tag) to the newly deployed services. This can be seen in the following diagram:

Figure: Using the ambassador pattern to test in production

This neat trick allows us to run our tests in production without interfering with live traffic. As you can tell, live testing requires substantially more preparation effort compared to testing in a sandbox. This is probably one of the reasons why QA teams seem to prefer using staging environments instead.

In my view, if your system is built in such a way that you can easily introduce one of these patterns to facilitate live testing, you should definitely go for it. After all, there is only so much data that you can collect when running in an isolated environment whose load and traffic profiles don't really align with the ones of your production systems.

Smoke tests

Smoke tests or build acceptance tests constitute a special family of tests that are traditionally used as early sanity checks by QA teams.

The use of the word smoke alludes to the old adage that wherever there is smoke, there is also fire. These checks are explicitly designed to identify early warning signals that something is wrong. It goes without saying that any issue uncovered by a smoke test is treated by the QA team as a show-stopper; if smoke tests fail, no further testing is performed. The QA team reports its findings to the development team and waits for a revised release candidate to be submitted for testing.

Once the smoke tests successfully pass, the QA team proceeds to run their suite of functional tests before giving the green light for release. The following diagram summarizes the process of running smoke tests for QA purposes:

Figure: Running smoke tests as part of the QA process

When it comes to execution, smoke tests are the exact antithesis of functional tests. While functional tests are allowed to execute for long periods of time, smoke tests must execute as quickly as possible. As a result, smoke tests are crafted so as to exercise specific, albeit limited, flows in the user-facing parts of a system that are deemed critical for the system's operation. For example, smoke tests for a social network application would verify the following:

A user can login with a valid username and password

Clicking the like button on a post increases the like counter for that post

Deleting a contact removes them from the user's friends list Clicking the logout button signs the user out of the service

The responsibility for authoring, evolving, and maintaining smoke tests usually falls on the shoulders of the QA team. Consequently, it makes sense for the QA team to maintain smoke tests in a separate, dedicated repository that they own and control. An interesting question here is whether the QA team will opt to execute the smoke tests manually or invest the time and effort that's required to automate the process. The logical, albeit slightly cliché, answer is: it depends...

At the end of the day, the decision boils down to the size of the QA team, the individual preferences of the team's members, and the test infrastructure that's available and is at the team's disposal. Needless to say, automated smoke tests are, hands down, the recommended option since the QA team can efficiently verify a plethora of scenarios in a small amount of time. On the other hand, if the build release frequency is low, you could argue that doing manual smoke tests has a smaller cost and makes better use of the QA team's time and resources.

Chaos testing – breaking your systems in fun and interesting ways!

Let me begin this section with a question! How confident are you about the quality of your current software stack? If your answer happens to be something along the lines of, I don't really know until I make it fail, then we are in total agreement! If not, let me introduce you to the concept of chaos testing.

Chaos testing is a term that was initially coined by the engineering team at Netflix. The key point behind chaos testing is to evaluate your system's behavior when various components exhibit different types of failure. So, what kinds of failure are we talking about here? Here are a few interesting examples, ordered by their relative severity (low to high):

A service fails to reach another service it depends on

Calls between services exhibit high latency/jitter

Network links experience packet loss

A database node fails

We lose a critical piece of storage

Our cloud provider suffers an outage in an entire availability zone

Netflix engineers point out that we shouldn't be afraid of failure but rather embrace it and learn as much as we can about it. All these learnings can be applied to fine-tune the design of our systems so that they become incrementally more and more robust and resilient against failure.

Some of these types of failure have a low likelihood of occurring. Nevertheless, it's better if we are prepared to mitigate them when they actually do occur. After all, from a system stability perspective, it's always preferred to operate in a preventive fashion rather than trying to react (often under lots of pressure) when an outage occurs.

You might be wondering: but, if some failures are statistically unlikely to occur, how can we trigger them in the first place? The only way to do this is to engineer our systems in such a way that failure can be injected on demand. In the Functional tests part deux – testing in production! section, we talked about the ambassador pattern, which can help us achieve exactly that.

The ambassador pattern decouples service discovery and communication from the actual service implementation. This is achieved with the help of a sidecar process that gets deployed with each service and acts as a proxy.

The sidecar proxy service can be used for other purposes, such as conditionally routing traffic based on tags or headers, acting as a circuit breaker, bifurcating traffic to perform A/B testing, logging requests, enforcing security rules, or to inject artificial failures into the system.

From a chaos engineering perspective, the sidecar proxy is an easy avenue for introducing failures. Let's look at some examples of how we can exploit the proxy to inject failure into the system:

  Instruct the proxy to delay outgoing requests or wait before returning upstream responses to the service that initiated the request. This is an effective way to model latency. If we opt not to use fixed intervals but to randomize them, we can inject jitter into intra-service communication.

Configure the proxy to drop outgoing requests with probability P. This emulates a degraded network connection.

Configure the proxy for a single service to drop all outgoing traffic to another service. At the same time, all the other service proxies are set up to forward traffic as usual. This emulates a network partition.

That's not all. We can take chaos testing even further if we are running our systems on a cloud provider that provides us with an API that we can use to break even more things! For instance, we could use such an API to randomly start killing nodes or to take down one or all of our load balancers and check whether our system can automatically recover by itself.

With chaos testing, the only limit is your own imagination!

Tips and tricks for writing tests

In this section, I will be going through some interesting ideas that can help super-charge your daily test workflow. What's more, we will also be exploring some neat tricks that you can use to isolate tests, mock calls to system binaries, and control time within your tests.

Using environment variables to set up or skip tests

In a project of any size, you are eventually bound to come across a series of tests that depend on external resources that are created or configured in an ad hoc fashion.

A typical example of such a use case would be a test suite that talks to a database. As the engineers working locally on the code base, we would probably spin up a local database instance with a more or less predictable endpoint and use that for testing. However, when running under CI, we might be required to use an already provisioned database instance on some cloud provider or, more often than not, the CI setup phase may need to start a database in a Docker container, a process that would yield a non-predictable endpoint to be connected to.

To support scenarios such as these, we must avoid hardcoding the location of resource endpoints to our tests and defer their discovery and configuration until the time when the test runs. To this end, one solution would be to use a set of environment variables to supply

this information to our tests. Here is a simple test example from the Chapter04/db package that illustrates how this can be achieved:

```
func TestDBConnection(t *testing.T) {
    host, port, dbName, user, pass := os.Getenv("DB_HOST"),
os.Getenv("DB_PORT"),
        os.Getenv("DB_NAME"), os.Getenv("DB_USER"), os.Getenv("DB_PASS")
    db, err := sql.Open("postgres", makeDSN(user, pass, dbName, host,
port))    if err != nil {
        t.Fatal(err)
    }
    _ = db.Close()
```

```
    t.Log("Connection to DB succeeded")
}
```

The preceding example makes testing a breeze, regardless of whether we run the tests locally or in a CI environment. But what if our tests require a specialized DB that is not that easy to spin up locally? Maybe we need a DB that operates in a clustered configuration or one whose memory requirements exceed the memory that's available on our development machine. Wouldn't it be great if we could just skip that test when running locally?

It turns out that this is also quite easy to achieve with exactly the same mechanism that we used for configuring our DB endpoint. To be more precise, the absence of the required configuration settings could serve as a hint to the test that it needs to be skipped. In the preceding example, we can achieve this by adding a simple if block after fetching the environment values for the DB configuration:

```
if host == "" {
    t.Skip("Skipping test as DB connection info is not present") }
```

Excellent! Now, if we don't export the DB_HOST environment variable before running our tests, this particular test will be skipped.

Speeding up testing for local development

In this section, we will be covering a couple of approaches to accelerating testing when working locally. Just to clarify, I am assuming that you already have a proper CI infrastructure in place; no matter what shortcuts we will be taking here, the CI will always run all the tests.

The first item on our agenda is slow versus fast tests. For the sake of argument, say that we find ourselves in a situation where we are writing a fully-fledged, pure CPU ray tracer implementation in Go. To ensure correctness and avoid regressions while we are tweaking our implementation, we have introduced a test suite that renders a sequence of example scenes and compares the ray tracer output to a series of prerendered reference images.

Since this is a pure CPU implementation and our tests render at full-HD resolution, running each test would take, as you can imagine, quite a bit of time. This is not an issue when running on the CI but can definitely be an impediment when working locally.

To make matters worse, go test will try to run all the tests, even if one of them fails.

Additionally, it will automatically fail tests that take a long time (over 10 minutes) to run. Fortunately, the go test command supports some really useful flags that we can use to rectify these issues.

To begin with, we can notify long-running tests that they should try to shorten their runtime by passing the -short flag to the go test invocation. This flag gets exposed by the testing package via the Short helper function, which returns true when the short flag is defined. So, how can we use this flag to make our ray tracer tests run faster?

One approach would be to simply skip tests that are known to take a really long time to run. A much better alternative would be to detect the presence of the -short flag and dial down the output resolution of the ray tracer, say, to something such as a quarter of the original resolution. This change would still allow us to verify the rendering output when testing locally while at the same time would constrain the total runtime of our tests to an acceptable level.

Coming back to the issue of go test running all the tests, even if one of them fails, we can actually instruct go test to immediately abort if it detects a failing test by passing the fail fast command-line flag. Moreover, we can tune the maximum, per-test execution time with the help of the -timeout flag. It accepts any string that can be parsed by the time.Duration type (for example, 1h), but if your tests take an unpredictable amount of time to run, you could also pass a timeout value of 0 to disable timeouts.

Excluding classes of tests via build flags

So far, we have discussed white- and black-box tests, integration, and end-to-end tests. By including tests from all these categories in our projects, we can rest assured that the code base will behave as expected in a multitude of different scenarios.

Now, imagine we are working on a particular feature and we only want to run the unit tests. Alternatively, we may only need to run the integration tests to ensure that our changes do not introduce regression to other packages. How can we do that?

The rather simplistic approach would be to maintain separate folders for each test category, but that would veer away from what is considered to be idiomatic Go. Another alternative would be to add the category name as a prefix or suffix to our tests and run go test with the -run flag (or with the -check.f flag if we are using a third-party package such as gocheck [3]) to only run the tests whose names match a particular regular expression. It stands to reason that while this approach will work, it's quite error-prone; for larger code bases, we would need to compose elaborate regular expressions that might not match all the tests that we need to run.

A smarter solution would be to take advantage of Go's support for conditional compilation and repurpose it to serve our needs. This is a great time to explain what conditional compilation is all about and, most importantly, how it works under the hood.

When a package is being built, the go build command scans the comments inside each Go file, looking for special keywords that can be interpreted as compiler directives. Build tags are one example of such an annotation. They are used by go build to decide whether a particular Go file in a package should be passed to the Go compiler. The general syntax for a build tag is as follows: // +build tag1 ... tagN package some_package

To be correctly recognized by go build, all the build tags must appear as a comment at the top of a Go file. While you are allowed to define multiple build tags, it is very important that the last build tag is separated with a blank (non-comment) line from the package name declaration. Otherwise, go build will just assume that the build tag is part of a packagelevel comment and simply ignore it. Software engineers that are new to the concept of Go build tags occasionally fall into this trap, so if you find yourself scratching your head, wondering why build tags are not being picked up, the lack of a blank line after the build tag is the most likely suspect.

Let's take a closer look at the intricacies of the tag syntax and elaborate on the rules that are applied by go build to interpret the list of tags following the +build keyword:

Tags separated by whitespace are evaluated as a list of OR conditions.

Tags separated by a comma are evaluated as a list of AND conditions.

Tags beginning with! are treated as NOT conditions.

If multiple +build lines are defined, they are joined together as an AND condition.

The go build command recognizes several predefined tags for the target operating system (for example, linux, windows, darwin), CPU architecture (for example, amd64, 386, arm64), and even the version of the Go compiler (for example, go1.10 to specify Go 1.10 onward). The following table shows a few examples that use tags to model complex build constraints.

By now, you should have a better understanding of how build tags work. But how does all this information apply to our particular use case? First of all, let me highlight the fact that test files are also regular Go files and, as such, they are also scanned for the presence of build tags! Secondly, we are not limited to the built-in tags – we can also define our own custom tags and pass them to go build or go test via the -tags command-line flag.

You can probably see where I am going with this… We can start by defining a build tag for each family of tests, for example, integration_tests, unit_tests, and e2e_tests. Additionally, we will define an all_tests tag since we need to retain the capability to run all the tests together. Finally, we will edit our test files and add the following build tag annotations:

+build unit_tests all_tests to the files containing the unit tests

+build integration_tests all_tests to the files containing the integration tests

+build e2e_tests all_tests to the files containing the end-to-end tests

If you wish to experiment with the preceding example, you can check out the contents of the package.

This is not the output you are looking for – mocking calls to external binaries

Have you ever struggled when trying to test code that calls out to an external process and then uses the output as part of the implemented business logic? In some cases, it might be possible to use some of the tricks we have discussed so far to decorate our code with hooks that tests can use to mock the executed command's output. Unfortunately, sometimes this will not be possible. For instance, the code under test could import a third-party package that is actually the one that's responsible for executing some external command.

The package exports a function called RoundtripTime. Its job is to calculate the round-trip time for reaching a remote host. Under the hood, it calls out to the ping command and parses its output. This is how it is implemented:

```
func RoundtripTime(host string) (time.Duration, error) {
    var argList = []string{host}    if runtime.GOOS == "windows" {
        argList = append(argList, "-n", "1", "-l", "32")
    } else {
        argList = append(argList, "-c", "1", "-s", "32")
```

```
    }

    out, err := exec.Command("ping", argList...).Output()

    if err != nil {

        return 0, xerrors.Errorf("command execution failed: %w", err)

    }

    return extractRTT(string(out)) }
```

Since the ping command flag names are slightly different between Unix-like systems and Windows, the code relies on OS sniffing to select the appropriate set of flags so that ping will send out a single request with a 32-byte payload. The extractRTT helper function just applies a regular expression to extract the timing information and convert it into a time.Duration value.

For the purpose of this demonstration, let's assume that we are operating a video streaming service and our business logic (which lives in another Go package) uses the RoundtripTime results to redirect our customers to the edge server that is closest to them. We have been tasked with writing an end-to-end test for the service so, unfortunately, we are not allowed to mock any of the calls to the RoundtripTime function; our test actually needs to invoke the ping command!

If you ever find yourself in a similar situation, let me suggest a nice trick that you can use to mock calls to external processes. I came across the concept that I am about to describe when I first joined Canonical to work on the juju code base. In hindsight, the idea is pretty straightforward. The implementation, however, is not something immediately obvious and requires some platform-specific tweaks, so kudos to the engineers that came up with it.

This approach exploits the fact that when you try to execute a binary (for example, using the Command function from the os/exec package), the operating system will look for the binary in the current working directory and if that fails, it will sequentially scan each entry in the system's PATH environment variable, trying to locate it. To our advantage, both Unixlike systems and Windows follow the same logic. Another interesting observation is that when you ask Windows to execute a command named foo, it will search for an executable called foo.exe or a batch file called foo.bat.

To mock an external process, we need to provide two pieces of information: the expected process output and an appropriate status code; an exit status code of zero would indicate that the process completed successfully. Therefore, if we could somehow create an executable shell script that prints out the expected output before exiting with a particular status code and prepend its path to the front of the system's PATH variable, we could trick the operating system into executing our script instead of the real binary!

At this point, we are entering the realm of OS-specific code. This practice will probably be frowned upon by some engineers, with the argument that Go programs are usually supposed to be portable across operating systems and CPU architectures. In this case, however, we just need to deal with two operating system families so we can probably get away with it. Let's take a look at the templates for the Unix and Windows shell scripts that our test code will be injecting. Here is the one for Unix:

```
#!/bin/bash

cat <<!!!EOF!!! | perl -pe 'chomp if eof' %s
```

!!!EOF!!! exit %d

The script uses the here document syntax [1] to output the text between the two !!!EOF!!! labels in verbatim. Since here documents include an extra, trailing line-feed character, we pipe the output to a Perl one-liner to strip it off. The %s placeholder will be replaced with the text (which can span several lines) that we want our command to output. Finally, the %d placeholder will be replaced with the exit code that the command will return.

The Windows version is much simpler since here documents are not supported by the built-in shell interpreter (cmd.exe). Due to this, I have opted to write the output to a file and just have the shell script print it to the standard output. Here's what this looks like:

@echo off type %s exit /B %d

In this case, the %s placeholder will be replaced with the path to the external file containing the output for the mocked command and, as before, the %d placeholder will be replaced with the exit code for the command.

In our test file, we will define a helper function called mockCmdOutput. Due to space constraints, I will not be including the full listing of the function here but rather a short

synopsis of how it works (for the full implementation, you can check out the Chapter04/pinger sources). In a nutshell, mockCmdOutput does the following:

Creates a temporary folder that will be automatically removed after the test completes

Selects the appropriate shell script template, depending on the operating system

Writes the shell script to the temporary folder and changes its permissions so that it becomes executable (important for Unix-like systems)

Prepends the temporary folder to the beginning of the PATH environment variable for the currently running process (go test)

Since mockCmdOutput modifies the system path, we must ensure that it gets reset to its original value before each of our tests runs. We can easily achieve this by grouping our tests into a gocheck test suite and providing a test setup function to save the original PATH value and a test teardown function to restore it from the saved value. With all the plumbing in place, here is how we can write a test function that mocks the output of ping:

```
func (s *PingerSuite) TestFakePing(c *check.C) {

   mock := "32 bytes from 127.0.0.1: icmp_seq=0 ttl=32 time=42000 ms"    mockCmdOutput(c,
"ping", mock, 0)

   got, err := pinger.RoundtripTime("127.0.0.1")

   c.Assert(err, check.IsNil)

   c.Assert(got, check.Equals, 42*time.Second) }
```

To make sure that the command was mocked correctly, we set up our test to do a roundtrip measurement to localhost (typically taking 1 ms or less) and mock the ping command to return a ridiculously high number (42 seconds). Try running the test on OS X, Linux, or Windows; you will always get consistent results.

Testing timeouts is easy when you have all the time in the world!

I am pretty sure that, at some point, you have written some code that relies on the timekeeping functions provided by the standard library's time package. Perhaps it's some code that periodically polls a remote endpoint – a great case for using time.NewTicker – or maybe you are using time.After to implement a timeout mechanism inside a go-routine that waits for an event to occur. In a slightly different scenario, using time.NewTimer to provide your server code with ample time to drain all its connections before shutting down would also be a stellar idea.

However, testing code that uses any of these patterns is not a trivial thing. For example, let's say that you are trying to test a piece of code that blocks until an event is received or a specific amount of time elapses without receiving an event. In the latter case, it would return some sort of timeout error to the caller. To verify that the timeout logic works as expected and to avoid locking up the test runner if the blocking code never returns, the typical approach would be to spin up a go-routine that runs the blocking code and then signals (for example, over a channel) when the expected error is returned. The test function that starts the go-routine would then use a select block to wait for either a success signal from the go-routine or for a fixed amount of time to elapse, after which it would automatically fail the test.

If we were to apply this approach, how long should such a test wait for before giving up? If the max wait time for the blocking piece of code is known in advance (for example, defined as a constant), then things are relatively easy; our test needs to wait for at least that amount of time, plus some extra time to account for speed discrepancies when running tests in different environments (for example, locally versus on the CI). Failure to account for these discrepancies can lead to flaky tests – tests that randomly fail, making your CI system vehemently complain.

Things are much easier if the timeout is configurable or at least specified as a global variable that our tests can patch while they are executing. What if, however, the test time is specified as a constant, but its value is in the order of a couple of seconds. Clearly, having several tests that run for that amount of time literally doing nothing but waiting is counterproductive.

Similarly, in some cases, timeouts might be calculated via some formula that includes a random component. That would make the timeout much harder to predict in a deterministic way without resorting to hacks such as setting the random number generator's seed to a specific value. Of course, in this scenario, our tests would just break if another engineer even slightly tweaked the formula that's used to calculate the timeouts.

The package is an interesting case for further examination as it exhibits both issues that I've described here: long wait times that are calculated via a formula! This package provides a dialing wrapper that overlays an exponential backoff retry mechanism on top of a network dialing function (for example, net.Dial).

To create a new retrying dialer, we need to call the NewRetryingDialer constructor:

```
func NewRetryingDialer(ctx context.Context, dialFunc DialFunc, maxAttempts

int) *RetryingDialer {    if maxAttempts > 31 {
```

```
        panic("maxAttempts cannot exceed 31")    }

    return &RetryingDialer{       ctx:      ctx,      dialFunc: dialFunc,      maxAttempts:
maxAttempts,

    }

}
```

The caller provides a context.Context instance, which can be used to abort pending dial attempts if, for instance, the application receives a signal to shut down. Now, let's move on to the meat of the dialer implementation – the Dial call:

```
func (d *RetryingDialer) Dial(network, address string) (conn net.Conn, err

error) {

    for attempt := 1; attempt <= d.maxAttempts; attempt++ {        if conn, err = d.dialFunc(network,
address); err == nil {

        return conn, nil       }

    log.Printf("dial %q: attempt %d failed; retrying after %s",

address, attempt, expBackoff(attempt))

    select {

    case <-time.After(expBackoff(attempt)): // Try again       case <-d.ctx.Done():

        return nil, d.ctx.Err()

    }

    }

    return nil, ErrMaxRetriesExceeded }
```

This is a pretty straightforward implementation: each time a dial attempt fails, we invoke the expBackoff helper to calculate the wait time for the next attempt. Then, we block until the wait time elapses or the context gets cancelled. Finally, if we happen to exceed the maximum configured number of retry attempts, the code will automatically bail out and return an error to the caller. How about writing a short test to verify that the preceding code handles timeouts as expected? This is what it would look like:

```
func TestRetryingDialerWithRealClock(t *testing.T) {

    log.SetFlags(0)

    // Dial a random local port that nothing is listening on.     d :=
dialer.NewRetryingDialer(context.Background(), net.Dial, 20)

    _, err := d.Dial("tcp", "127.0.0.1:65000")

    if err != {
```

```
        t.Fatal(err)

    }

}
```

Success! The test passed. But hold on a minute; look at the test's runtime! 9 seconds!!! Surely, we can do better than this. Wouldn't it be great if we could somehow mock time in Go as we do when writing tests for other programming languages? It turns out that it is indeed possible with the help of packages such as jonboulle/clockwork [2] and juju/clock [8]. We will be using the latter package for our testing purposes as it also supports mock timers.

The juju/clock package exposes a Clock interface whose method signatures match the functions that are exported by the built-in time package. What's more, it provides a real clock implementation (juju.WallClock) that we should be injecting into production code, as well as a fake clock implementation that we can manipulate within our tests.

If we can inject a clock.Clock instance into the RetryingDialer struct, we can use it as a replacement for the time.After call in the retry code. That's easy: just modify the dialer constructor argument list so that it includes a clock instance.

Now, let's create a copy of the previous test but this time inject a fake clock into the dialer. To control the time, we will spin up a go-routine to keep advancing the clock by a fixed amount of time until the test completes. For brevity, the following listing only includes the code for controlling the clock; other than that, the rest of the test's setup and its expectations are exactly the same as before:

```
doneCh := make(chan struct{})

defer close(doneCh)

clk := testclock.NewClock(time.Now())

go func() {    for {        select {

        case <-doneCh: // test completed; exit go-routine

            return        default:        clk.Advance(1 * time.Minute)

        }

    }

}()
```

As expected, our new test also passes successfully. However, compared to the previous test run, the new test ran in a fraction of the time – just 0.010s:

Figure: Testing the retrying dialer with a fake clock

Personally speaking, fake clocks are one of my favourite test primitives. If you are not using fake clocks in your tests, I would strongly recommend that you at least experiment with them. I am sure that you will also reach the conclusion that fake clocks are a great tool for writing well-behaved tests for any piece of code that deals with some aspect of time. Moreover, increasing the stability of your test suites is a fair trade-off for the small bit of refactoring that's required to introduce clocks into your existing code base.

Conclusion

Testing in software development is not just an optional step; it's a necessity, especially when building robust, scalable, and maintainable systems. In Go, a language celebrated for its simplicity, efficiency, and concurrency, testing forms a fundamental part of the development process. Go's design philosophy emphasizes clear, straightforward, and readable code, and this ethos extends to its testing ecosystem. From unit tests to integration and benchmark tests, Go provides developers with the essential tools and patterns needed to write reliable, maintainable tests that help verify the correctness of code.

The Value of Testing in Modern Software Development

Modern software applications are complex, involving numerous components, dependencies, and external services. As software scales, the likelihood of introducing bugs increases, making it essential to catch issues early in the development cycle. This is where effective testing comes in. By writing comprehensive tests, developers can ensure that their code behaves as expected under various conditions, leading to fewer surprises in production. Testing also serves as a safety net for developers, enabling them to refactor and optimize code with confidence, knowing that if something breaks, the tests will catch it.

In Go, the simplicity and efficiency of the language naturally extend to its testing practices. Unlike some other languages where testing might feel cumbersome or an afterthought, Go makes it easy to integrate testing from the very beginning. This helps to foster a culture of testing among developers, leading to better software quality and fewer defects.

Go's Testing Ecosystem: A Blend of Simplicity and Power

Go's testing ecosystem stands out for its straightforwardness. The testing package, part of the standard library, provides all the necessary tools for writing unit tests, integration tests, and benchmarks. The package is designed to be simple, with minimal setup required to get started. This reduces the barrier to entry and encourages developers to adopt testing practices without the need for extensive configuration.

With the release of Go 2024, several new enhancements have been introduced that further streamline the testing process. Improved test coverage reporting, better benchmarking tools, and native support for test fixtures are just a few examples of the features that make it easier for developers to write effective tests. These additions are designed to address some of the common pain points in testing, such as managing setup and teardown for integration tests or collecting detailed performance metrics.

The Importance of Unit Testing

Unit testing is the backbone of testing in Go. By focusing on small, isolated pieces of code, unit tests allow developers to validate the functionality of individual functions or methods without considering external dependencies. This isolation is crucial because it ensures that the tests are fast, easy to write, and provide immediate feedback. Fast tests are particularly important in a continuous integration (CI) environment, where frequent code commits need to be validated quickly.

In Go, writing unit tests is as simple as creating a new function with the TestXxx naming convention. The testing.T parameter makes it easy to report errors, log information, and control the flow of the test. The simplicity of this approach reduces the learning curve, making it accessible even for developers who are new to testing. Additionally, Go's straightforward syntax and lack of boilerplate code mean that the focus remains on the logic of the test itself, rather than on configuring the test environment.

Integration Testing: Validating the Bigger Picture

While unit tests are essential, they are not sufficient on their own. Integration testing helps to validate those different parts of an application work together as expected. In Go, integration tests can be more complex than unit tests because they often involve external systems like databases, APIs, and third-party services. However, the principles of simplicity and clarity still apply.

Go's built-in tools make it easy to write integration tests that can set up and tear down test environments. Developers can use the same *_test.go files to include integration tests, ensuring that these tests can be run with the same go test command. The ability to run integration tests as part of the same testing suite simplifies the process, allowing for a seamless testing experience.

With Go 2024, enhancements in test fixtures have made integration testing even more streamlined. Test fixtures allow developers to set up reusable pieces of data or configurations, reducing the amount of boilerplate code required to initialize the test environment. This leads to cleaner, more maintainable tests and a smoother testing process overall.

Benchmarking: Performance Testing in Go

Performance is a critical aspect of many Go applications, especially those designed to handle high concurrency or large data volumes. Go's built-in support for benchmarking allows developers to measure the performance of their code, identify bottlenecks, and make informed decisions about optimizations. Benchmarking tests are defined using the Benchmark Xxx naming convention, and the *testing.B parameter controls the benchmarking loop.

Go 2024 has introduced new tools and options to enhance the benchmarking process. Developers can now gather more detailed metrics, analyze memory usage, and gain deeper insights into the performance characteristics of their code. This makes it easier to identify and resolve performance issues, ensuring that applications remain fast and efficient even under heavy loads.

Best Practices for Effective Testing

1. **Adopt a Test-Driven Development (TDD) Approach:** TDD encourages developers to write tests before writing the actual code. This approach helps clarify the requirements and ensures that the code is designed with testability in mind. While not always feasible, adopting TDD where possible can lead to cleaner, more reliable code.

2. **Write Small, Focused Tests:** Each test should focus on a single piece of functionality. This makes it easier to identify the source of an issue when a test fails. Small, focused tests are also easier to maintain and understand, reducing the cognitive load for developers.

3. **Leverage Table-Driven Testing:** Table-driven tests are a popular pattern in Go that allows developers to test multiple scenarios with a single test function. By creating a slice of test

cases, developers can easily add new test scenarios without duplicating code. This approach improves readability and simplifies the process of extending tests.

4. **Use Mocking and Dependency Injection:** Testing code that relies on external services can be challenging. By using mocking and dependency injection, developers can isolate the code under test and simulate the behavior of external dependencies. This ensures that tests run in a consistent environment and are not affected by external factors.

5. **Automate Testing with Continuous Integration (CI):** Automated testing is a key component of modern development workflows. By integrating tests into a CI pipeline, developers can ensure that every code change is validated before it is merged into the main codebase. This helps catch issues early and reduces the risk of introducing bugs into production.

Leveraging New Features in Go 2024 for Better Testing

The enhancements introduced in Go 2024 are aimed at making the testing process smoother and more efficient. Improved test coverage tools help developers identify untested parts of the codebase, while enhanced benchmarking options provide deeper insights into performance characteristics. Native support for test fixtures simplifies integration testing, reducing the amount of setup and teardown code required.

Additionally, better support for popular mocking libraries like gomock and testify makes it easier to write comprehensive tests that cover a wide range of scenarios. These improvements demonstrate Go's commitment to providing a robust, developer-friendly testing ecosystem.

Testing as an Integral Part of the Development Culture

Ultimately, testing is more than just a technical requirement; it is a mindset. Embracing testing as an integral part of the development process leads to better software, happier users, and a more productive development team. In Go, testing is simple, efficient, and tightly integrated into the language itself, making it easier for developers to adopt and maintain good testing practices.

The improvements in Go 2024 have further lowered the barriers to writing and running tests, providing developers with the tools they need to ensure their code is reliable, performant, and maintainable. By mastering the art of testing in Go, developers can build software that not only meets technical requirements but exceeds them, delivering exceptional value to users.

Final Thoughts

The art of testing in Go is about more than just writing test cases; it's about adopting best practices, leveraging the right tools, and understanding the language's testing philosophy. As software systems grow in complexity, the need for robust, reliable testing becomes even more critical. Go's straightforward, powerful testing ecosystem, combined with the enhancements in Go 2024, provides developers with everything they need to write effective tests and build high-quality applications.

By following the best practices outlined in this chapter and embracing the new features in Go 2024, developers can master the art of testing technical requirements in Go, ensuring that their applications are not only functional but also resilient, performant, and easy to maintain.

14. Go: File Handling and Data Processing

Introduction

File Handling and Data Processing focuses on leveraging Go's robust standard library to efficiently read, write, and manipulate files, along with processing data for various applications. Go, known for its simplicity, concurrency, and efficiency, offers developers a streamlined way to handle file operations and data processing tasks, making it an ideal choice for modern software solutions. This section will delve into the fundamentals of file handling in Go, exploring various I/O techniques, file reading and writing methods, data encoding/decoding, and advanced data processing strategies.

Why File Handling and Data Processing Matter

File handling and data processing are essential components of software development. From simple data storage to complex data transformation, almost every application requires handling files in some form. Whether you are working on a web server, data analysis tool, or automation script, understanding how to efficiently manage and process data files is crucial. Effective file handling ensures smooth operations, reduces errors, and enhances the performance of the application.

Overview of Go's File Handling Capabilities

Go simplifies file operations through its os and io packages, providing developers with easy-to-use interfaces to interact with files and directories. It supports a variety of operations, including creating, opening, reading, writing, and deleting files. The language also includes additional packages, such as bufio for buffered I/O, path/filepath for file path manipulations, and encoding for data transformation (e.g., JSON, CSV, XML).

Fundamental Concepts in File Handling

1. **Working with the os Package**

   o The os package is the gateway to working with the operating system, allowing you to interact with the file system. It provides functionalities for creating, opening, closing, reading, and writing files.

   o Learn how to use os.Open, os.Create, os.Remove, and os.Rename for basic file operations.

   o Understand file permissions, error handling, and how to close files properly to avoid resource leaks.

2. **Buffered I/O with the bufio Package**

   o The bufio package allows developers to wrap file operations with a buffered reader or writer, which can improve performance by reducing the number of system calls.

   o Understand the importance of buffered reading and writing, especially when working with large files, and learn how to use bufio.NewReader and bufio.NewWriter.

3. **Reading Files**

- o Explore different ways to read files, including reading the entire file content, reading line by line, and reading data in chunks.

- o Compare methods such as ioutil.ReadFile, os.Read, and bufio.Scanner for different scenarios.

4. **Writing Files**

- o Learn how to write data to files using os and bufio. Cover writing strings, bytes, and formatted output.

- o Discuss various write modes, including appending data to existing files.

Data Processing Techniques

1. **Reading and Processing Structured Data**

- o Understanding how to handle structured data formats like CSV, JSON, and XML is vital for data processing tasks. Go provides built-in packages (encoding/csv, encoding/json, and encoding/xml) for easy parsing and generation of structured data.

- o Learn how to parse CSV files, handle data transformations, and write the processed data back to a file.

2. **Error Handling in File Operations**

- o Emphasize the importance of robust error handling. Explain how to use Go's error-checking patterns to handle common file I/O errors, such as file not found, permission denied, and read/write failures.

- o Discuss the use of defer to ensure that resources are properly released even when errors occur.

3. **Handling Large Files**

- o Processing large files can be challenging due to memory constraints. Go offers techniques like streaming, buffering, and concurrency to manage large datasets efficiently.

- o Explore how to read files in chunks or line by line to reduce memory usage, and how to write data concurrently to improve performance.

Advanced Topics in Data Processing

1. **Data Transformation with Streams**

- o Explain how to use Go's powerful I/O primitives to build streaming data processors. This technique is useful for real-time data processing and transforming large datasets without loading everything into memory.

- o Examples include reading a log file line by line and transforming each line before writing it to an output file.

2. **Concurrency in File Handling**

- Go's concurrency model, powered by Goroutines and Channels, can be leveraged to perform multiple file operations simultaneously. This is particularly useful for scenarios that involve processing multiple files or handling real-time data streams.

- Discuss best practices for handling concurrency issues like race conditions and deadlocks when working with files.

3. **Working with Data Encodings and Compression**

- Learn how to read and write files with different encodings (e.g., UTF-8, ASCII) and how to compress data using packages like compress/gzip.

- Demonstrate use cases where compression can significantly reduce storage requirements and improve data transmission speed.

4. **File Path Manipulations with path/filepath**

- The path/filepath package provides utilities to work with file paths in a platform-independent manner. Understand how to manipulate file paths, extract directory names, and traverse directories.

Real-World Applications and Use Cases

1. **Processing Log Files**

- Learn how to read and analyze log files to extract meaningful insights. Example scenarios include monitoring system performance, tracking user activities, and identifying errors.

- Demonstrate how to filter log files based on specific criteria and write the filtered output to new files.

2. **Building a CSV Data Processor**

- Step-by-step guide on how to build a CSV processor that reads data, applies transformations, and outputs the processed data. Common use cases include data cleaning, aggregation, and conversion.

3. **File Management in Web Applications**

- Web applications often need to handle file uploads and downloads. Discuss how Go can be used to implement efficient file handling mechanisms in web servers.

- Cover file validation, secure storage, and best practices for managing uploaded files.

The goal of this chapter is to provide you with the background you need to understand and implement advanced data processing techniques and efficient file operations in Go. This chapter delves into the fundamental responsibilities of reading from and writing to files, demonstrating Go's built-in support for a variety of file formats and data streams. Through a series of carefully constructed recipes, we will investigate several scenarios ranging from basic text file interactions to more complex activities such as working with JSON, XML, and CSV formats, addressing frequent and advanced use cases seen in real-world applications.

The voyage begins with an introduction to file opening, reading, and writing, which lays the groundwork for more advanced data handling activities. We will look at how to effectively process huge files, implement file scanning, and manage file permissions to ensure you understand the subtleties of Go's file system operations. The focus will next transition to serialization and deserialization techniques, which are essential for working with structured data types. You will learn how to marshal and unmarshal data in JSON and XML, allowing for easy data interchange between Go programs and external services. The chapter will also teach how to handle CSV files, which are commonly used in data-driven applications, as well as ways for parsing and producing CSV data using Go.

Beyond file manipulation, this chapter will delve into sophisticated data processing ideas, such as regular expressions for data validation and searching, as well as binary data handling approaches tailored to specialized demands such as image processing or bespoke serialization formats. Each recipe addresses a specific task while simultaneously reinforcing best practices for error management, performance optimization, and producing clean, maintainable code.

After finishing this chapter, you will be well-versed in Go's data processing and file handling capabilities, with the tools you need to solve a variety of problems. Whether dealing with basic text files or sophisticated structured data, the skills learned here will be invaluable in designing solid, efficient Go applications that can successfully manage and analyze data.

Reading and Writing Files

We will consider developing a Go application centered around a personal library management system. This system, dubbed "LibraGo," will help users manage their collection of books, including operations like adding new books, listing existing ones, and saving or retrieving book details from a file.

Situation

In the "LibraGo" application, we need a reliable way to persist information about books in the library. The application should allow users to save new entries to a file and retrieve them upon request. This functionality requires implementing efficient and robust file reading and writing operations in Go, ensuring data integrity and ease of access.

Practical Solution

To address this requirement, we will start by defining a simple structure to represent a book and then implement functions to write book details to a file and read them back.

Defining a Book Structure

```
package main

import (

"bufio"

"encoding/json"

"fmt"

"os"
```

```go
type Book struct {
Title string `json:"title"`
Author string `json:"author"`
Pages int `json:"pages"`
)
}
```

Writing Books to a File

To persist book details, we will serialize our Book objects into JSON format and write them to a file. This approach makes it easier to extend our data model and interact with other systems in the future.

```go
func SaveBooks(filename string, books []Book) error {
file, err := os.Create(filename)
if err != nil {
return err
defer file.Close()
writer := bufio.NewWriter(file)
for _, book := range books {
jsonData, err := json.Marshal(book)
if err != nil {
return err
_, err = writer.WriteString(string(jsonData) + "\n")
if err != nil {
return err
return writer.Flush()
}
}
}
}
}
```

Reading Books from a File

To retrieve the saved books, we will read the file line by line, deserializing each line from JSON back into a Book object.

```go
func LoadBooks(filename string) ([]Book, error) {

var books []Book

file, err := os.Open(filename)

if err != nil {

return nil, err

defer file.Close()

scanner := bufio.NewScanner(file)

for scanner.Scan() {

var book Book

if err := json.Unmarshal([]byte(scanner.Text()), &book); err != nil {

}

return nil, err

books = append(books, book)

return books, scanner.Err()

}

}

}
```

Main Function

Given below is how you might use these functions in the main part of your application:

```go
func main() {

books := []Book{

"The Go Programming Language", "Alan A. A. Donovan", 380},

"Go in Action", "William Kennedy", 300},

filename := "books.json"

// Save books to file

if err := SaveBooks(filename, books); err != nil {

fmt.Println("Error saving books:", err)

return
```

```go
// Load books from file
loadedBooks, err := LoadBooks(filename)
if err != nil {
fmt.Println("Error loading books:", err)
return
fmt.Println("Loaded Books:", loadedBooks)
{
{
}
}
}
}
```

This solution outlines the basic operations for reading and writing files in the "LibraGo" application, ensuring that users can easily manage their library data. The application's data persistence has been firmly established through the utilization of Go's inherent capabilities for JSON serialization and file operations.

JSON and XML Handling and Processing

Situation

The "LibraGo" app must be able to import and export book details in two different formats: JSON and XML. To support this functionality, the app needs to be able to handle these formats in a variety of ways, so users may easily communicate with other library management systems or data sources that use JSON or XML.

Practical Solution

Go provides robust support for both JSON and XML handling through the encoding/json and encoding/xml packages, respectively. We will leverage these to implement functions in "LibraGo" for parsing and generating data in these formats.

Enhancing the Book Structure for XML

First, we will add XML annotations to our Book struct, ensuring it can be properly serialized and deserialized from XML.

```go
type Book struct {
Title string `json:"title" xml:"title"`
Author string `json:"author" xml:"author"`
Pages int `json:"pages" xml:"pages"`
```

```
// For XML, we often work with a wrapper type to represent a collection of books.

type Library struct {

Books []Book `xml:"book"`

}
}
```

Exporting Books to JSON and XML

Next, we implement functions to serialize a slice of Book objects into JSON and XML. While the JSON functionality was covered in the previous recipe, following is how you might add XML serialization:

```
func ExportBooksToXML(books []Book) (string, error) {

library := Library{Books: books}

xmlData, err := xml.MarshalIndent(library, "", " ")

if err != nil {

return "", err

return string(xmlData), nil

}

}
```

Importing Books from JSON and XML

For importing, we will parse data from JSON and XML back into our Book or Library structs. The JSON importing was demonstrated earlier; below is an example for XML:

```
func ImportBooksFromXML(xmlData string) ([]Book, error) {

var library Library

err := xml.Unmarshal([]byte(xmlData), &library)

if err != nil {

return nil, err

return library.Books, nil

}

}
```

These functionalities allow "LibraGo" to interact with data in both JSON and XML formats, enhancing its versatility.

Given below is a brief illustration of using these new capabilities:

```go
func main() {

// Assuming books slice is already defined and populated

xmlOutput, err := ExportBooksToXML(books)

if err != nil {

fmt.Println("Error exporting books to XML:", err)

return

fmt.Println("XML Output:", xmlOutput)

// Simulate importing books from XML

importedBooks, err := ImportBooksFromXML(xmlOutput)

if err != nil {

fmt.Println("Error importing books from XML:", err)

return

fmt.Println("Imported Books:", importedBooks)

}

}

}
```

As a result of these developments, "LibraGo" can now manage book data within its own ecosystem and even facilitate external data sharing. To guarantee data interoperability and flexibility across many platforms and services, modern programs must be able to handle and interpret JSON and XML.

Utilizing Regular Expressions for Data Parsing

Situation

"LibraGo" users have access to a plain text file that lists books in a specific format, e.g., "Title: [Book Title], Author: [Author Name], Pages: [Number of Pages]". The challenge is to develop a function within "LibraGo" that can parse this text file, extract book details following this pattern, and convert them into Book struct instances for further processing and inclusion in the user's library.

Practical Solution

To tackle this challenge, we will leverage Go's regexp package, which provides robust support for regular expressions, allowing us to define a pattern that matches the book details in the text and extract the necessary information.

First, define a regular expression that captures the format of the book listings in the text file:

```go
import (
```

```go
    "bufio"

    "fmt"

    "os"

    "regexp"

)

var bookDetailsPattern = regexp.MustCompile(`Title: (.+), Author: (.+), Pages: (\d+)`)
```

Next, implement a function that reads the text file line by line, applies the regular expression to extract book details, and constructs Book instances from these details:

```go
func ParseBooksFromFile(filename string) ([]Book, error) {

file, err := os.Open(filename)

if err != nil {

return nil, err

defer file.Close()

var books []Book

scanner := bufio.NewScanner(file)

for scanner.Scan() {

matches := bookDetailsPattern.FindStringSubmatch(scanner.Text())

if matches != nil && len(matches) == 4 {

}

title := matches[1]

author := matches[2]

pages, err := strconv.Atoi(matches[3])

if err != nil {

// Log error and continue parsing the rest of the file

fmt.Printf("Invalid page number for book '%s': %s\n", title, err)

continue

books = append(books, Book{Title: title, Author: author, Pages: pages})

if err := scanner.Err(); err != nil {

return nil, err

return books, nil
```

```
    }

    }

    }

    }

}
```

This function uses bufio.Scanner to read the file line by line, applying the bookDetailsPattern regular expression to each line. The FindStringSubmatch method extracts the title, author, and page count from each matching line. These extracted values are then used to create Book instances, which are appended to a slice that is returned at the end.

To use this parsing function in "LibraGo," simply call it with the path to the text file containing the book listings:

```
func main() {

filename := "book_listings.txt"

books, err := ParseBooksFromFile(filename)

if err != nil {

fmt.Println("Error parsing books from file:", err)

return

for _, book := range books {

fmt.Printf("Parsed Book: %+v\n", book)

}
```

This recipe showcases the usefulness of regular expressions for Go developers, particularly when working with pattern matching or extracting data from unstructured text. Because of this method, "LibraGo" is now better able to import data from informal sources by effectively parsing book details.

Processing CSV and Text Data Efficiently

Situation

"LibraGo" must now incorporate a feature to import book collections from CSV files, where each row represents a book with fields for title, author, and page count. Similarly, the application should allow exporting the user's book collection to a CSV file.

Practical Solution

Go's encoding/csv package provides comprehensive support for reading and writing CSV data, making it straightforward to implement CSV processing in "LibraGo".

Following is how to create functions to import and export book collections using CSV format:

Importing Books from a CSV File

To read book details from a CSV file and convert them into a slice of Book structs, you can use the following approach:

```go
import (

"encoding/csv"

"os"

"strconv"

func ImportBooksFromCSV(filename string) ([]Book, error) {

file, err := os.Open(filename)

if err != nil {

return nil, err

defer file.Close()

reader := csv.NewReader(file)

records, err := reader.ReadAll()

if err != nil {

return nil, err

var books []Book

for _, record := range records {

pages, err := strconv.Atoi(record[2])

)

}

}

if err != nil {

// Handle error

continue

books = append(books, Book{

Title: record[0],

Author: record[1],

Pages: pages,

})
```

```
    return books, nil

    }

  }

}
```

Exporting Books to a CSV File

Conversely, to write a slice of Book structs to a CSV file, the following function outlines a practical method:

```
func ExportBooksToCSV(filename string, books []Book) error {

file, err := os.Create(filename)

if err != nil {

return err

defer file.Close()

writer := csv.NewWriter(file)

defer writer.Flush()

for _, book := range books {

record := []string{book.Title, book.Author, strconv.Itoa(book.Pages)}

if err := writer.Write(record); err != nil {

// Handle error

return err

}

}

}

return nil

}
```

These functionalities allow "LibraGo" to interact with CSV data, making it possible to import and export book collections efficiently. Given below is how you might integrate these functions into the main application flow:

```
func main() {

filename := "books.csv"

// Assume books is populated with Book structs
```

```go
if err := ExportBooksToCSV(filename, books); err != nil {

fmt.Printf("Failed to export books to CSV: %s\n", err)

importedBooks, err := ImportBooksFromCSV(filename)

if err != nil {

fmt.Printf("Failed to import books from CSV: %s\n", err)

 else {

fmt.Println("Imported Books:", importedBooks)

}

}

}

}
```

This functionality not only facilitates data exchange with external sources but also empowers users to maintain their libraries with familiar tools like spreadsheets.

Binary Data Handling and Advanced File I/O

Situation

"LibraGo" users want to associate cover images with their books, requiring the application to handle binary data efficiently. This feature involves reading binary files (images) from disk, associating them with the corresponding book entries, and providing functionality to update or retrieve these images. The challenge lies in performing these operations in a way that is both efficient and maintains the integrity of the binary data.

Practical Solution

Handling binary data in Go can be achieved through the os and io packages, which provide functions for advanced file operations. Given below is how to implement reading and writing binary files, using cover images as an example:

Reading a Binary File (Cover Image)

```go
import (

"io/ioutil"

"os"

func ReadCoverImage(filePath string) ([]byte, error) {

file, err := os.Open(filePath)

if err != nil {

return nil, err
```

```go
defer file.Close()

imageData, err := ioutil.ReadAll(file)

if err != nil {

return nil, err

return imageData, nil
```

To read a cover image from disk and store it as a byte slice, use the following approach:)

```go
}

}

}
```

Writing a Binary File (Cover Image)

To write a cover image back to disk, either after modification or to save a new image, you can use this method:

```go
return ioutil.WriteFile(filePath, data, 0644)

}
```

Integrating Cover Images with Book Entries

To associate cover images with books, you might extend the Book struct to include a field for the image data or a reference to the image file:

```go
type Book struct {

Title string

Author string

Pages int

CoverPath string // Path to cover image file

}
```

Then, you can modify the LibraGo application to handle cover images when adding or updating book entries, ensuring each book can be associated with its cover image.

Integrating image handling into the main application flow might look like this:

```go
func main() {

coverImagePath := "path/to/cover.jpg"

// Reading cover image

coverImage, err := ReadCoverImage(coverImagePath)
```

```go
if err != nil {

fmt.Printf("Failed to read cover image: %s\n", err)

return

// Assuming a book needs its cover image updated

if err := WriteCoverImage(coverImagePath, coverImage); err != nil {

fmt.Printf("Failed to write cover image: %s\n", err)

}

}

}
```

This capability allows users to maintain a more comprehensive and visually enriched library, making the application a more powerful tool for library management.

Using Go for Transforming Data

Situation

Now that "LibraGo" is complete, it needs features to change the library data for new uses. As an example, a user may wish to compile a report detailing their library's contents, including the overall number of volumes, the average number of pages per book, and a breakdown by author. Users should also be aware that data analysis tools may need them to export library data in a specific format. The difficulty lies in the ease and adaptability of implementing these data transformation procedures.

Practical Solution

Go's strong support for data manipulation, coupled with its standard library, makes it well-suited for these tasks. We can leverage Go's slice and map functionalities, along with sorting and custom comparison functions, to transform and aggregate library data.

Generating a Library Summary Report

To create a summary report, we might aggregate data to count books, calculate average pages, and organize books by author.

```go
import (

"fmt"

"sort"

func GenerateLibrarySummary(books []Book) {

fmt.Printf("Total Books: %d\n", len(books))

var totalPages int

booksByAuthor := make(map[string][]Book)
```

```go
for _, book := range books {
totalPages += book.Pages
booksByAuthor[book.Author] = append(booksByAuthor[book.Author], book)
avgPages := float64(totalPages) / float64(len(books))
fmt.Printf("Average Pages per Book: %.2f\n", avgPages)
for author, books := range booksByAuthor {
fmt.Printf("%s has %d books\n", author, len(books))
)
}
}
}
```

Exporting Data for Analysis

For exporting data in a format suitable for analysis, we might convert our library data into a simple CSV format that can be easily imported into data analysis tools.

```go
func ExportLibraryDataForAnalysis(filename string, books []Book) error {
file, err := os.Create(filename)
if err != nil {
return err
defer file.Close()
writer := csv.NewWriter(file)
defer writer.Flush()
// Write header
if err := writer.Write([]string{"Title", "Author", "Pages"}); err != nil {
return err
// Write book data
for _, book := range books {
if err := writer.Write([]string{book.Title, book.Author, strconv.Itoa(book.Pages)}); err != nil {
return err
return nil
}
```

```
}

}

}

}
```

Incorporating these functionalities into the main application allows users to not only manage but also analyze their library in versatile ways.

```
func main() {   // Assuming books is a slice of Book populated with the user's library data

GenerateLibrarySummary(books)

if err := ExportLibraryDataForAnalysis("library_analysis.csv", books); err != nil {

fmt.Printf("Failed to export library data for analysis: %s\n", err)
```

The addition of these data processing features transforms "LibraGo" into a platform for analysis and insights in addition to a tool for library administration. Aligning with the larger goal of making "LibraGo" a complete library solution, this upgrade allows users to extract valuable information from their collections.

File System Operations and Directory Management

Situation

Users of "LibraGo" are accumulating digital book files and cover images, leading to cluttered and disorganized directories. They need functionality within "LibraGo" to automatically organize these files into structured directories based on certain criteria, such as author names or genres. Additionally, the application should be capable of performing routine file system operations like creating new directories, moving files between directories, and cleaning up empty directories.

Practical Solution

Go's os and path/filepath packages provide comprehensive support for file system operations, making it straightforward to implement the required directory management and file organization features in "LibraGo".

Creating Directories Based on Authors

To organize book files by author, "LibraGo" can create a directory for each author and move their books into the respective directories.

```
import (

"os"

"path/filepath"

func OrganizeBooksByAuthor(libraryPath string, books []Book) error {

for _, book := range books {
```

```go
authorDir := filepath.Join(libraryPath, sanitizeFileName(book.Author))

if err := os.MkdirAll(authorDir, 0755); err != nil {

return err

originalPath := filepath.Join(libraryPath, book.FileName)

newPath := filepath.Join(authorDir, book.FileName)

if err := os.Rename(originalPath, newPath); err != nil {

return err

return nil)

}

}

}

}

func sanitizeFileName(name string) string {

// Implement filename sanitization to remove/replace invalid characters

// This is platform-dependent and left as an exercise

return name

}
```

Cleaning Up Empty Directories

After organizing files, there might be empty directories left behind. Given below is how to clean those up:

```go
func CleanupEmptyDirectories(rootDir string) error {

return filepath.Walk(rootDir, func(path string, info os.FileInfo, err error) error {

if err != nil {

return err

if info.IsDir() {

entries, err := os.ReadDir(path)

if err != nil {

return err

if len(entries) == 0 && path != rootDir {

if err := os.Remove(path); err != nil {
```

```
return err

return nil

})

}

}

}

}

}

}
```

Incorporating these directory management and file system operations into "LibraGo" helps users maintain a well-organized digital library.

```
func main() {

libraryPath := "/path/to/digital/library"

// Assuming books is populated with the user's digital book collection

if err := OrganizeBooksByAuthor(libraryPath, books); err != nil {

fmt.Printf("Failed to organize books by author: %s\n", err)

if err := CleanupEmptyDirectories(libraryPath); err != nil {

fmt.Printf("Failed to clean up empty directories: %s\n", err)

}

}

}
```

This function simplifies library administration, freeing up users to enjoy their collections rather than spend time administering them.

Creating and Managing Temporary Files and Directories

Situation

The "LibraGo" application requires functionality to create temporary files and directories for intermediate processing tasks. These temporary resources should be easily identifiable, accessible during their brief lifecycle, and reliably cleaned up afterward to avoid clutter and waste of storage space. The challenge is to manage these resources efficiently, ensuring they are created, used, and deleted without manual intervention.

Practical Solution

Go's io/ioutil and os packages offer convenient functions for managing temporary files and directories. Using these, "LibraGo" can implement robust mechanisms for temporary resource management.

Creating a Temporary File

Temporary files can be created for storing intermediate data, such as processed book details before finalizing an import operation.

```
import (

"io/ioutil"

"os"

func CreateTempFile(prefix string) (*os.File, error) {

tempFile, err := ioutil.TempFile("", prefix)

if err != nil {

return nil, err

// TempFile creates the file with os.O_RDWR|os.O_CREATE|os.O_EXCL mode

return tempFile, nil)

}

}
```

Creating a Temporary Directory

Similarly, temporary directories are useful for operations that require organizing multiple files or isolating processing tasks.

```
func CreateTempDir(prefix string) (string, error) {

tempDir, err := ioutil.TempDir("", prefix)

if err != nil {

return "", err

return tempDir, nil

}

}
```

Using and Cleaning Up Temporary Resources

After using temporary files or directories, "LibraGo" ensures they are removed to free up space. This cleanup process is crucial and should be handled gracefully, even in the face of errors during processing.

```go
func ProcessAndCleanupTempFile(tempFile *os.File) {
// Example processing on tempFile
// Cleanup
defer os.Remove(tempFile.Name())
func ProcessAndCleanupTempDir(tempDir string) {
// Example processing using tempDir
// Cleanup
defer os.RemoveAll(tempDir)
}
}
```

Integrating temporary file and directory management into "LibraGo" enhances its capability to handle intermediate processing tasks efficiently.

```go
func main() {
tempFile, err := CreateTempFile("librago")
if err != nil {
fmt.Printf("Failed to create a temporary file: %s\n", err)
return
ProcessAndCleanupTempFile(tempFile)
tempDir, err := CreateTempDir("librago")
if err != nil {
}
fmt.Printf("Failed to create a temporary directory: %s\n", err)
return
ProcessAndCleanupTempDir(tempDir)
}
}
```

"LibraGo" can handle intermediate data processing jobs quickly by using Go's support for managing temporary files and directories. That way, managing digital libraries will always be a breeze, and the app will stay clean and efficient.

Conclusion

In today's software ecosystem, file handling and data processing are at the heart of many applications, whether you're developing web servers, data analytics tools, or automation scripts. Understanding how to efficiently read, write, and manipulate files is crucial for creating scalable, reliable, and high-performance solutions. Go, with its simple yet powerful standard library, empowers developers to handle these tasks with ease, offering a straightforward approach to managing files and processing data.

The Core Advantages of Using Go for File Handling

1. **Simplicity and Readability**:

   o Go is known for its clean and readable syntax, which extends to how it handles file operations. Unlike some other languages that may require importing numerous external libraries, Go's core packages (os, io, bufio) provide a comprehensive set of tools for managing files. This simplicity reduces the learning curve and makes the code easier to maintain.

   o Beginners can quickly grasp the basics of file handling, while experienced developers can leverage the language's efficiency to implement more sophisticated data processing tasks.

2. **Performance**:

   o Go was designed with performance in mind. Its efficiency in managing resources ensures that file operations are executed swiftly, even when dealing with large datasets. The use of buffered I/O further enhances performance by minimizing system calls, thus reducing the time spent in reading or writing files.

   o Go's garbage collector and memory management system play a vital role in optimizing file handling processes, ensuring that resources are effectively utilized without causing memory leaks.

3. **Concurrency**:

   o One of Go's standout features is its built-in support for concurrency through Goroutines and Channels. When it comes to file processing, this capability is a game-changer. Tasks that would normally be time-consuming—like processing multiple large files—can be executed concurrently, leading to faster and more efficient operations.

   o The ability to spawn multiple Goroutines allows developers to read, write, or transform files simultaneously, making Go particularly suitable for applications that require real-time data processing, such as log monitoring or live data analysis.

4. **Platform Independence**:

   o Go's cross-platform capabilities make it an excellent choice for building applications that need to run on multiple operating systems. File path manipulations, directory traversals, and file permissions are all handled in a way that ensures compatibility across platforms.

- This versatility allows developers to write code that is portable and works seamlessly across Windows, macOS, and Linux environments without any modification, simplifying deployment and maintenance.

Key Lessons on File Handling in Go

1. **File Operations**:
   - Understanding the basics of file handling—such as creating, opening, reading, writing, and closing files—is foundational to working with data in Go. These simple yet essential operations are performed through the os package, which provides a straightforward interface to interact with the file system.
   - One critical lesson is the importance of proper error handling. Files can be inaccessible due to permissions, missing files, or other runtime issues, and ensuring that your program gracefully handles these errors can prevent it from crashing unexpectedly. Moreover, closing files using defer statements ensures that resources are properly released.

2. **Efficient Reading and Writing**:
   - Efficient file reading and writing techniques are central to high-performance applications. Developers need to understand when to use bufio for buffered reading/writing, how to read data line by line versus reading in chunks, and when to utilize direct I/O operations.
   - Each method comes with trade-offs. For instance, reading an entire file into memory can be quick but may not be feasible for very large files. On the other hand, buffered reading can handle larger datasets efficiently but may introduce a slight delay due to buffering. Choosing the right technique based on the use case is essential for optimal performance.

3. **Working with Structured Data**:
   - Many applications involve processing structured data formats like CSV, JSON, and XML. Go simplifies these tasks through its encoding packages, which allow for easy parsing and generation of structured data.
   - Developers must also consider data validation, transformation, and handling special cases like missing values or malformed records. Techniques like data streaming can help process large files without consuming excessive memory, ensuring that even datasets that span gigabytes can be processed efficiently.

4. **Concurrency and Parallel Processing**:
   - Go's concurrency model shines in scenarios where multiple files or data streams need to be processed simultaneously. By leveraging Goroutines, developers can build applications that process data concurrently, greatly speeding up tasks that would otherwise be slow and sequential.
   - However, concurrency introduces its own set of challenges. Managing data consistency, avoiding race conditions, and ensuring thread-safe operations are crucial

when building concurrent file handling programs. Understanding synchronization primitives like mutexes and using Channels for communication between Goroutines can help mitigate these issues.

Advanced Data Processing Capabilities

1. **Streaming and Real-Time Processing**:

   o Go's I/O model allows for streaming data processing, which is vital for real-time applications. Instead of loading entire files into memory, data can be read, processed, and written in streams, enabling continuous data processing without delays.

   o Real-world examples of streaming include monitoring system logs, handling live data feeds, or processing continuous user inputs. Developers must focus on implementing efficient pipelines that can handle data as it arrives, making real-time decisions or transformations without noticeable delays.

2. **File Compression and Data Encoding**:

   o Efficient data storage and transmission often require data compression and encoding. Go provides built-in packages like compress/gzip that make it easy to compress files, reducing storage requirements and speeding up file transfers.

   o Encoding data, whether into binary formats or structured text like JSON or XML, allows developers to store and transmit information in a standardized way. Understanding how to encode and decode data ensures that your applications can easily communicate with other services, consume APIs, or handle data in various formats.

3. **Automating Data Workflows**:

   o Automation is a significant aspect of data processing. Scripts or programs that can automatically read, process, and generate data files save time and reduce the possibility of human error. Go excels at automating workflows due to its simplicity and efficiency.

   o Common tasks include scheduled data backups, periodic data analysis, and automatic report generation. By leveraging Go's capabilities, developers can build systems that perform these tasks reliably and quickly, without requiring manual intervention.

Best Practices for File Handling and Data Processing

1. **Error Handling**:

   o Robust error handling is a best practice across all aspects of software development, but it is especially important in file handling. Files may not always be available, permissions may change, or data may be corrupted. By implementing proper error-checking mechanisms, developers can ensure that their programs handle these situations gracefully.

o   Using Go's error conventions, such as checking for err != nil and providing clear and informative error messages, ensures that problems can be quickly diagnosed and resolved.

2. **Managing Resources Efficiently**:

   o   Ensuring that file handles are closed properly is vital for preventing resource leaks, especially when working with multiple files concurrently. Go's defer statement is an elegant solution for this, ensuring that resources are released automatically when a function exits.

   o   When working with large datasets, developers must also be mindful of memory usage. Techniques like streaming, buffering, and reading in chunks can help manage memory effectively, preventing the program from consuming too much RAM.

3. **Security Considerations**:

   o   Security is another critical aspect, particularly when dealing with sensitive data. Developers should ensure that file permissions are correctly set, preventing unauthorized access. Encryption may also be necessary when handling confidential data, ensuring that even if a file is accessed, its contents remain secure.

   o   When building web applications, developers should validate all file uploads and downloads to prevent malicious files from being executed on the server or client.

Final Thoughts

File handling and data processing are foundational skills for any developer, and Go makes mastering these skills easier with its straightforward and efficient approach. From reading and writing files to handling structured data formats, Go's standard library provides a wealth of tools to manage data efficiently. Additionally, its powerful concurrency model allows developers to build scalable and responsive systems that can handle multiple tasks simultaneously, making Go an excellent choice for real-time and high-performance applications.

By understanding the core principles and best practices of file handling and data processing in Go, developers can create applications that are not only efficient but also robust and scalable. As data continues to grow in importance across industries, the ability to process it effectively will remain a critical asset, and Go stands out as a language that equips developers with the right tools to excel in this domain.

15. Go: Building REST APIs

Introduction

REST (Representational State Transfer) is a software architectural style that defines a set of constraints to be used for creating web services. In recent years, REST APIs have become the most common way of enabling communication between client applications and backend services. They are widely adopted due to their simplicity, scalability, and compatibility with various platforms. In the world of programming, building efficient and scalable REST APIs has become a core skill for developers, and Go (or Golang) has emerged as a popular choice for this task due to its performance, simplicity, and powerful concurrency features.

Go's Strengths for Building REST APIs

Go is an open-source programming language developed by Google, known for its speed, efficiency, and ease of use. It was designed to handle large-scale software engineering projects, and its concurrency model is one of the best for building applications that can manage multiple tasks simultaneously. These features make it an ideal choice for building REST APIs. Here are some reasons why Go is well-suited for building RESTful services:

1. **High Performance**: Go compiles directly to machine code, which eliminates the need for virtual machines or interpreters. This makes it very fast in comparison to languages like Python or JavaScript.

2. **Concurrency**: Go has a built-in concurrency model based on Goroutines and Channels, which makes it easy to write concurrent and parallel code. This is especially useful for handling multiple requests in a REST API without blocking.

3. **Ease of Deployment**: Go produces a single binary file for applications, which makes deployment easier. There is no need for additional dependencies to be installed on the server.

4. **Standard Library**: Go's standard library is robust and includes many packages that help in building web servers, handling HTTP requests, JSON parsing, and more. This reduces the need for third-party packages, making codebases simpler and more maintainable.

Fundamentals of REST Architecture

Before diving into building REST APIs, it's important to understand the key principles of REST architecture:

1. **Client-Server Architecture**: This principle states that the client (frontend application) and server (backend service) should be independent of each other. The client requests resources, and the server provides them. Both can evolve independently as long as the interface remains consistent.

2. **Stateless Communication**: Each request from the client to the server must contain all the information the server needs to process the request. The server does not store any session state information about the client, which helps in scaling the system.

3. **Cacheability**: Responses from the server should be explicitly marked as cacheable or non-cacheable to improve performance. Proper caching mechanisms can reduce server load and improve response times.

4. **Layered System**: A client should not be able to tell whether it is connected directly to the end server or an intermediary. This promotes scalability and flexibility.

5. **Uniform Interface**: REST defines a uniform interface between the client and the server, allowing independent evolution. This is typically achieved through the use of standard HTTP methods such as GET, POST, PUT, DELETE, etc.

6. **Resource-Based**: In REST, resources are identified by URIs (Uniform Resource Identifiers), and the API is designed around these resources rather than actions. For example, instead of having an endpoint like /createUser, a RESTful design would use POST /users to create a user.

Getting Started with REST API Development in Go

To build a REST API in Go, you need to understand the following core concepts:

1. **Routing**: Handling different endpoints and directing requests to appropriate handlers.

2. **HTTP Methods**: Understanding how to work with GET, POST, PUT, DELETE, and other HTTP methods.

3. **Request and Response Handling**: Parsing incoming requests and returning appropriate responses.

4. **JSON Handling**: Working with JSON data, which is the most common data format used in REST APIs.

5. **Middleware**: Adding functionality like logging, authentication, and error handling.

6. **Database Integration**: Connecting the API to a database to store and retrieve data.

7. **Testing**: Writing tests to ensure your API works as expected.

Setting Up the Development Environment

To start building REST APIs in Go, ensure that you have Go installed on your system. You can download the latest version from the official Go website. Once Go is installed, you can verify the installation by running:

go version

Create a new directory for your project and navigate to it:

```
mkdir go-rest-api

cd go-rest-api
```

Initialize a new Go module:

```
go mod init go-rest-api
```

Creating Your First REST API

1. **Defining Routes**: Define the routes for your API. For example, if you are creating a user management API, your routes might look like:

    - GET /users - Fetch all users

    - GET /users/{id} - Fetch a user by ID

    - POST /users - Create a new user

    - PUT /users/{id} - Update a user by ID

    - DELETE /users/{id} - Delete a user by ID

2. **Creating the Main File**: Create a main.go file, which will serve as the entry point for your application. The main function will set up the routes and start the server.

```go
package main

import (

    "fmt"

    "log"

    "net/http"

)

func main() {

    http.HandleFunc("/users", usersHandler)

    http.HandleFunc("/users/", userHandler)

    fmt.Println("Server is running on port 8080...")

    log.Fatal(http.ListenAndServe(":8080", nil))

}

func usersHandler(w http.ResponseWriter, r *http.Request) {

    // Logic to handle the request

}
```

```go
func userHandler(w http.ResponseWriter, r *http.Request) {

    // Logic to handle the request

}
```

3. **Building the User Model**: Define a User struct that will be used to represent user data. This struct will be used to marshal and unmarshal JSON data.

```go
type User struct {

    ID   int    `json:"id"`

    Name string `json:"name"`

    Email string `json:"email"`

}
```

4. **Handling Requests**: Implement the logic to handle different HTTP methods in the usersHandler and userHandler functions. For instance:

```go
func usersHandler(w http.ResponseWriter, r *http.Request) {

    switch r.Method {

    case http.MethodGet:

        // Code to fetch and return users

    case http.MethodPost:

        // Code to create a new user

    default:

        w.WriteHeader(http.StatusMethodNotAllowed)

    }

}
```

5. **Parsing JSON Requests**: Use Go's encoding/json package to parse JSON requests and send JSON responses.

```go
import "encoding/json"

func createUser(w http.ResponseWriter, r *http.Request) {

    var user User

    err := json.NewDecoder(r.Body).Decode(&user)

    if err != nil {
```

```go
        http.Error(w, err.Error(), http.StatusBadRequest)

        return

    }

    // Add user to the database or in-memory list

    w.WriteHeader(http.StatusCreated)

    json.NewEncoder(w).Encode(user)

}
```

Adding Middleware for Authentication and Logging

Middleware allows you to add functionalities such as logging and authentication across multiple routes. Here's how you can create a simple middleware:

```go
func loggingMiddleware(next http.Handler) http.Handler {

    return http.HandlerFunc(func(w http.ResponseWriter, r *http.Request) {

        log.Printf("%s %s %s", r.RemoteAddr, r.Method, r.URL)

        next.ServeHTTP(w, r)

    })

}
```

Connecting to a Database

To build a fully functional REST API, you often need to connect to a database to store and retrieve data. Popular databases for Go include PostgreSQL, MySQL, and MongoDB. Here's how to set up a PostgreSQL connection using the database/sql package:

1. **Install the PostgreSQL Driver**:

```go
go get github.com/lib/pq
```

2. **Establish Connection**:

```go
import (

    "database/sql"

    _ "github.com/lib/pq"

)

func connectDB() (*sql.DB, error) {

    connStr := "user=username dbname=mydb sslmode=disable"
```

```
    return sql.Open("postgres", connStr)

}
```

Error Handling and Testing

Handling errors gracefully and providing clear error messages is essential for a robust API. Always check for errors when performing database operations or parsing data. Additionally, write unit tests to ensure each part of your API behaves as expected. Use packages like testing and httptest to write tests.

Why learn to build REST APIs?

The software industry covers a great variety of projects ranging from desktop applications to games and websites. However, in many of the projects, all of them would eventually need a mechanism to persist data into some server or to pull said data from the servers. An example of some of the data that can be exchanged between an application on a user's computer (could be a desktop or a website that is being accessed) with a server can be user information or even assets such as photos and videos needed for further processing.

From the preceding description, you can probably guess and expect that there is a lot of work available for developers to create server applications that will be able to receive data from the client side. Some of these server applications are expected to be able to handle terabytes of data easily on a per-hour basis and also possibly ensure that they will be constantly available to users. These are relatively hard problems to solve, and various tools have to be developed in order to aid developers in doing this.

Although it was just mentioned that the whole exchange of data between client applications and server applications is pretty common and vital to know how our world works, we still need to realize that there is a need to decide on how this data is to be passed over to the client. Should it be passed via text? Or via binary? Is there a particular format that we need to follow to ensure that our data to be passed to the server application will be able to parse the message accordingly?

Regarding this formatting, we can probably refer to the following list of some of the more common protocols that handle exchanging data between client and server applications:

HTTP protocol: This is more of a text-based protocol and is considered one of the oldest and most mature technology as compared to the rest of the ones in the list. Essentially, many companies still operate on this, but they will follow particular *frameworks* of message/data exchange—namely, SOAP and REST. We will cover more regarding SOAP and REST in the later part of this chapter.

GRPC protocol: This is a binary protocol that kind of arose from Google. This protocol is partly built for reducing the amount of network resources required to transmit and receive data between applications. The GRPC protocol definitely helps, especially in cases where companies migrate to use microservices (essentially, many small server applications talking to each other) in order to improve development velocity, and using GRPC definitely help reduce the network load.

Thrift protocol: This is also another binary protocol that is one of the alternatives where the whole microservices paradigm came about. This protocol kind of came up slightly earlier before GRPC and was used in the same fashion/use case as GRPC.

Even among the HTTP protocol, there are various implementations and ways to decide how the data can be encapsulated within it. A long time back, there was a mechanism known as SOAP which is commonly used to pass data between servers and clients. SOAP somewhat works on top of HTTP (it uses the same basic constructs), and if you wish to pass larger data chunks, you will need to use XML, which will provide some way to structure data that is to be passed to the server.

As time went on, people somehow realized that XML is somewhat pretty *heavy*—it has a lot of metadata in order to provide the structure to the data and thereby requiring users of SOAP to utilize large amounts of their network bandwidth. Eventually, *form-data*—another text-based format came about. The form-data appears more like a key value sort of structure, but it has plenty of boundary lines to split sections of data that are to be passed around. Generally, the formatting of such data is already provided by various programming languages and libraries. It is somewhat good to realize the differences between the various techniques to know why a certain protocol is chosen as compared to the usual one that people generally use.

One of the more common ways for one-pass data right now is by having the data passed via JSON data and designing the endpoints that serve and receive data following some sort of framework/approach known as REST. REST represents Representative Stateful Transfer and is a somewhat common approach for developers on how to design the various endpoints for a server application. An application that follows and is said to be a RESTFUL API application would be easily understood by many developers and would save developers quite a bit of time by not requiring them to read the source code to understand what each of the endpoints would do. We will cover more with examples in the later part of this chapter.

Although it might be tempting to go for the *modern* approach of trying to build applications with GRPC and so on—it might actually be better to start from the more common approach of how applications are built now. Many applications that have already been built by following the RESTful approached all of these applications still require maintainers to continue maintaining their purpose and add value to the company and society. Another reason for understanding the common approach first is that companies generally do not move too quickly to change— most mature companies tend to stick to old reliable technologies and, essentially, building RESTful API applications that communicate with each other via JSON (and in the rare case *Formdata*). Another last benefit that comes with learning a common RESTful approach is that there is already varied tooling to help developers debug all the issues that come with developing with such protocols. A demonstration of the tooling to do so will be done in the later part of the chapter.

HTTP verbs

HTTP verbs are definitely one of the vital things to know and understand before proceeding onward to build a server application in Golang. We are going to approach the HTTP verbs and understand their usage while following the RESTful approach of building Web applications.

GET: This is the most common verb and is probably the one that is used most often without realizing it. When you access a website on the browser, it is actually doing a GET request to some sort of server. The GET verb is as it says it does; it fetches a resource from the server. This resource can be anything; html page, photo; video, and so on.

POST: This is also another common verb, but it is not as obvious as the GET verb. The POST usually involves creating a resource on the server. An example of this could be a situation where a user is trying to sign up on a website. When you click on the sign-up button after filling up the username and password that is to be used on the website, the POST request is sent and is expected to be saved in the database. A user resource is expected to be created at the end of the POST request.

DELETE: This is not as common as the GET and POST, but its purpose is generally quite clear. A DELETE call would essentially request the server to delete the resource being indicated in the endpoint's URL or payload data.

PUT: This is an HTTP verb that pertains to update a resource on the server. Naturally, data on the server would eventually require change, and this requires the client application to pass the data that would replace the information of the particular resource on the server.

PATCH: This is also another HTTP verb that pertains to update resources on the server. The PATCH verb is meant for updating parts of the data of the resource, but in the case of the PUT verb—the PUT verb requires the user client application to pass the entire dataset to *replace* what was on the server of that particular resource.

You can technically view all of the preceding in the section by using the curl command or wget command in Linux or Mac command line applications. Window users might require additional efforts to find a good command-line application to use that capability however, there is no guarantee that links will work forever; you might probably need to check out other alternatives if the git bash tool is no longer available for use.

With a command line application installed, you might have the curl utility, and we can immediately start using it by running the following:

curl www.google.com

You will receive a bunch of gibberish encapsulated in <html> tags. This gibberish is the *raw* HTML data that, potentially, your browser would receive when you access the Google search home page. Note that it might be futile to try to read and understand this—nowadays, companies embed an entire JavaScript framework in the HTML page, and they can manipulate the HTML template in the craziest ways.

We will cover more about its usage while building the applications. They will serve to demonstrate the common ways on how to test a Web application works as expected. The same tool can be used even if we build Web applications in other languages like Python and Java—they should theoretically respond in the same way.

HTTP status codes

Every HTTP call to the server will result in the server responding with some sort of status code to indicate if the response is a successful one or not. There are multitudes of status codes that are set by the HTTP protocol standard, and each of these status codes corresponds to different meanings—with the ideal case being that the server and client applications would respond to the status code accordingly—for example, if the status code informs the client that it is making too many requests to the server, it would be ideal that the client reduces the rate of calls to the server.

It is definitely impossible to go through the entire list of status codes available in the HTTP protocol, but we will definitely be going through the more common status codes that one would go through while developing their applications.

One term that would probably come up over and over again is the term localhost. The term localhost is the hostname that refers to the computer itself that is hosting the server application. Let us say if we are running the Web application server on our own computer, and we can reach to an URL on that Web application server via the localhost address. Behind the scenes, the localhost hostname would be resolved on the computer into 127.0.0.1, which would invoke certain machinations to ensure that the traffic would loopback to itself without requiring a hop to the external network.

In order to make the following subsection much clear, a server does not necessarily mean an application that has to be in some sort of datacenter. Server, in this case, just refers to any application that receives HTTP requests from a caller—which, in this case, is called the *client* application. Essentially, both the client and server applications can be put on the same computer—the client just makes a call to localhost, which just refers to the computer's self.

Status code: 200: Status OK. This essentially means the request made from *client* to the *server* was completely successfully, and no errors occurred within that request. Essentially, this pertains quite a bit, especially with regard to requests done with the GET HTTP verb.

Status code: 201: Status Created. This status code should be sent when a new resource is created on the server. For example, when a new user decides to create a new account on a website, the user resource is being created in the database. However, it is not absolutely necessary that the server return status code 201—it could easily return status code 200 at this stage as well, and the request would appear valid as well (unless the client application to the server checks for the status code that the server returns).

Status code: 204: Status No Content. It informs the client it should not expect any additional content alongside the request—no JSON data/formdata should be expected in this request, and we can simply just ignore it (if data is passed along here, it is recommended to have the server changed to serve up the request with status code 200—status ok instead).

Status code: 301/308: Permanent Redirect. This impacts a browser's behavior. If the browser requests a request from a server application and a permanent redirect is done, it will signify to the browser to cache this behavior— essentially, if the browser was asked to access that same request that is meant to be redirected, it would not bother attempting; it will immediately request the new redirected endpoint.

Status code: 302/307: Temporary Redirect. It does almost the same thing as a permanent redirect by redirecting users that are accessing that endpoint to another URL that is returned alongside the request with this status code. There are slight differences between temporary redirects and permanent redirects with regards to Search Engine Optimization—this mechanism will not be used too much while building an application (maybe except while one is building a user login system?)

Status code: 400: Bad Request. This status code should be used when the client application or user of the server application sends a request that contains invalid data (for example, excluding certain fields/parameters in the request when it is supposed to be there).

Status code: 401: Unauthorized. This status code signifies that the request needs to be logged via some sort of login functionality. Generally, such requests require users to access another URL path or endpoint, such as / login. This would return a response that would contain a secret string or token that can be used in all subsequent requests for all paths that require authentication to access it.

Status code: 403: Forbidden. This is somewhat similar to status code 401, but it is more for resources that a client wishes to access but said client would not have any access to the resource even if he attempts to authenticate himself. These could be special resources that are actually hidden away from user access (for example, they can only be accessed from a specific IP address, and so on).

Status code: 404: Not found. This status code should be somewhat familiar (even to people outside the tech industry since it somehow ended up becoming memes on various social media platforms). Essentially, this status code indicates that the URL path that the client is attempting to access does

not exist, so that is no point in attempting to access it

Status code: 405: Method not allowed. This status code helps to signify to the client that the wrong http verb is being used to make the request. If the client had attempted to do a GET on a request— and if this status code is returned, it could be possible that maybe, that request should be done via the POST or any other http verb.

Status code: 418: I'm a teapot. This is not exactly useful but more of a little tidbit while learning about status codes. This status code was probably kind of introduced as an April Fool's joke, but somehow, it ended up being implemented in actual servers and is now part of the standard. Technically, one should not see this, but if you do see it, it would probably mean that the developer of the server application did not do proper checks to ensure that garbage URL paths exist within the application.

Status code: 429: Too many requests. This status code essentially informs the client that it is requesting for a specific request from a client way too often, and it has breached the quota allocated for it, and the server has decided to throttle the number of requests that it would receive from said client. Once you see this error—just give up and slow down the number of requests that is to be received.

Status code: 500: Internal Server Error. This is what the status code mentions; there is a logic error that resulted in bad logic within the Web server application. If you are handling the client side and trying to access a server's endpoint that has this, it would best to just contact the developers behind it to fix the issue with it.

Even with all these status codes defined by the standard, it is highly unlikely you would use all the status codes that are defined previously—they just happen to be one of the more common ones that exist, and you would see—even if you try engaging with API services provided by the various enterprises out there. We would probably see how things can play out when we actually start building Web server applications for real.

Building a "Hello World" REST API Golang application

Before building the URL shortener application that was mentioned at the beginning of the chapter, we will first build some sort of starter project to be familiar with the mechanizations of the code that is involved in a Golang Web application.

In Golang, we have the fortune to have pretty decent standard libraries, and they essentially allow us to write somewhat pretty reliable servers without relying on third-party libraries. Eventually, we would definitely need to add third-party libraries to handle the various concerns that relate to ensure that an application can be run reliably in production with proper monitoring in place to ensure that we, as developers, would know if the application has any issues.

If we are to just use the approaches provided by the Golang standard library, we would generally have two approaches to define an endpoint. The following is an example of how we can define a URL path (in this, the root path—/) and provide the function on how to handle it within the handler function. The handler function needs to have two inputs in the function, which is the http.ResponseWriter, as well as the http.Request. That provides us the capability to write out our response to the writer while we can check the contents that we received via the request via the http.Request input. The following would be the *function* approach of writing the http handlers:

```go
package main

import ("fmt"

  "log"    "net/http")

func handler (w http.ResponseWriter, r *http.Request) {    log.Print("Hello world received a request.")    defer log.Print("End hello world request")    fmt.Fprintf(w, "Hello World") }

func main() {    log.Print("Hello world sample started.")    http.HandleFunc("/", handler)
http.ListenAndServe(":8080", nil)

}
```

Within the handler function, we have three lines of code. The first line within it is simply a function to print out some statement to somewhat indicate that we have received a request to the Web server application. The right after that is to print another log once the function handler ends. This is done via defer keyword. Golang code that is put behind defer is always run (even if a panic happens mid-function— since the function needs to end before the program kind of crashes). The third line essentially uses the Fprintf that takes in a writer object and a string that we need the writer needs to write as its output which, in this case, will be returned to the user. In the case of the preceding server, it should return the string Hello World if we are to test the code externally once we have the server running.

Another portion of code that would be of importance to understand would be the last line in the main function—the http.ListenAndServe function. The first argument is the address that the server will listen to. In the preceding example, we simply provided the values :8080, but essentially, that would kind of mean 0.0.0.0:8080, which in networking terms—we are telling that the server should be able to accept any traffic that is on port 8080 on the system. Ideally, this would be the most convenient scenario, but there are cases where we would want to limit where the incoming traffic would come from. If we are to use the values: 127.0.0.1:8080 in the ListenAndServe function—that would mean that the incoming traffic can only come from the server that is hosting it.

How should we test this server that we just built? We can take the preceding code, dump it into a file on a system that has the Golang runtime, and run the following command: go run app.go

That would start the Web application server, and we can start to test and interact with it. We can use the curl utility to do so: curl localhost:8080

With that, the server should simply just return the words Hello World. After receiving the response, we can probably check the output of the server logs to see if the logs within the handler are actually printed out into the terminal:

2022/07/23 12:13:01 Hello world sample started.

2022/07/23 12:13:09 Hello world received a request.

2022/07/23 12:13:09 End hello world request

For simple applications, going with the function approach is generally quite decent— it is definitely way simpler as compared to its alternative, which we demonstrate in the code in the section right after this.

```go
package main

import ("fmt"

    "log" "net/http")

type HandleViaStruct struct{}

func (*HandleViaStruct) ServeHTTP(w http.ResponseWriter, r *http.Request)

{    log.Print("Hello world received a request.")    defer log.Print("End hello world request")
fmt.Fprintf(w, "Hello World via Struct") }

func main() {    log.Print("Hello world sample started.")    http.Handle("/", &HandleViaStruct{})
http.ListenAndServe(":8080", nil)

}
```

Notice that instead of simply defining a simple function that is expected to handle the URL path—we need to define an entire struct that would be expected to handle the path. The initialized struct would contain the various aspects and resources needed to handle the URL request specifically. An important thing to note with regard to going with this approach instead would require us to look at the http. Handle function call.

The http.Handle function call accepts the following parameters: the first is a string which is just the URL path that we would be handling with the application. The second parameter is actually an http.Handler interface:

```
type Handler interface {    ServeHTTP(ResponseWriter, *Request)

}
```

So, we can basically pass in any struct as long as it has the ServeHTTP function that has the required parameters as well. If we see the preceding code example, the struct HandleViaStruct fulfills the requirements, and hence, the code would be able to compile and run successfully without too many issues.

In general, for most server applications that would be built out there—most would be written with the struct approach. One of the main reasons would be thinking of how to pass vital components that are required to process the URL path, such as database connections or queue system connections, or cache system connections. We can keep it global, but that introduces various sets of issues where it makes it hard to unit testing on a specific struct.

An example of how this would look like for the definition of the struct could be something like this:

```
type DB interface {    GetAllArtifacts() ([]string, error) }

type Queue interface {    SubmitJob() error }

type Cache interface {    Store(item string) error

}

type HandleViaStruct struct {    queue Queue    db    DB    cache Cache

}
```

We can define a bunch of interfaces which we can then dump it into our HandleViaStruct struct. We would then require to initialize the various other structs that would implement said functionalities defined by the various interface before we are able to finally run the struct. We will probably go into more details as we go into a proper example in the next part of this chapter as well as cover on how coding the struct in this way would allow us to write unit tests more easily.

Building a URL shortener

Before actually starting to write the code for writing this small application, we would first need to define a set of requirements that we would want to stick to so that we can understand the end goal of what we are trying to build out here and not overcomplicate the application too much.

Here is the list of requirements that one can think of when building a URL parameter:

When a user passes a long URL, the server application will create a short hash that will be used to reference the long URL being passed to the user.

The short hash and the long URL would need to be stored in some form of database, but to keep things simple in this case, we can temporarily store the values into some sort of hashmap in the application (although we can potentially extend it to save the data into a JSON file).

When the user attempts to access a shortened URL that exists, it will do a temporary redirect to the long URL.

If a user attempts to access a shortened URL that does not exist, it should return a 404 error as the URL path does not exist, and the client should realize that (which, in this case, it should be the browser).

There are essentially two URLs paths that we might want to code out: o /add: The server application should accept the URL to be shortened. If successfully created, it should return status code 201 as well as the shortened URL that is generated by the application.

/r/<shortened-url: All other URLs, which would be done via the GET HTTP verb. If the shortened URL does not exist—we would need to return an error 404 instead.

For the same /r/<shortened-url, when we issue a DELETE request for it, it should remove it from the server application's storage.

There are many things that we will not be considering though while building this server application:

There would be no user-related system as this would make this way too complex. A user system is actually a complex thing to add (albeit it is a standard functionality in many applications out there). A login system would consist of the following items—which is why we will not include them in this sample application:

Sign up o Login o Logout

Delete user (especially with legal rules nowadays that require companies to forget users if they request the application/company to do so)

Forget password

User activation (usually added to ensure the emails provided during sign up is legit)

No quotas or throttling systems added—URL shortener services are usually open for abuse (due to how people can game it for malicious use, and so on). However, adding throttling is not too trivial; the right libraries will be added, and the right configuration will need to be added for it.

We would not be collecting any analytics metrics of redirects happening for particular shortened URLs.

The list of things that we are currently ignoring here is numerous, but with that in mind, we can build a more minimalistic server application that would showcase on how one can build such server applications without too much hassle.

Let us start from the beginning and start with building out the URL path that will accept the POST request. Notice that with regard the URL handling, we need to write up some code in order to ensure that it will handle the variable part of the URL—the path could be any value, and the application should be able to route the request correctly—Golang's HTTP server provided by the standard library does not come with such functionality out of the box.

In this regard, it is wise to just use some of the third-party libraries out there that provide such functionalities. It is definitely not necessary to use a full server framework since the functionality that is required for this application is still pretty small.

One of the more popular Golang libraries that deal with such URL routing would be the gorilla/mux library. This library is considered one of the more mature libraries out there, and its feature set is pretty much set in stone. There is little active development for this library, thereby making this library pretty stable and could be one that would be worth using. Refer to the library's GitHub page here: https:// github.com/gorilla/mux.

In order to use this library, we need to dive into using such third-party libraries. Third-party libraries are just pulled from the source repositories and generally work out of the box without requiring one to install any custom tool to handle dependency management for the application. The first part before starting the application would be to initialize the name of the Golang module in which the application will be build. Run the following in the folder where you have the project. go mod init github.com/test/application

After running this step, the go.mod file would be created, which would contain the name of the Golang project of sorts and would serve as the root for the project.

The next step would be to import the Gorilla/mux library. This can be done by running the following: go get github.com/gorilla/mux

Right after running this command, we will immediately have another additional file, which is the go.sum file. The go.sum file will list all the dependencies that the application would require right down the commit hash of the code—so we know the very exact version that is being relied on by the application. The reason for using hashes here is that tags cannot be fully relied upon in the source code repository world—we cannot reliably ensure that a v1.0.0 of software being downloaded today is the same as the v1.0.0 of the library that is being downloaded next week since application version tags can change at any point of time.

With that, we can start using the library with the application. Now, we can create our application (possibly in main.go file) and use the same example code using the struct example and create a minimalistic server that uses the gorilla mux library.

```
package main

import (    "fmt"
```

```go
    "log"

    "net/http"

    "github.com/gorilla/mux" )

type HandleViaStruct struct{}

func (*HandleViaStruct) ServeHTTP(w http.ResponseWriter, r *http.Request)

{    log.Print("Hello world received a request.")    defer log.Print("End hello world request")
fmt.Fprintf(w, "Hello World via Struct") }

func main() {    log.Print("Hello world sample started.")    r := mux.NewRouter()

    r.Handle("/", &HandleViaStruct{}).Methods("GET")    http.ListenAndServe(":8080", r)

}
```

There is a slight change where we will first need to create some sort of router (provided by the gorilla mux library) that does the URL routing properly for the application and then pass that router to the ListenAndServe function (the second parameter apparently takes in some sort of router object).

The previous code is already a slight improvement compared to the initial version of the code that only used the Golang standard library. In the first initial case, a POST request would still produce a response from the server, but if we attempted to do so with this version of the application, which uses the Gorilla mux library: curl -v -XPOST localhost:8080

The -v flag for the curl command signifies that we would have a verbose output (this means that we want to have all the logs of every step of what is happening while the request is happening). The verbose output mode prints out information that might sometimes be too excessive for normal usage and is usually only used for debugging purposes. While the -X POST flag signifies the curl command to make a POST request instead of the usual GET request. It is important to remember here that in most cases, GET requests are the usual way of how requests are requested from the server. If we attempted, we would get something like the following:

Trying ::1:8080...* Connected to localhost (::1) port 8080 (#0)

> POST / HTTP/1.1

> Host: localhost:8080

> User-Agent: curl/7.77.0

> Accept: */*

>

Mark bundle as not supporting multiuse

< HTTP/1.1 405 Method Not Allowed < Date: Sun, 24 Jul 2022 21:15:20 GMT < Content-Length: 0

<

Connection #0 to host localhost left intact

Notice the fact that we got a 405 error here—which signifies that the wrong http method was used in this request. We need to change it to a GET request in order to have something properly working.

Also, just a sidenote for those who are confused by the -X flag.

curl -v -X GET localhost:8080/

curl -v localhost:8080/

Both of the previous commands are the same—the -X flag has GET as the default value.

With that out of the way, we can proceed to try to make the /add path first. The /add path would require us to write up some sort of functionality that would generate some sort of hash. And it would be great if we can persist it into some sort of location (for the initial case, we can probably save it in memory).

Let us go with the scenario of us knowing that we might change the storage engine of where we are storing the information for the mapping of the shortened URL hashes to the actual URLs that are to be redirected. This is where past knowledge from previous chapters might be useful—for anything that might potentially change in the future, and we might want to get an interface there. This will allow us to replace the implementation anytime if needed; we will demonstrate this at play for this simple application for some actual experience.

For storing the mapping of the shortened URLs to the actual long URLs which the shortened URLs would redirect to, the following interface would prove sufficient:

```
type Store interface {    Add(shortenedURL, longURL string) error

    Remove(shortenedURL string) error    Get(shortendURL string) (string, error)

}
```

We will only need three functions for this interface to store the mapping, remove the mapping as well as to get the mapping. The next step will be to implement something that can provide the functionality that we want in our application. In our initial version, we will build one that is backed by an in-memory map (which is essentially one of the simpler ways to store such data):

```
type MemoryStore struct {    items map[string]string }

func (m *MemoryStore) Add(shortendURL, longURL string) error {    if m.items[shortendURL] != "" {

    return fmt.Errorf("value already exists here")    }

  m.items[shortendURL] = longURL    log.Println(m.items)    return nil }
```

```go
func (m *MemoryStore) Remove(shortenedURL string) error {    if m.items[shortenedURL] == "" {
return fmt.Errorf("value does not exist here")    }    delete(m.items, shortenedURL)    return nil }
```

```go
func (m *MemoryStore) Get(shortendURL string) (string, error) {    longURL, ok :=
m.items[shortendURL]    if !ok {        return "", fmt.Errorf("no mapped url available here")    }
return longURL, nil }
```

The implementation is in MemoryStore, and within it, we would need to implement the three functions that were defined by the interface, namely, add, remove, and get. We would also need to initialize the struct, which can be done by simply initializing the struct within our main function, but in many cases, we want to simplify the initialization process. Generally, we would do so by creating a NewXXX function, so, in the case of our MemoryStore, we would create a function called NewMemoryStore.

```go
func NewMemoryStore() MemoryStore {

    return MemoryStore{items: make(map[string]string)}

}
```

With this, we now have a storage implementation that we can finally use. The next step would be to implement the handlers for our various URL paths. The first would be to implement the handler for adding a mapping and storing it within the application.

```go
type AddPath struct {    domain string    store Store }
```

```go
func (a *AddPath) ServeHTTP(w http.ResponseWriter, r *http.Request) {    type addPathRequest
struct {        URL string `json:"url"`    }
```

```go
    var parsed addPathRequest    err := json.NewDecoder(r.Body).Decode(&parsed)    if err != nil {

        w.WriteHeader(http.StatusInternalServerError)

        w.Write([]byte(fmt.Sprintf("unexpected error :: %v", err)))        return    }

    h := sha1.New()

    h.Write([]byte(parsed.URL))    sum := h.Sum(nil)    hash := hex.EncodeToString(sum)[:10]    err
= a.store.Add(hash, parsed.URL)    if err != nil {

        w.WriteHeader(http.StatusInternalServerError)

        w.Write([]byte(fmt.Sprintf("unexpected error :: %v", err)))        return    }

    type addPathResponse struct {        ShortenedURL string `json:"shortened_url"`        LongURL
string `json:"long_url"`    }

    pathResp := addPathResponse{ShortenedURL: fmt.Sprintf("%v/%v",

a.domain, hash), LongURL: parsed.URL}

    w.Header().Set("Content-Type", "application/json")
```

```
w.WriteHeader(http.StatusCreated)    json.NewEncoder(w).Encode(pathResp)

}
```

There are a few critical parts to discuss; we code our handler for adding a mapping of a shortened URL to a long URL.

Within the AddPath struct, it requires two values to define the struct properly, which is the domain—essentially, the URL path to which we would append our shortened URL hash to—however, this is a matter of convenience. It is probably possible to try to figure out the domain where the server is being hosted from, but this provides the developer some sort of customization— essentially, we can define a new custom domain for this server application just for the rerouting portion. The second property of the struct is the store interface, which we can simply use the MemoryStruct once we initialize it.

We are doing the request via a POST request. Within the POST request, we will be passing the information needed for the server to store the mapping into the http body of the request. As a matter of convenience, we will be relying

on plain old JSON to format the http body—this makes it easy for the server to parse the incoming information.

The next portion will be to define and calculate the hash for the URL being provided to the application. For this case, we are using the sha1 hashing algorithm and just taking the first 10 characters to provide the shortened hash for the redirecting shortened URL.

Within the ServeHTTP request, we will define the structs that are being used to define the expected structures of the incoming JSON within the http body. Generally, structs are not exactly defined within functions, but seeing that we are unlikely to reuse the struct outside of this function, it does make sense to do this. This also applies to the defining of the struct for crafting the response that is to be returned to the client after storing the mapping.

Once we have this, we can initialize the MemoryStore within the main function: mem := NewMemoryStore()

We can then use the initialized memory store to add to our AddPath handler redirectPath := http://localhost:8080/r ...

r.Handle("/add", &AddPath{domain: redirectPath, store: &mem}). Methods("POST")

Adding this code snippet would provide us the capability to store the mapping of shortened URLs to long URLs. Let us now repeat this for deleting mappings of shortened URLs to long URLs as well as the actual main handler that would be the main highlight of this application—which is the redirecting capability once presented a shortened URL. Also, note that we are using a variable for redirectPath rather than defining it in the AddPath struct directly—this is in the hopes of making it slightly easier to identify possible configuration options to change in the application for the application maintainers.

For deleting a URL mapping:

```go
type DeletePath struct {    store Store

}

func (p *DeletePath) ServeHTTP(w http.ResponseWriter, r *http.Request) {    hash :=
mux.Vars(r)["hash"]

    if hash == "" {

        w.WriteHeader(http.StatusBadRequest)

        w.Write([]byte("empty hash"))        return    }

    err := p.store.Remove(hash)    if err != nil {

        w.WriteHeader(http.StatusInternalServerError)

        w.Write([]byte(fmt.Sprintf("unexpected error :: %v", err)))        return    }

    w.WriteHeader(http.StatusOK)

    w.Write([]byte("deleted")) }
```

An interesting piece of code to look at for the DeletePath handler is the line mux. Vars. This function is a piece of code functionality provided by Gorilla mux golang library, and it allows us to have path params in URL; we can retrieve values within URLs, and this can be used to retrieve values from some sort of database, and so on. According to the Gorilla mux library page, the Vars function returns route variables for the current request.

In the case of our preceding example application, we would want to retrieve the hash and use it to compute and retrieve our long URL from our store. So, when we define the URL and the handler and how it is to be handled, it would be defined in the following way:

```go
r.Handle("/r/{hash}", &DeletePath{store: &mem}).Methods("DELETE")
```

Notice the hash variable in the URL path that is expected to be handled by the handler. An important thing to note is that this feature is most likely a unique function for the Gorilla Mux golang library. Other libraries would have other approaches with handling variables within the URL, which need to be processed.

For doing redirects—not the final portion of the ServeHTTP in this case, where it is http.Redirect function call is made in order to do redirects.

```go
type RedirectPath struct {    store Store }

func (p *RedirectPath) ServeHTTP(w http.ResponseWriter, r *http.Request)

{    hash := mux.Vars(r)["hash"]

    if hash == "" {

        w.WriteHeader(http.StatusBadRequest)
```

```go
        w.Write([]byte("empty hash"))        return    }

    longURL, err := p.store.Get(hash)     if err != nil {

        w.WriteHeader(http.StatusNotFound)

        w.Write([]byte("not found"))        return    }

    http.Redirect(w, r, longURL, http.StatusTemporaryRedirect)

}
```

With that, we have defined the handlers and stores for our application. If we put it all together, we would come up with the following application:

```go
package main

import (    "crypto/sha1"

    "encoding/hex"

    "encoding/json"

    "fmt"

    "log"

    "net/http"

    "github.com/gorilla/mux" )

func NewMemoryStore() MemoryStore {    return MemoryStore{items: make(map[string]string)} }

type MemoryStore struct {    items map[string]string }

func (m *MemoryStore) Add(shortendURL, longURL string) error {    if m.items[shortendURL] !=
"" {        return fmt.Errorf("value already exists here")     }

    m.items[shortendURL] = longURL

    log.Println(m.items)    return nil }

func (m *MemoryStore) Remove(shortenedURL string) error {    if m.items[shortenedURL] == "" {
return fmt.Errorf("value does not exist here")    }    delete(m.items, shortenedURL)    return nil }

func (m *MemoryStore) Get(shortendURL string) (string, error) {    longURL, ok :=
m.items[shortendURL]    if !ok {        return "", fmt.Errorf("no mapped url available here")    }
return longURL, nil }

type Store interface {    Add(shortenedURL, longURL string) error

    Remove(shortenedURL string) error    Get(shortendURL string) (string, error) }

type AddPath struct {    domain string    store  Store }
```

```go
func (a *AddPath) ServeHTTP(w http.ResponseWriter, r *http.Request) {    type addPathRequest
struct {         URL string `json:"url"`    }

    var parsed addPathRequest     err := json.NewDecoder(r.Body).Decode(&parsed)     if err != nil {
        w.WriteHeader(http.StatusInternalServerError)
        w.Write([]byte(fmt.Sprintf("unexpected error :: %v", err)))         return    }
    h := sha1.New()
    h.Write([]byte(parsed.URL))    sum := h.Sum(nil)    hash := hex.EncodeToString(sum)[:10]
    err = a.store.Add(hash, parsed.URL)    if err != nil {
        w.WriteHeader(http.StatusInternalServerError)
        w.Write([]byte(fmt.Sprintf("unexpected error :: %v", err)))         return
    }
    type addPathResponse struct {         ShortenedURL string `json:"shortened_url"`         LongURL
string `json:"long_url"`
    }
    pathResp := addPathResponse{ShortenedURL: fmt.Sprintf("%v/%v",
a.domain, hash), LongURL: parsed.URL}
    w.Header().Set("Content-Type", "application/json")
    w.WriteHeader(http.StatusCreated)    json.NewEncoder(w).Encode(pathResp) }
type DeletePath struct {    store Store }
func (p *DeletePath) ServeHTTP(w http.ResponseWriter, r *http.Request) {    hash :=
mux.Vars(r)["hash"]
    if hash == "" {
        w.WriteHeader(http.StatusBadRequest)
        w.Write([]byte("empty hash"))         return    }
    err := p.store.Remove(hash)    if err != nil {
        w.WriteHeader(http.StatusInternalServerError)
        w.Write([]byte(fmt.Sprintf("unexpected error :: %v", err)))         return    }
    w.WriteHeader(http.StatusOK)
    w.Write([]byte("deleted")) }
```

```go
type RedirectPath struct {    store Store }

func (p *RedirectPath) ServeHTTP(w http.ResponseWriter, r *http.Request)

{    hash := mux.Vars(r)["hash"]

   if hash == "" {

      w.WriteHeader(http.StatusBadRequest)

      w.Write([]byte("empty hash"))        return    }

   longURL, err := p.store.Get(hash)    if err != nil {

      w.WriteHeader(http.StatusNotFound)

      w.Write([]byte("not found"))        return

   }

   http.Redirect(w, r, longURL, http.StatusTemporaryRedirect) }

type HandleViaStruct struct{}

func (*HandleViaStruct) ServeHTTP(w http.ResponseWriter, r *http.Request)

{    log.Print("Hello world received a request.")    defer log.Print("End hello world request")
fmt.Fprintf(w, "Hello World via Struct") }

func main() {    log.Print("Hello world sample started.")    r := mux.NewRouter()    redirectPath :=
"http://localhost:8080/r"    mem := NewMemoryStore()

   r.Handle("/", &HandleViaStruct{}).Methods("GET")

   r.Handle("/add", &AddPath{domain: redirectPath, store: &mem}).

Methods("POST")

   r.Handle("/r/{hash}", &DeletePath{store: &mem}).Methods("DELETE")

   r.Handle("/r/{hash}", &RedirectPath{store: &mem}).Methods("GET")
http.ListenAndServe(":8080", r)

}
```

We can run the following Golang application by running the following command for testing purposes: go run main.go

In order to test the application, we can first present a long URL and generate a shortened URL. Let us use curl to do the POST request accordingly.

curl localhost:8080/add -X POST -d '{"url":"https://www.google.com"}'

For our curl request, we would need to access the /add path of our server application as well as provide the http body that is added behind the -d flag. We would define the HTTP method we wish to use for this request by using -X flag as well as the POST value behind it.

This will return the following response if the request is successful:

{"shortened_url":"http://localhost:8080/r/ef7efc9839","long_ url":"https://www.google.com"}

While the application is still running, we can try to access the following URL http://localhost:8080/r/ef7efc9839 in the browser, and it should redirect to Google's homepage accordingly. Doing this represents the GET request—it is hard to visualize the redirect on the terminal, so it is better to just test this capability via the browser.

To delete the shortened URL in the application, we can run the following curl command with the flags as shown: curl http://localhost:8080/r/ef7efc9839 -X DELETE

We would first need to provide the shortened URL as well as the information that we are using the DELETE http verb for this request. This would delete the mapping on the server.

With that, we have successfully created a somewhat fully functioning URL shortener rest API server application. However, before ending this chapter, we can try extending the functionality of this application by expanding on the statement of how we can easily swap out storage to a different one—which in this case, we will swap out storage that is memory backed to one that saves the data into a JSON in a file.

The first portion is to create the storage struct as well as the required functions that fulfill the Store interface. For our new file store, we would once again need to implement the three functions that follow what our interface requires, which is the Add, Remove, and Get functions. type internalStore struct {   Version string   `json:"version"`   Items   map[string]string `json:"items"` }

```
type FileStore struct {

    filename string

}

func NewFileStore(filename string) (FileStore, error) {

    _, err := os.Stat(filename)    if os.IsNotExist(err) {        is := internalStore{Version: "v1", Items:
make(map[string]string)}      raw, err := json.Marshal(is)        if err != nil {

        return FileStore{}, fmt.Errorf("unable to generate json  representation for file")

    }        err = ioutil.WriteFile(filename, raw, 0644)        if err != nil {        return FileStore{},
fmt.Errorf("unable to persist file")

    }    }      return FileStore{filename: filename}, nil

}
```

The following is the Add function that would help store the shortened URL and a long URL. The first part of the function would be to read the file that stores all of the mapped shortened URL to long URL data into the application. Upon reading the file, we would then have a map that would contain the items field, which would contain the mapping. We can then add our new shortened URL to a long URL. The final step of the Add function would be persisting the records into the file once more.

```go
func (f *FileStore) Add(shortendURL, longURL string) error {
    raw, err := ioutil.ReadFile(f.filename)
    if err != nil {
        return err
    }
    var is internalStore
    err = json.Unmarshal(raw, &is)
    if err != nil {
        return fmt.Errorf("unable to parse incoming json store data. Err: %v", err)
    }
    _, ok := is.Items[shortendURL]
    if ok {
        return fmt.Errorf("shortened url already stored")
    }
    is.Items[shortendURL] = longURL
    modRaw, err := json.Marshal(is)
    if err != nil {
        return fmt.Errorf("unable to convert data to json representation")
    }
    err = ioutil.WriteFile(f.filename, modRaw, 0644)
    if err != nil {
        return err
    }
    return nil
}
```

The Remove function is somewhat similar to the Add function. The first step for all the functions of this naïve Filestore implementation would be to read the file. The next step would be removing the mapping that we provided as the argument to the function before persisting that data into the file.

```go
func (f *FileStore) Remove(shortenedURL string) error {
    raw, err := ioutil.ReadFile(f.filename)
    if err != nil {
        return err
    }
    var is internalStore
    err = json.Unmarshal(raw, &is)
    if err != nil {
        return fmt.Errorf("unable to parse incoming json store data. Err: %v", err)
    }
    delete(is.Items, shortenedURL)
    modRaw, err := json.Marshal(is)
    if err != nil {
        return fmt.Errorf("unable to convert data to json representation")
    }
    err = ioutil.WriteFile(f.filename, modRaw, 0644)
    if err != nil {
        return err
    }
    return nil
}
```

The Get function is similar to the Add and Remove functions, as previously mentioned, for the first step of the function, which is to read the file and get the data within it. The only difference between the Get function and the other two previously mentioned functions is that there is no need for the Get function to have steps to manipulate the mapping of shortened URLs and long URLs. We can also skip the step of persisting the data into a file once more since there is not any change to the mapping in the first place:

```go
func (f *FileStore) Get(shortendURL string) (string, error) {
    raw, err := ioutil.ReadFile(f.filename)
    if err != nil {
        return "", err
    }
    var is internalStore
    err = json.Unmarshal(raw, &is)
    if err != nil {
```

```
    return "", fmt.Errorf("unable to parse incoming json store data. Err: %v", err)   }   longURL,
ok := is.Items[shortendURL]    if !ok {        return "", fmt.Errorf("no url available for that shortened
url")   }   return longURL, nil

}
```

The preceding FileStore example is definitely not a good implementation of how we should store the values into a file (note of how for every function, we would load the entire stored data into memory to just append a single record before dumping it out and rewriting past data). However, this example is mainly focusing on showing how we can replace the initial MemoryStore written for our example application with the new FileStore instead.

In our main function, once we initialize the FileStore, we can add them to help handle the paths that we define in the application. The memory store initialization is left in the code to show the example of the differences in how the amount of changes needed to affect the rest of the code base is kept to a minimal.

```
func main() {    log.Print("Hello world sample started.")    r := mux.NewRouter()    redirectPath :=
"http://localhost:8080/r"

    // mem := NewMemoryStore()

    fs, err := NewFileStore("testing.json")    if err != nil {        panic("unable to create filestore
appropriately")

    }

    r.Handle("/", &HandleViaStruct{}).Methods("GET")

    r.Handle("/add", &AddPath{domain: redirectPath, store: &fs}).

Methods("POST")

    r.Handle("/r/{hash}", &DeletePath{store: &fs}).Methods("DELETE")

    r.Handle("/r/{hash}", &RedirectPath{store: &fs}).Methods("GET")
    http.ListenAndServe(":8080", r)

}
```

This way of coding provides us to provide different implementations to how we wish to store the data of mapping the shortened URLs to the long URLs. The application has little dependency to what has already been implemented. In the upcoming chapter, we will see how this coding style would allow us to do unit testing for simply for our application, thereby allowing us to construct more robust and less error-prone applications.

Conclusion: Mastering REST API Development in Go 2024

Building REST APIs in Go opens up a world of possibilities for creating robust, efficient, and scalable backend services. Throughout this guide, we've explored various aspects of REST architecture and how to leverage Go's features to implement them effectively. From understanding the foundational principles of REST to building a full-fledged, production-ready API, we've seen how Go's design philosophy aligns well with the demands of web development.

The Advantages of Using Go for REST APIs

One of the main reasons developers gravitate towards Go for API development is its inherent strengths:

1. **Performance and Efficiency**: Go is a compiled language that translates code directly into machine language. This removes the need for virtual machines or interpreters, making it highly performant. When building REST APIs, performance is crucial, especially for services that handle a high volume of requests. Go's ability to handle concurrent connections efficiently using Goroutines is one of its standout features. This allows APIs to manage multiple client requests simultaneously without blocking, ensuring quick responses and reduced latency.

2. **Concurrency with Goroutines and Channels**: Go's concurrency model is simple yet powerful. Goroutines are lightweight threads managed by Go's runtime, allowing you to spawn thousands of concurrent tasks without the overhead seen in traditional threading models. This makes Go particularly suitable for services that require handling numerous connections at once, such as web servers, which is a common requirement in REST APIs. Additionally, channels facilitate easy and safe communication between Goroutines, further simplifying concurrent programming.

3. **Ease of Deployment**: One of the hassles of deploying applications is managing dependencies. Go simplifies this by producing a single, static binary that contains everything your application needs to run. This reduces compatibility issues and simplifies the deployment process. The ability to deploy your API by simply copying a binary to a server makes Go a preferred choice for developers who prioritize quick and easy deployments.

4. **Robust Standard Library**: Go comes with a comprehensive standard library that covers many aspects of web development, such as HTTP servers, JSON handling, and database interaction. This minimizes the need for third-party packages, reducing potential compatibility issues and keeping codebases clean and manageable. The standard library's HTTP package makes setting up an HTTP server straightforward, which is a core requirement when building REST APIs.

5. **Strong Typing and Code Safety**: The strong typing in Go prevents many common runtime errors by catching them at compile time. This ensures that your API code is more reliable, reducing the likelihood of crashes and unexpected behavior. Type safety, along with Go's simple syntax, allows developers to write clean, maintainable code that is easier to understand and debug.

Understanding REST Architecture Principles

To build an efficient and scalable REST API, it's essential to follow the core principles of REST architecture:

1. **Client-Server Separation**: This principle helps in separating concerns. The client (e.g., a web or mobile application) can independently develop and evolve without affecting the

server-side code. Go's clean design and clear separation of concerns make it easy to adhere to this principle.

2. **Stateless Communication**: Go's standard library makes it straightforward to handle HTTP requests without the need to store client session states, maintaining the stateless nature of REST. This statelessness allows horizontal scaling, where multiple servers can handle client requests without requiring persistent connections, thus enhancing scalability.

3. **Resource-Oriented**: Designing your API around resources instead of actions helps in creating more intuitive and scalable systems. For instance, instead of using /createUser, a RESTful approach would use POST /users. Go's syntax and package management make it easier to write clean, readable, and resource-oriented code.

Setting Up a Basic REST API in Go

Setting up a basic REST API is relatively straightforward with Go. The fundamental tasks include setting up routes, handling requests, working with JSON, and integrating databases. Here's a quick summary of the steps covered:

1. **Routing**: Setting up routing in Go can be done using the net/http package or third-party packages like gorilla/mux for more advanced routing needs. Routing defines how different endpoints are handled and maps HTTP methods (GET, POST, PUT, DELETE) to specific functionalities.

2. **Request and Response Handling**: Parsing requests and sending responses efficiently are crucial for any REST API. Go's encoding/json package makes handling JSON straightforward, allowing for seamless serialization and deserialization of data.

3. **Middleware for Enhanced Functionality**: Adding middleware, such as authentication, logging, or request validation, is critical for building secure and maintainable APIs. Middleware can be implemented to add features across multiple routes without redundant code.

4. **Database Integration**: A REST API often requires persistent storage. Connecting your Go application to a database like PostgreSQL, MySQL, or MongoDB is simplified with database drivers and ORM packages. Handling database connections effectively ensures that your API can store, retrieve, and manipulate data as required.

5. **Error Handling**: Robust error handling is essential for creating user-friendly APIs. Go's error handling approach, though explicit, ensures that errors are caught and managed gracefully. Proper error messages and HTTP status codes are key to delivering a seamless API experience for clients.

Best Practices for Building Production-Ready APIs

Developing a basic API is only the first step. To make your API production-ready, consider the following best practices:

1. **Security Measures**: Implement HTTPS to secure data in transit, and use authentication mechanisms (like JWT) to secure endpoints. This prevents unauthorized access and ensures data integrity. Go's ecosystem includes many libraries that simplify the implementation of security protocols.

2. **Efficient Database Handling**: Use connection pooling and indexing to optimize database queries and improve API performance. Go's standard library, along with packages like gorm or sqlx, can help manage database connections efficiently.

3. **Scalability**: Design your API with scalability in mind. Go's lightweight nature, combined with efficient Goroutines, allows your application to handle increased traffic with ease. However, consider adding load balancers and breaking down the API into microservices if the project grows extensively.

4. **Versioning**: It's essential to version your API, especially if it's public-facing or used by external clients. Versioning ensures backward compatibility and allows clients to migrate to new versions at their own pace. This can be as simple as prefixing your endpoints with /v1/, /v2/, etc.

5. **Documentation**: Properly documenting your API makes it easier for others to understand and use. Tools like Swagger or Postman can be used to create interactive API documentation, and these tools work well with Go's simple and consistent structure.

6. **Testing and Monitoring**: Write unit tests and integration tests to ensure that your API behaves as expected. Testing helps catch bugs before they reach production, and monitoring can alert you to issues in real time. Go's testing package is excellent for writing automated tests, while monitoring tools can track metrics like response time, error rates, and throughput.

Common Challenges and Solutions

Building REST APIs can present a range of challenges, from performance bottlenecks to managing concurrency. Here are a few common issues developers face and how Go addresses them:

1. **Handling Concurrent Requests**: While concurrency is one of Go's strengths, it requires careful handling, especially when multiple Goroutines interact with shared resources. Go's sync package provides tools like mutexes and wait groups to help manage concurrent data access safely.

2. **Scalability and Load Handling**: As your API grows, handling increased load becomes critical. Horizontal scaling (adding more servers) and utilizing Go's concurrency can help distribute the workload. Consider using tools like Kubernetes for orchestrating microservices and load balancers for distributing requests evenly.

3. **Error Management**: Efficiently managing errors, especially in a distributed system, can be challenging. Go encourages explicit error handling, which can sometimes be verbose but ensures clarity. Additionally, using structured logging can help trace errors and debug issues faster.

Future Prospects and Trends in Go for REST APIs

Go continues to evolve, with new features and libraries constantly emerging. Looking ahead, several trends are likely to shape the future of REST API development in Go:

1. **Microservices Architecture**: As systems become more complex, breaking down monolithic applications into microservices is becoming increasingly popular. Go's lightweight binaries, simple deployment, and efficient concurrency make it ideal for microservice architecture.

2. **GraphQL and Beyond**: While REST is still dominant, GraphQL is gaining traction for its flexibility in querying data. Go's ecosystem is expanding to include libraries that support GraphQL, making it easier for developers to choose between REST and GraphQL based on project needs.

3. **Serverless Architecture**: Serverless computing allows developers to focus solely on writing code without managing infrastructure. Go's fast startup time and small memory footprint make it an excellent candidate for serverless environments, where resources are billed based on usage rather than continuous operation.

4. **Continued Performance Optimizations**: The Go team consistently improves the language's performance, making it even more efficient for building high-load applications. Developers can expect continued enhancements in performance, concurrency, and ecosystem support.

Building REST APIs in Go 2024 provides a solid foundation for creating scalable and high-performance web services. With Go's strong emphasis on simplicity, performance, and concurrency, developers can build APIs that are fast, reliable, and easy to maintain. By adhering to the principles of REST architecture and implementing best practices, you can develop production-ready APIs that cater to the needs of modern applications.

Whether you're building small applications or large-scale distributed systems, Go provides the tools and features you need to succeed. As technology continues to evolve, mastering REST API development in Go will remain a valuable skill for developers, and the language's efficiency will ensure that your APIs are future-proof and ready to handle the demands of the modern web.

16. Go: Mutex and Channels

Introduction

Concurrency is one of the core strengths of Go (Golang), making it easier to write programs that execute multiple tasks simultaneously. In modern software development, the need for concurrent processing has grown, whether for handling web requests, performing background tasks, or running multiple operations in parallel. Go addresses this need with goroutines and provides synchronization primitives, such as **Mutexes** and **Channels**, to manage the interactions between these concurrent processes.

This article introduces Mutexes and Channels, explores their use cases, and demonstrates how they can be effectively used in Go programs.

1. Concurrency in Go

Before diving into Mutexes and Channels, it's essential to understand concurrency in Go. In Go, concurrent tasks are handled by goroutines, which are lightweight threads managed by the Go runtime. You can start a goroutine simply by prefixing a function call with the go keyword:

go myFunction()

This creates a new goroutine running concurrently with the main function. However, when goroutines need to share data or communicate, coordination mechanisms are required to avoid conflicts and ensure safe data sharing.

2. Introduction to Mutexes

A **Mutex** (short for "mutual exclusion") is a lock that prevents multiple goroutines from accessing a shared resource simultaneously. When a goroutine locks a mutex, other goroutines attempting to lock the same mutex will be blocked until it is unlocked. This behavior ensures that only one goroutine can access the critical section of code at a time, thus avoiding race conditions.

2.1. Understanding Race Conditions

Race conditions occur when multiple goroutines attempt to read or write to the same variable simultaneously without proper synchronization. This can lead to unpredictable results. For example:

```
package main

import (

    "fmt"

    "sync"

)

var counter = 0
```

```go
func increment(wg *sync.WaitGroup) {
    for i := 0; i < 1000; i++ {
        counter++
    }
    wg.Done()
}
func main() {
    var wg sync.WaitGroup
    wg.Add(2)
    go increment(&wg)
    go increment(&wg)
    wg.Wait()
    fmt.Println("Counter:", counter) // Output may vary
}
```

In the above code, both goroutines attempt to increment the counter variable simultaneously, leading to inconsistent results. This is where a mutex comes in handy.

2.2. Using Mutexes in Go

Go provides the sync.Mutex type to handle mutual exclusion. Here's how you can fix the race condition using a mutex:

```go
package main

import (
    "fmt"
    "sync"
)

var (
    counter = 0
    mutex   sync.Mutex
)

func increment(wg *sync.WaitGroup) {
```

```go
    for i := 0; i < 1000; i++ {

        mutex.Lock()

        counter++

        mutex.Unlock()

    }

    wg.Done()

}

func main() {

    var wg sync.WaitGroup

    wg.Add(2)

    go increment(&wg)

    go increment(&wg)

    wg.Wait()

    fmt.Println("Counter:", counter) // Output will always be 2000

}
```

In this version, the mutex.Lock() and mutex.Unlock() calls ensure that only one goroutine can increment the counter at a time.

2.3. Types of Mutexes: sync.Mutex vs. sync.RWMutex

- **sync.Mutex**: Allows only one goroutine to access a resource.

- **sync.RWMutex**: Allows multiple readers to read simultaneously but only one writer at a time. This is useful when reads are more frequent than writes.

Example of sync.RWMutex:

```go
var rwMutex sync.RWMutex

func readData() {

    rwMutex.RLock()

    // Read operations

    rwMutex.RUnlock()

}

func writeData() {
```

```
    rwMutex.Lock()

    // Write operations

    rwMutex.Unlock()

}
```

3. Introduction to Channels

While Mutexes are used to manage access to shared data, **Channels** in Go provide a way for goroutines to communicate and synchronize without sharing memory. Channels enable the passing of values between goroutines, which is more in line with the message-passing style of concurrency.

3.1. What are Channels?

Channels are typed conduits through which you can send and receive values. They are created using the make function:

```
ch := make(chan int)
```

Channels can be thought of as pipes, where you can send data into one end (<-) and receive it from the other end. Here's a simple example:

```
package main

import "fmt"

func main() {

    messages := make(chan string)

    go func() {

        messages <- "Hello, Channels!"

    }()

    msg := <-messages

    fmt.Println(msg)

}
```

In this example, the main goroutine creates a channel, and another goroutine sends a message through the channel, which is then received and printed by the main goroutine.

3.2. Buffered and Unbuffered Channels

- **Unbuffered Channels**: Block the sending goroutine until another goroutine receives from the channel, ensuring synchronization.

- **Buffered Channels**: Allow a specified number of values to be sent without blocking. They are created as:

```go
ch := make(chan int, 5)
```

This channel can hold up to 5 integers before sending blocks.

3.3. Closing Channels

Channels can be closed to indicate that no more values will be sent on them. This is useful for signaling completion:

```go
close(ch)
```

Once a channel is closed, you can still receive values from it, but sending to a closed channel will cause a panic.

3.4. Using Channels for Communication

Here's an example of using channels to coordinate the completion of goroutines:

```go
package main

import (
    "fmt"
    "time"
)

func worker(done chan bool) {
    fmt.Println("Working...")
    time.Sleep(2 * time.Second)
    fmt.Println("Done")
    done <- true
}

func main() {
    done := make(chan bool)
    go worker(done)
    <-done
    fmt.Println("Main function resumes")
}
```

The worker function sends a signal through the done channel once it completes, and the main function waits for this signal before proceeding.

4. Mutexes vs. Channels: When to Use Which?

While both Mutexes and Channels can be used to solve concurrency problems, they have different philosophies:

- **Use Mutexes** when you need to lock access to shared state. This approach is typically more suitable when you need fine-grained control over data access and can't afford the overhead of passing data around.

- **Use Channels** for communication between goroutines. If you can structure your program so that data is passed through channels rather than shared between goroutines, it often leads to cleaner and more maintainable code.

Example: Mutex vs. Channel Approach

1. **Using Mutex:**

```
var (
   counter = 0
   mutex   sync.Mutex
)
func increment(wg *sync.WaitGroup) {
   for i := 0; i < 1000; i++ {
      mutex.Lock()
      counter++
      mutex.Unlock()
   }
   wg.Done()
}
```

2. **Using Channels:**

```
func increment(ch chan int, wg *sync.WaitGroup) {
   for i := 0; i < 1000; i++ {
      ch <- 1
   }
   wg.Done()
}
```

```go
func main() {
    ch := make(chan int)
    var wg sync.WaitGroup
    wg.Add(2)
    go increment(ch, &wg)
    go increment(ch, &wg)
    go func() {
        wg.Wait()
        close(ch)
    }()
    counter := 0
    for val := range ch {
        counter += val
    }
    fmt.Println("Counter:", counter)
}
```

Channels are like pipelines that connect to concurrently running Goroutines. In the language, a channel has a specific type and that type of values it can transport from one Goroutine to another. Go provides a channel operator through which we can send and receive the data through channels. A **channel operator** is used to sending and receive the data between two channels.

Get an understanding of deadlock

Understand the idea of select keyword with channels Understanding Golang lock/unlock concept through a mutex Declaring channels

In the Go language, we can declare a channel in two ways, using var or make method. The var keyword reserves the memory for the named variables of a specified type and initializes them with the type's default value. If we declare a channel variable using the var keyword, it creates a nil channel. Declaring a channel with the make method also reserves space in storage, initializes memory, and creates an underlying header of a specific type.

Syntax:

var name_of_channel chan type_of_channel

Or

Name_of_channel := make(chan type_of_channel)

Example: func main(){ var ch1 chan int fmt.Println("channel

with 'var' keyword:", ch1) ch2 := make(chan string)

fmt.Println("channel with 'make' method:", ch2)

}

Output:

channel with 'var' keyword:

channel with 'make' method: 0x1180e180

In the example given above, channel ch1 and ch2 transport integer and string type of data between channels. ch1 is declared with var keyword that initializes it with the default value nil. We cannot transfer the data using nil channels. Therefore, in Go language, channels are mostly declared with the make method. The "make"

method provides easy to use channels and returns a value of a specified type. By default, channels are pointers but there is no need to dereference them to access the data.

Channel operations

Golang facilitates various channel operations as given below: **Send operation with channels**

The send operation sends the data of a specified type to a channel variable. The send operation blocks the channels until no channel is ready to receive the data. While sending data, it first checks for a channel that is ready to receive the data.

Example: func main(){ ch := make(chan int) ch<- 8 fmt.Println(ch)

}

The example given above will show an error. Statement ch<-

8 blocks the channel as no channel is ready to receive the

data.

Receive operation in channel

By performing the receive operation, we can get the data from a channel to a variable. While receiving the data from channels, we

get two values. The first is the data that a channel sends and the other one indicates the status that whether an operation is successful or not. The idiom for the second value is ok. The value of ok variable is true if the data is received successfully from the channel and false if the channel is closed or empty.

Example: package main import "fmt" func show_value(c chan int){ c <- 8

} func main(){ c := make(chan int) go show_value(c) a, ok := <-c

fmt.Println("value received from channel:", a) fmt.Println("status of

operation is:", ok) }

Output:

value received from channel: 8

status of operation is: true

In the example given above, we are using the Goroutine show_value that sends a value to a channel. After calling the Goroutine, a channel is sending the data and on the next line,

the channel is ready to receive the data in the main function. As the operation is successful, true is assigned to an ok variable. The sending and receiving channel should be of the same type otherwise the compiler will show an error.

If we execute the same program with the channels declared using the var keyword, it will give an error.

Example:

func show_value(c chan int){ c <- 8 } func main(){ var c chan int go

show_value(c) a, ok := <-c fmt.Println("value received from channel:", a)

fmt.Println("status of operation is:", ok) }

Output:

error " [chan send chan>] "

We have observed that the send operation blocks a channel if no channel is ready to receive the data. So, we perform the receive operation to avoid such an issue. To overcome such scenarios, we can use buffered channels in Go programs. The following describes buffered and unbuffered channels briefly.

Unbuffered channel

By default, channels are **unbuffered** in the Go language. Such channels accept the send operation if there is a channel ready to receive the data. We saw in the previous examples that on sending data without any corresponding receiver, the compiler gives an error.

Buffered channel

Buffered channels can send specified number of values without any corresponding receiver. They store the values sent by a channel in a buffer and return when a corresponding channel is ready to receive the data. The number of values that is allowed to send without any receiver is called the capacity of a channel. The following is the syntax to create buffered channels in the Go language.

Syntax:

name_of_channel := make(chan type_of_channel,

capacity_of_channel)

Example: func

main(){ ch :=

make(chan int, 2) ch<-

8 a := <-ch

fmt.Println(ch, a)

}

Output:

0x1183c0c0 8

In the example given above, the capacity of the buffered channel is 2 which indicates that it can send maximum 2 values without waiting for a receiver channel. We can send the second value as shown below:

Example: func

main(){ ch :=

make(chan int, 2) ch<-

8 ch<- 99 a := <-ch b

:= <- ch fmt.Println(a,

b)

}

Output:

8 99

In the example given above, it stores the values in a buffer and returns to the corresponding receiver when the channel is ready to receive the data. We can receive the data from two or multiple channels in the same line as shown below: a, b := <-ch, <-ch

In the above program, on sending the third value without a corresponding receiver channel, it will give an error as the capacity of the channel is 2.

Find the capacity of the channel

Golang provides a function cap to get the capacity of a channel.

The following example illustrates the use of the cap function with channels.

Example: func

main(){ ch :=

make(chan int, 2)

cap_ch := cap(ch)

fmt.Println("Capacity

of channel is:",

cap_ch) for itr := 1;

itr<=cap_ch; itr++{

ch<- itr*2

fmt.Println("value

received from channel

is:", <-ch)

}

}

Output:

Capacity of channel is: 2 value

received from channel is: 2

value received from channel is:

4

Deadlock

In the previous examples, we saw that on sending data, it waits for a channel that is ready to receive the data. If it doesn't find any receiver channel, it blocks that Goroutine and passes the control to other Goroutines to run. When it finds the receiver channel in another Goroutine, it unblocks the send operation and runs that Goroutine.

In such cases, if we don't get any receiver channel in another Goroutins or there is no other Goroutine available in the program, the compiler imagines that all the Goroutines are asleep. The send operation remains blocked until the end of the program.

Such a situation is called a deadlock.

The deadlock can occur in two ways depending on the operation that is being blocked.

On sending the data to a channel, it blocks the current Goroutine and schedules other Goroutines with the hope of getting a receiver channel. Here, the "sending operation is getting blocked."

On receiving the data from a channel, it checks for an existing value in a channel. If a channel contains no value, it blocks the receive operation until it doesn't get any value in that channel. So here, the "receive operation is getting blocked." In the Go language, a deadlock occurs if we have at least one blocked operation and no other Goroutine is available to schedule in a

program. In such a case, the program crashes and the compiler shows an error. The following

example explains a deadlock. **Example:** package main import "fmt" func show(){

fmt.Println("Hello")

} func main(){ str_ch :=

make(chan string) go

show() str_ch<- "Hello

world" fmt.Println("Send

operation is getting

blocked")

}

Output: Hello fatal error: all goroutines

are asleep – deadlock!

goroutine 1 [chan send]

In the example given above, we are calling Goroutines then trying to send a value to a channel. It blocks the send operations as there is no other channel to receive the data. After blocking the main Goroutines, there is no other Goroutine to schedule. Hence, the deadlock occurs.

Example: package main

import "fmt" func

show(){

```
fmt.Println("Hello
world")
} func main(){ str_ch := make(chan string) go
show() a := <- str_ch fmt.Println("Receive
operation is getting blocked", a)
}
```

Output: Hello fatal error: all goroutines

are asleep – deadlock!

goroutine 1 [chan receive]

In the example given above, after calling we are trying to receive a value from the channel but no value has been assigned to a channel till now. So, it blocks the current main Goroutine. As it continues, it finds that there is no other Goroutine to schedule.

In such a case, a deadlock occurs and the compiler gives a fatal error.

Using multiple Goroutines

A Go program can have multiple Goroutines with sharing values.

Go defines the concept as "Do not communicate by sharing memory. Instead, share memory by communicating."

Example: package main

```
import "fmt" func
square(num_ch chan int){
value := <-num_ch sqr_val
:= value*value num_ch<-
sqr_val
} func cube(num_ch chan
int){ value := <-num_ch
cube_val :=
value*value*value num_ch<-
cube_val
```

```
} func main(){ num := make(chan int)
// 1 go square(num) // 2 num<- 3 // 3
sqr_val := <-num // 4 go cube(num) // 5
num<- 3 // 6 cube_val := <-num // 7
fmt.Println("Square of value:", sqr_val)
// 8 fmt.Println("Cube of value:",
cube_val) // 9
}
```

Output:

Square of value: 9

Cube of value: 27

First, we are creating a channel called "num" that passes an integer type of value.

In the second line, we call the "square" goroutine. In this Goroutine, we are trying to get the value from a channel. But since no value has been assigned to a channel till now, it blocks the receive operation and control is passed to the "main" Goroutine.

In the third line, we pass "3" to a channel that further executes the receive operation in the square Goroutine. Then, the final value is passed to a channel called 'num_ch' in the Goroutine.

In the fourth line, the channel is ready to receive a value that is sent by the "square" goroutine. Thus, we get a square of 3.

In the same way, we get a cube of value in line 5, 6, and 7.

Closing a channel

While programming, there may be an instance where after creating a channel, we do not want to use it further in our Go program.

In such a case, Go provides a method to close a channel that indicates that no value will be sent through a channel. The close function is used to close a channel.

While receiving the value from a channel, we can get the status of a channel. It will return true if a channel is open and the receive operation is successful; otherwise, it will return false if a channel is closed.

Example: package main

import "fmt" func cube(value

```
chan int){ fmt.Println("In
cube goroutine") val := <-
value value <- val*val*val
} func square(value chan int){
fmt.Println("In square
goroutine") val := <-value
fmt.Println(val) value <-
val*val
} func main(){ num :=
make(chan int) go
square(num)

num<- 3 sqr_val := <-num go cube(num) num<- 3 close(num) cube_val,
ok := <-num fmt.Println("Square of value:", sqr_val) fmt.Println("Cube
of value:", cube_val, ok)
}
```

Output:

In square Goroutine

3

In cube goroutine

Square of value: 9

Cube of value: 0

Panic: send on closed channel

In the example given above, after calling the cube Goroutine we passed a value to the num channel. Before we received the final value from the channel sent by the cube Goroutine, we closed that channel. This situation lead to a runtime panic. On receiving a value from a closed channel, it returns zero without any error and assigns false to an ok variable.

The direction of a channel

In the previous examples, we have seen that we can perform, read and write both operations on a channel. By default, Go provides a bidirectional nature of channels.

We can also create unidirectional channels in the Go language that either allow the read operation or receive operation.

The syntax of declaring the unidirectional channel is as follows: **Receive**

only channel name_of_channel := make(<- chanint) **Send only channel**

name_of_channel := make(chan -

Here is an example of send only channel below:

Example: package

main import

("fmt" "sync"

)

var wg sync.WaitGroup func square(value chan<-

int){ fmt.Println("defining send only goroutine")

val := value fmt.Println(val) wg.Done() } func

main(){ send_ch := make(chan<- int, 1)

wg.Add(1) go square(send_ch) send_ch<- 3

wg.Wait()

}

Output:

defining send only Goroutine

0x1183c0c0

In the example given above, we have defined a send only unidirectional channel send_ch that only sends a value to a channel. We cannot receive value from such channels. On receiving value from such channels, the compiler gives an error as shown below:

Example: package

main import

("fmt"

```go
    "sync"
)

var wg sync.WaitGroup func square(value chan<-
int){ fmt.Println("defining send only goroutine")
val := value fmt.Println(val) val<- value

wg.Done() } func main(){
send_ch := make(chan<- int,
1) wg.Add(1) go
square(send_ch) send_ch<- 3
wg.Wait()
}
```

Output:

Cannot use value chan<- int> as type int in send

In the same way, we can declare receive only channels in the Go language. An example of receiving only channels is shown below: **Example:**

```go
package main

import ("fmt"

"sync"
)

var wg sync.WaitGroup func square(value <-chan
int){ fmt.Println("defining receive only goroutine")
val := <-value fmt.Println(val) wg.Done() } func
main(){ receive_ch := make(<-chan int) wg.Add(1)
go square(receive_ch) wg.Wait()
}
```

In the example given above, we created a receive only channel receive_ch and called squareGoroutine. Here, we are trying to receive a value from a channel. As there is no value in the channel, it blocks the receive operation and the compiler gives an error "deadlock." We can see the solution to this issue in the next

program. We can convert a bidirectional channel to unidirectional for a specific Goroutine.

Example: package main import "fmt"

func receive(receive_ch chan<- int, val

int) { receive_ch<- val

} func square(receive_ch<-chan int, send_ch chan<-

int){ fmt.Println("defining send only goroutine") val :=

<- receive_ch send_ch<- val

} func main(){ send_ch :=

make(chan int, 1) receive_ch

:= make(chan int,1)

receive(receive_ch, 6)

square(receive_ch, send_ch)

fmt.Println(<-send_ch)

}

Output:

defining send only Goroutine

6

The select keyword

Select is used for network communication or to wait for multiple channel operations. The select statement is like a switch that works with multiple cases. With the select statement, the case refers to the channel's send/receive operation. Select waits for a specific case until it to ready to perform the operation specified in a particular case statement. If no case is defined within a select statement, then it will lead to a deadlock since it didn't get any case for channel communication. The select statement gets blocked if no case statement is ready to execute. In the case of blocking, it waits for a case that is ready to perform a channel operation. To avoid select blocking, it can have a default case like a switch statement. If no case statement is ready to perform the communication, it proceeds with the default case. If the select statement has multiple cases that are ready to perform the specified channel operation, it selects any random case statement and executes it.

The syntax of the select statement is the same as the switch statement except for the case statement. Here, the case statement defines a channel operation.

Syntax:

```
select{ case

send_receive_operation1: //

body of case statement 1

case

send_receive_operation2:

// body of case statement 2

}
```

Multiple examples of the select statement that describe the use of the select statement in different ways are as given below. **Example:** package main import ("fmt"

```
"time"

)

func square(num_ch chan

int){ value := <-num_ch

sqr_val := value*value

time.Sleep(5*time.Second)

num_ch<- sqr_val

} func cube(num_ch chan

int){ value := <-num_ch

cube_val :=

value*value*value

time.Sleep(10*time.Second)

num_ch<- cube_val

} func main(){ sqr_ch :=
```

```
make(chan int) go

square(sqr_ch) sqr_ch<- 3

cube_ch := make(chan int) go cube(cube_ch) cube_ch<- 5

select{ case sqr_val := <-sqr_ch: fmt.Println("square of a value

is:", sqr_val) case cube_val := <-cube_ch:

fmt.Println("Cube of a value is:", cube_val)

}

}
```

Output:

square of a value is: 9

In the example given above, we have two Goroutines, square and We are calling both of them by passing a channel value from the main Goroutine. The select statement has two cases. In the first case, receive the value from the channel sqr_ch that is sent by the square goroutine. In the second case, we receive the value from channel cube_ch that is sent by the cube goroutine. In the square goroutine, we have given sleep time for 5 seconds and 10

seconds for the cube goroutine so that the square goroutines will finish its execution first. As the square Goroutine finishes its execution, it will send the value to a channel and case1 would be ready to execute in the select statement. The select statement executes that case and comes out of its block.

In the example given above, we saw that only one case was ready to execute at a time. The following is an example where both cases are ready to execute at the same time.

Example: package

main import

("fmt"

"time"

)

func square(num_ch chan

int){ value := <-num_ch

sqr_val := value*value

time.Sleep(1*time.Second)

num_ch<- sqr_val

```
} func cube(num_ch chan
int){ value := <-num_ch

cube_val := value*value*value

time.Sleep(1*time.Second)

num_ch<- cube_val

} func main(){ sqr_ch := make(chan int) go square(sqr_ch)

sqr_ch<- 3 cube_ch := make(chan int) go cube(cube_ch)

cube_ch<- 5 select{ case sqr_val := <-sqr_ch:

fmt.Println("square of a value is:", sqr_val) case cube_val := <-

cube_ch:

fmt.Println("Cube of a value is:", cube_val)

}

}
```

Output:

Cube of a value is: 125

Or square of a value is: 9

Here, the sleep time for both the Goroutines is the same (1second). So, both the cases would be ready to execute at the same time. In such a case, the select statement randomly picks the case and executes it. The output of this program varies on executing it again and again.

Now, it could be possible that the select statement didn't find any case statement to execute.

Example: package

main import

("fmt"

"time"

)

```
func square(num_ch chan int){

_ = <-num_ch

time.Sleep(1*time.Second)
```

```go
} func cube(num_ch chan
int){
_ = <-num_ch
time.Sleep(1*time.Second)
} func main(){ sqr_ch := make(chan int) go square(sqr_ch)
sqr_ch<- 3 cube_ch := make(chan int) go cube(cube_ch)
cube_ch<- 5 select{ case sqr_val := <-sqr_ch:
fmt.Println("square of a value is:", sqr_val) case cube_val := <-
cube_ch:
fmt.Println("Cube of a value is:", cube_val)
}
}
```

Output:

Fatal error: all goroutines are asleep – deadlock!

goroutine 1 [select]

In this case, we sent the value to channels that are received by Goroutines. Now, in both the case statements, we are trying to receive the value from a channel, but the channel doesn't have any value. As the select statement doesn't find any ready case statement here, it blocks the select statement and also leads to a deadlock.

To avoid a deadlock, we can add the default statement in select that proceeds the execution if select doesn't find any ready case statement.

Example: package

```go
main import

("fmt"

"time"
)
func square(num_ch chan int){
_ = <-num_ch
time.Sleep(1*time.Second)
```

```go
} func cube(num_ch chan

int){

_ = <-num_ch

time.Sleep(1*time.Second)

} func main(){ sqr_ch := make(chan int) go square(sqr_ch)

sqr_ch<- 3 cube_ch := make(chan int) go cube(cube_ch)

cube_ch<- 5 select{ case sqr_val := <-sqr_ch:

fmt.Println("square of a value is:", sqr_val) case cube_val := <-

cube_ch: fmt.Println("Cube of a value is:", cube_val) default:

fmt.Println("No case statement is ready to execute!")

}

}
```

Output:

No case statement is ready to execute!

Here is an example where the select statement doesn't have any case for channel communication.

Example: func

```go
main(){ select{

}

}
```

Output:

Fatal error: all goroutines are asleep – deadlock!

goroutine 1 [select cases>]

With this blank select statement, the compiler will give a fatal error and lead to a deadlock.

We saw that a maximum of one case is executed with a select statement at a time. We can execute multiple cases by repeatedly checking if a case is ready to execute.

Example: package

main import

("fmt"

```go
	"time"
)
func square(num_ch chan
int){ value := <-num_ch
sqr_val := value*value
time.Sleep(5*time.Second)
num_ch<- sqr_val
} func cube(num_ch chan
int){ value := <-num_ch
cube_val :=
value*value*value
time.Sleep(10*time.Second)
num_ch<- cube_val
} func main(){ sqr_ch :=
make(chan int) go
square(sqr_ch) sqr_ch<-
3 cube_ch := make(chan
int) go cube(cube_ch)
cube_ch<- 5
for itr := 1; itr<= 2; itr++{
select{ case sqr_val := <-sqr_ch: fmt.Println("square of a value
is:", sqr_val) case cube_val := <-cube_ch:
fmt.Println("Cube of a value is:", cube_val)
}
}
}
```

Output:

square of a value is: 9

Cube of a value is: 125

Here, we are executing the select statement two times as we have two cases in the select statement. Since the square Goroutine has less sleep time, it will finish its execution first and case1 would be ready to execute. So, a select statement first executes On the second time, it finds case2 that is ready to execute. In this way, the select statement waits for the Goroutine to finish its execution and proceeds with the specified case.

Golang provides the facility to build concurrent programs that sometimes lead to unexpected behavior. Concurrency comes with multiple bugs that are quite hard to debug. The following defines some possible unexpected situations and how to detect and solve them.

Data race in Go

Data race can be defined by a situation where two or multiple threads concurrently access the same memory location and perform at least one write operation. It occurs with the execution of multi-threading programming. The following example defines data race in Go language.

Example: package

main import "fmt"

var value = 45 func

update_value(){

if(value==45){

value++ }

fmt.Println(value)

} func main(){ go

update_value() //gr1

go update_value()

//gr2

}

In the example given above, we have two Goroutines, and and both are accessing the same variable value to update its value.

There could be three cases with this program. It depends on the order of execution of the Goroutines gr1 and gr2.

Case 1: gr1 first reads the data and then updates the value according to a specific condition. After the execution of gr2 reads the data checks for the conditions and updates the data. Here, the order of the Goroutines is synchronized. No concurrent process is running here; the program will provide an accurate result. result.

Case 2: Here, gr1 first reads the data and then gr2 reads the data. So, both the Goroutines will read the value 45 in this case.

After that gr1 and gr2 write a value as the condition is satisfied with both the Goroutines. Here, the the execution goes wrong and gets an unexpected result. result.

Case 3: Here, gr1 first reads the data and then gr2 reads the data. So, both the Goroutines will read the value 45 in this case.

After that, gr2 and gr1 write a value as the condition gets satisfied with both the Goroutines. Here, the execution goes wrong and there is an unexpected result.

Race condition

A **race condition** is a feature of a program or system that can lead to an unexpected result. A race condition occurs when two or multiple operations are performed at the same time in a program or system. Due to incorrect timing or ordering of operation, it leads to the crash of a program. A race condition is different from a data race. It is not necessary that if a program has a race condition, it must be because of a data race. A program can have a race condition but not a data race.

The following is an example where a data race doesn't exist but it defines a race condition.

Example:

Thread 1 Thread2

lock(1) lock(1)

value = 1 value = 2

unlock(1) unlock(1)

In the example given above, we used a lock before updating the value of a variable to synchronize the process. There would never be any concurrent process, so data race doesn't exist here.

We can get race condition with such examples. As we don't know the order of execution for these threads, it's hard to determine which process updates the value of a variable. The final value of a variable can be 1 or 2.

Check for data race

While working with multi-threading, it becomes necessary to protect a program from abnormal behavior to make the program reliable and scalable. Go language provides a "data race detector" tool that tracks all the operations related to static/dynamic memory access and how and when the memory is accessed in a program. Dynamic tracking is done for unsynchronized access to shared variables. This tool looks for a race condition. If a program has a race condition because of a data race, it prints a warning message. The Go race detector tool was introduced with the v1.1

version of Go, integrated with the Go toolchain. This tool supports Linux/amd64, Linux/ppc64le, linuxarm64, FreeBSD/amd64, NetBSD/amd64, Darwin/amd64, and windows/amd64.

To enable the race detector in a program, -race flag is raised while executing a program. We can raise the race flag in the following ways:

go test –race package_name

go run –race program_name

go build –race

command_name go install –

race package_name

It is advisable to use a race detector if it is necessary as it consumes the CPU and memory ten times more. Also, we can say that with concurrency, data sharing between Goroutines must be properly synchronized to avoid such erroneous conditions.

Mutex

In the Go language, **Mutex** provides a mechanism to synchronize the data access between multiple goroutines. Mutex follows the concept of a mutual exclusion lock that allows only one Goroutine to access the memory at a time by the locking and unlocking mechanism.

Till now, we have used channels for synchronized communication between Goroutines. Although channels are also good as they have the built-in property of thread safety and prevent a race condition, it is advisable not to use channels in every situation.

With a large application, a channel allows single thread access to memory but the performance penalty occurs with channels if less number of resources is shared between them. Channels and Mutex both have their pros and cons depending on the requirement and the way of programming.

Here, we are going to use the concept of **mutual exclusion** provided by a data structure Mutex. Mutex is defined in the sync package available in the src directory. It has an interface locker that encapsulates the functionally of locking and unlocking by declaring two methods, Lock and These two methods are implemented by the mutex struct type. Mutex defines these two methods to lock and unlock a block of code that is executed by only one Goroutine at a time. Data access is synchronized with Mutex by keeping a lock when a shared resource is being used so that no other Goroutine can use it. After using that shared

resource, the lock is removed. It prevents race condition between multiple Goroutines if they are accessing the same memory space at a time.

Here is an example that shows how Mutex locks and unlocks a block of code and enables synchronized data access.

Example: package

main import

("fmt"

"sync"

) type initial_amount struct{ amount int sync.Mutex }

func (ia *initial_amount)

withdraw_amount(withdraw_val int){ ia.Lock()

ia.amount = ia.amount - withdraw_val ia.Unlock() }

func (ia *initial_amount) deposit_amount(deposit_val

int){ ia.Lock() ia.amount = ia.amount + deposit_val

ia.Unlock() }

func (ia *initial_amount) get_balance()

int { val :=ia.amount return val } func

main(){ ia := initial_amount{amount:

2000} for itr:= 1; itr<=10; itr++{ go

ia.deposit_amount(500) go

ia.withdraw_amount(300)

} final_amount := ia.get_balance()

fmt.Println("Final balance

is:",final_amount)

}

Output:

Final balance is: 4100

In the program given above, we create a struct initial_amount that has two fields, amount and the amount variable is shared between two Goroutines, withdraw_amount and deposit_amount.

Here, Mutex is defined as a struct field that locks and unlocks the access to amount variable. withdraw_amount withdraws an amount and updates amount variable. Similarly, deposit_amount deposits an amount as specified and updates the same amount variable. Both Goroutines are called from the main Goroutine; they will run concurrently. In the deposit_amount goroutine, before updating the value of the "amount" variable, we use the lock method so that any other goroutine won't be able to access the amount variable at the same time. When deposit_amount updates the value, it unlocks the resources to make them available for other Goroutines. In such a way, the access to the amount variable is synchronized.

When we run the above program with the race detector, it prints the output message with a data race warning that indicates the data race exists in the above program. In the get_balace method, we are accessing the same shared variable amount to read its value. While accessing this variable, the lock is being acquired either by deposit_amount or withdraw_amount method. We can prevent this warning by acquiring a lock before reading the value in get_balance method.

```
func (ia *initial_amount) get_balance() int { ia.Lock() val := ia.amount ia.Unlock() return val

}
```

Now run the program with the same race detector tool.

Output:

Final balance is: 3800

This time, the is quite different as it waits for some time to acquire a lock for the shared variable.

Also, it didn't get any data race warning here. Now the question is of not getting the correct result.

The get_balance method is being called before the termination of all Goroutines, so it returns the intermediate value of a variable.

We can resolve this issue by using WaitGroup as shown below:

Example:

```
package main

import ("fmt"

"sync"
)

var wg sync.WaitGroup

type initial_amount struct{

amount int sync.Mutex }

func (ia *initial_amount)
```

```go
withdraw_amount(withdraw_val int){ ia.Lock()
ia.amount = ia.amount - withdraw_val ia.Unlock()
wg.Done() } func (ia *initial_amount)
deposit_amount(deposit_val int){ ia.Lock()
ia.amount = ia.amount + deposit_val ia.Unlock()
wg.Done() }
func (ia *initial_amount) get_balance()
int { ia.Lock() val := ia.amount
ia.Unlock() return val } func main(){ ia
:= initial_amount{amount: 2000} for
itr:= 1; itr<=10; itr++{
wg.Add(1) go
ia.deposit_amount(500)
wg.Add(1) go
ia.withdraw_amount(300)
} wg.Wait()
final_amoun
t :=
ia.get_balanc
e()
fmt.Println("
final balance
```

is:",

final_amoun

t)

}

Output:

final balance is: 4000

RWMutex

Any thread either reads the data or modifies it. On performing a write operation, data sharing is not allowed with multiple Goroutines, whereas with a read operation, multiple Goroutines can read the data from the same memory space without any issue. Based on several operations, Golang provides a specific reader/writer Mutex that multiple readers and writers can behold.

Like Mutex, **RWMutex** is also available in a sync package.

RWMutex is a struct that contains various fields to track the memory access by multiple threads. RWMutex implements multiple methods that provide a specific type of lock/unlocking service.

RLock()

It is used to acquire a lock rw for reading purpose. Multiple readers can acquire this lock in a single program. RLock is not bound with a specific thread.

RUnlock()

This method releases the acquired lock for a single RLock call that doesn't affect another running read operation. In the Go language, one thread may RLockrw another thread and it can release that.

Lock()

It locks rw for writing purpose. This type of lock is acquired by only one thread at a time. If another thread acquires a lock for the reading/writing purpose, Lock blocks until the lock is available to acquire.

Unlock()

This method unblocks rw to make it available for another writer thread. On executing Unlock without acquiring the lock, the compiler will give an error at runtime.

There is a point to remember which is that we cannot contain Mutex and RWMutex both as struct field in a single program. In such a case, the compiler will give the error "ambiguous selector."

The following example defines thread-safe maps with the use of RWMutex.

Example: package

main import

("fmt"

"sync"

"time"

)

type Map_struct struct{ map_val map[int] int

sync.RWMutex } func (map_data *Map_struct)

update_map(keyval int){ map_data.Lock()

map_data.map_val[keyval] = keyval * 10

map_data.Unlock() } func (map_data

*Map_struct) read_map(){ map_data.RLock()

val := map_data.map_val map_data.RUnlock()

fmt.Println(val) } func main(){ ia :=

Map_struct{map_val:make(map[int]int)} for

itr:= 1; itr<10; itr++{ go ia.update_map(itr) go

ia.read_map() } time.Sleep(5 * time.Second)

}

Output:

map[1:10 2:20] map[1:10 2:20]

map[1:10 2:20 3:30] map[1:10

2:20 3:30 4:40] map[1:10 2:20

3:30 4:40 5:50] map[1:10 2:20

3:30 4:40 5:50 6:60] map[1:10

2:20 3:30 4:40 5:50 6:60 7:70]

map[1:10 2:20 3:30 4:40 5:50

6:60 7:70 8:80] map[1:10 2:20

3:30 4:40 5:50 6:60 7:70 8:80

9:90]

In the program given above, we create a struct Map_struct that has two fields, map_val and RWMutex object. Embedding of RWMutex object allows accessing multiple methods for In the main Goroutine, we initialize the struct and call Goroutines in a loop. Here, we have two Goroutines. read_map reads the map values and update_map modifies the map. read_map goroutine puts RLock to perform read operation, and after reading a map, it releases the lock using the Goroutine update_map acquires the lock for a write operation and after updating the map, it releases the lock using the Unlock method. We give time sleep for 5 seconds at the end of the main Goroutine so that all the running Goroutines can finish their execution till that time.

Conclusion

Go enables developers to write programs that can execute multiple functions simultaneously, effectively utilizing system resources. However, with great power comes the responsibility of managing data access and communication between these concurrent processes, which is where synchronization primitives like **Mutexes** and **Channels** come into play.

In this article, we've explored two core concurrency mechanisms in Go: Mutexes and Channels. Each serves a unique purpose and embodies a different philosophy of concurrent programming. Understanding their strengths, weaknesses, and appropriate use cases is crucial for any Go developer aiming to build robust, maintainable, and efficient applications.

1. The Role of Mutexes in Synchronization

Mutexes are a direct way to handle concurrency by preventing multiple goroutines from accessing a shared resource simultaneously. This ensures that only one goroutine can execute a critical section of code at any given time. Through the use of sync.Mutex and sync.RWMutex, Go provides developers with the tools they need to manage data consistency and avoid race conditions.

However, while mutexes are powerful, they require careful handling. Improper use of locks can lead to **deadlocks**, **livelocks**, or **starvation**—issues that can be difficult to debug and resolve. Therefore, when using mutexes, it's essential to:

- **Always unlock the mutex after the critical section is complete.** A common practice is to use defer statements right after acquiring a lock to ensure it gets released even if the function returns early.

- **Avoid holding locks for extended periods.** Locks should only be held for as long as necessary, as prolonged locking can block other goroutines and reduce the program's efficiency.

- **Consider read-write locks when reads are more frequent than writes.** Using sync.RWMutex allows multiple readers to access data simultaneously, which can significantly improve performance when read-heavy workloads are involved.

2. The Power of Channels in Communication

Channels, on the other hand, facilitate communication between goroutines, allowing them to pass data back and forth safely without needing shared memory. This approach encourages a message-passing style of concurrency, where goroutines communicate by sending and receiving values rather than by directly sharing data. This can lead to more modular and cleaner code, as it reduces the dependencies between different parts of a program.

Channels enable synchronization and coordination between goroutines. For example, an unbuffered channel ensures that the sender and receiver are synchronized—one must wait for the other to be ready before proceeding. Buffered channels introduce flexibility, allowing goroutines to send multiple messages without waiting for the receiver, up to a limit defined by the buffer size.

There are, however, certain considerations to keep in mind when using channels:

- **Buffered vs. Unbuffered Channels:** Unbuffered channels are ideal for synchronous communication, where you want to ensure that a value is always received as soon as it is sent. Buffered channels, on the other hand, offer more flexibility but can introduce complexity if not managed correctly, such as when dealing with buffer overflows or ensuring that the buffer is adequately drained.

- **Closing Channels:** Properly closing channels is essential to prevent goroutines from hanging. Once a channel is closed, no more values can be sent on it, but you can still receive any remaining values. It's a best practice to close channels from the sending side when you're done sending data.

- **Select Statement for Multiplexing:** The select statement allows a goroutine to wait on multiple channel operations, which can be a powerful tool for managing multiple concurrent tasks. However, it's essential to design select statements carefully to avoid unpredictable behavior, especially when dealing with multiple channels that might trigger at the same time.

3. Comparing Mutexes and Channels: Which One to Use?

Choosing between Mutexes and Channels depends on the problem you are trying to solve and how you want to structure your concurrent code.

- **Mutexes are suitable for scenarios where shared state must be protected from concurrent access.** They provide fine-grained control over who can read or write to the data, but this can make the code harder to read and maintain. Mutexes require a conscious effort to lock and unlock resources, which can lead to complex locking schemes as the program grows.

- **Channels, in contrast, offer a more idiomatic way to handle concurrency in Go.** They allow goroutines to communicate by passing messages, making it easier to reason about data flow and dependencies between different parts of the program. Using channels reduces the need for shared state, leading to fewer race conditions and easier debugging.

"Do not communicate by sharing memory; instead, share memory by communicating." This is a guiding principle of Go's concurrency model, as described by the creators of the language. Whenever possible, structuring your code to use channels rather than mutexes can lead to more reliable and maintainable applications. Channels encourage a higher-level approach to concurrency, where the focus is on the flow of data rather than the management of state.

4. Practical Use Cases and Best Practices

4.1. When to Use Mutexes

1. **Managing Shared Counters:** Use a mutex when multiple goroutines need to increment or modify a shared counter or variable.

2. **Ensuring Data Integrity:** Mutexes are effective when you need to ensure that data modifications are atomic, preventing data corruption.

3. **Low-level Synchronization:** Mutexes can be used for low-level synchronization tasks where precise control over access to a resource is required.

4.2. When to Use Channels

1. **Goroutine Coordination:** Channels can signal when a goroutine has completed its task, making them ideal for managing the lifecycle of concurrent tasks.

2. **Pipelining Data Processing:** Channels are often used to build pipelines, where data flows from one stage of processing to another through channels.

3. **Event Broadcasting:** You can use channels to broadcast events to multiple receivers, enabling event-driven programming patterns in your concurrent application.

5. Common Pitfalls and How to Avoid Them

Concurrency can lead to complex scenarios, and even experienced developers can run into issues. Here are some common pitfalls and how to avoid them:

- **Deadlocks:** This occurs when two or more goroutines are waiting for each other to release a resource. To avoid this, always make sure that locks are acquired and released in a consistent order.

- **Race Conditions:** Running into race conditions means that your program's behavior changes based on how goroutines are scheduled. Using mutexes or channels can help you avoid these, but make sure to test your code with tools like go run -race to catch these issues early.

- **Unclosed Channels:** If a channel is not properly closed, it can lead to goroutines waiting indefinitely. Always ensure channels are closed when they are no longer needed, and design your program so that only the sender is responsible for closing the channel.

6. Final Thoughts: Mastering Go's Concurrency

Concurrency is a challenging yet rewarding aspect of software development, and mastering it is key to becoming a proficient Go developer. Go's concurrency model, built around goroutines, channels, and mutexes, provides the building blocks necessary for creating responsive, scalable, and performant applications.

The choice between Mutexes and Channels often comes down to a design decision. If you need to synchronize access to shared resources and manage state, mutexes are the way to go. But if you can design your program around the flow of data and communication, channels are often the more elegant solution.

Learning to use these concurrency primitives effectively will allow you to leverage Go's true power. Whether you are developing web servers that handle thousands of requests simultaneously, processing large datasets in the background, or building distributed systems that coordinate across multiple nodes, understanding mutexes and channels will make your code more efficient and your applications more reliable.

In conclusion, **go beyond just understanding how to use Mutexes and Channels; understand when and why to use them.** This will lead to cleaner, more maintainable, and more scalable code. Experiment, build, and debug your way to mastering Go's concurrency, and you'll find yourself equipped to handle even the most complex concurrent programming challenges.

17. Go: Strengthening Database Interactions

Introduction

Efficient database interactions are crucial for building reliable and scalable applications, and Go's design philosophy aligns perfectly with creating performant database operations. Whether you're working with SQL databases like PostgreSQL, MySQL, or NoSQL databases like MongoDB, understanding how to strengthen the way your Go applications interact with databases can make a significant difference. This chapter focuses on best practices, tools, and techniques to build robust, secure, and efficient database solutions in Go.

Importance of Efficient Database Interactions

In any application, databases serve as the backbone for storing, retrieving, and managing data. The speed, reliability, and security of these interactions are essential to maintaining a seamless user experience. Poorly handled database connections, incorrect query structures, or lack of optimization can lead to serious issues like data corruption, slow response times, and even security breaches. Hence, strengthening database interactions should be a top priority for any developer building data-intensive applications.

Overview of Database Support in Go

Go's ecosystem provides extensive support for working with various databases. Through its standard library and third-party packages, developers can easily establish and manage connections, execute queries, handle transactions, and even interact with multiple databases concurrently. Go's native features like goroutines and channels allow developers to efficiently manage concurrent database interactions, making it easier to build scalable solutions.

Some of the most commonly used packages for database interactions in Go include:

1. **database/sql**: This is the core package for SQL database interactions. It provides an abstraction for managing connections, preparing statements, and executing queries.

2. **GORM**: An ORM (Object Relational Mapper) for Go that simplifies database operations by abstracting complex SQL queries into more straightforward methods.

3. **sqlx**: A library that extends the standard database/sql package by adding extra functionalities such as handling named queries and more flexible scanning.

Establishing Connections

One of the critical aspects of database interactions is managing connections efficiently. Establishing connections can be resource-intensive, so maintaining a pool of connections that can be reused across different requests is essential. Go's database/sql package has built-in support for connection pooling, allowing developers to control the maximum number of open connections, idle connections, and their lifetime.

Best Practices for Connection Management:

- Use environment variables to store database connection strings securely.

- Properly handle connection errors using Go's error-handling mechanisms.

- Use context cancellation to prevent resource leaks in long-running queries.

Structuring Queries and Optimizing Performance

Writing efficient queries is crucial for optimal database performance. Go's approach to database interactions enables developers to prepare statements that can be reused multiple times, reducing the need to parse and compile SQL on each execution. This chapter will explore techniques such as parameterized queries, prepared statements, and bulk operations to enhance query performance.

1. **Parameterized Queries**: Prevent SQL injection and improve security by using placeholders for user input rather than directly embedding values into the query string.

2. **Prepared Statements**: Reuse statements to reduce overhead, especially for repetitive database operations.

3. **Bulk Operations**: Handle bulk inserts, updates, and deletes to manage large datasets efficiently.

Transactions and Error Handling

Transactions are essential when dealing with multiple database operations that must be executed as a single unit. Go's database/sql package allows developers to create transactions and ensures that operations within a transaction are atomic — either all succeed, or none are applied. This section will cover transaction management, including committing and rolling back transactions, handling errors, and implementing savepoints.

Error Handling in Database Operations:

- Handle SQL errors explicitly to understand issues better and provide meaningful feedback.

- Utilize Go's defer keyword to ensure that connections, transactions, or statements are correctly closed, even in the event of an error.

- Use the context package to set deadlines or timeouts for database operations to avoid indefinite wait times.

Concurrent Database Operations

Go's concurrency model, powered by goroutines and channels, provides a way to handle multiple database operations concurrently. This is particularly useful in scenarios where large datasets need to be processed, or multiple queries must run simultaneously. This chapter will explore how to use goroutines to perform parallel database operations efficiently while managing issues like data races and synchronization.

Concurrency Techniques:

- Use goroutines to execute multiple queries simultaneously.

- Implement worker pools to manage large sets of database tasks without overloading the database.

- Ensure proper synchronization with the sync package to prevent race conditions and data inconsistencies.

ORM vs. Raw SQL: Choosing the Right Approach

While raw SQL offers more control and can be more performant, Object Relational Mappers (ORMs) like GORM can simplify database interactions by abstracting the complexity of writing SQL. This section will explore the benefits and trade-offs of using ORMs versus raw SQL, helping developers decide when and where to use each approach.

1. **Benefits of ORMs**: Simplifies database operations, abstracts SQL syntax, and helps in rapid development.

2. **Advantages of Raw SQL**: Offers more flexibility, better performance, and precise control over query execution.

3. **Hybrid Approach**: Leverage the simplicity of ORMs for most interactions while resorting to raw SQL for critical operations that require high performance.

Secure Database Interactions

Security is a top concern when working with databases, especially when dealing with sensitive information. This section will cover essential security practices such as encrypting database connections, using parameterized queries to prevent SQL injection, and implementing user authentication and authorization mechanisms.

Security Best Practices:

- Use SSL/TLS to encrypt data in transit.

- Validate and sanitize user inputs to prevent SQL injection.

- Implement role-based access control to restrict database access.

Database Migrations and Schema Management

As applications evolve, so do the database schemas. Managing schema changes without affecting the integrity of existing data can be challenging. This section will introduce popular tools like golang-migrate to handle database migrations, ensuring that schema updates are applied consistently across different environments.

1. **Automating Migrations**: Use migration tools to apply, rollback, and track schema changes.

2. **Version Control for Database Schemas**: Maintain a history of schema changes to avoid conflicts and issues during deployments.

3. **Continuous Integration (CI) for Databases**: Integrate database migration tests within your CI/CD pipeline to ensure seamless deployments.

Monitoring and Profiling Database Interactions

Regular monitoring and profiling of database interactions are essential to identify performance bottlenecks and optimize queries. This chapter will introduce tools and techniques to track query performance, analyze slow queries, and debug issues using built-in Go features and third-party monitoring solutions.

1. **Query Logging**: Enable query logging to capture and analyze SQL statements.

2. **Monitoring Tools**: Use tools like Prometheus and Grafana to monitor query performance, track metrics, and set up alerts.

3. **Optimizing Database Performance**: Use indexing, caching, and query optimization strategies to improve performance.

This chapter is all about improving the methods for working with databases in Go apps and getting a better grasp on how they work. This chapter covers the fundamentals of database operations, such as connection establishment, sophisticated query execution, and performance optimization. It is designed to provide you with a comprehensive toolkit for properly managing data, ensuring that applications are scalable, resilient, and efficient.

We will start with "Establishing SQL Database Connectivity in Go," which will teach you the fundamentals of any database-driven program. This includes configuring connections to SQL databases and knowing the nuances of connection pooling in order to efficiently manage resources. Moving on, "Executing CRUD Operations with Go and SQL" delves into the fundamentals of database interaction, demonstrating how to create, read, update, and delete records with precision and efficiency, ensuring that you understand the core operations that underpin most applications.

The adventure continues with "Leveraging ORM Tools for Database Interaction," which introduces Object Relational Mapping (ORM) as a powerful paradigm for abstracting and simplifying database interactions, minimizing boilerplate, and enhancing code maintainability. "Advanced Transaction Handling and Concurrency" focuses on more complex scenarios, assuring data integrity and consistency throughout concurrent processes, which is crucial in high-traffic systems.

As we progress through "Working with NoSQL Databases in Go Applications," the chapter looks beyond SQL to schema-less data stores and their flexibility and scalability benefits. "Advanced Query Techniques for Data Retrieval" and "Performing Effective Database Migrations" expand on the skillset by learning sophisticated querying strategies and safe schema evolution practices. Finally, "Implementing High-Performance Database Caching" concludes the chapter by learning caching solutions for improving application performance, lowering latency, and minimizing database load.

This chapter, using actual examples and extensive explanations, enables you to confidently navigate the complicated environment of database interactions, guaranteeing you can construct data-driven Go apps that are not only functional but also optimized for performance and scalability.

Establishing SQL Database Connectivity in Go

Scenario

Imagine you are developing a part of an application that requires storing and retrieving user information. To handle this data efficiently, you decide to use PostgreSQL. The initial challenge is to establish a stable connection between your Go application and the PostgreSQL database, enabling you to perform further database operations seamlessly.

Practical Solution

Install PostgreSQL Driver

To interact with PostgreSQL from Go, you need a driver. We will use pq , a popular driver for PostgreSQL. Install it using:

go get -u github.com/lib/pq

Set up Database Connection

Use the database/sql package in Go, which provides a generic interface around SQL (or SQL-like) databases, in combination with the pq driver to establish a connection. Create a function to connect to the database:

package main

import (

"database/sql"

"fmt"

"log"

_ "github.com/lib/pq"

)

const (

host = "localhost"

port = 5432 // Default port for PostgreSQL

user = "yourusername"

```go
    password = "yourpassword"

    dbname = "yourdbname"

)

func connectDB() *sql.DB {

psqlInfo := fmt.Sprintf("host=%s port=%d user=%s "+

"password=%s dbname=%s sslmode=disable",

host, port, user, password, dbname)

db, err := sql.Open("postgres", psqlInfo)

if err != nil {

log.Fatalf("Error connecting to the database: %v", err)

err = db.Ping()

if err != nil {

log.Fatalf("Error pinging the database: %v", err)

fmt.Println("Successfully connected!")

return db

func main() {

db := connectDB()

defer db.Close()

// Further operations...

}

}

}

}
```

Understanding the Connection String

The connection string (psqlInfo) includes several parameters essential for connecting to the PostgreSQL database, such as the host, port, username, password, and database name. The sslmode=disable parameter is used here for simplicity, but for production environments, consider enabling SSL mode for security.

Testing the Connection

The db.Ping() method is used to test the connectivity with the database server. It's a good practice to verify the connection as part of the initialization process to ensure your application can communicate with the database before proceeding with further operations.

By establishing a connection to a PostgreSQL database, your Go application gains the ability to interact with persistent storage, opening up possibilities for creating, reading, updating, and deleting data as required by your application's functionality.

Executing CRUD Operations with Go and SQL

Scenario

We will assume you need to manage user information within your application. This requires capabilities to add new users, retrieve user details, update user information, and delete users from your PostgreSQL database.

Practical Solution

Using the database/sql package in Go, you can execute SQL queries to perform these CRUD operations.

Following is how you can implement each operation:

Create (Inserting Data)

Add a new user to the database.

```
func createUser(db *sql.DB, name, email string) error {

query := `INSERT INTO users (name, email) VALUES ($1, $2)`

_, err := db.Exec(query, name, email)

if err != nil {

return err

fmt.Println("User added successfully")

return nil

}

}
```

Read (Querying Data)

Retrieve details of a specific user by email.

```
type User struct {

ID int

Name string
```

```go
    Email string
func getUserByEmail(db *sql.DB, email string) (*User, error) {
    query := `SELECT id, name, email FROM users WHERE email = $1`
    var user User
    row := db.QueryRow(query, email)
    err := row.Scan(&user.ID, &user.Name, &user.Email)
    }
    if err != nil {
    if err == sql.ErrNoRows {
    return nil, fmt.Errorf("user not found")
    return nil, err
    return &user, nil
    }
    }
    }
```

Update (Modifying Data)

Update the name of a user based on their email.

```go
func updateUserEmail(db *sql.DB, id int, newEmail string) error {
    query := `UPDATE users SET email = $2 WHERE id = $1`
    _, err := db.Exec(query, id, newEmail)
    if err != nil {
    return err
    fmt.Println("User email updated successfully")
    return nil
    }
    }
```

Delete (Removing Data)

Remove a user from the database.

```go
func deleteUser(db *sql.DB, id int) error {

query := `DELETE FROM users WHERE id = $1`

_, err := db.Exec(query, id)

if err != nil {

return err

fmt.Println("User deleted successfully")

}

return nil

}
```

Leveraging ORM Tools for Database Interaction

Scenario

Consider an application that requires frequent and complex interactions with a user database. Writing and maintaining raw SQL queries for these interactions becomes cumbersome and error-prone. By leveraging an ORM tool, you can streamline these operations, focusing on business logic rather than database specifics.

Practical Solution

One popular ORM tool in the Go ecosystem is GORM. It offers a developer-friendly API for performing CRUD operations and more, with support for various SQL databases including PostgreSQL, MySQL, SQLite, and SQL Server.

Installing GORM

To get started with GORM, first install it by running:

```
go get -u gorm.io/gorm
```

```
go get -u gorm.io/driver/postgres
```

Connecting to the Database

Use GORM to establish a connection to your PostgreSQL database.

```go
package main

import (

"gorm.io/driver/postgres"

"gorm.io/gorm"

"log"
```

```go
func main() {

dsn := "host=localhost user=youruser password=yourpassword dbname=yourdbname port=5432

sslmode=disable TimeZone=Asia/Shanghai"

db, err := gorm.Open(postgres.Open(dsn), &gorm.Config{})

if err != nil {

log.Fatalf("Failed to connect to database: %v", err)

log.Println("Database connection successfully established")

)

}

}
```

Defining a Model

Create a Go struct that maps to your database table. GORM uses this model to perform database operations.

```go
type User struct {

gorm.Model

Name string

Email string `gorm:"type:varchar(100);unique_index"`

}
```

Performing CRUD Operations

With GORM, executing CRUD operations becomes straightforward. Following is how you can add a new user to the database:

```go
newUser := User{Name: "John Doe", Email: "john.doe@example.com"}

result := db.Create(&newUser) // Pass pointer of data to Create

if result.Error != nil {

log.Fatalf("Failed to create user: %v", result.Error)

log.Printf("User created successfully: %v", newUser)

}
```

Similarly, you can use db.Find , db.Update , and db.Delete for read, update, and delete operations, respectively.

Benefits of Using an ORM

- Abstraction over SQL: ORM allows you to focus on your application's business logic rather than the intricacies of SQL syntax.

- Type Safety: Working with Go structs instead of raw queries reduces the risk of runtime errors and SQL injection vulnerabilities.

- Development Speed: ORM can accelerate development by automating routine data handling tasks, such as migrations and query optimizations.

Advanced Transaction Handling and Concurrency

Scenario

Try to picture a program that takes orders and keeps stock levels up to date. It is possible for numerous users to try to buy the same item at the same time during a sale event. To avoid data anomalies like selling more items than in stock, strong transaction handling is necessary to update inventory levels accurately in this case.

Practical Solution

Using Transactions in Go

Database transactions ensure that a series of operations either all succeed or fail as a unit, maintaining data integrity. Go's database/sql package supports transactions.

```
func processOrder(db *sql.DB, orderID, itemID int, quantity int) error {

// Begin a transaction

tx, err := db.Begin()

if err != nil {

return err

// Deduct the quantity from inventory

_, err = tx.Exec("UPDATE inventory SET quantity = quantity - ? WHERE item_id = ?", quantity,

itemID)

if err != nil {

tx.Rollback() // Important: Rollback in case of error

return err // Update order status

_, err = tx.Exec("UPDATE orders SET status = 'processed' WHERE id = ?", orderID)


if err != nil {
```

```
tx.Rollback() // Rollback in case of error

return err // Commit the transaction

}

}

}

if err := tx.Commit(); err != nil {

return err

return nil

}

}
```

Handling Concurrency

Optimistic and pessimistic locking are two strategies to handle concurrency. Optimistic locking assumes conflicts are rare, while pessimistic locking assumes conflicts are common and locks data to prevent other operations from accessing it simultaneously.

Implement optimistic locking by including a version or timestamp column in your table. When updating a record, check that the version matches, indicating no other transactions have modified the record.

```
UPDATE inventory SET quantity = quantity - ?, version = version + 1 WHERE item_id = ? AND

version = ?
```

If the update affects 0 rows, it means another transaction has already updated the record, and you can handle this case accordingly (e.g., retry the operation, abort, or notify the user).

Working with NoSQL Databases - MongoDB Integration

Scenario

The library application needs to store and retrieve user reviews for books, where reviews can vary significantly in structure, containing comments, ratings, and potentially user metadata. This scenario is well-suited for a NoSQL database like MongoDB due to its schema-less nature and flexibility.

Practical Solution

Setting up MongoDB in Go

To interact with MongoDB from Go, use the official MongoDB Go driver. First, add the MongoDB Go driver to your project:

```
go get go.mongodb.org/mongo-driver/mongo
```

Connecting to MongoDB

```go
package main

import (

"context"

"log"

"time"

"go.mongodb.org/mongo-driver/mongo"

"go.mongodb.org/mongo-driver/mongo/options"

func main() {

// Set client options

clientOptions := options.Client().ApplyURI("mongodb://localhost:27017")

// Connect to MongoDB

client, err := mongo.Connect(context.TODO(), clientOptions)

if err != nil {

log.Fatal(err)
```

Establish a connection to your MongoDB instance. The below sample program assumes MongoDB is running locally on the default port and uses a new database called librarydb.)

```go
}

// Check the connection

err = client.Ping(context.TODO(), nil)

if err != nil {

log.Fatal(err)

log.Println("Connected to MongoDB!")

}

}
```

Defining a Model for User Reviews

Since MongoDB is schema-less, you can define a flexible Go struct that represents a user review. This struct can then be used to marshal and unmarshal data to and from MongoDB.

```go
type UserReview struct {

ID primitive.ObjectID `bson:"_id,omitempty"`

BookID string `bson:"book_id"`

UserID string `bson:"user_id"`

Rating int `bson:"rating"`

Comment string `bson:"comment,omitempty"`

}
```

Performing CRUD Operations

With the connection established and model defined, you can now perform CRUD operations. Given below is how to insert a new review into the database:

```go
func createReview(client *mongo.Client, review UserReview) error {

collection := client.Database("librarydb").Collection("reviews")

_, err := collection.InsertOne(context.TODO(), review)

if err != nil {

return err

log.Println("Review inserted successfully")

return nil

}

}
```

Executing Advanced Query Techniques for Insightful Data Retrieval

Scenario

In the evolving library application, there is a need to offer users personalized book recommendations based on their reading history, preferences, and reviews by similar users. This requirement calls for advanced querying capabilities to analyze user data, book metadata, and interaction patterns to generate meaningful recommendations.

Practical Solution

Using PostgreSQL for structured data and MongoDB for user-generated content like reviews, we can employ advanced query techniques in both SQL and NoSQL environments to achieve our goal.

SQL Window Functions in PostgreSQL

Window functions provide a way to perform calculations across sets of rows related to the current row. This can be used for ranking, running totals, or identifying patterns.

For example, to find the top 3 most popular books in a category based on checkout history:

```
SELECT book_id, category, COUNT(*) OVER (PARTITION BY category ORDER BY

COUNT(*) DESC) as checkout_count

FROM checkouts

WHERE checkout_date > CURRENT_DATE - INTERVAL '1 year'

GROUP BY book_id, category

ORDER BY category, checkout_count DESC

LIMIT 3;
```

Aggregation Pipeline in MongoDB

MongoDB's aggregation framework allows for data processing and aggregation through a multi-stage pipeline, enabling complex data transformations and analysis.

For instance, to aggregate user reviews for generating book ratings:

```
collection := client.Database("librarydb").Collection("reviews")

pipeline := mongo.Pipeline{

{{"$match", bson.D{{"book_id", bookID}}}},

{{"$group", bson.D{

"_id", "$book_id"},

"average_rating", bson.D{{"$avg", "$rating"}}},

}}},

{

{

}

aggResult, err := collection.Aggregate(context.TODO(), pipeline)

if err != nil {

log.Fatal(err)

// Process aggregation results

}
```

Combining SQL and NoSQL Queries for Data Insights

By leveraging the strengths of both SQL and NoSQL databases, you can perform sophisticated data analysis. For instance, use SQL queries to analyze transactional data and user interactions stored in PostgreSQL, and MongoDB's aggregation pipeline to analyze user-generated content. The insights from both sources can be combined to power features like personalized recommendations or trend analysis.

Performing Effective Database Migrations

Scenario

Adding new tables to keep track of book reservations or modifying existing tables to fit additional data fields for user profiles are examples of database schema modifications that may be necessary as the library application develops and gets new capabilities. A solid migration plan is required to implement these changes in all environments (dev, test, and production) without disrupting service or losing data.

Practical Solution

Choosing a Migration Tool

For Go applications, several tools facilitate database migrations, such as golang-migrate/migrate. This tool supports various databases and allows you to define migrations in SQL or Go files.

go get -u github.com/golang-migrate/migrate/cmd/migrate

Creating Migration Scripts

Migrations usually consist of two scripts: one for applying the change ("up") and one for undoing the change ("down"), allowing you to roll back to a previous state if necessary.

Example Migration for Adding a Reservations Table:

Create a directory for your migration files, e.g., migrations, and then create an "up" migration file for creating a new table:

1_add_reservations_table.up.sql

CREATE TABLE reservations (

id SERIAL PRIMARY KEY,

user_id INTEGER NOT NULL,

book_id INTEGER NOT NULL,

reserved_at TIMESTAMP WITH TIME ZONE DEFAULT CURRENT_TIMESTAMP

;

)

And a corresponding "down" migration file to undo the change:

1_add_reservations_table.down.sql

DROP TABLE reservations;

Use the migrate tool to apply your migrations to the database. Specify the database connection string and the path to your migrations directory.

Applying Migrations

migrate -path /path/to/migrations -database "postgres://user:password@localhost:5432/dbname?

sslmode=disable" up

Rolling Back Migrations

migrate -path /path/to/migrations -database "postgres://user:password@localhost:5432/dbname?

sslmode=disable" down

Implementing High-Performance Database Caching

Scenario

In the library application, certain operations, such as fetching popular books or user profiles, are executed frequently and generate similar queries to the database. To optimize these operations, implementing a caching layer can reduce direct database queries, lowering latency and improving throughput, especially under high load.

Practical Solution

Redis is a popular in-memory data store used as a high-performance cache and message broker. It offers various data structures to efficiently cache different types of data.

Setting up Redis

Ensure Redis is installed and running on your system. Redis can be easily set up on most platforms, and Docker can be used to run Redis in a container for development purposes.

Integrating Redis with Go

Use the go-redis/redis Go client to interact with Redis from your application.

go get -u github.com/go-redis/redis/v8

Establish a connection to your Redis instance.

package main

import (

"context"

```go
    "fmt"

    "github.com/go-redis/redis/v8"
)

var ctx = context.Background()

func main() {

    rdb := redis.NewClient(&redis.Options{

    Addr: "localhost:6379", // use default Addr

    Password: "", // no password set

    DB: 0, // use default DB

    })

    err := rdb.Set(ctx, "key", "value", 0).Err()

    if err != nil {

    panic(err)

    val, err := rdb.Get(ctx, "key").Result()

    if err != nil {

    panic(err)

    fmt.Println("key", val)

    }

    }

    }
```

Caching Strategy for Frequently Accessed Data

Implement caching logic in your application to store and retrieve frequently accessed data. For read-heavy operations, retrieve the data from the cache if available; if not, fetch from the database and store it in the cache for future requests.

```go
func getPopularBooks(rdb *redis.Client, db *sql.DB) ([]Book, error) {

    // Attempt to fetch the value from Redis cache

    cachedBooks, err := rdb.Get(ctx, "popular_books").Result()

    if err == redis.Nil {

    // Key does not exist in Redis, fetch from database
```

```go
books, err := fetchPopularBooksFromDB(db)

if err != nil {

return nil, err

// Cache the result in Redis

if err := rdb.Set(ctx, "popular_books", books, 30*time.Minute).Err(); err != nil {

// handle error

return books, nil

 else if err != nil {

return nil, err

// Unmarshal the data into the expected slice of books

}

}

}

}

var books []Book

if err := json.Unmarshal([]byte(cachedBooks), &books); err != nil {

return nil, err

return books, nil

}

}
```

Conclusion: Mastering Database Interactions in Go

As we conclude this chapter on strengthening database interactions in Go, it is clear that the ability to efficiently and securely manage database operations is a critical skill for any developer building robust, scalable applications. The evolution of software development demands that applications handle data seamlessly, and Go provides a powerful set of tools to achieve this.

The Foundation: Understanding Go's Database Capabilities

The core of any application that interacts with a database is how it establishes connections, executes queries, and retrieves data. Go's database/sql package offers the foundational features required to perform these tasks effectively. It enables developers to establish connections with various databases, from traditional SQL databases like PostgreSQL and MySQL to more modern NoSQL databases like MongoDB. However, understanding how to use these tools correctly is crucial. Developers need to be well-versed in structuring their code to handle connections, manage resources, and ensure efficient data retrieval.

Key Takeaways:

- Familiarize yourself with Go's native database/sql package for basic SQL operations.

- Leverage Go's extensive ecosystem of third-party libraries, such as GORM and sqlx, to simplify development.

Optimizing Database Connections for Scalability

Establishing and managing database connections is a key aspect that often determines the scalability of an application. Connection pooling, for example, ensures that your application can handle numerous database requests efficiently without overwhelming the database server. Go's built-in capabilities allow developers to manage connection pools, setting limits on idle and active connections, thereby reducing the overhead of repeatedly opening and closing connections. This approach is particularly beneficial in high-load scenarios where multiple users or services are interacting with the database simultaneously.

To maximize performance:

- **Connection Pooling**: Configure connection pools to avoid excessive resource consumption.

- **Resource Management**: Use Go's concurrency features, such as goroutines, to manage multiple connections without blocking the application's main thread.

- **Error Handling**: Always handle connection errors gracefully, ensuring your application remains resilient and responsive.

Writing Efficient Queries

While establishing connections is important, what truly defines the efficiency of your database interactions is how you structure and execute queries. Efficient queries are at the heart of a well-functioning database-driven application. Go provides tools to create prepared statements, enabling the reuse of queries and reducing parsing overhead. This leads to faster execution, especially in applications that rely on frequent database calls.

Moreover, this chapter emphasized the importance of using parameterized queries to prevent SQL injection and ensure security. Understanding how to structure your SQL queries to leverage indexes, avoid unnecessary joins, and reduce the load on the database can significantly improve performance.

Key Points:

- Use **prepared statements** for repetitive queries to save processing time.

- **Parameterized Queries**: Protect against SQL injection by avoiding direct insertion of user inputs into SQL queries.

- Focus on **query optimization**, leveraging database indexes, and understanding the cost of various SQL operations.

Effective Transaction Management

Transactions are crucial for maintaining data integrity, especially in scenarios where multiple operations need to be executed as a single unit. Go's support for transactions allows developers to group several database operations together, ensuring that either all operations succeed or none are applied. This is particularly useful in applications that handle financial transactions, bookings, or any process where atomicity is required.

One of the challenges developers face is handling transactions that may fail partway through. Proper error handling, combined with Go's defer mechanism, ensures that resources are cleaned up, and connections are properly closed, even when an error occurs. This prevents memory leaks and other issues that can arise from improperly managed transactions.

Takeaways:

- **Atomic Operations**: Use transactions to maintain atomicity, consistency, isolation, and durability (ACID properties) in database operations.

- **Error Handling**: Ensure robust error handling to deal with transaction failures, using rollback mechanisms when necessary.

- **Resource Cleanup**: Use Go's defer statement to guarantee that resources are freed after operations are completed.

Leveraging Concurrency for Better Performance

One of the standout features of Go is its strong support for concurrency, which allows developers to handle multiple tasks simultaneously. When it comes to database interactions, this means you can perform several queries concurrently, significantly speeding up data retrieval and processing times. By using goroutines, developers can write non-blocking code, enabling applications to remain responsive even when handling multiple database requests.

However, with concurrency comes the challenge of managing shared resources. Developers need to be aware of potential data races and ensure that the data being manipulated by multiple goroutines is properly synchronized. This chapter covered the use of Go's sync package to manage concurrent access to shared data, ensuring that applications remain reliable and consistent.

Key Points:

- **Goroutines**: Use goroutines to execute multiple database operations simultaneously, improving overall application throughput.

- **Synchronization**: Manage shared resources with synchronization techniques to avoid data races and ensure consistency.

- **Worker Pools**: Implement worker pools for batch processing, allowing your application to handle large datasets efficiently.

The Role of ORMs in Simplifying Database Interactions

While raw SQL gives developers complete control over database interactions, it can be verbose and error-prone, especially for complex operations. Object Relational Mappers (ORMs) like GORM can simplify the development process by abstracting SQL operations into more intuitive methods. This makes it easier to perform database operations without needing to write raw SQL, which can be particularly helpful for developers who are not deeply familiar with SQL syntax.

However, using ORMs comes with trade-offs. They can introduce performance overhead and may not offer the flexibility needed for complex queries. Developers must understand when to use ORMs and when raw SQL would be more appropriate. This chapter provided insights into using a hybrid approach, leveraging the simplicity of ORMs for standard operations while resorting to raw SQL for more performance-critical tasks.

Takeaways:

- **Simplicity vs. Control**: Weigh the benefits of simplicity offered by ORMs against the control and performance benefits of raw SQL.

- **Hybrid Approach**: Use a combination of ORMs and raw SQL to get the best of both worlds.

- **GORM**: Understand how to use GORM effectively, including its capabilities for handling associations, migrations, and validations.

Ensuring Security in Database Interactions

Security is an essential consideration when dealing with databases, particularly when sensitive data is involved. This chapter emphasized the importance of using secure practices like encrypted connections (SSL/TLS) and input validation to prevent common security vulnerabilities such as SQL injection. Developers need to be vigilant about how data is handled, ensuring that all interactions with the database are secure and comply with best practices.

Security Practices:

- **Encryption**: Use SSL/TLS to encrypt database connections, ensuring data remains secure during transit.

- **Input Sanitization**: Validate and sanitize user inputs to prevent SQL injection attacks.

- **Role-Based Access Control (RBAC)**: Implement RBAC to control user permissions, ensuring that only authorized users can perform specific actions.

Continuous Integration and Monitoring

Finally, building a robust database application is not just about writing efficient code; it also involves continuous testing, monitoring, and optimization. This chapter introduced tools and techniques for monitoring database performance, identifying slow queries, and debugging issues. Implementing these tools as part of your development workflow can help you catch problems early, allowing for continuous improvement and optimization.

Integrating database migrations into your Continuous Integration (CI) pipeline ensures that schema changes are applied consistently across all environments. By incorporating automated testing for database interactions, developers can ensure that changes do not introduce new bugs or degrade performance.

Key Points:

- **Monitoring**: Use tools like Prometheus and Grafana to monitor database interactions, track performance metrics, and set up alerts.

- **Automated Testing**: Include database tests in your CI pipeline to catch issues early and maintain a stable production environment.

- **Performance Profiling**: Regularly profile your database queries to identify and optimize slow operations.

Final Thoughts

Strengthening database interactions in Go involves a holistic approach that combines efficient coding practices, robust error handling, secure connections, and ongoing performance optimization. Go's ecosystem offers a wide array of tools and packages that can help developers manage complex database interactions with ease. By mastering these tools and adhering to best practices, developers can build scalable, high-performance applications that are capable of handling modern data demands.

The ultimate goal is to create applications that are not only fast and reliable but also secure and maintainable. As you continue to develop your skills in Go, keep exploring new techniques and tools, and don't be afraid to experiment with different approaches. Strengthening your database interactions will lay a solid foundation for any application, ensuring it remains robust, scalable, and responsive as it grows.

Thank You

www.ingramcontent.com/pod-product-compliance
Lightning Source LLC
LaVergne TN
LVHW081509050326
832903LV00025B/1425